This Walk Ain't Easy!

But, Help Is Along The Way

Felicia Joy Devine

Copyright © 2022 by Felicia Joy Devine

All rights reserved. No part of this publication may be reproduced, distributed, or transmitted in any form or by any means, including photocopying, recording, or other electronic or mechanical methods, without the prior written permission of the publisher, except in the case brief quotations embodied in critical reviews and other noncommercial uses permitted by copyright law.

ISBN: 978-1-63945-332-0 (Paperback)
          978-1-63945-335-1 (Ebook)

The views expressed in this book are solely those of the author and do not necessarily reflect the views of the publisher, and the publisher hereby disclaims any responsibility for them.
Writers' Branding

1800-608-6550
www.writersbranding.com
orders@writersbranding.com

Contents

Acknowledgments

Foreword

Chapter 1: Exposure 12

Chapter 2: Acceptance 25

Chapter 3: Trust... 89

Chapter 4: Waiting 152

Chapter 5: Deliverance 207

Chapter 6: Healing 291

Chapter 7: Restoration 325

Chapter 8: Ministry 340

Survival Guide for Walkers

Psalm 121 (KJV)

1 I will lift up my eyes to the hills—from whence comes my help? 2 My help comes from the LORD, Who made heaven and earth. 3 He will not allow your foot to be moved; He who keeps you will not slumber. 4 Behold, He who keeps Israel shall neither slumber nor sleep. 5 The LORD is your keeper; The LORD is your shade at your right hand. 6 The sun shall not strike you by day, nor the moon by night. 7 The LORD shall preserve you from all evil; He shall preserve your soul. 8 The LORD shall preserve your going out and you're coming in from this time forth, and even forevermore.

Acknowledgments

Dear God,

Thank you, God for your son Jesus! Thank you, God for being there for me in spite of me! Thank you, God for "Setting Me Up" with your plan, then you activated your wonderful soldiers who were/are charged with guiding, teaching and supporting me throughout my process. Sometimes I got so caught up in the battle that I did not acknowledge that you were right there. I have no doubt that All of My Help Comes from you Lord and I am so grateful!

Deacon Sylvester Devine and Deaconess Hattie Ruth Devine, In Loving Memory

You were my wonderful praying, worshiping parents. Thank you for "training me up" the right way and exposing me to God. I found my way back! I miss you both so much but, its funny how, it doesn't' hurt like it did when I first lost you. Only God can fill the void that was left because I cherished you both. I find peace in the blessing that God gave me you for parents and this was truly an act of love. Because of you I have a loving family. My big brothers, Leon and Junior, my big sister Vanessa, my precious baby girl Amber Joy, nephews Ellis and Terrance and nieces, Shonda, Courtney and Kayla. Of course my darlings Carl and Bill who have joined you at rest.

Amber (Pooh) Joy Devine

Baby girl you are such a blessing to me. You are kind, compassionate, understanding, smart and articulate. I just love you so much! As a matter of fact, I like you more than I love you if that's even possible. Pooh for so long our motto was *"Me and you against the world"* but God showed us that wasn't the case. Always remember how He carried us.

As you continue on your own journey allow God to lead you, guide you and carry you through your process.

My Pastor, Rev. Gilbert Pickett, Sr.

Thank you for allowing God to work through you. My Church home at Mount Horeb is where I finally understood that it is about our individual relationship with God and not the people, place or the religion. Thank you for your teaching, guidance, and support. It was through you that I unveiled my spiritual gifts of exhortation and teaching. Thank you for allowing me to do some of the things that I now know were part of my "Set-Up" like the Women's Conference and the Bible School Workshops, before I even realized where he was leading me and understanding my purpose. Thank you for your mentoring and input. My auntie, Harridell Lewis, is an Evangelist in South Carolina. The first time I brought her to our church she heard you preach and said to me, "That man of God is truly anointed." She was so right. It's no wonder she still can't get enough of your sermon tapes. You are truly that "Shepherd" who speaks words of wisdom and have changed my life. I thank you for allowing God to use you. I thank you for being you, and I love you.

Gina (Niecy) Denise Lewis

Thank you for your no pressure approach to leading me to Jesus. You have done a lot of things for me especially being my personal cheerleader and best friend. I have to say nothing compares to you bringing me back to church. You saved my life. Keep spreading your words of wisdom. I know you hate when I get mushy but I love you. I know you know that but I just needed to say it publicly.

Leslie E. Phillips

To my sister with "Half a Mind". Thank you for believing in me when no one else did. Thank you for your unwavering support and love. You are such an inspiration to me and I think you know how much you mean to me. You are truly a blessing and I thank God for bringing us together. You are my prayer partner, my accountability partner and my dear sister-friend. We have taken so many steps in this journey to purpose together. We have laughed, cried, fussed, wanted to give up but God gave us each other to encourage and support each other. Our relationship truly shows what happens when two come together in his name anything is possible. I just can't wait until the world sees what He has given you through your awesome plays.

Cynthia Davis

Thank you for your unwavering support and keeping me on track. I would not have been able to complete this without you. Who would have thought you teaching me how to use the computer prior to getting saved was part of my set-up. It's so cool that now, we are saved and you are still teaching me, guiding me and saving me from my *non-tech, I must have a deadline self.* I love you, my sister.

Isabelle and Mozelle Perry

You are my wonderfully supportive cousins. Thank you for your love and support. I can't remember a time you were not there for me. I love you both.

My Sisters in Christ

Denise Thomas, Juliet Morton, Michelle Pearson, and Patricia (Patty) Lemon. You are awesome women of God. The way you have demonstrated love, compassion and strength and trusting in God is so inspiring. I am so proud to call you my sister-friends.

Kim Dennis-Walker

My little (BIG) sister in Christ, you brought me the Word before I found my way back. You encouraged, inspired, guided and supported me through some of the darkest points in my life. You are one powerful sister. Thank you and I love you.

Donnesa Williams

You are truly an angel. You are a prayer warrior. Thank you for being my conscience before I knew conviction. Thanks for reminding me who was in charge and that I had to relinquish control. You helped me to realize that God was "Setting Me Up." It's all been a part of his master plan. Thank you for your leadership in the Sister Circle. You helped me make it happen and I love you!

Alison A. Edwards, In Loving Memory

You taught me so much about myself and strength and most importantly unwavering faith.

To The Women I Met Through the MHBC Ministry

Minister Renee Rivera, God sent you to encourage me, Evangelist Tameka Jacobs, God sent you to inspire me, Rev. Cynthia Green, God sent you to inform me, Minister Kim McGuire, God sent you to teach me, Evangelist Martinez, God sent you to comfort me, I love and thank you all.

To My Supportive Sisters and Brothers in Christ

Carol Campbell, Candice Jarvis, Sandra Mapp, Nicola Bryant, Mildred Parham, Carolyn Phillips, Harrison (Lee) Washington and Deacon Eddie Johnson.

God Sent You to Teach Me

Evangelist Harridell Lewis (Auntie), Rev. Jackie Jones, Rev. Marjorie Harris, Rev. Dr. Angela Moses, Elder Gail Chandler, Rev. Que English and Deaconess Darlene Morgan.

To The Encouragers, Folks on TV and Radio

Bishop T.D. Jakes, Pastor Paula White, Pastor Cheryl Brady, Joyce Meyer, Rev. Frank Reid, Pastor Jamal Bryant, Pastor Creflo Dollar, Pastor Joel Osteen, Pastors Floyd and Elaine Flake, Jan and Paul Crouch and the rest of TBN Praise the Lord family. I cannot forget Mr. Steve Harvey, Ms. Yolanda Adams, Pastor Donnie McClurkin, for your morning inspirations.

Foreword

What is the lesson in abuse, addiction, molestation, imprisonment, death, rejection, or sickness? Essentially, what are God's plans for us while we are walking in our valleys trying to get to the top of the mountain? God answered these questions before they were even asked. Unconstrained by time, emotions, or circumstances, He sees all and is aware that someday His children will turn and walk away from Him. He is waiting for us to come out of the darkness with provisions available for the way back to Him. In the end, nothing will have been meaningless. God's light coming forth out of the darkness—from exposure to trust to waiting to deliverance to healing to restoration to ministry—all conceived from the very essence that is of God in order that He might fulfill His ultimate plan for us.

Each of us has a purpose, a reason for being here, that no one else can tell you. But we can find out from God by beginning a relationship with Jesus Christ. In *John 14:6-7,* Jesus said, "I am the way, the truth, and the life. No one comes to the Father except through Me. If you follow Me and do what I say, your life will change." He then talked about taking the first step to starting a relationship with Jesus and anybody that takes that first step toward building a relationship with Jesus Christ will have a very fulfilling life.

Cynthia Davis

Exposure

The First Set of Footprints:
Exodus 3:1-14

Exposed! Uncovered! Busted! Found Out! Unraveled!

These are just a few of the terms that seem to describe what I was feeling when my life as I knew it blew up in my face. You see I had been doing well on my career path; things were moving in the right direction, a positive direction. My personal life had some road bumps and my intimate relationships were shaky. Nothing prepared me for the blow I was about to receive which subsequently changed my life.

Married! What do you mean Married? I can't believe he came to my job wearing a wedding band. How do you date a man for seven years, have a child with him, deal with his mother's cancer and subsequent death and my mother's Alzheimer's disease together, and he up and marries someone else while, in my mind, we are still together. I tried my best to hold it together while he was in my presence. I looked at him and said, "I can't believe you! How could you betray me like this?" At this point, you are probably wondering what he said. He said ab-so-lute-ly nothing! What could he say? He was standing there with this expression on his face as if he should be mad at me as if I did something wrong. I don't know what pissed me off more, that look on his face or what he had done to me. I wanted to punch him in his face but I didn't. Not because he didn't deserve it but because I was at my job. I then asked, "What could I have possibly done for you to treat me this way?" Again, no answer. I looked at him and said I wish you both get exactly what you deserve in this marriage. It took everything in me to stop the tears from falling while I was in his presence. I turned around and walked away and went back into the office building where it felt like the walls were closing in on me. My legs felt wobbly, I was sick to my stomach, I felt like I was going to pass out. The worst part was I really wanted him to stop me and wake me up from this nightmare, tell me I had just been "Punked" or on "Candid Camera" or something! But it didn't happen; this was reality, my reality. I couldn't believe it. We broke up on January 2nd and he got married the previous December. Yes! He got married prior to breaking up with me. I was crushed, I felt like my best friend was taken away. I remember feeling why is this happening to me? How could he do this to me? I trusted him. I loved him unconditionally. How could he leave me to raise our child alone? I always had his back, even when he was losing good jobs, getting too drunk to function. No matter what, I had his back. Why didn't he have my back? When did this begin? Where did I go wrong? Why is this happening to me?

    I went back to work but I could not concentrate. I could not function. Work was the one place I usually felt whole. I was Miss Guided, MG, an expert in my field. Even when everything else went wrong in my life I had my many accomplishments at work to fall back on. My self-esteem and self-worth were tied to my work. For the first time, I could not focus on my job. I couldn't take feeling this way and having to sit in this office. I didn't want to go into the field because I could not deal with people. I decided to leave early. I went out for drinks with a friend, to try and numb the pain but it didn't work. It seemed as if the more I drank, the more sober I became. The more sober I became the more it felt like I was reliving what happened earlier that day over and over in my mind. I was so broken. I was not prepared for this. Since the drinks weren't working I decided to go home. When I got home I was even more distraught. I had to look at my beautiful little girl that he has chosen to abandon and deal with my mom whose memory was diminishing every day. The funny thing is both of them could tell something was wrong with me. My daughter said, "Mommy you look so sad." I don't want you to be sad. My mother looked at me and said, "Baby what's wrong?" I wanted to curl up in her arms like I did when I was a child and let her rock me until this pain went away. It's funny;

in all her own madness she could feel her baby's pain. I refused to let either of them see me break down because mama had enough to deal with and Pooh, that's my baby girl would be experiencing pain soon enough but it didn't have to start now. I just went about my normal routine cooking, straightening up the house, and getting them both ready for bed. After awhile they both fell asleep. Now I had my time alone. I could allow myself to feel again, to let it out! The house felt cold and empty. It had been like this for a while. He was clearly not around as much and acting distant prior to today, but this night was different it felt like a broken home. I looked in on my daughter as she slept. She was so peaceful so innocent so angelic. I checked on my mom and she too was peaceful. I called my best friend Wisdom to tell her what this man had done to me. I screamed, cried and I told her I felt so humiliated so stupid. I had told her how unhappy I was in this relationship prior to this but because of our daughter, I felt a need to try and make it work. I think I felt worse because he was not doing his part and I stayed with him. Wisdom listened to me and then said, "Why don't you come to church with me on Sunday." When I am going through tough times, I turn it over to God and that's where I find peace." I told her to be quite honest I was not trying to hear that. I was so hurt and so angry. I asked her why God would allow me to hurt like this. She said, "As hard as it may be some times God does not want the things for us that we may want for ourselves." She tried to offer some additional words of comfort but I really wasn't trying to hear her out. I did not want to be comforted because at this point, I was angry and I wanted to stay that way. I really didn't want to hear about how this God, in time could make things better. I wanted to feel better now and besides, I didn't understand why he let it happen in the first place. I got off the phone and felt a need to go for a ride. I had to get out of this cold empty house. I knew if they woke up, I didn't have the energy to hide this pain I was experiencing. I wouldn't be able to look at either of them in the eye without falling apart. I called Wisdom back and asked if she could sit with them while I went out to clear my head and she did.

    I jumped into my car and got right on the parkway. The road was open and it felt good to drive. It was a rainy night and I remember

Exposure

thinking I love the rain. But not tonight, I had some difficulty seeing between the rain and my tears. I was so distraught. I turned on the radio and Mary J. Blige came on singing "I'm Not Gonna Cry." The funny thing is the song talks about not crying and the longer I listened to the words of the song the more I wanted to cry. I felt like the song was telling my story. I mean there were some subtle differences, for me, it was seven years, not eleven and I was not his wife. Wow, wife! The thought of not being his wife and him marrying someone else hurt so deeply. I feel so used, so abused, so mistreated and so disrespected. I just listened to the words of this song and my heart just bled and bled.

I have all kinds of thoughts racing through my mind. This pain feels familiar even though this has never happened to me before. The storyline may have changed but the hurt and pain, that's a place I know too well. Why does stuff like this keep happening to me? Why can't I find Mr. Right, why do I keep finding Mr. Wrong or even worse, Mr. Right Now? I don't get it I had two loving parents who were married for over 40 years. I want that, what they had, why can't I have that? What happened? Why am I always in these dysfunctional relationships? My parents made me feel like I was a princess. I had a normal childhood; I didn't grow up in dysfunction. Or did I? Sometimes, you can grow up in craziness and not know it because it's your norm. These are some of the thoughts I wrestled with as I tried to make sense out of the nonsense that I was facing. The social worker in me said think back to when this could have possibly started. Maybe it was something in my childhood. Maybe it is some deep dark unresolved issue. Whatever it is I am determined to find out because this pain is cutting me like a knife and I don't want to live like this anymore. I'm going to try and retrace my steps. I don't know what it could be because I was treated like a princess growing up.

A Misguided Child

Let's see how do those stories usually start? Oh yeah, once upon a time there was a little girl named Guide. Now Guide was born to a Devine family who were very happy when she came to them. The immediate family consisted of three sons, a mother, and a father. The family was initially from South Carolina. The parents and the three boys moved to New York in search of a better life for their young family. In case you haven't figured it out yet, I am that little girl named Guide. As far back as I could remember, I was told when I was born my father drove around to friends and families' homes "yelling I got me a girl!" He was so excited and so was the rest of the family for him. My mom was also very excited. She said every woman wants a little girl a "doll" she can dress up, especially after having three boys. I was so loved I was raised and treated like a little princess by my entire family.

My mother and father were Christians, they were raised Baptist and were members of separate churches in their home state South Carolina. My dad was a Deacon in his church. My aunts say my grandmother always felt he was supposed to be a minister but did not follow his true calling. My mother was very active in her church and served in a variety of capacities. Mama was a virtuous woman and you knew she had a special connection with God. That woman could make a little bit go a long way. Both of my parents were strong believers in God and served Him in their own way. My parents brought us to church because they believed in *Proverbs 22:6, "Train up a child in the way he should go: and when he is old, he will not depart from it."* I guess their understanding of that scripture was to take your children to church and once they get there the rest would work itself out. As I look back I kind of question some of the initial training I got in church. It seems a little contradictory.

In the Baptist church, we bless or dedicate the babies. The difference between Christening and blessing or dedication in most cases is the use of water. In the Baptist faith, people are not immersed in the water until they are "ready" to accept the plan of salvation for themselves. Then the full body is immersed in water as an act of symbolism to be made clean. The old you dies and the new you emerges. To bless a child in the Baptist church means to have the minister openly pray for the child and in some churches use oil to anoint the baby. Some of my friends are Catholic and are very clear and strict about the role and religious standing of the Godparents. They even have criteria and/or qualifications for these people. The Baptist church has no criteria that I know of. If it's one thing I did learn it was the rules according to church. It seems as though this was a man-made ritual adapted from the Catholic Church. Most people believe that it's the Godparents' role and responsibility to keep the child spiritually connected in support of and at times in lieu of the parents. The more "worldly" folks believe that the role of the Godparents is I.C.S.H. = In Case Something Happens. People who fall into this category think being a Godparent means step in and take charge of the child. If that's the case, then why perform the ceremony in church? Too often the selection of God parents is detached from its original intent. A lot of Godparents are not even saved. So you ask the question, how can an unsaved person step in to be a spiritual guide when they are not equipped themselves? I need to get back to figuring out why stuff happens to me. My mind is so crazy! I am always thinking about more than one thing at a time. I know you must be saying what do Godparents have to do with why I'm so messed up? Maybe that's why I am so messed up. I am so easily distracted. Maybe I was distracted when I met that jerk and I missed that he was a jerk. Oh yeah, OK I have to stay focused and get back to my soul searching,

My Godparents loved me dearly. They wanted the best for me and they were good people but they were not saved at the time. My parents were saved and understood the spiritual connection involved in becoming Godparents. For some reason, they compromised their beliefs and conformed to modern-day standards and pressures. They chose two loving family members who the only time I remember being in church with them was weddings and funerals. Now, remember I was a part of a family who went to church regularly. What I do remember about my Godmother was she was the life of the party and family gatherings. Although unintentional, I think this was the beginning of my *misguided* training. It was kind of an unspoken message that you can have one foot in the world and one foot in the church. It was at this point I unintentionally became misguided. This marks the beginning of my journey, the beginning of my Christian experience, or as I heard some people say, "The Walk." I was exposed to God but I believe I was given mixed signals. "The Walk" can be defined as the change process a person goes through as they increase their faith in God, find their God-given purpose for life, and commit themselves to building and uplifting the kingdom of God.

The funny thing is everybody knows before a person learns to walk, you must crawl. During the crawling stage, you are cared for, dependent on others to guide and protect you. You are led because you are not mature yet, therefore you follow. Because of the whole Godparent thing, I think it's safe to say that I was given a mixed message from the start. My walk was already compromised. From this point on I will refer to myself as Miss Guided. There I go again. Maybe I keep getting off track because I'm reaching for somebody else to blame for this crazy situation I am in. I don't know! I am just gonna go with it. To be quite honest it's easier for me to focus on babbling than deal with the pain I feel inside. Now I guess I'm trying to social work myself. I know that's not "good practice" but I'm gonna do it anyway. It's better than me ramming this car into something. So let's go back to my religious upbringing, that's a good place to start.

Religion!

What do you mean my life is already planned? Sunday school, why did they call it that? Maybe it's because it was just that. I learned how you are supposed to behave (act) on Sundays. I learned that there were 66 books in the Bible, how to behave in church, and that there were Ten Commandments that should not be broken. I also learned that I had to say my grace before I ate my food and pray before I went to bed. I learned that I had to memorize the Lord's prayer, my grace, the 23rd *Psalm,* and *John 3:16.* I never learned why though. I learned the difference between right and wrong, mostly around stealing and obeying my parents.

Going to Sunday school wasn't so bad because it was basically reading comprehension. I was good at that in regular school. I always scored three grades above reading level and was in a special creative writing class when I was little. All the lessons I learned in Sunday school did not stick with me as I was growing up. EXCEPT ONE, your life is already planned out for you. God already knows what will happen. I remember having a lot of questions about that. I also remember not getting good enough answers which left me puzzled. I remember feeling . . . that was deep! That lesson never left me even though I didn't quite get it. The thing is no one ever told me that I needed to check in with God for guidance. I mean really, if you know that someone has the answers to your questions, wouldn't you consult them? Isn't that the reason why we see doctors, lawyers, teachers, to get answers from them? Don't get me wrong, I was always taught to pray but it was one-sided. I learned to go to God to ask for stuff. I was never taught that God speaks back to you. Maybe this is why my initial walk was around the block. You know what happens when you walk around the block, it's circular, you end up right back where you started from.

When you set out on a planned journey or excursion you know your destination. A person doesn't necessarily know what he may encounter along the way, but you usually know where you are going. You are exposed to new things that are foreign but you learn survival skills, you adapt, change, conform you grow. It seemed that I learned a lot about rituals in church. I mean the dos and don'ts. Most of what I learned went out the window when I attended my first church meeting. It was crazy the same people who taught me about respect and the dos and don'ts of the church were mean and rude in the church meeting. I felt misguided again. I learned you can act one way in church service but outside of service you could do anything you wanted or speak to people any way you wanted. Well, at least that's what I saw the adults doing.

One good thing about coming to church was I also got to see some of my school friends. My church was physically the largest and most beautiful Baptist church around. It's funny, as I think back; there was an in-crowd within the church. These were the women who gave the biggest events and were always on the program. My parents were not that visible. I mean they were active in their auxiliaries but not with the "in-crowd." I remember as a child wishing that they were more popular. I guess that's why I became so active in the church; I was always in something or doing something. It's funny more people knew me in the church than my parents and they were members before we got that big beautiful church; shoot they were members before I was born.

I think my foundation was weak because I was religion and event focused when I should have been God-focused. I needed a relationship with God, but I was misguided. I had friends that were of other religions and some I thought were pretty cool and others I just didn't get. Those friends who were Catholic, I thought were cool because they could go to church stay only an hour, and could wear pants. Women and girls wearing pants to church was one of our don'ts in the Baptist church. Other classmates were Jehovah's Witnesses. I felt sorry for them because they had to be removed from class when we had birthday parties and other fun Holiday stuff. I also had family members who were Jehovah's Witnesses who seemed disconnected from the family. I never got that. There were Jewish kids in my class and most of my teachers were too. I never really got the Jewish thing. I guess I connected that to being white which really blew me away when I heard that Sammy Davis, Junior was Jewish. I really didn't get them either. On second thought I guess my reading comprehension wasn't that great because wasn't Jesus Jewish? It's funny how disconnected you can be and not really know.

I remember going to church every Sunday but I was never complete. I waited for our turn to sing or usher but never connected. It was never complete. Prayer time in church gave me the opportunity to bow my head and catch a nap. Sitting up in the choir loft you were on display so you could not dose off in front of everyone. As I think about it now, they must have been praying for a long time for me to get a nap in. I also remember the sermon was your time to completely zone out. I dreaded this part whether I was in the choir loft or in the pews. I remember being sooooo bored. Don't get me wrong every now and then I would hear a sermon that caught my attention.

> *I remembered a sermon based on Exodus 3:1-11: Exposure to God—What a great opportunity and privilege it must have been for Moses to not only be approached by God but also exposed to God! As believers, we are taught to "seek God" in all aspects of our lives. Here in the text, we see a blessed honor bestowed upon the once Prince, now Shepherd being approached by and exposed to God by God Himself! The exposure in verse 4, "Moses, Moses," and the response, "Here I am" did not quite match up with the reaction. In verse 6, Moses hid his face in fear, and in verse 11 he questions his ability. We must come to understand the involvement of God in our lives. God is very much aware of who we are, even prior to*

us being aware of His presence. As Moses soon discovered, that God not only makes us aware of His presence, but also of His power. Though Moses felt unworthy for the task of being the emancipator of the children of Israel, the power of God, "I AM WHO I AM" in verse 14 was the power that Moses needed to complete the task. Each encounter we have with God can be seen an opportunity for God to expose himself to us in various ways. Let us not only look forward to His presence, but also His power.

This sermon stuck with me because it was something I could relate to. This made me understand a little better what I learned in Sunday school regarding your life being planned out for you. But then again, I was so young and immature that I didn't really get it as I should have. What I did get from that sermon was God is powerful.

When I was a Junior Usher, disappearing to the basement at the beginning of the sermon and returning to the Sanctuary once it was over was the norm. In all fairness to the ministers of that time maybe I was conditioned from a baby. When the sermon would start my mom would spread her handkerchief over her lap and rock me to sleep. I guess this was so she could hear the Word without me disturbing her. After I grew up, I guess I never loss the urge to take that nap when it was preaching time. Back then I would get comfortable and hope I would not drool too much, didn't want to mess up my Sunday best. Trust me my mama did not play when it came down to our church clothes. She made sure we all looked good. My entire family, Dad and my brothers had suits, yes plural and "Florsheim" shoes. My mom and I had shoes, purses and gloves that matched our outfits. Mom always had a hat and on Easter I would get a special outfit and a bonnet.

Its funny I remember thinking those of us that went to church every Sunday were so different from those who came on Easter and Christmas. Now that I look back, I realize that the only difference was I was physically in the building every week but I did not have a real connection to anything except the other youth. For the most part I was well behaved. I tried to do the right thing. Not because of my Christianity but because I was afraid of my mother. I knew she would spank me because she cared about what people thought, and I better not embarrass her. I think that's what kept me out of trouble. I lived my life trying not to embarrass my mom. Don't get me wrong my mom was a Christian woman she believed in God. She knew Jesus. She had a relationship with him. But for me, on the other hand, I was exposed to God but did not make the connection. This left a void in my life.

Not So Precious Memories

I was also exposed to some other stuff that I was too young to sort out. Instead of truly accepting God I was left to accept less than I deserved, because I did not know who I was and who I belonged to. Again, I was misguided. Little did I know my mind was being shaped but it was formed with a deficit? If you don't understand who you are and who you belong to, I guess you are left to try and figure it out on your own.

I remember when I was 6 years old, my brother would pick me up from the bus stop and we would come home together. My mom worked in a school about 10 minutes away so she got home shortly after we did. I got out of school at 2:30 p.m. or so and she got out at 3:00 p.m., by the time I got on the bus and was dropped off near my house, the time would be about 3:15 p.m.; my mom would be getting home between 3:20-3:30 p.m. My brother had to meet me at the bus stop and stay with me until mom came home. On this particular day, my brother had to go outside for something. I don't know if he left something somewhere or somebody had something of his or he went to the store. It was something he had to go get and he said he needed to get it before my mother came home. So, he ran out the door and he told me to lock the door and he'd be right back. I mean no sooner than he had walked out somebody knocked at the door. I wasn't tall enough to look out the window or the peephole and thought it was Junior because he had just left, so I opened the door and it was this guy from up the block. He asked me if my brother was home and I told him no and then he asked if anyone else was home. He was looking around and I was so naive and really not getting what's going on. So, the guy asked me if he could come in and I said nobody's home and I'm not supposed to let anybody in. Somehow, he convinced me to let him come in because he was not a stranger and he lived on the block. It made sense to me and my six-year-old mind. So, I let him in and he sat on the couch. He started talking to me telling me I was a pretty little girl. Some of the details are really, really fuzzy now but the jest of it was he was trying to come on to me. I sensed and or felt something wasn't right so I went and sat on the other side of the room in a chair. I didn't know anything about sex. I didn't know any of that kind of stuff yet. But I just sensed something wasn't right He said, "Don't sit on the chair, the chair is not comfortable come and sit here by me. Maybe we can sit and watch television or talk or get to know each other; I have a little sister like you." The conversation went something like that. I don't remember what the full dialogue was. All I do remember clearly was he started to touch me. When he touched me, it didn't feel right. I didn't know what he was getting ready to do but I know it didn't feel right. I remember saying to him, "Don't touch me; my Mom is going to be home you better leave." He would not leave. I remember him pinning me down on the couch, rubbing on me, and trying to loosen up his pants. While fighting him off, I heard my mother's key turn in the door. He jumped off of me. My mom entered the room and yelled, "What are you doing here? Get away from my daughter!" He ran out of the house. By the time my brother, Junior, came back, my mother was hysterical. When she saw Junior, she just started hitting him and screaming asking why he left me in the house alone. She demanded to know what was going on. Junior said, "But I told her I was just going out for a minute and she knows she is not supposed to open the door." My mother turned to me and began screaming, "Why did you open the door?" Lots of family members came over and the police were involved. At some point, my family and next-door neighbors were standing outside. The guy's family came up the block and everyone was outside arguing. I don't know whether my brother beat the guy up or took something and hit him in the head but he was hurt. His family came up to our house because they wanted to fight. My extended family, my dad's sisters lived in New York at the time so they were out there with their husbands and boyfriends. Everyone came over to the house because my mother was so upset when she walked in and realized what could have happened to me. Now that

I am a mother, I can relate to that fear. She was also thankful at the same time that nothing happened, but she wanted to instill in me that I could not open the door to anybody. I know I should not have been there by myself, but she needed me to understand that I could not open the door for anybody. The problem is she didn't say it in a way that made me feel like it wasn't my fault. She left me feeling like it was my fault that the incident happened. I haven't thought about this in years, I remember feeling if only I didn't open the door! I allowed this to happen! I opened the door! My mother's reaction; the screaming, and yelling, and crying made me feel like I deserved what happened to me because I opened the door.

Acceptance

The Second Set of Footprints:
Romans 10:9-10

Lord I Accept You! But . . .

I remember identifying myself as a Baptist but never a Christian honestly it was only a year ago that I truly realized what a Christian was. I remember begging my mother for permission to get baptized when I was about eight. She would not let me but she did by the time I was 10. I had seen enough people go up to the front to know how to answer the Shepherd's questions. Getting baptized for me meant I could join the children's choir and have some of the communion snacks. That was my sole agenda. Again, there was no connection. Back then you were not allowed to do so if you were not baptized. The ironic thing was my mom didn't want me to get baptized until she felt I truly understood what I was doing. When she finally did, I still did not get it. I just knew how to answer her questions about it. What was most important to me was getting to try those communion snacks. They were like the forbidden fruit.

As I look back over my early Christian education, it seemed that I learned a lot about rituals and rules. It's funny how a lot of what I learned went out the window when I attended my first church meeting. It was crazy because the same people who taught me about respect and the rules were mean and rude and did everything but curse. I remember asking my mother if we could go home because I felt certain people were being picked on. I did not know a lot back then but I did realize that people should not be getting their feelings hurt in the church. It bothered me deeply and I just wanted to go home.

I joined a few auxiliaries in my teenage years, they were like clubs. My understanding of auxiliary membership meant dressing. Listening to the adults talk about how we were true believers because we attended church every Sunday, attended rehearsals during the week, and attended meetings while the other people who came to church only on holidays were not. And oh yes, when they came on those holidays, they made the church crowded and uncomfortable.

There was a popular group in the church called the Hostess Club. If you belonged to that group, your events were attended by everyone, they dressed the best, they spoke the best, they drove the fancy cars, had nice homes, and their kids were involved in the more expensive activities like cotillions and fashion shows. I remember thinking they were God's special people. My parents were members of other clubs which were not part of the "in-crowd." So, we did not participate in certain events. Although, I was asked to participate in the "in crowd" events because I was very popular (I was president at one time or another of each of the youth organizations—Junior Ushers, Choir, and Youth Council), unfortunately, my mother did not feel comfortable unless I was on the program and if I wasn't I couldn't participate in the "in crowd's" events. As a teen, it really didn't feel good to be on the outside of that group.

I also remember our church decided to vote out our Shepherd. The church was divided because a lot of people did not want him to leave. This was another time when people were acting mean and hateful and verbally wounding each other. Even some of the ministers were mean. The sad part of it all was when the Pastor left half the church left with him. My mom said she didn't want the Pastor to leave either but she was not leaving her church.

I was very confused about church throughout my teenage years by the way people treated each other. I wished I had somewhere to go to feel comfortable because there was so much going on in my house. I felt like I could not find peace anywhere.

Don't get me wrong, I had a strong family unit but things were always up and down at home. For the most part, things were intact. I mean my father was a hard worker and had a real presence in our home. My father went to work every day and had a hustle—his Gypsy

Cab. My mom was basically a housewife with jobs here and there, but always there for our family. I had three brothers and a cousin (also like a brother to me) who lived with us from the time I was six months old. I was the baby and only girl, spoiled by all the men in my life growing up. I wonder, what happened? So you know that means I was spoiled. I loved having three brothers and my brother-cousin. Each was different but spoiled me in their special way. My oldest brother Lee is 13 years older than I am and always seemed like a father figure. We didn't get close until we were adults. My brother, Junior, is seven years older than me and the closest to my age; then there was Carl who was 10 years older.

My brother Carl was a troubled soul. He was so talented. As a small child, he loved to draw. Actually, he was pretty good at it until he fell through a glass door and cut his hand. After his accident, he was never able to draw again because of the damage he caused to his hand. Losing the ability to draw hurt Carl deeply. My mom said that a piece of his spirit was lost when he could no longer draw. I think that loss touched him deeper than anyone of us realized.

Carl had a gentle spirit. He was always smiling and loved children. He taught me how to talk, walk and ride my bike. He was very good to me. He nicknamed me baby Disster and Sheba which was short for the Queen of Sheba. Carl was the one I was closest to. The sad thing about Carl was he also was the one who had a troubled life. Carl just . . . Well, he was on drugs and I really did not clearly understand or know what was truly going on because I was so young at the time. I remember people in my family talking about drugs and I remember young people, in the neighborhood dying from drugs. They were shooting drugs with needles. I remember thinking in my childish mind I hate needles when I have to get them from the doctor. Who would want to give themselves shots? Well anyway they were dying from Heroin overdoses. My brother Carl was hooked on it too. I remember hearing a story about Carl. Apparently, a girl he was dealing with in his teenage years had a venereal disease and gave him the disease and he did not tell my parents out of fear. He saw something was wrong and he did not say anything until it was too late. As a result the infection took over and it resulted in him having to have one of his testicles removed. He became involved with another girl during his teenage years and he attempted to become intimate with her, but she laughed at him because he only had one testicle. Family members said he never got over that. His self-esteem took a beating. Between that and not being able to draw was more than he could handle. Those two events, I believe, started messing with his head, which led him to drugs to ease his pain.

Things were so crazy at home, one minute everything was fine and the next minute everything was crazy. The night before my 8th birthday party, Carl decided that he was going to go out and get high; he overdosed and ended up in the hospital. The family was back and forth in deciding if I was going to have a birthday party because Carl was being released from the hospital that day. When they finally decided that the party was on, it was like a cloud hanging over the party because Carl was upstairs sick. He was recuperating from the overdose but what I did not understand back then was he was probably also going through withdrawals. He had been doing heroin for a while but nobody knew. It was so sad because he was just so sweet.

When I was seventeen, around the holidays, Carl had been on drugs for years, and he finally was getting off the drugs through a Methadone program. He said this was going to be his year. He kept repeating this statement throughout the Christmas season—"This is gonna be my year." I could tell he meant it. We all thought he meant that he was going to turn his life around. No more drugs because he had not been getting high. Little did we know, on a Saturday morning Carl was going to wake up and make some major declarations? I should say the night before he went and played cards with my brothers and their girlfriends. The next morning he got up and came over to give my mother a gold chain with a diamond H which was her first initial. Now, this was a big deal for a drug addict. He had come a long way. Money was not spent on gifts, expensive ones at that. Money was usually spent on drugs but not at this point in his life. He was saving money and doing well. He had even saved enough to get his bass guitar and amplifier out of hock. Carl had taken up playing the Bass guitar. He was really good at it. He had a band and my mother would let them practice in our garage. They played at a few clubs and they were really pretty good. He loved music. Music made him so happy and he got back some of

Acceptance

the use of his hand. The problems with playing in the band though were the "gigs" as he called them. There was a lot of getting high in that world. Carl got deeper and deeper into that life. He was so far gone he pawned his guitar and amplifier. One day he got tired of his addiction. He realized he truly had a problem and got on methadone to get off Heroin. The problem was he hated the methadone. He said it made him higher and sicker than heroin ever did. By the time he came to see us that life changing Saturday morning, he had weaned down to a very low dosage. He was in a committed relationship and engaged. All he wanted to do was to get his guitar back and play again.

I will never forget, he came into my room and woke me up. I threw my pillows at him because I wanted to sleep. He told me how proud he was of me because I was graduating from high school. I thought this is crazy; I am in my junior year. I wasn't graduating until the next year. I playfully told him, "Get OUTTA MY ROOM," it was too early in the morning and I wanted to go back to sleep. He left the house and his fiancé came by shortly after. She was like, well where is he? He and I were supposed to go into the city together to get his Bass guitar back. My brother loved his instrument. The band wrote songs and they would also play other peoples' music. They would play for different parties and get paid. My mom was real good about supporting our dreams and supporting what it was we wanted to do, so he had all the equipment he ever wanted. But Carl's drug habit took over everything and he started to pawn his stuff. That Saturday morning, he was on his way to get his stuff back. Little did I know that would be the last time I would see my brother. Carl went into the City, his fiancé followed right behind. She was like where did he go, I have to catch up with him, I can't believe he left me, he just left the house. So, she left our house and tried to catch up with him but she didn't. She called us up later and said she wasn't able to catch up to him. By Saturday night Carl had not come home. It was scary because she did not hear from him and did not know where he was. Sunday rolls around and she still didn't hear from him. My older cousins came by and they were just sitting with my mother. No one felt right. I think we all knew something was wrong. By Monday morning my mom called the morgue. I was upset because she was calling the morgue. I called my brother Lee and told him that mama was calling the morgue to look for Carl and he got upset. He went off on my mother like he never had before. He said, "Why would you call the morgue looking for my brother?" He said, "Call the police, call the hospitals." I will never forget, my mama stated that God told her to contact the morgue. Shortly after her making this statement to me, she made the phone call, came into my room and told me that Carl was gone. I did not believe her. So, she called the neighborhood funeral home and asked the funeral director to go with her to the morgue to identify the body and make arrangements and he agreed. She also called my father at work and told him to meet her there. My brother Junior called to check in, because we were all alerted and alarmed by Carl's disappearance. My brother Lee called and told him what was happening. Junior said he knew where the morgue was and was going to meet our parents there as well. When they got there, it was him. Carl was in the morgue. My brother was gone. He was 27 years old. I was devastated; my brothers were devastated my mom and dad were devastated. Mama was so strong and she moved forward and did what needed to be done. It's funny when I think back to that Sunday night when I went to sleep, I dreamt that Carl had died. I saw the entire funeral. That's what's so crazy. And then I woke up to find out that he was really gone. I remember sitting there just out of it. My aunts were from a holiness church and had given me some stuff they called Spirits of Ammonia. It was something that was supposed to keep us calm. I remember being at my brother's funeral feeling like I was having an out of body experience. I remember feeling high throughout the entire service. They gave it to me and Junior. It made me numb; it was a crazy feeling. I kept reflecting on the day before when we went to make sure his body was acceptable for viewing. Based on his appearance, I had a hard time accepting that it was him. The person in that casket did not look like my brother to me. I remember thinking for years my brother is not dead. You see, my brother Carl was really light skinned. His nickname was red because he was so light. At the time, I didn't know that the skin on dead people turn darker the longer they are kept out of the ground. So, Carl had gotten quite a few shades darker than he normally was. I just told myself it wasn't him. My beautiful, sweet, loving big brother Carl was gone. Years later, talking about Carl's death to my mother, she said she never really got over it. She said you never think that you are going to bury your child; the parent expects to go first. You never get over that. Mama said God helped her to deal with it. I remember wondering why God didn't help me with it.

Mr. Contender Sucker Punched!
Loving Him till it Hurts

I was heartbroken; I met my first boyfriend during my freshman year in High School, Mr. Dis-ease. He was being sent to his grandparents' house by his mother in West Virginia for the entire summer. Has she lost her mind? I remember thinking how could she do this to us? Yeah, I had a lot of drama with me back then. Didn't she realize how much in love we were? Didn't she realize how close we were? I just knew I was going to die from a broken heart. Oh the dramatic mind of a 15-year-old. It was what it was and those were my thoughts. I just knew this was going to be the worst summer ever. I had just completed my freshman year in high school and I had a cute boyfriend that was going to be a senior. He was really smart, could write beautiful poetry and he was from the projects in Manhattan. I felt I had "every girl's" dream, the perfect mix of a guy who was intelligent, artsy, and knew how to negotiate the streets; he wasn't a punk by any means. All I knew was I loved him and he was in love with me. He treated me so well. When he came around to meet my family, he was so nice and tried to be so helpful. He would offer to take out the garbage and look for other things he could do to be helpful. I was crazy about him! Why couldn't his mother understand that she was ruining my life? Mr. Dis-ease was gone less than a week when I received his first letter. I was thrilled. I remember thinking he loved me so much that he wrote me a letter right away. I wrote him right back telling him how much I missed him and would just die if I didn't see him.

I was bored to death and didn't know what I was going to do. Then it happened. I got my first real job at a summer camp at my church. I was a Daily Vacation Bible School Counselor. I liked little kids and I was happy that I would make some money so I could put off my impending death for at least until after summer youth employment was over.

So, I started my first day of work. I was a little nervous because I didn't know what to expect. We worked Monday through Thursdays, with Fridays off. My first week was relatively easy the campers did not start right away so the counselors were there getting the administration's expectations and getting to know each other. Then it happened. I saw this guy, 6 ft. 2 in. tall, dark skin smooth as chocolate, he was gorgeous. All of a sudden, I had butterflies in my stomach. My heart would flutter every time he walked into the room. There was something about him that was magnetic. His friend liked my friend and they had already connected but me I became really shy. I remember thinking what about Mr. Dis-ease? How could I be attracted to someone else? Then again, what about Mr. Dis-ease, he's away and I can hang out with this guy until he gets back. That is if I ever get my nerves up to speak to him. Then it happened. He came over to me and spoke with the deepest voice I had ever heard. It was wonderful. I remember thinking oh my God he is gorgeous. It was love at first sight. He introduced himself and asked my name and smiled. Little did I know that smile would change my life as I knew it then? There was something about him that was familiar. He was strong but also sensitive. It was as if he knew I was shy and made it easy for me to talk to him, again, I just knew I was in love.

We began to talk and I found out that he played basketball and was quite good at it. During the school year, he attended a Catholic high school and was on a basketball scholarship. During the summer he played in summer leagues. He was going to be playing that weekend in the neighborhood park and invited me to come to watch him. I remember saying to myself what am I going to wear. I agreed to attend and got my girlfriends together and we went to watch him play. He was amazing! The crowds were cheering for him, everybody in the neighborhood loved him, and he had skills. Again, I just knew I was in love. I remember thinking that this basketball star liked and wanted me! I was thrilled, all smiles. It didn't hurt that my girlfriends also thought he was fine. But as good as I was feeling there was a wrench thrown in my fairytale man. One of my friends told me that they heard he had a girlfriend in the neighborhood. They also said that he has been known to hit her. I thought this was the most ridiculous thing I had ever heard of. Not the girlfriend part because I could understand that. I still had not gotten around to telling him about Mr. Dis-ease. It was the hitting part. Not my new interest! He was just so sweet, so cute and so smooth.

After the game, I approached him and I asked him about the girl and the hitting. He said she was his ex-girlfriend and the hitting was blown out of proportion. He said that she jumped in his face like she was a man so he "mushed" her out of his face. He said you have to understand that there are some girls that don't know how to be a girlfriend. There can only be one man in the relationship and she didn't get that, so that's why they broke up. He then told me how much he liked me and we would never have that problem. He then told me that his grandmother just bought him a car and he wanted to know if I wanted to go for a ride so we could be alone and talk. I remember thinking that I had died and gone to heaven, I now had a boyfriend who was a basketball star that everyone in my neighborhood knew and loved, he is gorgeous and he had a car. I had hit the jackpot. But I remember thinking what was I going to do about Dis-ease? I just didn't know. I figured I would worry about that later.

We went out on our first date; he took me to The International House of Pancakes. I just knew we were going to McDonald's, Burger King or White Castle but we didn't. We went to what was considered a restaurant. Again I was impressed, not to mention I also loved that when we left we jumped into his car not a bus or the train. I felt grown up. We continued to have a wonderful summer until one day I got a phone call from his supposed to be ex-girlfriend cursing at me, calling me all sorts of names, and saying I needed to stay away from her man. I didn't understand, he told me they were broken up. I immediately called him and told him what had transpired and he said he would handle it. He said not to worry she was just mad and trying to get him back. He said she just hates that he loves me now and not her. I remember thinking oh my God, he loves me. I figured OK I would let my man handle it. Later in the week, he did not come to work and I conveniently ran into her on her block. We walked the kids from the camp through her block from the park on our way back to the church.

Boy, how crazy was that? My friends, the other counselors, about 30 little kids and I were standing outside of her house. She was sitting on the steps and I asked her if she was who she was. She said yes. I told her not to ever call my house again under any circumstances. In my mind, I had agreed to let him handle her saying that she was his girlfriend part but I needed to handle her disrespecting me by calling my house.

It was clear that the two of them had talked. She told me that she didn't want him anyway. She said she was tired of him and she deserves better treatment. Later that night she called my house to apologize. She explained that she was really upset because he told her he was interested in me but he still wanted to see her. She said that he told her he was her first (sexual partner) and that should mean something. She said they got into an argument and he smacked her and told her how things were going to be. She said she loved him so much that she thought that if she could get me to stop seeing him they would work out their issues. She also told me that she was going to leave him alone because her parents found out he was hitting her and forbade her to see him again. I remember thinking that this was crazy. How could she say she was in love with someone who hits her? I also remember thinking as a virgin, how could you give yourself to someone who was so mean, she was describing a monster and the guy I knew was nothing but nice to me.

I remember my mother had real problems with me seeing this guy. She especially did not like the fact that he had a car. She said I could go to the movies or out to dinner but I could not get into the car with him. I remember thinking this was ridiculous. Why should we have to take public transportation when he had a car? Besides this was one of the perks in the relationship. What did she know anyway? So what we did was I would meet him around the corner and we were on the go. I now understand why my mother didn't want me in that car. A lot of kissing and hugging took place in that car. As I look back it opened up the door for some things I truly wasn't ready for. The more I was with him the more I wanted to be with him. And the more I wanted to be with him the more urges I started to have. I mean Mr. Dis-ease and I would kiss but this was different.

Acceptance

As the summer went on, we became very close. One day we got off work early and I told my mom I was going to my friend's house but I didn't I went to his house. He and I started kissing and hugging and he invited me to his bedroom. We went upstairs where we continued with the kissing and hugging and he asked me if I were a virgin and I said of course. He then told me how much he loved me and he wanted to take our relationship to the next level. I remember shaking but I felt like I loved him too and wanted to show him how much. So, he started to remove my clothes and I continued to shake. I was so scared. I told him that I always dreamed of this moment but I thought it would be with my husband. You have to remember I was a church girl. I had morals and values. I remember him saying then I guess we will have to get married someday. He always knew the right thing to say at the right moment. That's how he hooked me. No matter what he said to me I believed it. As we started to get into the act I began shaking even more and told him I was not ready. I remember he was wonderful. He said I don't want to push you into anything you are not ready for. He was so understanding and comforting. There we were lying in his bed with no clothes on and he said this has to be right for both of us. I want you to remember your first time for the rest of your life with good thoughts. He said let me just hold you in my arms. We don't have to do anything you are not ready for. I am not going anywhere and we will wait. It was this moment that made me fall in unconditional love. This moment was pivotal in our relationship. The way he handled this situation made me trust him with my life. You see I had six girlfriends who I grew up with and we always discussed our virginity. We talked about the best thing was to wait until marriage because this is what we were taught in Sunday school. But we told ourselves if we fell in love before then it would be OK. We just could not have sex with anyone else because that would make you a slut. By this point, out of the seven of us, five had lost their virginity. Some of the stories were really sad because they were not connected to the boys any longer, or the boys were rough or they just hated it.

About two weeks later we tried again and succeeded. To this day I remember that experience as being something beautiful at that point I was committed to him for better or worse. But that day I saw a different side of him. It was beautiful until the act was over. He got a little weird. He then cradled me in his arms and told me how much he loved me, and said that I now belong to him. I remember all kinds of red flags went up for me. I had mixed emotions about this statement; I asked him what he meant. He said you said it yourself what we did was special. I am going to be the first and the last you make love to. I was the first and when we get older, we will get married and I will be the last. He then said, "But let me tell you something. There will be a lot of time between now and then and we both have to finish high school and college before we get married. During that time, you may start to think about dealing with someone else but that is not going to happen, you belong to me." I remember laughing and saying, "Well that is just as long as you remain true to me." He then smiled a sinister smile, clinched me tightly and said, "What I do should not and will not make a difference." He then leaned over and grabbed what I thought was a gun. I had never seen a real gun so it could have been a lighter made out of a gun, but it didn't matter because I thought it was a real gun at the time. He held it to my head and said, "Let's get a few things straight. As I said you belong to me. I love you, and sometimes guys do things with hoes they won't do with their girl. This does not mean that you could be with someone else, it just means that you are to keep yourself like a lady and be there just for me." He said, "I have an image to uphold and I can't have people thinking you are out there. Plus, I am not going to tolerate it. Always remember, I will take you out before I see you f.... someone else. I mean that, do you understand?"

I remember responding in a very submissive voice yes I understand. He said "I am serious MG, do you understand what I am saying to you?" I guess I wasn't forceful enough or convincing enough, frankly, I was stunned. How could someone who was so gentle turn into someone so threatening? I responded again forcefully, I quickly learned how to play his game. I grabbed him back and said why are we are having this conversation; I don't want anyone but you. He then made love to me again and switched back to that sensitive guy who had taken my virginity earlier. He said, "I know it hurts baby but the more we do it the better you are going to feel." Now that I look back it seems as though the more we did it the more control he had over me.

Acceptance

    As the summer came to an end, it was a few days before we had to go back to school, we were hanging out in the neighborhood, and I asked him to walk me home. The rumors were still circulating about him messing around with his ex. I questioned him about it, and he said it wasn't true. I told him that he needed to make up his mind about what he wanted; I decided to tell him about Dis-ease which really made him very angry. I told him that Dis-ease was away for the summer and when I went back to school, I was going to break up with him based on the fact that we are now in a relationship. He was really angry about the fact that I had not told him about Dis-ease. I then said to him at least Dis-ease was in West Virginia. I told him that I knew he was lying about f . . . . with his ex. He then said, "Don't curse at me." I told him that I don't know what she put up with, and I heard about him hitting her but I would not tolerate it. He told me that I needed to be put in check. He said, "You cursed at me and that's not ladylike and you suck your teeth at me, and I will not have you disrespecting me." I told him that I think he must have lost his mind. I wasn't his property, I am his girlfriend. I reminded him that I was not his ex and he better not threaten me. He said, "Curse and or suck your teeth at me one more time and see what happens." Honestly, part of me felt like I wanted to see what he would do, the other part saw he was serious and I had flashbacks of the gun incident so I didn't say anything. At this point, he began to tell me how things are going to be from now on. All I remember is he said something that didn't sit right with me. Now let's face it. I was 15, I sucked my teeth at anything and everyone, it was a reflex reaction. I sucked my teeth and didn't realize I had done it until I felt his hand that could palm a basketball like a grape come crashing down across my face. I was stunned! I could not even fight back. I was paralyzed. He then said, "You see you took me there." I trembled in fear. He said, "Now, let's get a few things straight. First of all, get rid of Dis-ease immediately. Second, when you speak to me you better watch what you say and how you say it, and third, don't you ever suck your teeth at me again." He continued our talk by telling me, "This has been a long time coming. I haven't hit you before this because I didn't want to get into it with your brother because we are cool. But if we got to throw, then so be it. I am not going to have my women disrespect me.

This Walk Ain't Right! But, Help Is Along The Way

I ain't no punk. You just remember you brought this on yourself. It is as if you wanted me to hit you." It's funny, I felt I did bring it on. I felt that I taunted him, so I guess I deserved it. I never told my brothers, my parents or even my best friend, Wisdom, because I blamed myself. This was a major turning point in our relationship.

So, I went back to school and I tried to break it off with Dis-ease but it was so hard I just couldn't. I mean I didn't want to be with him and I would not kiss him or anything but I could not bring myself to tell him because I didn't want to hurt him. I started hanging out during school hours. I left school early one day with my friends and showed up outside of the [1]"Contender's" school to meet him. He acted a little strange. He wasn't really happy to see me. He asked why I was there so early. I told him I had a half-day. He gave me a look like he knew I was lying. The next day, he decided to come by my house and pay me a visit after school. We went for a walk around the corner. He asked me if I broke it off with Dis-ease and I tried to explain, but all he wanted to hear was yes. I could see how visibly angry he was getting and I tried to proceed with caution. I admitted that I had not and asked permission to explain the situation, hmm permission, that's funny. How did I get here? As I explained, he said I better break it off tomorrow and then asked me if I had been cutting classes. I said no, yes, I lied but I figured how he would know. At that moment, it happened again. He smacked me in my face and said don't lie to me. I then told him I had cut a few classes, but what's the big deal. He then started to explain that school was important and I should take it seriously and he went on and on and on. The crazy part is I should have been mortified by his behavior, but I liked the fact that he cared enough to discipline me. I felt like he was right because I should not have cut school and I should have told Dis-ease. He told me I better go to class or he was going to really hurt me.

The next day I went back to school and broke things off with Dis-ease. He was devastated. I also started attending classes regularly. I came home from school and called the Contender and asked him to come over so we can talk. I told him that I broke things off with Dis-ease. He then did the unthinkable. He broke up with me. He said he can't be with someone he could not trust. He said he can't get past my lying to him. I just didn't get it. Why didn't he see that I was afraid of him and that's why I lied? He told me about a girl that he went to school with who wants to get back together with him. I didn't even know about this girl. This explains his behavior, the other day when I showed up at the school. I was devastated. I pleaded with him to give me another chance. He refused. This was the beginning of him having me fully under his control. I was miserable. I cried every day, I lost so much weight. When he saw me again after a few weeks he asked what was going on, he said I was too skinny, I told him I would gain weight if he came back to me. I asked him to make love to me one last time. I figured maybe this would bring him back into my life. He did but the crazy thing was he reminded me of what he said the first time and said even if we are not together, I cannot be involved with anyone else. He said he had to regain his trust for me and this would be the only way because as far as he was concerned, Dis-ease and I were messing around because Dis-ease did not know I wasn't his girl. He was playing mind games with me and I knew it, but I didn't care because somewhere down the line I only cared about getting him back.

During the time of me and the Contender's breakup, I got back together with Dis-ease. But I didn't tell the Contender. He got back together with me, and I broke up with Dis-ease again. This on-again off-again pattern lasted for months. The abuse from the Contender got worse. I was totally under his control. If he wasn't hitting me to control me, he was breaking up with me or just being mean.

One day, I was at my school and the Contender decided to come up to see me with a group of his friends. My two girlfriends from the neighborhood were also dating two of his friends. We went to school in Manhattan. One of my girlfriends was seeing one boy from Manhattan and another from East Elmhurst but she was open and honest with both of them. I think that worked in her favor because the challenge was on them.

Everyone in the neighborhood knew I belonged to the Contender. Even when we would break up and he told them that no one else could date me and he had me in check. He liked to show that I was under his control. I guess that's why he lost it when he and his friends came to my school and me and my friends walked out of the building with the other guys. The guys at school were pursuing us and we wanted to remain as friends. There wasn't really anything going on that day. The Contender and his friends were standing outside the building when we were dismissed from school. One of my friends Miss "Sweetie" came out of the building holding hands with the new guy she was dating. It was sad because the guy who wanted her back came with flowers for her but she didn't want to get back together with him. My other friend "Miss Mouthy" came out of the building next and her boyfriend was standing outside. She tried to give me a heads up because she knew I was walking out with Dis-ease, who was begging me to come back to him, but I was not having it. I was still so in love with the Contender and also afraid of him so leaving him was not an option. But to be on the safe side, Miss Mouthy said hello to the guys as loud as she could so I would know the Contender was waiting for me. I remember coming out of the building and walking toward him and he was so angry. He thought I was messing around because Miss Sweetie was holding hands with the new guy. I remember we introduced them all which was a very awkward feeling. Needless to say, me and Miss Mouthy said goodbye to the other guys and left with our guys. That was a long ride home. The whole time we were walking down the street. The Contender would not talk to me or even look at me. I tried to play off what I was feeling by talking to everyone else. I remember getting on a crowded train and everybody ran into one of the subway cars. As I got ready to get on the train, the Contender pulled me back by my arm and guided me into another car. When the doors closed, my back was on the door. He stood in front of me. I remember it like it was yesterday. He stood there looking down at me without saying a word. I remember the mean look on his face as this 6 ft. 2 in. young man glared down at me. I was only about 5 ft. 3 in. and thin, because he had me so stressed by the break-ups and make-ups and the hitting that I was losing weight like crazy. He wasn't a heavy guy, but he was bigger and stronger than I was. So, we're on the train and we rode with him glaring at me not saying anything all the way to Queens. I was so glad to get off that train and on the bus. Usually, I would take a different bus than the rest of the crew because I lived, as they called it "The Boondocks," even though it was all the same neighborhood. I was in a different direction from the

Acceptance

rest of them. This particular day, I had an appointment at my dentist's office that was on the same bus line as the rest of the crew. So I got on the bus, sat down, he sat across from me. He would converse with his boys but I would catch him looking at me every now and then, it was crazy because he would laugh and joke with them but when he would look at me he was clearly angry. So we all rode the bus to the last stop and Miss Mouth and her boyfriend argued all the way down the street. Miss Sweetie tried to console her heartbroken ex-boyfriend. Then I started to walk in the direction to my dentist. The Contender finally spoke to me asking where I was going. I told him to the dentist and he said he would walk with me. I really didn't want that, but I could not risk him getting even madder. At least he was not swinging on me he was just mad. To be quite honest I could deal with that because he was always angry about something or another. It was the smacking me in my face I could not deal with. So, as we are walking he's still not talking. So I begin to talk. I immediately try to explain that things were not the way they appeared. I told myself that I wanted to appeal to that side of him that was kind to me, gentle and loving. You see in my mind I made him treat me the way he treated me. It was my fault because I provoked him that first time to see just how far he would go. It was really twisted when you think about it. I had heard that he hit other girls but instead of me having the attitude he will not treat me that way and if he does I am walking. No, not me I wondered why he hit them and not me. I thought it was because he didn't care as much for me. So, I provoked him. The sad part is he went for it and once he hit me the first time I didn't know how to get him to stop. I told myself that it wasn't a big issue. It wasn't like he did it every day; it was only when I did something he did not approve of. He said he had to put me in check, "deep check." I think another reason I let him get away with this is because he and I became involved in things we should not have been doing at our age and I felt a lot of guilt behind that. Here I am so active in church how could I be doing this. So, getting back to my story, as we walked he listened and I could tell he wasn't angry as he was initially. We finally reach my dentist's office. The dentist was located on the second floor of a three-story walk-up. I tried to say goodbye at the door but he stopped me. He asked if I wanted him to go home and get his car and pick me up to take me home. I told him my mom would be picking me up so he said let me walk you upstairs then. So, we got to the top of the stairs and he leaned over to kiss me goodbye. It was at that moment that he leaned down and put his hands around my neck and said, "The next time I come to your school and I see you with Mr. Dis-ease I am gonna knock all your teeth out and you won't need a dentist. Do you understand what I'm saying?" I said, "Yes, I understand." He kissed me on the lips and said to call him when I got home. I remember feeling like thank God, he didn't hit me.

After the dentist incident, it seemed like things really went downhill from there. The Contender was so abusive to me. It wasn't just physical abuse I was also mentally abused. I had to dress the way he wanted me to. Back then all the girls were wearing Chinese shoes and jelly shoes. It was the style. He hated them and I was not allowed to wear them. If we were alone, he would get physical about it but if we were around a group of people he would not acknowledge me. I remember one time he went to a basketball camp for a couple of weeks during the summer. I wore my Chinese shoes the whole time he was gone. I remember I heard he was back and I was out in my Chinese shoes. I remember running home to change them because he had a car and he could have rolled up on me at any time. Just as I got home, he was pulling up to my house. I ran into the house and told him I would be right back. I changed those shoes. I remember hoping that he didn't see my feet when I ran into the house. When I came back out, he didn't mention it so, I knew he didn't see them. But you better believe he looked at me from head to toe. It was as if I had to pass an inspection.

The mental abuse continued. He would say and do horrible things because he felt I *needed to be put in check*. Most of the time, I suffered in silence. From my point of view, I guess he was gracious enough not to embarrass me publicly. I really think that it had something to do with my brother Junior finding out and kicking his butt. You see by this point in the relationship, he realized that I wasn't telling anyone what was going on. So, he recognized that he needed not to let anyone find out because they would tell. It's funny, when I would get the strength to not deal with him he would pour on the charm and pursue me, pamper me but as soon as he realized I was reeled back in he would mistreat me. He would mess around with other girls; break up with me to teach me a lesson because he knew I would be miserable. The sad part about it was I always saw him, he lived in my neighborhood and he was my best friend Wisdom's cousin. Wisdom and I knew of each other in elementary and Junior High School. We did not like each other very much. I always thought she was a bully and was mean and she thought I was stuck up and full of myself. When we got together, he gave me her telephone number as another place I could reach him because he was always there. One day my mother had a heart attack and went to the hospital. I was not able to go but I was going crazy waiting home to get some news as to how she was. I attempted to reach him at Wisdom's house but he wasn't there. At first, she was distant on the phone, not very warm or friendly. When I explained why I was trying to reach him she immediately showed genuine compassion and concern. She told me he was not there but she would find him. When she wasn't able to locate him she left word for him to meet her at my house. She came over and we sat and talked on the steps for a while and connected immediately. I knew then that she was a special person because she did not have to come over to sit with me, especially since she didn't like me. From that day on Wisdom and I were cool and have been best friends for 30+ years.

So, I suffered in silence not even telling Wisdom what he was doing. I think she had an idea but because he left no marks and she never witnessed it, she had no proof. His best friend Big Brother (BB) knew what was going on though. He and I became really good friends. He and Wisdom tried to get something going but it never really played out for some reason. He was there at times when the Contender would become aggressive with me. He was able to calm him down. I used to confide in him about what was really happening. He used to tell me to not say much when I was around him because for some reason, I really set him off. I remember the day I finally got away from him for good. I was on the phone with BB. While we were on the phone the Contender came to BB's house. The Contender asked BB who he was on the phone with and BB told him it was me. Why did he do that? In retrospect, I don't think BB was thinking clearly. The Contender and I were not really speaking because I had enough of his mess. I was tired

This Walk Ain't Right! But, Help Is Along The Way

of the way he treated me and I knew I would be going away to college so I would be free of him. I didn't plan to tell him how to contact me once I left and he would not be able to find me.

So, BB and I were on the phone and the Contender tells him to let him speak to me. We immediately got into an argument. At this point in our relationship, I would argue back at him and I guess he realized that he was losing the hold he had on me. He was losing control. So, the Contender gets off the phone. I could hear him in the background ranting and raving. BB was trying to calm him down. He said I am sick of her and I'm going to teach her a lesson once and for all. So I'm on the phone talking crap mostly because I knew he couldn't hear me. At some point, he picks up another extension and hears what I was saying and goes off. So, BB told me to apologize so he would stop acting the way he was acting. The Contender was like no, that's it and left the house. BB told me that the Contender had left and I think he's coming to your house. He asked if anyone was home with me. I told him no. He said don't answer the door because he is really mad. I was like I don't care I have had it and I'm not putting up with his mess anymore. Before I knew it my bell was ringing, BB said, "Don't open the door I'm on my way there." I will get him to leave. The funny thing is like a nut I opened the door. The first thing he does is check out if anyone is home with me. When he realized I was home alone he came after me. He was smacking me in my face pushing and pulling on me. He grabbed me by my neck at one point. I was fighting back this time. I was trying to get away from him. I tried to run up the stairs and he grabbed my leg and pulled me back down with my head hitting each step. Finally, I kicked him between his legs and ran up the stairs. I went into the kitchen and got the biggest butcher knife I could find and came after him. He was doubled over in pain but he saw the look in my eyes. I was going to kill him. I had enough. He started saying you are crazy. I was like you have not seen crazy yet. At this point, BB was banging on the door yelling MG let me in. I came charging at the Contender who was hurting from the kick to the groin and couldn't get up to get me. He stumbled back and opened the door for BB himself. BB talked me down took the knife and got him out of my house. I remember going into my bathroom after it was all over and looking in the mirror. My hair was a mess; I was sweating and crying. I was a mess! Through my blurred vision, I could see what appeared to be a handprint across the side of my face. I remember thinking what happened to me? How did I get to this place? I felt so ashamed. I allowed myself to go through this. Nobody knew except BB and I can't let anybody know now. I figured I will go to bed and tell my mother I have a headache when she gets in and that way nobody will see me. The handprint will be gone in the morning and if not I will leave out for school making sure I don't run into anyone. I was used to playing things off.

I really didn't understand why this happened to me. I loved him so much. It's funny I was not used to being treated this way. For the most part, I was a spoiled brat. My brother Jr. called me Cadillac legs because my father or mother drove me everywhere I wanted. During my teenage years, I was very active in the church. I was a part of everything a young person could be a part of. The only thing was I had a terrible secret. I was in a relationship at 15, he was my first love who physically abused me and I suffered in silence throughout my late teenage years and until I went away to college. I guess I didn't tell anybody because I knew if someone asked me why I put up with that treatment, I would have to admit I had sex out of marriage and at this young age. Besides, if I told my brothers, my cousin, and my father they would have killed him. I loved him too much to jeopardize his safety. Wow!!! How sick was that! I was consumed with guilt, hurt, pain, confusion, and just wanting to know why? The good thing was after that crazy night the Contender never hit me again. So I went away to college armed with my new red bible with my name engraved on it and a check from the Church Scholarship Committee. I was ready. My secrets and I were off to explore bigger and better things. No more suffering in silence.

Mr. Man Submit! Submit! Submit!

I was so happy to get to college. I was finally free of the *Contender*. I really did not like the way things went down. I really should not have ever put up with the way he treated me and I felt very guilty about that. I beat myself up about the fact that I lived in the house with five men and I allowed someone to physically abuse me. Not to mention my crazy mother! She would have done more damage to that young man than the five men could have ever done. One thing about my mother, you don't get to mess with her kids. I also did not like that I pulled a knife on him because that wasn't me. I was so grateful because it could have turned out worse. Shoot I could be in jail instead of college. I was grateful to God. I promised myself that I would never allow myself to be abused again.

Throughout my teenage years, I always worked after-school jobs and full-time jobs in the summer. I was used to having my own money. When I started college, I quickly realized that I needed a job. I mean my parents were sending me money but $50 a week was not what I was accustomed to. One of my suitemates was an upperclassman and she managed the campus snack bar. She got me a job working with her. This was perfect I didn't have to leave campus to work and it paid more than work-study and the hours weren't limited.

At work one day this guy came into the snack bar. He was gorgeous with all these muscles and clothes that were so stylish. I remember saying, "Damn, he's fine." The sad part is I thought he would never be interested in me. I asked my co-worker to let me take his order and she did. He struck up a conversation and I remembered wondering, is he just being nice or might there be some interest. After he got his food, he sat down at one of the tables. I had to stop myself from staring I was really taken aback by this guy. So he ate his food and then left. I felt that he was flirting but I wasn't really sure. I was a little guarded. I didn't trust my judgment because of my last relationship. My self-esteem was also in the toilet because of the abuse. I was a mess but I was interested. I told my friends about him as we were walking back to the dorms. I would get dressed up to go to work in case I ran into him. That would have been fine if I worked in an office. I worked at the snack bar. I was wearing heels to make sandwiches, sling burgers, and sweep floors. Unfortunately, I didn't see him again for a while. Just as I had given up on the thought of seeing him again, he walked into the snack bar. I knew I had to say something to test the waters. I said, "I haven't seen you in a while. I was afraid you didn't like the sandwich I made." He laughed and said, "No, I only have classes twice a week and I am a commuter, I work construction full-time so I'm not here

Acceptance

every day." Then he said, "Besides, that's why I am back. It was so good I could not wait to come back for more."

For the next couple of weeks, this was our encounter a few short words about the meal with a flirtatious twist. Boy, was I starting to like this guy. Then one day it happened he asked if I lived on campus. I told him I did and then he asked if I like ice cream. I said yes again. He then asked if he could take me out for ice cream and talk so we could become acquainted. I could not believe it I was thrilled and impressed!!! I remember thinking ice cream? I thought that was so cute, so sweet. He wasn't asking to take me for a drink to ply me with alcohol and then try to get in my pants. He was asking to get to know me. I agreed to the ice cream date. The coolest part of it all was he actually took me to a place called *Ye Olde Ice Cream Parlor*. I mean one of those places straight out of the fifties movie. I felt like I was living out a scene from the TV show "Happy Days." We had so much fun. He was one of the nicest guys I had ever met. I remember thinking he is such a real man. This was the beginning of numerous dates.

We went to the finest restaurants, shows, and concerts. This guy was amazing considering my last relationship. He would read reviews in the newspapers of restaurants and then based on that take me and at times my cousin and friends. He would pay for everything. I remember thinking, *"This guy was too good to be true."* He did not smoke, do drugs but on occasion might have a Heineken and only one Heineken although he kept my refrigerator fully stocked with them. He worked out four times a week and was really a manly man; he was the type of guy who would pull out your chair, open doors for you; always a gentleman. If we went to the movies it had to be on premiere night and if it was too cold or too hot I was told to wait in the car until he actually got the tickets. He felt his women should not have to stand in line or be uncomfortable. This guy worked full-time for a lucrative construction company on Long Island and was in the union so he made a lot of money. He was 20 years old had $25,000 in the bank that he saved in two years. He also had a little black book with all the people who owed him money in it totaling a pretty hefty sum. He always kept a crisp $100 bill in his wallet which he never spent. He said as long as that bill was in his wallet he would never be broke. He wore designer clothes and designer cologne. He always looked and smelled fantastic. He was a member of a Baptist church on Long Island and sang in the choir.

I went back home to visit during a holiday break and I went to church and took him with me. I sat up on the balcony with my new boyfriend *The Man*. He grew up in a Baptist church just like me. He was still active in his church, attending every Sunday. He was a commuter so his college experience was very different from mine even though we ended up at the same place. I remember sitting in church that day and not having a connection anymore. I felt I was now like one of those holiday churchgoers. I wanted to get back to school ASAP, that was what I was connected to. Hanging out, partying, no curfew, no parents and no rules, no pretending everything was OK. I started to think I had no real connection to the church so why was I going. Sitting there I began feeling uneasy about how I was feeling about church. How could I feel this way? I was in church my entire life. I began to justify my feelings in my mind. I was becoming the queen of justification.

I told myself it wasn't my fault that I lost the connection. It was the people in the church's fault. I felt the people were hypocrites to teach you that stuff. When I say stuff, I mean how you are supposed to treat one another with love and then they fight in the church. I really felt uncomfortable around the drama but didn't know why. It just didn't sit right with me.

The biblical stuff they were teaching me I just didn't understand. I didn't understand the King James Version of the Bible. It felt like I was reading Shakespeare. They made us memorize scriptures that were never explained to me or even told me why I had to memorize them in the first place. I knew the *23rd Psalm*, the *Lord's Prayer, Psalm 100* and *John 3:16*.

John 3:16 I knew was special because everybody in my church knew that one and people recited it with pride. Not me, it was just another one of those scriptures we had to learn. There were so many contradictions. I thought God is so complicated, but then I said no it's the religious people that are complicated. So I decided that there were just too many rules in church and I did not feel connected so I stopped going. The truth is church made me uncomfortable because

Acceptance

I was not following the rules to live by. Rather than follow the rules I chose to make my own rules. I just didn't get it. I thought maybe there is a missing piece to this puzzle. I even thought maybe I should change my religion. I mean I believed that there was a God but it was the rest that was really cloudy for me. I even thought about leaving the Baptist faith altogether but I was taught our denomination was right and all the rest were wrong. Besides, the way I rationalized things and the way my warped mind saw things I just couldn't see it. I felt the Muslim women had to wear all those clothes and I sweat too much. The Jews and the Jehovah's Witnesses didn't celebrate Christmas and clearly, that wasn't an option for me. The African Methodist Episcopal, I had no clue as to what they were or what they believed. And the Catholics were interesting but you had to take classes to understand all their rules, and you already know how I felt about all the rules associated with religion. So I told myself I wasn't really missing anything. It's funny, Mr. Man never took me to his church. I don't remember him asking and I don't remember me asking to go. So I decided that there were just too many rules in church and I did not feel connected so I stopped going.

Wow as I reminisce about this guy, I wonder how I let him get away. Oh yeah, I remember . . .

This relationship lasted about two years. Although he was a great guy I always felt like there was something missing. I used to feel guilty about feeling that way because I kept comparing him to the Contender. I wondered how I could possibly find fault in this relationship when the last one was so bad. So I would just suck it up and say MG you should be grateful for what you have because you know where you were.

Although I worked, he would not allow me to pay for anything. I don't just mean when we went out on dates, I mean things I needed like snow boots, toiletries etc. He discouraged me from asking my parents for things I needed while I was away at college. At first, I thought he was really generous but then I began to see that he was controlling. Although I had a problem with it I didn't say anything because he was such a great catch. Even my mother thought so. I thought I was on the right track because she and I rarely agreed on anything. I was still a pain in the neck teenager. You know although the college experience was important to my mom, I wasn't sure of what she wanted more for me to get a degree or come back with a successful husband. Mr. Man was a small business management major and I was a journalism major.

I went to class one day, and my journalism professor/advisor told me that I was a great writer, but I needed to think about relocating for a short time after college. He said it is hard to break into journalism in New York without having worked somewhere else in the business first. I told Mr. Man this and he laughed. I asked what was so funny and he said, "If we are together, that's not going to happen." I asked why and he said, "What am I supposed to do while you are running around the country?" I said you will have a business degree you can come too. He laughed again and said, "Think not, I am not chasing my women around the country. Besides you won't need the experience because you won't have to work if we get married." I said what does that mean. He said, "The Bible says it's a man's responsibility to take care of his family so there would be no need for you to work." He said, "The women's responsibility was to submit to her husband so he sets the rules for the family." I then asked why you think I am going to college? He said, "So when we have our children, they will have educated parents. The fact that they would know we both went to college would let them know they had to go to college." I started to realize that this was not the relationship for me because he wanted someone who was submissive. I didn't remember much from my religious upbringing but I remember that women were supposed to be submissive. I also remember thinking I can't leave him because I can't do better than him. Look at the relationship I was in before. Little did I realize I became that submissive woman. I was acting like his wife but I did not have a ring or a license.

I heard that he was cheating on me with a girl that lived in one of my cousin's friend's suite. I asked him about it and he told me she was a friend he met in the library. He told me that I had nothing to worry about because I had him. He said I am a man of my word and I honor my commitments. I am the real deal, not that riff-raff you were accustomed to. I remember that statement stung. He was always saying mean things like that and felt it was OK as long as he was being a responsible man. I investigated this situation regarding this girl and found that she was from the Caribbean working on her degree but wanted to be married. She admitted to her friends that she was the submissive type naturally and had no problem being that way. It's funny when I heard that I felt the two of them should be together. I felt in my heart that he was cheating and although this could have been my reason to break up with him I couldn't. I was not happy but I felt I could not do better. I became what he wanted me to be, I was so unhappy. I was so submissive that I did not realize that others saw it and were appalled by my behavior.

Mr. Man's best friend was an older guy who I guess returned to school to start his life over after leaving the military. He lived on campus, was divorced had kids and he happened to be a black belt in Karate. When I first moved on campus this guy tried to talk to me and pursued me with a vengeance. There was something about him; although he was attractive I just wasn't interested. One day I was in my suite alone with him and he tried to date rape me but I was saved by my suite mates arriving at the right time. When Mr. Man told me about their friendship I told him what had happened. He told me I must have misread the situation because his friend was a great guy. Not only did he not believe me but he insisted that we double date with him on a regular basis. And of course, it has to be the way he wanted because he was "The Man."

I remember waking up one morning feeling like I had a nightmare. No, I really didn't think it, it was a fact that I woke up to another day in my life that felt like a nightmare. Mr. Man had no respect for my dreams and aspirations. He was so controlling. I clearly could tell he was cheating and it pissed me off. I just could not take it anymore. The straw that broke the camel's back for me was when I interviewed and secured a residential advisor position, which meant I would be in charge of one of the dormitories on campus. It was a major accomplishment for me and I was so proud of myself. Rather than support and encourage me, Mr. Man patronized me and made me feel as though my accomplishments were useless and a waste of time. We got into a major argument and I asked him to leave my room. After a couple of days, I called him to try and makeup, but he told me that he could not forgive me for asking him to leave and he didn't want to be with me anymore. I was devastated. Later that day I went to Pathmark to get some groceries and he was with that girl. Boy, did they seem like a happy couple. I called him and asked him what that was about? I thought you said that you were not cheating and now you are with this same girl. He said he didn't get together with her until I kicked him out of my room. As far as he was concerned we had broken up. I said you got together with her the next day? I will never forget his answer. He said, "Yeah what's wrong with that? You act like there should have been some kind of mourning period." I was too through. Later I heard they got married have a set of twins and are driving twin BMWs and a beautiful house.

After we broke up, I pledged a sorority. One of my big sisters was extremely hard on me. I wasn't surprised because she dated The Man's best friend. I thought we had become friendly when we went through those double dates I had to endure. After I became a member, she told me she was hard on me because she did not respect me. She said she watched how I allowed myself to be treated by Mr. Man and she felt I needed more backbone. The lessons she tried to teach me when I was on line were her attempts to enhance my self-worth. Wow, I didn't realize that people could see what I hated about myself. You know it's funny although he was not the man for me it still hurts. I gave this man my all.

Mr. Forbidden Fruit: When It Seems Too Good To Be Bad!

"The Man" and I broke up the week before classes started my junior year. This story, believe it or not, may be the hardest for me to reflect on. Mr. Forbidden Fruit (FF) was the best and worst man I dealt with, this man, gave me all I needed, wanted with no strings attached, he made me feel like I was a Queen. When I reflect back, the way you perceive things is relative to what you may be experiencing at the time. The sad part is I believed that for years, you see when The Man and I broke up he was there. I tried to tell myself and believe that I was not going to get into a relationship but he roped me in. I think to some extent I roped him as well, boy did I love this man. But I think I am getting ahead of myself. Well, the story begins.

Acceptance

I was working as a Resident Advisor at my college. This particular day I worked in the office assigning students to their new dorm rooms. I had to escort people who were on the waiting list to their rooms when their names came up on the list. I took a student to his room and there he was, The Forbidden Fruit (FF). I was sad because The Man and I had just broken up and most people on campus did not know. He told me I was too beautiful not to smile. Why are you so serious? I smiled and then he said there you go? I knew it would be hard to be more beautiful than you are but that smile clinched it. I left the dorm and went back to the office. Little did I know he asked the guys in the suite about me and was told that I was dating The Man. No one knew we had broken up yet. A couple of days later I ran into FF on campus. He tried to talk to me but I was so hurt and confused that I managed to let him down gently. A few nights later I was on campus with my cousin and a couple of girlfriends trying to get a ride off campus to get something to eat. Splitting up to look for rides to no avail; we regrouped and talked about how unsuccessful we were. While I was talking to my cousin FF walked up. He seemed thrilled to see me as we greeted each other. My cousin said, "Don't speak to him, I asked him to take us off-campus and he said no." He looked so surprised. I then said, "I can't believe it you mean to tell me that my cousin asked you for a ride off-campus and you told her no?" He then hemmed and hawed blown away by the fact that we were cousins and said if I would have known you needed a ride we would be there already. I said well, then I guess you need to make up for your mistake. He agreed and we were off. We left campus got some food and some drinks and all went back to my room and hung out. Everybody left and he and I sat up talking for hours at least until daybreak.

FF left early the next morning. I can't remember the last time, if ever I was able to sit and talk with someone and connect like we did. He told me he had a girlfriend but she lived far away. He said he didn't get to see her much and he gets lonely at times. The sad part of this was the girlfriend lived in my neighborhood. She was older than me so we didn't travel in the same circle. Once I found out who she was I knew I would never try and pull him because that would be wrong. That shows you how crazy I was. I didn't think it was wrong to mess around with him but to try to take him was wrong in my mind. I told him about my recent breakup and how I had no intention of getting into another relationship any time soon. We agreed to be friends with benefits and that's exactly what happened. We became the best of friends seeing each other through the good and bad times in our lives. FF didn't go to school. He worked full time and had graduated a couple of years before. He lived on Long Island and would come to the school to visit his fraternity brothers during the week. This was cool because he had a car and he would come to get me and take me off campus for meals and we would just sit up and talk for hours. Well unfortunately our friendship became extremely intimate and that made things worse. We were so connected. I think it was because we were not trying to have a relationship and we were honest with one another. We made a pact that if either of us saw the other falling too deep into the relationship; the other should put a stop to things. We were both lonely and provided each other with the attention we needed. The funny thing is at one point he started coming up to the school every day even on weekends. We drew closer and closer.

Before I knew it, I was in love yet again. This time I just knew I would not get hurt. I expected my friend to see I was falling in and pull back. Unfortunately, he was falling in too but he would not pull back. I had to be the one to put a stop to this. I wasn't trying to break up a relationship because I knew how it felt when someone is cheating on you. He felt we were cool because I said I didn't want a relationship. My last two were so toxic I needed to give myself some time. So after about 8 months, I cut off the affair. That's a good word because that's what it was. It was right before the summer break. This was really hard because we were so close. About a month later I got a call from him while I was home for the summer. He told me he had to see me because he had to talk to me. He asked if he could come to pick me up so we could talk. I agreed but could not imagine what he had to talk to me about. We drove out to his house where he prepared a nice meal for us and he told me that he was engaged. I tried to play it off but I was crushed. He said he didn't want me to hear it from anyone else so he wanted to make sure I heard it from him. I thanked him for telling me and went through the formalities of saying that he didn't have to go through all of this because we didn't have a relationship and we agreed to no ties. He said both of us know that we mean more to each other than that. I knew this but I would not agree because we were never supposed to discuss our feelings especially now. It's crazy this discussion lead to intimacy and the whole affair started all over again. This crazy sin-filled affair lasted for years. Yes, that means I dealt with him during his marriage and later during my marriage. What a messy situation. The guilt I felt was enormous but I just couldn't stop. It was almost as if I were addicted to him. I would cut him off periodically but we would always land back together.

Daddy's Dying?

Happy New Year! It was January 2nd and all I remember saying... What? Tumor? What do you mean he has what appears to be a tumor the size of a grapefruit in his intestine. He came here because his stomach has been bothering him and he hasn't had an appetite. I don't understand this. My father has Parkinson's disease. He's being treated for this and is at the VA hospital all the time having tests run. Why was this not detected? How is this possible? Why is this happening to my daddy, my hero the greatest man whom I feel ever lived? These were the thoughts and questions I had when the doctor told me that he was pretty sure my dad had cancer. I remember I was alone with the surgeon on an elevator going to look at the x-rays of what turned out to be a malignant tumor the size of a grapefruit.

I can't begin to describe the feeling that went through me knowing my daddy, the strongest, sweetest most supportive and not to mention the best role model in my adult life, was in this vulnerable state. My heart was broken because all I knew was he did not deserve to be going through this. Why him? Why is he facing surgery? All I knew was they just needed to get the tumor out so I could bring my daddy home ASAP. Daddy had the surgery but when they opened him up they said that the tumor was in a good place where they could remove it. But the bad news was that the tumor touched many of his organs due to its size. This resulted in cancer spreading to numerous organs. Daddy spent a week in the hospital and was sent home to recover. They said there was nothing they could do. It was only a matter of time. I remember thinking time for what? They sent him home connected us with doctors and gave us equipment and said what he would be getting is considered in-home Hospice care. I WAS DEVASTATED BY THE NEWS!! I remember thinking; oh my God they are saying my daddy's going to die. How could this be possible? He had a stomach ache and now they were telling me he was going to die. Let me back up for a minute. I need to say how much I loved my father. Heck everybody loved this man. He was so loved that we had to sit through two funerals. Wait a minute I am getting ahead of myself. Let me go back. So the doctors sent my dad home. Me, my mom and my husband were in the house to care for him. My brothers and brother-cousin clearly could not deal with the situation.

Daddy was a trooper about his cancer. He did not complain at all. He was very cooperative about his medication and chemotherapy appointments. He only gave us trouble with his eating he was not hungry. He was wasting away to nothing but never complained. I remember my best friend Wisdom knew he loved chitterlings or as we say "chitlins." She made him some and we were able to get him to eat those.

My poor mother knew she was losing the love of her life. I remember she felt if she used a tablespoon to feed him she could get more food into him before he would say he didn't want anymore. He asked me to feed him because she pushes him too hard. He said I can't eat that much. I explained to him that she is just worried about him and feels if he eats, he will be well. Look, this was the man who had been with her for the past 40 years; he was there when she lost her mother, her siblings, and the birth of their four children, and the death of their middle son. She was losing an integral part of herself. I could not even begin to relate to what she must be going through. She was so strong and dealt with her pain in silence. It was things like the way she fed him that let you know she felt like she was fighting for her life.

During daddy's final days I would snuggle up next to him on the couch in the living room and watch TV as long as he felt like sitting up. I remember thinking how much I loved him. I reflected on the fact that this was the man who was always there for me. He would drive me everywhere when I was a child and always made sure I had money

Acceptance

in my pocket. When I went to college, he would drive out to see me, bring me money, and bring relatives to the campus because he was so proud that I was going to college. This was my daddy! He walked me down the aisle at my wedding. His Parkinson's disease had him very shaky. Before my wedding, he said he didn't know if he would be able to walk with me because he did not want to throw me off or mess up my moment. I told him, if my daddy didn't walk with me then I wasn't walking. We would walk at his pace and everyone would just have to wait until we got there because I was not going anywhere without my daddy. I should have taken that as a sign not to marry that man. But that's another story we will get to later. It was also my daddy who my husband went to when he was addicted to crack and feared smoking away his paycheck. My daddy would take that man to work to get his check, cash it bring the money home to me after dropping him off at a train station to go get high. My daddy told me he went on, but baby I brought you the money from his check to pay your bills. That was my daddy, he always made things better. He was always there for me. God, I loved that man.

We spent quality alone time together on that couch. The time span was not long because he would want to return to bed for comfort, but the quality of the conversations was so deep. The time we spent saying nothing with me laying on his shoulder was priceless. I remember thinking that my big strong daddy seemed so weak and frail but I still had a need to lean on him. I needed to feel and enjoy his presence because I knew I was losing him. These are the moments I will cherish forever. This was a very difficult time for me. Here I was the baby of the family and I really had to step up to the plate. I had to feed him, coordinate his care, converse with the doctor who was wonderful enough to come to the house to give him his chemo. A couple of times I remember my mom was not around and he could not go to the bathroom to urinate. I could not get him on the bedpan and I remember I had to hold his penis in my hands to help him urinate in the urine receptacle. I realized at that moment that my big strong daddy was leaving me. But I could not allow myself to feel that pain. I had to take care of him, my mother and my drug-addicted husband. I was also a full-time graduate student working full time as a caseworker with a full caseload of troubled teens.

I had to hold it together until I got into bed at night. I would cry myself to sleep every night.

One night I had to get him back into bed and I began to sing to him. His favorite hymn was *Blessed Assurance.* I sang to him while brushing his hair. He always liked for me to play in his hair when I was growing up. It always made him sleepy, peaceful. As I finished the song, he said I like that song. I told him I know. I realized at that moment he wanted to let go but something was stopping him. I then told him that I will take care of mama. I remember praying over him and asking God to take him because I could see he was suffering and that I know he would be at peace if he were in heaven. I never thought I would ever pray for something like that. All I knew is I loved this man and I did not feel he should suffer for our selfish need to have him around. He sighed in relief and went off to sleep. A day or so later he took a turn for the worst and we had to take him back to the hospital.

I went to visit him in the hospital and he was a little out of his mind because of the amount of morphine they were giving him. When I got there, he was sitting straight up in his bed and said, "There's my baby. I thought you were not going to be able to find me." I said, "Hi daddy you look good and strong today." He said, "I had to stay up because these people moved me to another room." He said, "I told them they better not move me and not tell my daughter. My daughter is coming here and she will set you people straight and lay you out if she can't find me." I chuckled. I found it funny that even though he was clearly not in control of his mind he knew I would not let anyone mess over him. I just said that's right daddy.

The next day I went to visit my daddy. I remember it as if it were yesterday it was a Thursday, and he wasn't doing so well. Mama was there when I got there. She said he had been sleeping all day. His breathing was really deep. His legs were so swollen which was an indication that his kidneys were failing. I remember mom saying let's sing to him. We sang *Blessed Assurance*. After we finished, mom told him to just rest. She told him not to worry about us we would be OK. She said your boys will be OK, and your little girl will be OK and she would be OK. At that moment his breathing became really rough. It's sounded like a rattle. Mom freaked out and so did I. She started screaming don't leave

Acceptance

me. I went to get the nurse and they said there was nothing they could do but to make him comfortable. After we lost it, daddy's breathing calmed down as if he knew he could not go then. I really think he was waiting for my mom to say she would be alright. To this day I don't know if she realized what she was saying because she was clearly not ready. I remember calling my family and telling them that we were losing him and no one wanted to believe or accept it. I left the hospital and I knew I would not be back. Although I did not want him to suffer I could not watch him die. I did not want to be there when he took his last breath. I went to work on Friday and I was a mess. I called my friends and told them I didn't want to go to the hospital and I didn't want to go home. I went over to their house. I needed a moment to breathe and accept the fact that I would not ever hold him or speak to him again. I knew this in my heart. My mother was so angry with me because I did not come to the hospital. I told her I could not see him like that and I did not want to see him die. She was so distraught she hung up on me. My friend drove me home at about 11:00 that evening. When I got home my mother's car was in the driveway with the light on. She had just come in and was so tired and distraught she did not close the car door properly. The front door was also ajar. My heart sank. I knew from what I was seeing he was dead. I locked up the car went upstairs and found her lying on the bed with her clothes on. She told me he was sleeping all day. He did not wake up to speak to her at all. She said she came home for a nap and she was going back. I locked the house up and we both went to bed. Mom woke me up at 6:00 Saturday morning telling me daddy was gone. She got the phone call before she could get back there. We held each other and cried. We went to the hospital with my brothers and sister-in-law and found my daddy in his bed so peaceful. He really looked like he was sleeping. I never saw someone right after they died before. He looked better at that moment than when he was alive. I remember thinking, No more suffering, no more pain, he was at peace but no more daddy!

This Walk Ain't Right! But, Help Is Along The Way

Crack's in My Marriage

What do you mean he died two weeks ago? This was my response to the news that my ex-husband had passed away from some rare brain disease. I lay in my bed thinking back and saying hmm Mr. Dis-ease died from a physical illness—isn't that ironic. This man lived a roller coaster life that could best be described a continuous state of Dis-ease. The interesting part is that I married into his dysfunction adding yet another layer onto my own unresolved issues. It's funny I married him because I knew he would always look out for me and never do anything to intentionally hurt me. How could I not marry him? He was my first love. I was so convinced that there was no greater love than this. When I think back and remember our history I added to his disease.

I remember I was in the ninth grade all gussied up in my latest back-to-school fashion. I probably had someone on my butt, Jordache, Gloria Vanderbilt, Calvin Klein, Sergio Valente, don't quite remember who, but I know someone was chasing my behind. That's what we did back then. I know some of you can remember the latest Pro-Ked or Uptown sneakers in every color with the three lines going around the sides. Or maybe it was a pair of Adidas, Puma or Pony. All I know is I had to have them because they were the style.

Getting back to the story, I had convinced my mother to allow me to go to high school in Manhattan to pursue my love for vocal music. Don't get me wrong, I was not going to be the next Stephanie Mills or Natalie Cole, I was a choral singer. I started off in the celestial children's choir in my church and then graduated to the youth ensemble young adult choir. I was also a part of the school choir and a member of the Queens Borough Wide Chorus. Auditioning and being accepted into the Talent Unlimited High School was a great accomplishment for me. I was ready for a new adventure. Living in Queens always felt like I lived in New York but I was missing something. It's funny there are a lot of books, songs, and TV shows that portray the city as a trap door that leads you down the wrong road. As a teenager, you feel that this is what adults tell you so you won't have fun. As an adult, I look back and realize that each day I went to the city I entered into the "temptation playground."

Acceptance

So I'm in the chorus in the soprano section and I asked my friend Missy who was the cute guy in the tenor section. I thought he was handsome. He always wore a sports jacket with his pants even jeans. I guess growing up in the house with five men attending church regularly gave me a real appreciation for men in suits and sports jackets.

I thought he was so cool, he looked mature. I found out that he was a junior and that increased my interest. After we were introduced, we got acquainted quickly. We had a lot of the same interests. We both loved all types of music and Dis-ease was a poet. His poetry was amazing. He had a real sensitive side. He was very well-mannered, smart, and was a gentleman. He wasn't as tall as I would have liked but I wasn't taller than him so that was OK. He was an honor student but by no means was he a nerd. Dis-ease also had a street-smart side to his personality. You see I felt I had the best of both worlds. I had a man who is intellectually gifted but also a little thuggish. Growing up in the projects in Manhattan exposed him to a body of knowledge that helped him to survive the streets of New York.

Mr. Dis-ease and I would talk for hours about our upbringing, our hopes, and dreams. One of the things that I remember that troubled Mr. Dis-ease the most was his Asthma. He talked about how his asthma ruined his childhood. He didn't have the relationship he wanted with his father. He said he disliked his father because he called him a mamma's boy and a punk because he was always so sickly. The Asthma attacks during his childhood years were frequent. Dis-ease found comfort from his mother until a school guidance counselor told his mom that Asthma is psychological. She clearly had it all wrong. What she should have said was psychological trauma can bring on an asthma attack. Because his mother was very active in the PTA, respected the counselor, and had little knowledge of asthma she believed her. The next time Dis-ease had an Asthma attack in school his mother came up there and gave him a spanking in front of the entire class. She told him to stop faking because the attacks were all in his mind. Later a doctor explained how ridiculous the counselor's comments were but it was too late. The damage to Dis-ease's self-esteem was already done. Can you imagine how he must've felt and the teasing he had to endure from the other children? He said it took years for him to live that down.

This Walk Ain't Right! But, Help Is Along The Way

My heart broke for him. Dis-ease masked his pain through his poetry and smoking reefer (that's what we called it back then). I felt sorry for him and developed strong feelings for him.

One day I was on my way to school and passed out in 59th street and Lexington Ave. train station. I told my mom that I was sick but I think she thought I just didn't want to go to school that day. I came home and went to the doctor who said I had pneumonia. I remember Dis-ease begging my mom to see me and after a week he wore her down. She liked Dis-ease, how could you not. During this time Dis-ease would sit and watch TV with me read to me and recite some of his poetry and my feelings grew for him. How could they not, Dis-ease was such a great guy. So over the next few months Dis-ease and I began to get closer. We started to kiss and hug and do the things youth do when they spend too much unsupervised time together. We started to talk about taking our relationship to the next level. We were trying to figure out where this would happen. The summer fell upon us and Dis-ease's family sent him away to West Virginia until school started. We were both sick over this. We pledged our undying love for each other and vowed to write to each other every day. We wrote a couple of letters back and forth but then I stopped writing.

It was that summer I worked at my church as a counselor at the daily vacation bible school. I forgot about poor Dis-ease until the end of the summer. When Dis-ease came back from the summer I knew I had to tell him the truth. I also knew I had to break up with him because I was now involved with *the Contender*. Little did I know but this was the beginning of an on-again off-again relationship with Dis-ease. Dis-ease was hurt by the break-up and always wanted to get back together. I was so wrong during that time because my heart belonged to *the Contender*. Every time we broke up I would go back to Dis-ease because he was always waiting with open arms and a good heart. This on again off again continued all the way up until I went away to college.

I will never forget I walked into my college math class which was already a fate worst than death because I hated math, and who was sitting in one of the seats but Dis-ease. I remember I was pissed off. How the heck did he find me? I felt like he was stalking me. Dis-ease did not live on campus but he commuted on public transportation to and from the school for three hours since he could not get a dorm room. Somewhere in our on-again off-again relationship, I lost respect for Dis-ease. He was just too nice and we all know nice guys finish last. The funny thing was I never took the time to figure out what was wrong with me that I didn't want a nice guy. I don't know when it happened, but the relationship became one-sided and I stopped caring about Dis-ease's feelings. I easily slipped into using him. The only thing I can say in my defense was I was pretty messed up myself considering what I went through with the Contender. Math was my worse subject and of course, Dis-ease volunteered to tutor me. I agreed. Dis-ease tutored me for a while and then he decided he was going to make a major move to win me back. Unfortunately, he didn't have enough money to pull off all that he planned. Although the night was amazing he ran short on money for the cab back to campus. I in my selfishness was appalled. I left him in the cab and told him I would get money from my dorm room and went to bed. I heard a loud knock at the door for about 20 minutes until someone let them in the suite. They came to my door and I pretended to have forgotten. I gave him the money closed the door and did not think twice about him. I was just pissed off that I had to shell out my money. Looking back now I can't believe I did that to him. I didn't see him anymore after that and he dropped out of college. I ran into one of our H.S. friends and they told me he had died. I felt really bad about how I treated him and wished I could make it up to him, but it was too late.

One day I was in Manhattan and I was coming out of a McDonald's and who do I run into but Dis-ease. I looked at him as if I saw a ghost. I told him I heard he was dead. He laughed and said wow guess it got out. I was so angry with you that I told my boys if you ever asked about me to say I died. We both laughed and I told him I deserved that and apologized and asked him to forgive me. He said he did. We went out for a drink and played catch up. It was so nice hanging out with him again. We exchanged numbers and began dating again. I decided that I was going to stay with him no matter what. He was the only person who loved me and treated me the way I deserved to be treated. I was first in his life and I didn't have to worry about him because he would always take care of my heart. We dated for about a year and decided to get married. I had some reservations about marrying Dis-ease because although he was very smart he never finished college and as a result, he took a lot of dead-end jobs. He still suffered from low self-esteem and liked to get high. He mostly smoked reefer but he got into powder cocaine (blow) with another friend of mine. I remember thinking this might be a problem but everyone I knew sniffed blow on occasion besides, it wasn't like it was crack.

Dis-ease and I planned to get married on September 17, 1988, his birthday. We decided to get married at the church I grew up in. After 4 years of being away at school I had not really attended church. I was still a member because my mother was still putting money in my envelopes because she said that would keep me active and connected.

As part of the wedding criteria at the church, we went to a session of premarital counseling and the pastor was really great and made a lot of sense. He talked about marriage and what it meant. He said we should not enter into it lightly. I remember thinking I should not get married to this man. I remember talking to my best friend Wisdom who had the strength to call her wedding off before it was too late. I told her I thought Dis-ease was messing around on me because he was pulling disappearing acts. She said, "He is not messing around on you. That nut loves you too much, that's clear." She said, "He is messing with that stuff." I said what stuff? She said, "Crack!" I was like he doesn't smoke crack. He sniffs coke and puts it in reefer but no crack. She said, "Choose to believe what you want." Deep down I knew she was right but I was getting married in two weeks. My invitations were out, everything was booked, I had family coming in from out of town. I didn't have the nerve to call it off. My pride couldn't take it. I remember going with my cousin, my maid of honor for a final fitting three days before. I told her I just wasn't sure if I should do this. She said, "Look, we can call this off right now. I will make the calls." I remember feeling I should take her up on it but I couldn't.

Two days before the wedding I went to meet Mr. Forbidden Fruit. We talked at length about the situation and he told me that I probably just had pre-marital jitters. He reminded me of when he went through it. I told him he should not use himself as an example because we were still messing around and he's married. I told him I don't even

Acceptance

know why I'm asking him for advice. As a matter of fact, we started messing around again two weeks after he got married. He was on his honeymoon for those two weeks. That said he was using the wrong example to encourage me. Then he said the thing that made me go through with it. You can't call it off now your parents will be devastated and embarrassed.

We had a beautiful wedding with a huge bridal party. After the wedding, I had a surprise birthday after-party for him at our brand new apartment. The party lasted all night as planned and we were taken to the airport that morning to catch a flight out for our honeymoon in Mexico. Mexico was awesome; we had a private pool on our balcony which had a magnificent view of the countryside. I just knew my life was finally on the right track. But then we came home and the honeymoon was over. It seemed like everything went downhill. When Dis-ease started staying out nights and I didn't know what was going on.

One night I went to sleep and Dis-ease was not home as usual. The bed we slept in had a dual-purpose headboard. It opened up on top and you could store linens and blankets in it. We used to hide the emergency house money in there. I woke up in the middle of the night and there were two large white men standing in my bedroom with Dis-ease. It was about 4 o'clock in the morning. In my grogginess, I asked him what was going on. Dis-ease said he owed them money and they brought him home to get their money. I asked why the hell he brought them to our bedroom while I was sleeping. Why didn't he just get the money himself? I was so naive to stuff like this. He said they do not trust me. They think I might come out of the bedroom shooting so they insisted they come in with him. I remember I was so scared. He gave them the money and they left. Needless to say, we got into a big argument after that. I noticed his wedding band was missing. I asked him where it was. Our bands were matching and they had diamonds in them, he said he lost his down the sink. That wasn't the case he had sold it for drugs. As time went on things got worse. I was carrying the bills all by myself. Every time he got paid, he had a story. One day he came home and told me he fell asleep on the train and got robbed. This jerk knew he needed to make it believable so he cut up his leather jacket to show me how he was robbed. I was done! I decided to move out of that expensive apartment that I could not afford alone. We moved back to my parents' house. He was so pathetic, that when he got paid he would have my father take him to the bank to cash his check. Then he would go on a binge for the entire weekend. I wouldn't see him until Monday. I remember one day we went out to dinner and it was his payday. He wanted to try and patch things up between us. We were in Manhattan and he wanted to go pick up his check which was one train stop from the restaurant. He told me to stay there have another drink and he would meet me back there. He never returned. When I got home the police called and told me he was in the hospital. He was doing crack and had an Asthma attack and was sent to the hospital. I asked the cop is he dead? They said no. I said DAMN! I was pissed off because that means I had to still deal with him. I know the policemen thought I was crazy. The straw that broke the camel's back for me was when he started to take our VCRs out the house. Then one day he took my entire paycheck that I cashed and had not put it in the bank yet. I was asleep and heard the front door close which woke me up. He ran out of the house with the money in his hands. He dropped two 20 dollar bills on the floor; it was as if he left a trail. That was it for me. I was putting him out. I didn't care about the for better or worse marriage vows. He had to leave!

The next day I got a call from a counselor who told me that he went to the employee assistance program at his job. She was calling to inform me that he was going into a rehabilitation center in Florida that day. He was afraid to call me because he had stolen my money. I didn't believe her at first. The next day I received a call from a rehab in Florida calling on his behalf to say he arrived. He got on the phone briefly. He said that he would be there for a month. They had a family week that was a part of the program so he wanted me to come down. The rehab would pay for my airfare. I talked to my brother Lee and he said I should give him a chance because Dis-ease is trying to get help. My parents said the same thing and Mr. Forbidden Fruit encouraged me to go as well. I was in graduate school working on my Master of Social Work Degree (MSW) at the time. I told everyone if I could get excused from my classes I would go. Although the rehab said I could stay there, that was not going to happen. I was going to get a hotel to stay in nearby. I flew down there and they had a limo waiting to pick me up at the airport to take me to my hotel to check-in. The limo waited and then took me to the rehab. I got down there the week of our first wedding anniversary. I brought the top of our wedding cake and a bottle of sparkling apple cider. I was really going to try and stand by and support my husband. I was so depressed about this situation. I could not believe this was how we were spending our first wedding anniversary.

From Counselor to Client!

I couldn't believe it they put us in a classroom-type situation. I remember thinking I am on a break from school and now my life is a social work intervention. They start off by explaining that addiction is a disease just like any other illness. They talked about the fact that people don't look at it that way and are not sensitive to it because in most cases it's self-inflicted. The instructor really had a way of helping you look past your pain and anger. But then they go through this whole thing about how you can't be an enabler or co-dependent so now I'm confused. I felt like they were telling me to give him a chance but then it felt like they were telling me to leave him. I was so confused. Then they sent us to another room and we had to participate in a group counseling session. This was really difficult for me; here I was in social work school learning the techniques and strategies to run social workgroups. Shoot I was running groups at my full-time job and now I'm in "the group" not as a facilitator or leader but a participant. It was clear to the rest of my group that I was uncomfortable. I didn't feel like sharing. All of a sudden, they started giving me a hard time for not speaking up. I felt like they attacked me because I was a social worker. They tried to rip me apart to get me to share. I remember being so angry with Dis-ease for putting me in this situation. They accused me of thinking I was better than them. It wasn't that I felt better than them I was just in so much pain and such a state of confusion. I was so lost, hurt and embarrassed. T'   t thing was after they attacked me and broke me down. I felt   'ittle wounded but better. Sometimes I don't know why you have to go through these things but there is a way out and something always happens to make it get better.

I remember Dis-ease was able to get a special day pass to spend our anniversary with me at the hotel. I had mixed feelings about this because I tried to tell myself that we were in Florida in a nice hotel with a really nice pool celebrating our first anniversary. This would have been cool, but the reality was he was on a day pass from a rehabilitation center because he was addicted to crack and we happened to be in Florida. We talked and he apologized and promised that he would make this up to me and didn't want to lose me. He said I was his world and he did not know what he would do if he lost me. He reminded me that he loved me since he was 16 years old and begged me to give him another chance. I agreed if he refused to use drugs again and follow the discharge instructions. He agreed and we ate that nasty old cake and toasted to a new life with our sparkling apple cider. We made the best of a very difficult situation. I went back home the next day without him because he had another two weeks before he completed the program.

When Dis-ease got home I made up my mind that we were going to start over. For the first time in who knows how long I began to pray. It's funny I didn't even know what to say because it was so long since I prayed. I remember it was a long laundry list of what I wanted from God. Not once did I thank him for what he had done for me. I was just so detached from God that I didn't even feel right praying. So Dis-ease came home and at first, he was on fire. He wanted to do all he could do to stay off the drugs. The plan was that he had to attend 90 meetings in 90 days. He regularly attended his meetings. Each day he went to a meeting for the first month and a half. Then he started to miss meetings telling me he would make them up. Instead of going to a meeting each day he tried to double up thinking he could do his 90 meetings in 90 days by going to multiple meetings to make up for days he missed. Before I knew it he had stopped going to meetings and slowly pulling disappearing acts again. He was back out there again. I remember feeling like DAMN! Here we go again. He went back to Florida. This time I refused to go back down there with him. I was done I told myself. He had a counselor call me and they said you know that relapse is part of recovery. The counselor al

Acceptance

to do what I had to do for myself. That's exactly what I was thinking. I had it with Dis-ease and his disease. I knew he would be coming back home but I also knew it was only a matter of time before we would break up because I was done with him, his drugs, and yes the marriage.

Dis-ease came home and he tried to attend the 90 meetings in 90 days but again he did not complete them. I was very cold towards him and I could hardly look at him because he really disgusted me. I remember thinking why he doesn't just overdose. I know that was wrong but I was fed up. He started hanging out again and not coming home. I remember one night I said to myself when he comes back that's it. Sure enough, that's it for me! When he came home, I was so angry and I put him out! He checked into another program this time here in New York. He called and I told him I hoped he gets well but we were through. I didn't hear from him for about six months. I filed for divorce. He contacted me a few months later. I told him I needed to serve him with the papers. He told me he had been clean and sober for months. The sad part was it didn't matter to me. I told him I loved him but was not in love with him. I also told him I married him because I knew how much he loved me. The problem is I came to realize that he loved me more than he loved himself. I told him he had to get well and focus on himself for a change. He told me he was saved and had been attending church and he would discuss the divorce with his pastor. I told him to do what he needed to do but I was not coming back to him. Our marriage was over. He signed the papers and we were divorced. We later became friends. He used to come over to visit and we would read the bible together. It's too bad we didn't do this when we were married. I remember thinking he has truly changed.

He used to visit my mom in the nursing home and read the bible to her as well. He was coming to see me on a regular basis and then he stopped. I wondered what happened to him. I tried calling him and there was never an answer. I thought he went back to the drugs. About six months later his brother called me and said he died. Apparently right after I saw him the last time he got sick and went into the hospital. He had some rare brain disease and slipped into a coma for months and died. His brother tells me all of this two weeks after he died. I was so distraught. Why couldn't he have called me two weeks ago so I could have gone to his funeral? I wish I would have known earlier I could have gone to the hospital to visit him. It was truly over. He was dead. He was finally free of the tormented life he led. The one consolation I had was I knew before he died, he found God. Death has been such a big part of my life. When you come from such a large extended family you experience so many deaths.

Mr. Manhattan Slick AKA The Hustle Man

Wow, that was some past. All that I went through and now I meet Mr. Manhattan Slick. When I met this man, I was totally out of my league. There was nothing that I had been through that prepared me for the rollercoaster ride I was about to get on. It's funny that I put it that way because when I met him it was just as if I was at a theme park waiting to get on the much talked about, much-publicized new rollercoaster of the year. If you are a rollercoaster lover you know what I'm talking about. That feeling you get when you were looking forward to going to the park and excited about getting there. You have so much energy and you're nervous but it's a good kind of nervousness because you know what's to come is going to be exciting, and memorable. So you build up your nerves and you go for it. Well, I went for it, and it was truly the ride that changed my life forever. I think I'm getting ahead of myself again. Let me go back in time a little.

When I got out of my marriage I was at a good place in my life. I realized that I needed to focus on myself and get better with a lot of stuff. I had gained a lot of weight and I was not happy with the way that I looked. I was working for a foster care agency as a supervisor/program coordinator and the administration had changed and I was not feeling them at all. My really close friend Miss Insight and I were both on a mission to make ourselves over. We wanted better jobs, better outward appearances and were feeling a need for a spiritual connection as well. I should say Miss Insight was further along on the spiritual piece than I was. I admired her because once she decided to go back to church, she started trying to find a church home. She kept going to churches until she found her place of worship. She traveled to a church in Brooklyn for a while even though she lived in Queens. No matter how late we hung out she would go to church. Miss Insight like me went to church as a child. What I didn't realize was she started to establish a relationship with God as a child. Remember I only knew religion. She told me about the time when she went to church and she was about 13 years old. The pastor did an altar call and she went up to pray. Miss Insight said she believed in prayer because she watched her mother pray and believe. She said although her family didn't have much her mother didn't worry about taking care of her family because she had a relationship with God. This relationship was visible to Miss Insight and she wanted that. I remember her telling me that she went up to the altar and the minister started to pray over the people and all of a sudden, her body started to shake like she was having convulsions. The next thing she knew she was waking up from being knocked out cold on the floor. She said there were people praying over her and around her. She said when she got up she felt so peaceful and so much joy. She will never forget what that felt like. Then that nut tells me she has never felt that since. She said, unlike the time she went to another place of worship and they did an altar call asking all the women to come to the altar. She said she went up and the pastor said when I wave my hand the Holy Spirit will enter into each of you. She said she remembers not really believing what he was saying. Then all of a sudden, all the women in front of her started falling out, dropping like flies. She said she was like I got to go down too because I don't want to be the only one standing. All of a sudden, she dramatically went down to the floor by making herself fall out. She said it was obvious she was faking it and she was so embarrassed. She said she was on the floor trying to figure out how she could get up in a dramatic form as she went down. She said she got up and realized that there were people behind her still standing. She said she felt like they were looking at her saying, "You didn't catch no spirit." She said she was so embarrassed. I could not help but fall out laughing. I mean I had tears rolling down my face. Look at the lengths that we go to just to fit in, even in church. We both had to agree that there is peer pressure at church but you have to be careful with that. You might mess around and hurt something trying to "play church."

So Miss Insight and I went to the gym 4 days a week. After a few months, the weight just started dropping off. During this time period

This Walk Ain't Right! But, Help Is Along The Way

I started seeing this guy Mr. Mama's Boy. Insight and I went to a club one night and were having drinks at the bar. Mama's Boy was staring at us from across the room. Insight picked up on it from the start. I was totally oblivious to him and his staring until she brought it to my attention. He sent some drinks over via the bartender and he came over to talk with us. I was very shy in these kinds of situations. Miss Insight was shy too when she was interested in someone, but when she wasn't she was really playful and an excellent ice breaker when I felt awkward. So she started a conversation and we all hit it off right away. He asked me to dance and I had enough drinks so I agreed. I was also shy about dancing too. So we hung out till the club closed and we exchanged numbers and started to date after that. We had a good relationship for a while. We would go on trips to Virginia Beach, the Poconos, and places like that. We really got along well. He was divorced and had a son and was very close to his family. His sister lived in New Jersey and she would come to stay with the family every weekend in Brooklyn with her son. She was also divorced. Their father would pick her up. She never took the train or bus she had to be picked up. Mama's Boy was from a Baptist family and his father was a Deacon at their place of worship.

The church was honoring Mr. Mamma's Boy's father and he asked me to attend the banquet. Insight and I went out shopping for something for me to wear. During our shopping trip, I thought wow, I have no church clothes. How did I come so far from how I grew up? I remember a time I would have been able to just go into my closet and find something. I was so far from my upbringing. So we went shopping and I was so happy because I had lost weight and I was able to buy a smaller size. If I do say so myself I looked good really good in my cream suit and cream shoes and stockings. I looked like a church lady. I was ready to play my part. I say play my part because this was when I was meeting the family and his church family. I knew what to do, how to act, when to sit, and when to stand. I knew the hymns. I was trained and armed with my religion. There was a sermon preached that day and I had no connection to the message. It was a nice function but all I really remember is what I was wearing.

Acceptance

Then it happened. Mama's Boy's family went down south to visit family and the father took the grandmother to a revival one night. They got into a horrible car accident and the father had to be airlifted to a hospital. It was touch and go for a while because he was in critical condition. He got better but he was still very sick so they flew him home and he continued to recuperate at home. The accident caused significant damage to his internal organs especially his kidneys. It didn't help that he needed pain meds and anesthesia for his surgeries. The impact on his kidneys caused him to need dialysis. This was a difficult time for Mama's Boy and his family. He tried to step up and do more for the family in his father's absence. As a result, we were not spending as much time together. We would make plans and they would always seem to get canceled. This was starting to bother me but I let it go because I understood that he was trying to make the best out of a difficult situation. I continued to hang out with my girl Insight and went to the gym regularly. I had lost 50 pounds. I was feeling really good about myself, better than I had felt in years. Insight and I were developing training programs for staff at work and facilitating them. I felt really good about where my life was and who I was becoming. Since the father was out of commission Mama's Boy had to pick his sister up on the weekends. This meant our Friday nights were done. I was not feeling this. The straw that broke the camel's back was the night we had tickets to a play. I was dressed and waiting for him to pick me up and he called and said he could not go because he had to pick up his sister. I was livid. I told him we could not see each other anymore because I was not happy in this relationship. I had been through so much in my life and I had finally gotten to the place where I promised myself I would not just settle for less than I deserved, so I thought.

This was a turning point in my life. I felt really good about this break-up. I was putting myself first for a change. The Contender even tried to come back into my life. I was like you have got to be kidding me. I was in such a healthy place but I still felt like something was missing. Not knowing what to do with these feelings I just went shopping. This was my new favorite thing to do because I had dropped so much weight. I loved trying on new clothes in smaller sizes. I was really feeling the new me although I felt a void. I told myself the void I was feeling was because I was 31 years old and had completed school had a great career but no kids. I thought I would probably not have a child because I was getting too old. I always believed that couples should be married when they had children. Since I was not married and didn't even have a boyfriend I felt me having children was not going to happen.

Miss Insight and I got a group of young people together and went on our annual weekend retreat. This was a weekend designed to take youth away and work with them on much-needed skills before they transition out of the foster care system. We had been coming up to the Catskills for years with different groups of young people. Although this was a working weekend there was something special about spending this quality time with the youth at such a vital time in their lives. It was coming up here and the connection I made with the youth that encouraged me to go to graduate school. I didn't have the time to connect in this way with my young people when we are in the city. This was a weekend I would look forward to year after year. This year there was new staff working at the retreat site. I don't know who trained these people but they were borderline racist and had a hard time connecting with our young people.

At the end of the night, Insight and I got our youth settled into their cabins and decided to go to our van and sit there for a while talking and listening to music. We needed to vent to each other about the way we felt these people were responding to our youth. Insight and I were very protective of our kids and we both had a real hard time letting go of the anger we were feeling.

The van also had all the snacks we brought up because we could not take them inside because we might attract bugs and animals. As we were sitting in the van, we noticed that another van was parked next to us. Insight rolled her window down and started to talk to this guy in the van. She asked him what he was doing in there all alone. He laughed and said just relaxing and thinking. He then asked her what she was doing. He could not see me at first because I was in the back of the van getting some snacks. When she told him that we were in there talking and munching he came over to check out our snacks. He got in the passenger seat and Insight began to question him about who he was and what he did. He was the coordinator of a young father's program which immediately caught my interest. He brought a group of his guys up for the weekend to focus on developing their skills. I was impressed because he was teaching young men how to be good fathers. How cool was that? So we talked for a while and Insight decided to go in for the night. I sat outside talking to Mr. Manhattan Slick until daybreak. It was such an awesome conversation. I thought he was so cool. I noticed him when we all first checked in but for some reason, he had a fishing hat on and looked like an older man. The next day I saw him in the daylight and I thought he was gorgeous. I was blown away. I remember thinking wow what a difference daylight makes. So at the end of the weekend, we exchanged numbers. I remember talking to Miss Insight on the phone the next day. I said, "I'm not going to call him first." As I was speaking to her, he beeped in on my other line.

We started talking every night and the more I talked to him the more I wanted to talk to him. Although I was really feeling this guy I was really guarded about taking care of me. I was not looking for a relationship. I just wanted to have someone special that I could spend time with, no commitment. I guess I wanted what I had with Mr. Forbidden Fruit without the wife or husband. Mr. Manhattan Slick told me that he was living with someone but they were on the verge of breaking up. He said she knew that he was seeing other people so right now it was convenient because his kids—a boy and a girl were coming in from Florida for the summer. He said after that he was going to get his own apartment. I agreed to see him but we were going to keep it platonic. We went out on our first date which was a harbor cruise one of my cousins was giving. It was magical. At one point the ship pulled over and we watched a fireworks show. It was so awesome and so romantic. Well, so much for platonic, that did not happen we became everything to each other quickly. As a matter of fact, he started to profess his love. I did not respond back even though I felt the same way. I knew this was moving too fast and felt it was too good to be true. As time went on, I told him I was also in love. We spent more and more time together. I met his kids and we hit it off right away. They were 10 and 11. He was a teen father himself and that's why he worked so well with this population. After his son left, he informed me that his daughter was going to stay with him. He said he told the woman he lived with he was in love with me and he would be moving out soon. She flipped. Apparently, she thought this was a phase he was going through and she would get him back since he was living there. She called me and started to say some really mean things and I decided that I didn't want this drama in my life. I told him I didn't want to see him anymore. He called and called but I would not answer my phone. He brought flowers to my job. He came to my gym looking for me. He laid it on really thick. I should have run away at that point. Because I had feelings for him I didn't. I listened to what he had to say. He said he was going to find a place for them both to live. He said his daughter staying made things harder because he needed a bigger apartment than planned and he really could not afford it. He asked me if I would be willing to get a place with him. I told him this was too soon and I needed to think about it because I was not ready to live with a man and take on raising a child.

MMS joined the program that I was a part of and began co-facilitating workshops with me. At one point, we were assigned to do a workshop with parenting teens in Westchester County. When I called for directions, I was told that there were no parenting teens in the group of 30 youth. We were not prepared for that because our workshop design was for parenting teens. In the car on the ride up, I redesigned the entire workshop. He took the design and presented the workshop like he had done it a thousand times. We were so in sync. I was really surprised because the only person I could train with like this with was Miss Insight, so again I was impressed.

Some time went on and I realized that he was not coming around as frequently as he had been. I questioned him about it, but he lied. One night I got a phone call from the woman he lived with. She called to ask if I was still seeing him. I said yes, I was. She then told me they were back together. I was blown away. Did I mention I thought I was pregnant? We talked for hours. It was a trip because she played me. She got me to tell her a lot of stuff about us because I was so angry with him. She told me a lot of stuff as well. Apparently, he decided that he was going to make the relationship work because he needed a place for him and his daughter and he couldn't find something he could afford. So he decided that he was going to work things out with her. The

Acceptance

problem is he failed to tell me about his big plan. I was livid. She played it off like she was also livid but that was a front. She was just happy she was getting her man back. This call was to make me mad and get me out of the picture. The only good thing about this situation is she was more pathetic than I was. I called him and asked him to meet me so we could talk. He admitted everything and we decided to part our ways. The only problem was this potential pregnancy. Sure enough, I took the test and found out I was pregnant. This was the beginning of my rollercoaster ride. To make a long story short he pretended that he was going to be involved in the baby's life. When I went to my doctors appointments, he wasn't there. When he was supposed to pick me up from places, he did not show up. When I asked him to sign his rights away, he didn't. When I asked him to give the baby his last name, he didn't sign the papers. He was not there when she was born. As a matter of fact, he did not see her until she was six months old. I had my baby alone. Although I acted as though that didn't bother me, I was so hurt for me and my child. I felt so guilty, how could I have gotten into this situation. I felt now my dysfunctional behavior is starting to affect others. I brought my beautiful baby into this mess. The hard part was I could not understand how I got here. I was raised better than this. I had morals and values and my life was a movie of the week. I could not understand how he could work with young fathers and turn his back on his own child.

So now my baby was born and I wanted to have the child blessed. My mother wanted her blessed at the place of worship I was raised in. I refused because if you were not married the babies were blessed in the basement, not the sanctuary. I had such a problem with that. I can see them holding something against me but no one was going to the backdoor, my baby girl. I was so hurt and angry with Mr. Manhattan Slick. He truly hustled me into thinking he was a great guy. Every time I had to go through something alone I would think about how he was walking around living his life and I am in pain. There was a side of me that hated him.

When my baby was about two months old I got really fed up with him. The baby had some stomach problems and she had to go for x-rays. I remember praying one of those rescue prayers. I wanted my baby to be OK.

I tried to call him because I needed his medical history. "She" answered the phone and said he wasn't there and would answer the questions. She was not sure about a lot of things on the list. Mr. Manhattan Slick called me back and was very cold and distant.

One day I read an article in Essence magazine that said mothers who don't attempt to get child support for their children are negligent. The article said it's business, it's not personal. That money belongs to the child and if you don't try to pursue it you are a negligent parent. I felt so guilty I decided to take him to court. When I went to file the papers they said I had to have two hearings but they could be held at the same time. I had to establish paternity since we were not married and then I could file for child support. By the time the court date came, she was six months old.

The court date finally arrived and he did not show up. This was really uncomfortable for me because I'm in the same family court that I have worked for many years on my foster care cases. I had been out of the game for a while because I left the agency and now I was working as a city-wide consultant. I didn't have to go to court anymore. I remember thinking maybe no one will recognize me. I always had this thing about being embarrassed. After a couple of court dates, he finally showed up. I thought we were going to have a problem with the whole paternity thing. He surprised me and showed me a glimpse of the man I first met and fell in love with. When the judge ordered the paternity test he spoke up and said no. He said, "I don't want my baby to go through any unnecessary pain having her blood drawn. I waive my right she is my child." He was not working and the judge said she was going to order a child support order and he would just have to be in the arrears until he got a job. When we left the court, we talked and he asked me if he could see the baby. I called my mom who was keeping her and told her we were coming. When we got home, he took one look at her and said, "Wow, she is beautiful." He said she looked just like her older brother when he was a baby. He played with her gave her a bath read her a story and put her to bed. We talked and agreed that we would put our differences aside for her sake. We agreed

Acceptance

to parent her together. It's funny that's all I really wanted. I had such a wonderful father and I wanted my baby girl to have the same. After a couple of months of spending time together and caring for our baby, we got back together. His daughter went back to live in Florida. He moved out of the woman's house and got his own apartment.

Mr. Manhattan Slick living in his own apartment was a rollercoaster ride as well. He was cheating on me with the woman he used to live with and whoever else. We broke up again, got back together, and this went on until he moved out. During this time period, he moved in with his mother. She was diagnosed with cancer and had to have surgery. She went to a special hospital because his family was Jehovah's Witnesses. This hospital was known for bloodless surgeries and in the event that she was not doing well, they would be able to accommodate her. After hours of surgery, they found cancer in so many places but removed as much as they could. The doctors gave her three months to live. Meanwhile, my mother was diagnosed with Alzheimer's disease. We were both going through it. This drew us closer. We alternated with the doctor's appointments for our mothers. If he could not go I would and vice versa. Things were rough but we were good. He and I took trips together, raised our child, and collaboratively cared for our mothers. He did a lot of things that really got on my nerves and I remember wanting to leave him so many times. He would take my car and not come in time for me to go to work, get really drunk and act totally out of control, disappear for days at a time. He was a mess. A lot of it had to do with his mom getting sicker, finally, she passed away. My mom was still alive but her memory got worse and worse. After his mother died, he really changed. He was not coming around as much he was not taking my mom to her appointments; he was not picking up our daughter, he was drinking so much. Honestly, I really did not want him around; he was really a pain in the neck. In October we went away together to work on our relationship and it was a disaster. We argued while we were there and all the way home on a four-hour drive. We were in such a bad place. Although things were this way, I still felt I needed to wait and give it some time because I felt he was still grieving. His mother had just died in April. He became more distant, constantly lying and claiming to be working all the time.

Then the holidays came. He did not spend them with us. He claimed it was against his religion. He became a Jehovah's Witness when it was convenient, holidays, birthdays, etc. Then it happened. One of my childhood friends, Miss Mouthy called me and told me that she had to let me in on what was going on. Miss Secrets another childhood friend told her that Mr. Manhattan Slick got married. Technically we were still together. He told her and for some reason, she did not tell me because he confided in her.

Miss Secrets is one of the seven I spoke about in the beginning of my relationship with the Contender, she knew my secret when I was being abused. She witnessed it first hand when the Contender smacked me so hard one night and I lost my earring. I remember me; Miss Secrets and the Contender were looking for that earring in the dark on the ground and in bushes. She kept my secret back then. Maybe that was an indication of what was to come, this time she kept my man's secret from me. To add insult to injury she knew this for a while. It's funny I knew things were bad between us but I thought this too shall pass. It's funny how you can use biblical references to support what you want and your actions even though you are not living biblically. It's also funny how you can go from being unhappy in a relationship to being miserable outside of the relationship.

After hearing about Mr. Manhattan Slick's marriage, I was blown away. I immediately called his house and a woman answered the phone. I said is this Mr. Manhattan Slick's girlfriend. She said yes this is and I believed she said this is his wife. I didn't ask her to repeat it because I was afraid to hear the answer. This was the beginning of my nightmare with this man. I purchased a new car and allowed Mr. Manhattan Slick to use my old car to make it easier for us to make our mothers' appointments and pick up our daughter. Unfortunately, I never took the registration out of my name because we were together as a couple. We always had each other's back, at least I thought. Mr. Manhattan Slick had accumulated thousands of dollars' worth of parking tickets in my name. I decided to take a trip; I felt a need to getaway. My timeshare was coming up and I felt this would be the best time to go and clear my head. The night I was supposed to leave I went to the store to get a few things. I turned the corner and this car came out of nowhere

Acceptance

coming at me on my side of the street. I could not believe it. He hit my new car. Just that quick! There were six thousand dollars in damages. Thank God I walked away without a scratch. Needless to say, I was not able to go on my trip. I was so depressed. One of my girlfriends I knew from college called me to catch up on each other's lives. I was telling her about my car accident and she said you had an accident? I say yes and she asked when and I told her. She then said, you are not going to believe this, but I see an Evangelist and she is my spiritual advisor and she has the gift of prophecy. She said that she went to see her and the woman told her that one of her friends had a car accident but she was fine. She then said God spared her life because she has something he wants her to do. She told her to bring her friend to see her. Now, I'm not going to lie, I was thinking what kind of mumbo jumbo is this? I had not seen my friend in a while and I decided to go along with it so I could hang out with her. I'm not gonna lie I was wondering if she was losing it with this prophecy stuff. She picked me up and my college roommate met us there as well.

When we got there, the woman took me into a room so she could speak to me privately. She told me that she sees I have been in a lot of pain but this was going to pass. OK, so I'm thinking my friend probably told her this stuff about me. Then she told me she saw me writing a book. She saw me at a book signing and I was going to be a successful writer. She said she saw me and my daughter very happy and laughing and enjoying each other's company. She had me intrigued at this point. She started telling me things that most people would not know about me. I was amazed. I asked her about my weight and she said you are going to lose that weight but you have to lose the weight off your mind first and then you will lose the weight off your body. I remember when we were leaving, she said to my girlfriend, you guys better stick by her she's going places. She is going to write books and she's going to be very successful. I remember thinking this lady is crazy, I don't even like to read books so how am I going to write a book.

God of a Second Chance

Wow! I really didn't mean to recall all of that. Now, I am truly more miserable than I was when I got in this car and more miserable than I have ever been in my entire life. Reliving all of that has left me feeling like I wish I could find a bridge and drive off of it. If it wasn't for my mom and Pooh (my daughter's nickname) I think I would just end this misery I call a life. Wait a minute, where am I? I lost track of where I was going I was so deep in thought. When I got into the car, I was so distraught that I just wanted to drive. I didn't give any thought to where I was going or how much gas was in the car. I was just going. I didn't even notice when the gas light came on. As I continued to drive, the car started to slow down. I can't believe it, on top of everything else, my car runs out of gas. Really? This can't be happening! I am on a road where I can see nothing for miles around. I felt so alone, so hurt, so tired so depleted. I was so lost, both physically and mentally. The rain had stopped but it was foggy. I could barely see my hand in front of my face. It was clear that I was in the middle of nowhere. I was scared because I didn't know if there were wild animals around or some undesirable people who might "get me." I could see a light in the distance behind the fog. I felt if I could get to a safe area some light would shine on my situation. So I got out of the car and started to walk towards the light. It seemed further than I expected. I walked and I walked and it seemed as if it was getting darker. I wanted to turn back but I could not see anything behind me. If I went back it seemed as if that would have been more difficult to find my way. I felt so lonely, so lost, so tired, and so weary. I dropped to my knees and started to cry. I screamed out to God asking why he allowed me to feel such pain. I screamed and I cried out to God. I don't want to live like this anymore. Please stop the pain! Please stop the pain! After, I felt better. I guess I needed to get it off my chest. I pulled myself up and continued to walk to seek help. The fog started to move away and I could see the light a little more clearly. It was still at a distance though. I could see a fence from the distance. I walked toward it and reach out in front of me to brace myself. Even on a good day, I am clumsy. So I knew I needed to be careful. The last thing I needed the way I was feeling is

Acceptance

to fall. With my luck, I will break something and be left lying here, in the middle of nowhere for some wild animals to eat me. Thank God the fence was not that high. It was high enough to keep whatever lives there in but low enough for me to climb over. I remember thinking I hope there's someone in there to help me find my way.

As I got closer to the light, I saw a man standing in the distance in what looked like a robe. There were a bunch of white things near him. I thought they were sheep spread out all around him. He looked like a Shepherd. I remembered thinking this is crazy. How far did I drive? But even if I drove far I felt like I am looking at something from another time period. Now I think I'm going crazy. If this were the desert, I would think I was seeing a mirage. This is just a little outside of New York City. That's it I have completely snapped. I have been through so much that my mind is gone, depleted because now I am seeing things. I begin to question whether I should continue walking because now I am afraid. I'm losing my sanity and I am afraid of most animals. But something inside of me was driving me to continue to walk towards the shepherd. As I got closer, I realized that my eyes were deceiving me. There was a man standing and he did have on a robe but he was a minister, a Pastor standing in the middle of a patch of grass. What I thought was sheep were parishioners all dressed in white sitting on the ground listening to what the Pastor was saying. This is too funny. He looked like a shepherd tending to his sheep from a distance. It's funny how your eyes play tricks on you. Ironically, He is a Shepherd tending to his congregation which is his flock. I do remember that much from Sunday school. As I approached them, he continued to talk, but when he saw me he stopped talking to acknowledge my presence. If I wasn't so messed up in the head I would have been embarrassed because I was clearly interrupting something. At this point, I was so self-absorbed and so deeply wounded that I just kept coming towards them.

The shepherd asked, "Can I help you? You seem like you may be lost." So I said boldly, "Please help me. I am so lost. I don't know where to turn." I told him what happened to my car. He said, "We will help you with the car, but it seems as though you need more than gas." I said sarcastically, "I do, I need a new life. Can you help me with that?" He said, "As a matter fact, I can if you are willing." Willing? Are you kidding me I can't go on like this?" I asked, "What are you offering me religion? I had religion when I was younger. It didn't work then and I doubt if it's gonna work now. Besides I have chosen so many wrong paths and done so many things that I know God would not be pleased. I can't even begin to tell you how many commandments I've broken in my life." He listened to me and then he started to talk to me. "Well first of all," he said. "I am not offering you religion, I am encouraging you to have a relationship with God. Secondly, the God we serve is a forgiving God, I guess you missed the part about Jesus dying for our sins when you were religious." He then smiled and said, "The question is can you forgive yourself?" I immediately felt so connected to this Shepherd; he understood exactly what I was feeling. He offered me an invitation to a different life and told me that I have to be willing to change. This change of Life must begin and end with God in it. I told him I don't think God wants me because I have sinned so much since I was baptized. He told me, "God is a forgiving God." He broke it down for me by telling me that I needed to truly accept Him. I needed to confess that I am a sinner and how I want God to be a driving force in my life and repent from sin and believe that he will give me another chance. He went on to explain that I can read about the acceptance of God in the Bible.

The Shepherd Speaks On Accepting God

Acceptance of God—Romans 9:9-10: Praise God that Salvation is free! Paul helps the Roman Church and the modern day believer to understand the simplicity of accepting Christ as Lord and Savior. Confess and believe! No longer are the rituals for atonement of Sin in the Old Testament needed for a new life in the Kingdom of God. John 3:16 lets us know that "God so loved us, that He gave us Jesus Christ" for the saving of our souls. Acceptance of God through Jesus Christ also gives us access to the power of the Holy Spirit. God in His love had a plan to rescue us or save us from the plight of eternal punishment for our sins. It is Jesus acting as our substitute taking our place. He suffered for us. Based on Jesus' death for sin, forgiveness and admission to Heaven is available for each and every one of us.

Wow! I had only been talking to this man for a few minutes and he told me what *John 3:16* was about. That was one of those scriptures my church had me memorize when I was religious. Now that I understood it, I decided at that point to accept God into my life.

The Shepherd told me that I had to go on a journey. There was a mountain behind him called Mount Horeb. The top of the mountain is where you go to meet God. The Shepherd said that each of us possesses a spiritual gift and there is a purpose for our lives that has been predestined by God. We each have an assignment here on earth. He told me that I needed to find out what my assignment is. This was all so new to me. I attended church from birth to age 18 and I had never heard this before. He told me that I will have to climb this mountain to renew my life. He explained that it's a journey to my purpose and although there would be tough times I should not give up. He also said when I arrive at the top I will be filled, and equipped to walk in purpose. So I asked him, do I have to do this alone? He said no; remember God will be with you, He has designed the path for you. You are also going to meet some women on your journey. These women are your sisters in Christ and they will share their experiences with you, and keep you encouraged. They will minister to you and believe it or not you will minister to them as well. He also said he would check in with me at various points during my journey to ensure that I am truly following the path and completing the necessary steps. This sounded a little crazy to me. I remember sitting there wondering how did I get to this place. I was puzzled but I did realize that since I started to talk to him the pain had subsided. So I said I guess I will be living on this mountain? He said yes that's the best way to do it. Turn away from your old life and start anew. I told the Shepherd that I will start tonight. I have to go home and pack. I also have to find a place to live that's big enough to take my mother and daughter with me as I embark on this journey. He said don't worry about that. Everything you will need will be provided. I knew he was right; I had to move I had to leave the past behind me.

This Walk Ain't Right! But, Help Is Along The Way

I agreed and realized that I needed a clean start. I went home and got mama and Pooh, packed up, and moved into a house on the mountain.

My last job was being taken over by a college. It was also a new start for my career as well. So we moved into the house and I started a new job at the college. As the Shepherd said my problems were nowhere near over. I had financial issues due to the state Mr. Manhattan Slick left me in. This man ran up $10,000 dollars in parking tickets in my name. The Sherriff was taking $250 per paycheck from me to pay off the balance. How embarrassing it was when my boss called me into her office to inform me of what she had to do. The saddest part is he went off into his new life and I was not even getting child support.

I started to think about why I agreed to try this church thing again. I had no real connection to the church in the past so why was I going back now. I stopped going to church when I was in college. Another reason I didn't go to church was that when I was in college, I did not have church clothes like I used to because tuition had to be paid. I was taught you don't come to church if you don't have the right clothes. Then after college, I was broke. A recent graduate and I had no money. I remember you had to pay your money or you would not be considered an active member. I went back for funerals and to get married. I wanted to go back when I had my child but my friends were wounded in the church when they had their babies out of wedlock. I did not want my baby to be the next target. My friends were told that their babies cannot be blessed in the church if you were not married when you had them. They were so hurt and I hurt for them. I had so many excuses. I decided that there were just too many rules in church and I did not feel connected so I stopped going. So here I am back in church. Maybe things will be different this time. At this point what did I have to lose?

When I got to the house I got settled in my new life. I decided to go for a walk. I proceeded to climb up the mountain. I was seeking a place I could be alone. It was beautiful on the mountain. I felt safe there. When I started my walk, I was welcomed by a group of the Shepherd's helpers. They were so warm, so nice, so welcoming. They gave me gifts, a bible which was described as food for thought, sort of a survival guide, an MP3 player pre-loaded with gospel music, a portable DVD player with sermons by the Shepherd, his friends, and other Shepherds who were tending their own flocks. "There was contact info in case I needed." There were also invitations to functions that would be taking place around the mountain, rest stops where I could get replenished if I became thirsty and a list of other congregations that lived on the mountain. I was also given a list of poisonous things I should avoid. I was feeling wounded but encouraged and equipped. Although my circumstances had not changed, I felt different. There was a true sense of hope. I had not felt this before. I could now see a light at the end of the tunnel. Little did I know the people could not fully prepare me for what I was about to encounter.

As I climbed the mountain my MP3 player began to play the song *"In the Midst of It All"* by Yolanda Adams. I thought wow this woman can really sing. It wasn't just her voice it was the words and the message she was conveying. I felt this song way down deep in my soul. It literally knocked the wind out of me. I had to stop and take a rest. I knelt down to the ground and before I knew it I was overcome with emotion and began to cry. I cried like I had never cried before. I screamed out to God asking him to take this pain away. This pain dug so deep that it had become a part of who I was. I did not want to carry it anymore. I continued to listen to the song and Yolanda talked about how people she was close to could not help her but she learned to depend on God. At that moment I started to get it. I realized that only God could get me through this. Then the next song came on the MP3 was Donny McClurkin's *"Stand"*—*What do you do when you done all you can and it seems like it's never enough. You just stand and let the Lord see you through.*

I felt a little stronger and began to catch my breath. I calmed down and realized that the songs were so encouraging. I can't wait until I get to that place when this pain and anguish I feel would be behind me. I can't wait until I can encourage others like I was just encouraged. After I rested, I felt strong enough to continue climbing the mountain and so my journey continues.

Wow climbing this mountain was harder than I thought. The mountain had high and low points. I was not prepared for some of the weather conditions on the mountain. I did not realize that the temperature would constantly change as I reached different points in my walk. As the nighttime approached you could feel the temperature drop. It was so cold and dark. I also grew tired of walking and looked for a good place to rest at one of those rest stops the Shepherd mentioned. I began to settle in for the night. Although I was so tired, I could not sleep.

I decided to watch a DVD of one of my new Shepherd's sermons. This sermon was on Christian development. He spoke about it being a process. He spoke of how when you first come to Christ you are a babe and you should continue to grow. You should not be in the same place from one year to the next. I really took this in. I guess the fact that I was a social worker that studied and taught human development was why I could relate to Christian growth and development so well. I was able to understand and connect this information to my knowledge of development and understand the gradual process. The part that I forgot to compare is that there are internal and external factors that influence the developmental process.

I did not realize some of the people I would meet on the mountain were going through their own stuff and working out their issues on this same mountain as well. I thought the people on Mount Horeb had already arrived, been to the top, met God and were perfected, sent back to help me and others like me. I remember thinking they would have all the answers. I also thought the people on the mountain were all good. That there was no bad in them because let's face it, they met God.

Little did I know there was a lot I was unaware of? It really didn't matter because I was in a good place. I have decided to accept God into my life. I decided to sleep at the rest stop. Before I closed my eyes I took out the MP3 player and listened to some more gospel music. The song the "*Battle is Not Yours*" by Yolanda Adams was playing and then "*Open up My Heart*" also by Yolanda Adams.

I prayed the Lord's Prayer because that's what I memorized from my childhood and then asked God to bless my family and friends. I remember thinking as I drifted off to sleep, this Yolanda Adams lady sure can sing. I also felt her words expressed exactly how I felt. Wow, what powerful songs. I felt such a sense of peace. I can rest now.

Trust

The Third Set of Footprints:
Proverbs 3:5-6

Trusting What's Divine!

Wow, it's morning. I slept better than I have in a while. I'm having one of those where am I moments. Oh yeah, I moved to this mountain. What is this truly about? I got up and went back to the house. Walking back was helpful; a morning walk to clear my head before getting ready for work was a good thing. Much to my surprise I ran into the Shepherd. This guy seems to be everywhere. If I didn't know better, I would think he was stalking me. No let me stop playing. At least I still have my sense of humor in all this madness I've been dealing with. He asked me how I was doing. I told him I was alright. He reminded me that walking up this mountain will not be easy and not to give up because there is help along the way. He then told me that I had learned two valuable lessons prior to moving onto the Mountain. Some people call them valley experiences. My valley experiences opened up my eyes and taught me some invaluable lessons. The first, about being exposed to God and believing that He truly exists. I learned that it doesn't stop there. I was left with the desire to want more. I wanted a better understanding. You have to be willing to get to know Him to understand Him. The second step is truly accepting God into my life. I now understood that there is a relationship that needed to be accepted, pursued and developed. The first two steps in this walk I entered into blindly, partially because I was lead by external factors, my parents, life circumstances and I really didn't realize what I was getting myself into, until the second time when I truly accepted God.

The Shepherd told me that God has been watching over me even though I was not looking to Him for love, validation, guidance and support. He then said, "Now that you have truly accepted establishing a relationship with God, there are six additional steps or lessons that I needed to learn." He asked me to consider each lesson as a step in the right direction and not to give up no matter how challenging things may get. Going through this process is necessary, in order to make this a true, growing and long lasting relationship with God. I'm not going to lie; I remember thinking, what have I signed up for? It was scary. Then I remembered I have nothing to lose. I am miserable and I can't take living and feeling the way I feel so I will take the chance and see what God has to offer me.

The Shepherd encouraged me and said, "The next four steps in this process are the core elements of the walk. These necessary steps will introduce four pathways to gaining and maintaining an essential connection which is crucial in building and maintaining a relationship with God." He said, "The steps you are about to face should be viewed as entry points to pathways that you will continually revisit and strengthen throughout your Christian Development Process." At this point I was like HUH? What does that mean? He laughed and said, "You will be introduced to four areas you will get acquainted with now but you will gradually develop a deeper understanding in each area as you continue your Christian walk throughout life." I didn't quite get it but I still don't even know how I got here so I guess it will be revealed to me as I continue to climb this mountain. The Shepherd saw I was struggling with what he explained to me. He then suggested that I attend the New Climber's class he developed which may help me to better understand the process. The Shepherd said, "It's not easy climbing Mount Horeb." He said he developed the class to assist all new climbers in their journey. I agreed to come to the class being offered. I asked when could I take this class and he said there was one this evening. I went to work and when I got off, I attended the class.

The facilitator handed out a document that was developed to assist in the climb up Mount Horeb. It was called Understanding the Walk through Model. She began to describe the model by explaining:

Trust

The Walk-Thru Model

FOOTSTEPS *Process of Change*	RELATIONSHIP GOALS Connection Point	SCRIPTURE REFERENCES Biblical Support	VIRTUES Admirable Quality	COURTSHIP Integrating Issue	RELATERS Footprints
STEP I EYE OPENER	ACKNOWLEDGE GOD'S EXISTENCE	EXODUS 3:1-14	REVELATION	ONSET OF AN ISSUE	EXPOSURE TO GOD
STEP II THE DIFFERENCE	ACCEPT GOD'S PLAN OF SALVATION	ROMANS 10:9-10	FREE WILL	WILLINGNESS TO ADDRESS THE ISSUE	ACCEPTANCE OF GOD
STEP III DIVINE PERFECTION	BELIEVE THAT GOD HAS THE MASTER PLAN	PROVERBS 3:5-6	FAITH	BELIEF THAT THE ISSUE WILL BE RESOLVED	TRUSTING IN GOD
STEP IV CREATION	UNDERSTAND THINGS HAPPEN IN GOD'S TIME	ISAIAH 40:31	ENDURANCE	UNDERSTANDING THAT RESOLUTION TAKES TIME	WAITING ON GOD
STEP V REDEMPTION	KNOWING YOU MUST LET GO AND LET GOD	2 TIMOTHY 4:18	RELEASE	REALIZE THAT YOU ARE IN A GIVE AND TAKE SITUATION	DELIVERANCE
STEP VI GRACE	UNDERSTAND THERE IS A PROCESS	LUKE 8:43-48	PURPOSED	ITS GETTING BETTER BUT NOT RESOLVED YET	HEALING BY GOD
STEP VII. SPIRITUAL PERFECTION	GOD BROUGHT YOU THROUGH	JOB 42:10-17	PEACE	RESOLUTION	RESTORED BY GOD
STEP VIII RESURRECTION	BE A WITNESS, GIVE BACK, SERVE GOD IN EXCELLENCE	MATHEW 20:28	WISDOM	A WILLINGNESS TO HELP SOMEONE ELSE	MINISTER FOR GOD

A Christian is defined as a person who believes in Jesus Christ as Savior. This belief is the cornerstone of the relationship that is developed between the individual and the Father, Son and Holy Spirit (Ghost). Relationship can be defined as a significant connection with emphasis on the way those who are in the relationship behave toward and feel about one another. This is a reciprocal process.

Development is the process of change; it is a progression, a course of action. When a person becomes a Christian, it is often described as an event i.e. "The day I became saved or the day I joined the church." Christianity is not that cut and dry. Although salvation is a choice, Christian development is not an event it is a developmental process. The process begins with knowing who God is, who Jesus Christ is, why He came, why He died, why He was resurrected and then accepting Him into your life, and allowing the Holy Spirit to adapt your lifestyle to emulate and promote Jesus' actions, His works of kindness, helpfulness and concern for others.

The Walk Thru Model is a methodology that charts the process of "The Relationship Walk." The chart outlines the process people go through as they develop and strengthen their relationship with God. The model connects the processes of Christian Development and Relationship Building through a conceptual framework that serves a dual purpose. The Walk Through suggests a marriage between that which is considered developmental and that which is considered relational. This theory serves as a spring board to a continuum that introduces relationship goals that are rooted in scripture with clearly identified virtues.

The second concept within the framework is the "The Courtship" phase, which suggests that the believer uses a strength-based approach to facing and overcoming life's challenges through the use of The Relaters. This is a cyclical process. The Christian understands that God will walk him through each and every issue he is facing while simultaneously building and strengthening his relationship throughout the process.

The relationship building process is often referred to as "The Walk." This walk has many similarities to a physical walk or a footrace. The Christian Walk can best be compared to a Marathon. A marathon is a long distance race that is lengthy and difficult at times. It is a test of endurance. Prior to the Walk, participants must understand the relationship between knowing where he begins and knowing where he is going or "the geographic route" of the marathon. He has written instructions telling him which way to go and how to get there. He must utilize them to be successful in the race. The walker must also have a willingness to honestly assess his mental, physical and emotional capabilities prior to and throughout the course of the walk. The body gives the walker signals and messages that should not be ignored and must be considered in order to progress and complete the journey.

As the walker begins the journey he must recognize that he is not alone. This is a well-organized event with a built-in support mechanism that is coordinating the entire process. The walker must acknowledge he will sometimes be **exposed** to conditions or face situations he is not prepared for like inclement weather, attire that is not conducive to walking and things that challenge his sense of direction. Although he is faced with these challenges *he **accepts** the fact that he must reach his destination so he perseveres. He remembers that he started this walk for a reason. Although the task at hand may be difficult he does not turn back, he does not give up. He **trusts** that he will arrive at his destination if he looks to the coordinator for direction and stays on the right path.*

*While walking, he encounters setbacks and detours such as construction sites where injuries occur and **waiting** for the appropriate traffic signals that appear to be faulty. He may become dehydrated. In addition, he may feel as though he has become weakened. One of the great things about a marathon is the coordinator knows what to expect, He knows the walkers' needs. During the process the coordinator **delivers** water to the walkers to quench their thirst he must not hold on to it he must drink it to become revitalized.*

*At the end of the marathon the walkers reach the finish line. They are filled with mixed emotions. They are happy they completed the race but are tired, sore, and depleted. Before they can receive the benefits of completing their task they must rest, they must become revived therefore undergoing a **healing** process. The walker must get back his energy. Once his energy has been **restored** they reflect on the process, celebrate their accomplishments, show gratitude to the coordinator for his direction and allowing the walker to participate in such an invaluable, life altering experience. Most of the major marathons or races are covered by the media who want to interview the walkers. This is the walker's opportunity to share what he did, how he did it, what were the struggles, the challenges, the high points and the low points and how he became victorious. This is his opportunity to **minister** or give back, guide, support and encourage someone who may be interested in walking or participating in a marathon.*

The Relationship Walker and the Marathon Walker have similarities such as:

1. *The Marathoner's goal is to cross the finish line. The Relationship Walker is a journey and the goal is obedience / total surrender / to fulfill the Great commission.*
2. *The Marathoner has a road map: The Relationship Walker also has a set of written instructions, the Bible.*

3. *The Marathoner must listen to his body: The Relationship Walker must listen for God's voice for guidance.*
4. *The Marathoner can quit or keep going: The Relationship Walker has free will and self-exploration.*
5. *The Marathoner has an Organizer: The Relationship Walker's organizer is God.*
6. *The Marathoner sometimes faces challenges: The Relationship Walker faces trials and tribulations.*
7. *The Marathoner doesn't give up: The Relationship Walker grows through adversity.*
8. *The Marathon is a lengthy process: The Relationship Walker waits for God*
9. *The Marathoner takes the water: The Relationship Walker gives and takes.*
10. *The Marathoner heals: The Relationship Walker understands the healing process*
11. *The Marathoner's strength is restored: The Relationship Walker gains purpose.*
12. *The Marathoner gives interviews: The Relationship Walker Testifies*

A new believer begins the walk with the understanding that there is a God, makes a decision to accept him into his life, learns to trust Him, learns to wait on Him, experiences deliverance, begins to heal, becomes restored, and by the end of the process becomes a witness to others. By no means am I suggesting that once a person has gone through these stages "the walk" is over. The steps the believer takes during the relationship building and change processes are called Relaters. The relaters are like footprints, where you can look back, trace your steps, and remember where God has brought you from. These steps can best be described as life experiences, tough situations and challenges. Some refer to these as tests, trials and temptations. The Christian is now encouraged to use the relaters as a focal point to gain a broader understanding of "The Walk." Each step the Christian takes deepens their relationship with God, builds stamina, and prepares him for the next stage of development.

The facilitator also stated that the model charts the course or outlines the lessons that must be learned as you go through your journey. Each person in the class has to complete the journey lessons in order to gain insight into their purpose for their existence.

I thought this is so deep. I also thought, what have I agreed to? The facilitator then stated that all of us are not going to make it through because some people give up before they become completely enlightened. Those who complete the journey may be on different time schedules and that usually depends on which step you are on when you begin. Then there are some who take longer because they get stuck on a step. Each step has a built-in Bible study and the document serves as a roadmap highlighting points of interest. The facilitator suggested that each of us read through the document and determine where we were in our journey and make that our starting point. I determined that I was already exposed and am now on step two, learning how to accept. I knew that my next place to go was step three, learning how to trust.

As I was leaving the class the Shepherd appeared again. How does he do that? It felt like he came out of nowhere. He asked what I thought about the class. I told him it was interesting. I did not share with him how blown away I really was. He said the next step is learning to trust God. He also advised me to get involved in the activities and services that take place on the Mountain. He told me to read my Bible which is God's Word, and that there are worship services on Sundays both at 8:00 am and 11:00 am. In addition, he said, that there are Bible study sessions during the week. There are ministries that are set up to help people who are in need. I thought ministries? Is that what we use to call auxiliaries? He also said that people tend to grow spiritually when they are helping others in need. He said I could choose whichever worked for me but I needed to stay connected. I needed to be focused so I could access help and gain knowledge towards developing a true relationship with God. I fearfully agreed because I did not know what was in store for me. I told the Shepherd I would see him later and went off to prepare for work the next day.

I am really glad that it just so happened that my job was closing. At first, I thought it would be difficult moving from such a small agency to a large University. I don't know, but I felt this change could not have come at a better time. I have been so miserable for so long. I really need to change my entire life, I need a fresh start. Working at the University will give me the perfect opportunity to put the past behind me. At least that is what I thought.

We moved to this University and although it sounded good, working here was challenging. By this point in my career, I had my undergraduate degree in Journalism, a Master's degree in Social Work, and many years' experience in training, staff development and program design and development. There were a lot of things that were different here. I am not very happy, there's something missing. My previous CEO had an entirely different vision for the company. I didn't realize it then but she and I were on the same page. My new CEO had a different vision. I guess I am having trouble with this because when you apply for a job you apply to places where you would like to work or share the vision. At least that's the way I look at a job search. The problem was my company was taken over so we didn't have many choices. I guess I should be happy that at least I had a job. No matter how miserable I was.

I got a call at work today from one of the young people I used to work with who is older now and a Christian. She told me that God told her to call me and tell me to step out on faith because he had bigger things for me to do than I'm doing right now. I told her that I was doing some outside consulting work with families and that is such a prayer-driven rewarding experience. So she suggested that I do it on a full-time basis. I asked her was she out of her mind. Look, I have a daughter who I am supporting by myself; I can't walk away from a job with medical benefits to consult with no benefits. I felt I needed a safety net. She told me that God would be my safety net. I told her I believe that God can do anything but I'm not ready to take that chance because I had my child to think about (So much for my belief).

A few days later another friend of mine told me that she was in prayer with her prayer partner and God told her to tell me to leave my job and begin to consult on a full-time basis. She said that I was supposed to be making a difference in people's lives and I needed to reach more people in Jesus' name. Although this sounded good, I told her as I told the last person that I could not do that because I needed medical benefits for my daughter. She said you have to trust that God will provide you with benefits. You have to be obedient. I told her I had to think about that, I really wanted to get her off the phone. I remember thinking I believe in God and all but I am not leaving my secure job for something I wasn't sure about. Now I had been working as a consultant a couple of nights per week making really good money. This consulting I was providing was the same opportunity that was given to me by God through this same friend I'm talking to. Remember I said earlier Mr. Manhattan Slick ran up $10,000 in parking tickets in my name. The Sheriff's Department was garnishing my paycheck at $250 per pay period. I did not know what I was going to do because he would not pay the bill nor give me my money back. This same friend called me up and said she had too many projects and God told her to turn this over to me. There were two contracts. One contract was for parenting classes once a week at $200 per week and the second was at $250 per week for domestic violence. Not only did God give me my money back he gave me overflow. The funny thing is I had no problem believing that God told my friend to give me the consulting jobs. I quickly accepted those gigs. Why was it so hard for me to accept that God told her that there was a special purpose in my life? I had a hard time believing that one and I was not leaving my day job.

For reasons beyond my knowledge, I believed there was a God and I accepted Him into my life but I didn't trust Him to see me through so I could not take that leap of faith. It's funny, doing the training sessions is where I truly learned how to pray. I prayed the hardest for God to get me through them. Although I had the skills, I doubted myself because collecting the paycheck was one thing, but being responsible for people whose families were at risk was a whole different story. These people's lives were in shambles. I didn't want to mess them up further. So I prayed to God to give me what I needed to help them. I felt so humbled and knew that I was brought there for a reason. It's amazing how I had worked in the world of foster care for over 20 years. I worked to get kids back home after being in care; I worked to get kids adopted; I worked to get young people toward self-sufficiency but there was something different about the work I was doing within these groups. Let's face it I was going into the hood working in their environment and they saw me as a means to get their kids back or prevent their families from falling apart. I prayed before each session and I found this so rewarding. The strangest part was we would always get into a discussion about the power of God. I remember the discussion got so deep that the group members asked if we could pray at the end of the sessions. I told them that I could not make it an official part of the group because of the regulations, but whoever wanted to stay after the groups were over we could join together in prayer. It was amazing! Everyone stayed. I couldn't believe that I was fearful in the beginning about doing these sessions. These were the sessions I enjoyed the most. Why was it that I was having so much trouble stepping out on faith and doing this full time?

Unfortunately, during this rewarding time in my life, my day job decided to reduce my hours from 5 days to 4 days per week. This meant a reduction in salary. I was angry. My pride was taking a real beating. I knew I had more experience and credentials as well as a better reputation in the field than others that were kept at full-time status. Once the anger started to diminish I took this as a sign that maybe I should have listened to my friend. I said OK. I am going to take some consulting jobs on Fridays and build up my business so I would be able to leave. Well, it didn't happen. I got used to having a short week and spent less money. I still did not move in the direction I was being called to.

A few months later I was put in charge of an event that I knew was cutting edge. The people in my field loved the event but my director, who I didn't seem to see eye to eye with, decided that he should lay me off. The problem with him was his ego and pride were bigger than mine. He and I had different approaches to the work and how staff should be treated. For some reason, he always got on my nerves. He told my supervisor to come in from her vacation to lay me off. I was blown away. Again, I was livid because I knew I had more experience and education than some who were not layed off. My pride was in the toilet. I remembered thinking what would people say? Where will I work? What will I do about medical coverage for my daughter?

On Sunday morning I decided to go to the 11:00 am worship service. It was lively and the music was great. It was what I remember from childhood but better. I guess part of it was that the Shepherd's sermon was so relevant to what was happening in my life. His sermons were interesting and he seemed to really get it. I mean he was able to explain what I needed to hear. I remember thinking that's why he stalks people so he can have access to their experiences and use those experiences as encouragement in his sermons. I was so excited about going to worship services. I would go get my friend Wisdom and we were off to worship. I just loved going to worship service. I was getting to know people as well.

Wisdom introduced me to some people and I met others on my own. Some of these people offered such warm smiles and made me feel so loved. This is great! I don't think I will ever leave this mountain.

A woman approached me this same Sunday and asked me to join her ministry. I wasn't sure what she was talking about. I love the Lord and all but I didn't want to be no minister. I guess she saw the look of bewilderment on my face and began to explain that the ministry she was talking about was Body and Soul. After, I realized that "ministry" was the new buzz term for what we used to call auxiliaries back in the day. I still wondered if she was crazy. I thought, I am clearly overweight, I smoke, drink and although I am not sickly, I am also not the most health-conscious person. I remember thinking this lady is really sweet but she has lost her mind. She said she felt I would be an asset because of my social work background and I could bring my training and expertise to the mental health side of the ministry. Once she said that I was in. You see my self-esteem and self-worth are directly tied to my career. This is the one thing I have always been good at, working with people and helping them to feel better about themselves and their situations. It always made me feel good to help people out of dark places. It is what has always given me a lift. You see, I could avoid dealing with my own stuff if I could focus on someone else. The joy was I came out feeling better when they came out feeling better. So as far as I was concerned this was a win-win situation. I agreed to work with this group, this ministry. There were some awesome women in this ministry. They are all committed to helping people and ensuring that people get vital information that assists in caring for and developing their minds, bodies, and souls. This is where I met Miss Understood. She was such a fireball. This young woman has such a love for life and is full of energy. I can't explain it but I was really drawn to her. She was funny, organized, and had the acting ability. She used to make me laugh because she was so dramatic. I remember telling her that she used situations within the ministry as prompts for "acting." It was as if someone would say and "scene" and she would do her portrayal of the irate women, or the comical women or the sensual women "and end scene." I teased her and told her she used us for material and she was great in each role. Some people would react in a wounded manner when she would go into her "role." I would always burst into laughter. I thought she was the most talented creative person I ever met. I guess I also saw her differently than others. I believe that "behavior is purposeful." People don't do stuff without a reason. We may not know or understand why people do the things they do, we may not even like it but there is a reason. Therefore I knew she would not fly off the handle for just any reason. Miss Understood had this excellent acting ability that was thrown in the mix of things. She would crack me up! I guess I have been around so many unstable people in my career and life that I knew she was just theatrical. The funny thing about it is once she realized why I was laughing at her she would tell me to shut up and laugh too. We hit it off and became quick friends.

At the same time my worship attendance increased, I realized I needed to work on my individual relationship with God. At first, I attended the 11:00 am worship service because that's the service I attended as a child. Something led me to try the 8:00 am service. I immediately realized I liked the earlier service. I valued the intimacy of the service and remained focused on my relationship with God. I wasn't distracted like I was in the later service. Maybe it's because it was time-limited. Maybe it was because the focus was on praise and worship, the scripture, the prayer, and the sermon. It wasn't about how you were dressed, the announcements, the choir, and the people. I was focused and was able to begin my journey toward understanding the individual purpose that everyone was talking about.

I started to read my Bible more. I got the New Living Translation version which seemed to make my comprehension of the Bible clearer than the King James Version. I actually understood what I was reading. Reading the Bible was hard for me for several reasons. First, I didn't understand King James. Secondly, I wasn't that into reading. I like to write. Sometimes I don't even like to read what I've written myself. The story had to be great for me to read a book. I love stories. When I got my NLT Bible, I realized that the Bible was a book of stories. As a child, I wasn't ever able to comprehend what I was reading because I could not get past the early English content.

Laid off from work, I had nothing but time on my hands. I began attending more activities during the week. One particular night, I went to Bible Study and the Shepherd taught us about spiritual gifts. He said that every member of the body of Christ had a spiritual gift that is outlined in the three books of the Bible—*Romans, Corinthians,* and *Ephesians*. He gave us an inventory, which was like a quiz, and explained that we should answer the questions and our score would determine our gifting. When I completed the inventory, I came out with Exhortation as my primary gift. I felt that I scored something I didn't know the meaning of. I asked the Shepherd and he explained that Exhortation was to encourage and uplift people within the Body. He then asked if I was doing that and I felt I had not within the Body. Wisdom chimed in and asked, "Are you crazy? That's all you do, with everyone you know. That's who you are." I thought about it. I always associated that with my social work training. I researched the gift and I realized this is who I am. Now, I had an understanding that my spiritual gift was exhortation. This is why I was a good social worker and so compassionate toward people. I still had questions because I was not doing this within the Body. I could not even see myself doing this exhortation because I didn't know enough about the Bible and most people in church knew more about this God stuff than me.

As time went on, I realized that the ministry I was a part of put a lot of focus on the physical aspect of health. I knew this is very important and the Lord knows we all need to physically take better care of ourselves. I just needed more.

I don't know what was going on around me, but I felt like people who were coming to worship were so wounded and needed emotional healing. I also noticed that people seemed as if they were losing sight of why we were there and argued over frivolous things. For example, in one ministry meeting I went to people were arguing over chicken. At yet another meeting, the ministry members were arguing whether they should donate a dollar to something. And still, a female congregant came into worship service very late and was mad because she could not sit where she wanted. She even went as far as to point out that she purchased a pew during a pew drive so she should be able to sit in it. These frivolous encounters were beginning to distract me more and more. It was that same old stuff I witnessed at my childhood church. I felt so strongly about these distractions I finally decided that we need to do something about it. I went to my friend Wisdom and told her that we needed to plan a women's conference to bring our women together. She thought it was a great idea. I took it to various ministry leaders and they felt it didn't fit within the focus of their ministries. I disagreed but what could I do. I mentioned my idea to Miss Understood who came to me later and told me she thought this was a good idea. I then went to a few other worshippers, I knew and really respected, they too told me that Mount Horeb was not ready for a women's conference. I was crushed. I couldn't understand why people on the Mountain didn't want to focus on developing spiritually and coming together. I went back to my friend Wisdom and told her my feeling of defeat. She told me not to give up and to take it to the Shepherd. I took her advice and approached the Shepherd with my idea. He told me to write a proposal. It's funny my love of writing came in handy here. My skills from work would also come in handy. I thought what a coincidence. Throughout my social work career, whenever I worked on work plans or developed programs, I was taught to bring the people who would be involved or doing the actual work to the table. So I got my group together, me, Wisdom and Miss Understood—and we came up with what we thought was a great plan for what we named a Women's Spiritual Conference. I took the results of our planning session and wrote a proposal. The Shepherd felt it was a great idea and agreed to let us have it. I was so excited about this new project. I went to the next worship service and the choir sang *If You Can Use Anything Lord You Can Use Me*. I got so into it. I really meant every word.

    I remembered thinking, I now know what I'm supposed to do, and it's to present conferences, women's spiritual conferences. I was so happy. I felt the rest would be easy because I have been putting conferences together and facilitating them for years. I mean, I know

I am not a facilitator for this religious stuff but I can put a conference together with my eyes closed. I was a little nervous. This was a religious event and God knows I really don't know much about that. I figured its OK because I remembered what the older people would say—God knows your heart.

I continued to understand that my purpose was to uplift and encourage. I also understood why I have always had such a bad reaction to those who wound people especially, in the church. At this point, I was beginning to experience situations and understand that satan would use people both in and out of the church to discourage and distract me from fulfilling God's purpose for me. The hard part is when you are experiencing the tests and temptations, it's hard to admit that this is for your own good because it feels so bad. I had this dual process going on and I felt my life became a living hell.

It took a while for the Women's Spiritual Conference to make its debut which we entitled *Sister to Sister: Together We're Better with Christ*. Our group thought the conference would be perfect to bring women together. For some reason, people didn't respond well to our invitation. This was the first time I felt wounded in the church. What I experienced when I brought the idea to the congregation and what I experienced in trying to get people to register was mind blowing. The women were very mean. I was so hurt. It was like planning a party and nobody came. I felt that satan was really busy trying to distract us from why we were having the conference in the first place. We were so wounded by the lack of response to our good intentions that we started to take it out on each other. The night before the conference I had a bad argument with Miss Understood that ended in both of us saying we were not attending.

We were both so new in our Christian walk that we did not know or realize that God was getting ready to make a major move that would impact the rest of our lives and satan was not pleased. He figured he would cause dissension amongst us and we would give up. People heard that we were arguing and tried to justify their not coming by saying that we were not saved enough and there was not enough God in what we were trying to do. The funny thing is that God showed up and showed out.

Wisdom called me and Miss Understood and talked us into coming; reminding us that we had worked too hard to let this end this way. Then God sent Rev. Jackie to us for encouragement. She said she had been doing conferences for years and it takes time to build so don't be discouraged. She opened us up at the conference and then it happened. God showed up and took over the entire weekend. He showed us that momentous weekend that those who were supposed to be there were there. We had an awesome time and were on fire when we entered the sanctuary that Sunday morning. During the conference planning and execution, I learned several things. I learned that we had a lot of growing to do. I learned that God will step in and turn situations around into what He wants them to be. I learned that just because people are in church doesn't mean that they are nice people. Each person has to allow for growth no matter how long they have been in church. Lastly, I learned that as people of Christ, we are assigned to bring new Believers into the Body of Christ with the spirit of support and encouragement, not drive them out with the spirit of meanness. When I get older, I hope to remember that when I am dealing with younger women, I must guide them not hurt or misdirect them.

At least the conference made me feel better about my church life. My work life was still dim but the conference planning experience is where I truly started my trust walk. By the second conference, I learned that we could plan until we were blue in the face but God will show up and make it what He wants it to be. This is when I began to trust God because I knew this was the beginning of something bigger than me.

Miss Understood and I made up at the conference and developed a great sister friendship. She also taught me about trusting God through her testimony. Shortly after the conference, we were sitting and talking and she told me her story.

Miss Understood: You've Been Part of A Set Up!

According to my mother, I was very friendly. I would go up to people at the drop of a hat. She was scared about that. She was afraid someone was going to take me. I know my family used to tease me about buying me a wig because I didn't have any hair. My mother used to say, "Leave my baby alone she's going to have some hair." My brother was jealous of me. We were a year and a half apart. My mother said he used to take his teddy bear and hit me with it. He would say, "I don't want that ole baby in my crib" because I had his crib. My mother said I was a very quick birth. They didn't have time to shave her or get her clothes off. Before she knew it I was here. She said, I don't know what happened to your father he disappeared. When I looked around, he was gone. He was excited or whatever. She said unlike my brother, she was in labor for three days with him, but with me it was no time; I kind of burst into this world. She said, "It was like Tadahhhh!!!"

I had braces on my feet when I was an infant. My mother said they took me to Mississippi to visit my great grandfather and he didn't like the bars on my feet and tried to take them off. My mother said she told him that I had to wear them to straighten out my feet. But he didn't like that so he tried to remove them anyway. During toddlerhood is when she said we would go outside and she was concerned because I was very clumsy especially in the summertime.

I remember walking to my elementary school. There wasn't a traffic light and it was a busy street and so one of my parents had to walk me. I remember my father coming behind me. He would watch me cross the street because I wanted to be a big girl. He would watch me cross and when I would get to the other side I would stop and wave and say, "Daddy I made it." The rest of the way I would make my way to school. My childhood was happy although my father took sick when I was in the fourth grade. I was brought up around both sides of my family. I remember being happy. We never lacked anything. In terms of food and clothing, we never lacked but I knew we were poor. When we were small my mother said my father had brain surgery. We were small so I don't remember that. I also remember they said he was kicked in the head by a mule when he was in Mississippi and they didn't take him to the hospital. I truly believe that triggered what happened to him. Then my father became an alcoholic and he had seizures. I don't know if it was a combination of everything and all that together but I realized that my father started to lose it.

One Saturday morning we woke up and he was fussing with somebody in the bathroom. He was saying, "You can't come in here, you can't do this now my wife is about to cook." I remember it woke us up. He was the only one up and he was talking and we had a window in the bathroom and he was outside of the bathroom door. We were standing in the kitchen looking at him and my mother said, "Who are you talking to?" It was no one there. Of course, she called the police and my father was taken to Elmhurst Hospital. He didn't stay though. He came home and something else must have happened because the next thing I know my father was institutionalized at Creedmoor. I guess I was about nine or ten then. I did not see my father for a while when they first took him away. My mother knew the situation and knew how he was and she was up in the air about if she should take us. I remember being in the kitchen crying saying, "I want to see my daddy. I want to see my daddy. I want to see my father."

My mother took us and I remember going to see him and I remember being devastated because of the medication he was on; had him so drugged up his speech was gone. We couldn't comprehend anything he was saying. He knew who you were and he wanted to speak and tell us something but he couldn't. I remember sitting there with my hands over my eyes so the tears wouldn't fall. I was devastated. I remember my brother being cool. He was OK; maybe because he is a boy and was older than me. My mother saw that and said ok, let's go. That didn't stop me from going to see him though. In my mind, that was my father and I needed to see him so we continued to see him. My mother would continue to see him on a regular basis. She went every weekend as we got older we, my brother and I would go see him on our own. We would have him home on special occasions like Father's Day, Thanksgiving, Christmas, Mother's Day whatever. So basically, when I was little we went from everything was fine to one day he was gone. He was never the same again. We knew he would never come home for good. He was never in his right mind again; whatever medication he was on he was going to be on for the rest of his life. I really don't know if that was truly the case because I was a kid. I often wonder if it happened to us being grown would it have turned out that way. You know my mother, being from the south and not knowing and she was limited to what she knew. She had to really go on what people told her and you don't know if the right decisions were being made. Maybe it's the institution they had him in, maybe it was the medication they had him on. I don't know. I really don't know if he would have been in the same situation if we were older.

I remember my brother went to see a psychiatrist when we were young after my father was institutionalized. But I never had to. I knew I had my memories of my father. I also remember that prior to my father getting sick he was an alcoholic also. I have memories of him being drunk. Maybe he was upset because he saw his own father get killed. I really don't know my father's side of the family that well; nothing really about them. I really knew my mother's side. I mean when my father came in drunk he either went one of two ways. I'm still not sure why. Sometimes he became violent wanting to hit my mother. I mean he would go after her and run and I remember also I guess I don't know.... when my father would get drunk we would do things to him knowing that he was in a state like put matches on his toes to try and get his attention. He was there and he would be drunk and passed out but we would try to get his attention. I am recalling some of the stuff now like I remember him falling asleep in the chair I just remember him um... most of the time he was drunk. We would see him out in the street drunk. Um, he had his friends up the block. I guess at one point.... I guess he stopped working. I don't know if he was working or not working I really don't know that part. My father would be up at the corner sitting up on the corner with his friends getting drunk and stuff and falling out and stuff. So my father was an alcoholic. I guess a lot of that was coming from a lot of the stuff he experienced growing up in Mississippi back in that time. My father died at the young age 46, dead! I was 21 or 22. My father was too young to die. I am at the age now or past the age when he died. Diabetes runs in my family. My father was a diabetic. My father's side of the family was diabetics. My great-grandmother had her legs amputated. I remember seeing her when I was about 9 or 10 years old. It was the first time and the only time. They said my father had a combination of a heart attack and a stroke. He was just so young. He died at 46. You know what has always bothered me? I just don't know what happened to him and whether my mom and my grandmother were given the right information. I just don't know. He was too young. My father was speaking fine before he left. I'd go to see him and he is on this damn medication and it's not making any damn sense. It just didn't make any damn sense to me. You know? He spoke and he was fine before then. He didn't have a stroke or anything beforehand. But they put him in the institution and . . . . I have no idea. I wonder did they give him some type of treatment. I have no idea. But I know when we went to see him, he knew things. He knew our names, he knew our cat, and he knew he wanted to come home. That was the biggest thing he wanted was to come home. I remember every time we would get ready to leave, he would walk us out and you would see this look on his face as we were about to go, and that used to BREAK MY HEART! I mean you couldn't take him home and you knew he wasn't coming home. And this was your fah . . . this was your father . . . . I mean . . . . you know . . . . I . . . . EVEN NOW, all these years later I am crying over it. YOU SEE I STILL HURT, I keep trying to fight back the tears but I can't. IT HURTS MY HEART THAT MY FATHER'S LIFE . . . . WASN'T MUCH OF A LIFE . . . . This hurts my heart. Sometimes I think of my mother too at a young age. Taking care of her kids, she was left as a single mom to take care of her kids and stuff but she didn't give up. Mom had faith in God that I couldn't even begin to imagine. Sometimes when I think about their lives it really bothers me.

My mother had a nice voice for singing. She wanted to go into nursing and she didn't. That bothers me, that she didn't achieve things. That's why it's important that I do what God has given me to do. What I feel that I need to do. I CANNOT . . . . I REFUSE TO GO THROUGH THIS LIFE AND SAY I DIDN'T TRY . . . . I DIDN'T GIVE IT A CHANCE . . . . AND THAT'S SO IMPORTANT TO ME. That's why I tell kids and my own son, YOU GO FOR WHAT YOU KNOW. YOU GO FOR IT BECAUSE YOU DON'T WANT TO EVER HAVE ANY REGRETS. It breaks my heart because it is from a different time and I know how difficult that time was to take care of children. That's the way they were raised. They were domesticated. They had to take care of their children, they sacrificed. I try to tell my son don't sacrifice. Find a way to make it work. You can do what you still need to do and still raise your child because it can work. It can. So it just bothers me that I always felt that my father got the short end of the stick. Getting kicked in the head by a mule, seeing his father get killed and other things he probably went through living in Mississippi that I don't even know about. They said my father was no joke! He was fearless. They said one time they had to talk him down really hard and long to stop him from going home and getting his gun and going after some white man in Mississippi. It was something about being gay or something. Maybe he tried to come on to my father and he wasn't having it. There are probably more stories that I need to get from my aunts. I have no idea I don't know what happen . . . . I know he loved my mother. I just feel like he didn't get a fair chance to live his life. I don't even know what my father was good at or talented at. I know he was very much into guns. As a matter of fact, my brother has one of my father's guns, a shotgun. I don't know my father's, father's side of the family. I don't know anything about them. My father is the oldest of four children. My grandmother had him when she was 13 so maybe that has something to do with it.

My mother took us to church when we were small, since I was an infant. We went to Sunday school when I was like six or seven. I remember growing up in the church. For as long as I can remember I remember being in the church. We grew up African Methodist Episcopal. I was active; I was on the choir, usher board, youth department. I was secretary of the Sunday school when I was a little older, when I was 11 or 12. It was funny my mother at first wasn't going to church. She used to send me and my brother. She grew up Baptist with her siblings in the south. A couple of her brothers were deacons. Her father was in the church, I remember she would get us up and get us ready for Sunday school and then she would get back in bed. She would fix us breakfast and everything. My mother started going to church, getting back in the church when my brother and I got a little older. I remember we were like nine or ten. My mother would come to our programs and stuff like Easter and Christmas. She would work with us and make sure we had our parts, anything that we were involved in. My grandmother, my father's mother was a member of the church. That's how I think we got involved in it. The church was right up the block. As far as I remember as long as I was able to read and write I remember being brought up in the church. I was about 10 and 12 when I joined the church; I joined because of peer pressure. I figured it was the thing to do. I was never baptized as a child. At our church, we didn't have a baptismal pool and we didn't go out for that. I was christened as a baby of course but never baptized. The first time I was baptized was when I got here on Mount Horeb. I think I was religious as a child. I don't think I had a relationship with God. Although I felt I used to talk to God I didn't have a relationship. I knew all the right things to say and do; even my brother knew things like the Apostles' Creed and the Ten Commandments. We knew them not just a little or a one-liner. We knew the actual verses. That's how we were taught. I think it was a religious thing, a place we would go. We were never really taught; it's not like anyone ever took us aside and told us there was a difference between religion and relationship. Maybe they did but I can't remember. If they did, it just didn't stick. I remember my mother catching the Holy Spirit a lot. I remember me and my brother holding our breath. You see my mother started coming to church after my father was institutionalized. We used to have Altar calls like most churches and my mother would go up there and she would be the last one up there. My brother and I would hold our breath when we would see her going up. I used to hate to see her coming because I knew she would be the last one up there. I had a hard time with that. My brother and I had a hard time with that. I guess with everything that was going on with her she saw this as her opportunity to let it out. She would just let it out. Sometimes it would take two people to go up and get her. Sometimes she would be up at that alter for a long, long time. When they would come to get her she was just no good. She would get back to her seat and just be stretched out. Every now and then she would go up and she would be alright. She would regroup and come right back. But the times that she didn't, which was most of the time she would have to be taken back to her seat. I can remember my friends looking over at us and then I would look at my brother. I hated that part. I hated, hated, and hated altar call. I don't know how my brother felt about it but I hated it. And when she got up there, she would cry out. She would wail. I mean wail. Oh, I used to hate that. Oh, I hated altar call. It wasn't that I was embarrassed, it was her pain and to see your mother like that. My mother was a strong woman. We grew up with my mother being strong. I always remember my mother in the kitchen where she sat. She was always talking to God, she was always praying and she was always singing. My mother wasn't a drinker or a smoker. She called herself smoking one time and she would light it and put it back out. She wasn't a smoker. Her thing, her refuge, her relief was God, it was Jesus. That's what I grew up with knowing her strong faith. She trusted in God. I remember feeling I wish I could grow up with a faith like my mother. I don't want to turn to anything to ease the pain. I would turn to alcohol and turn to weed to ease the pain. I wanted to numb it so I could go to sleep. I am that person who when I am in pain I will pop a pill in a minute. My mother won't, she just deals with the pain. I found myself doing it because it was easier, it was quicker it was just better than having to deal with the pain or cry myself to sleep. I know in the morning I will still have to face it. I knew that but when I didn't feel like it I wouldn't. I know what I would turn to a good drink or a good joint. Sometimes I would use the over-the-counter sleeping pills so I could get a good night's sleep. It's funny because I knew what I would turn to was wrong. I needed to open up the Bible. What I started doing was talking to Him and asking for help. Some days I needed help just getting out the bed. You have good days and bad days. I think people lie when they say every day is a good day. Sometimes you feel bad during this walk and that's the truth. Some days you question everything. You are like why am I going through this and some days you don't even care. You just want to numb it.

During my teen years, I was still going to church. Then I got pregnant at 15 and I decided not to go back. It wasn't like someone in the church said something to me about it. People knew. I don't remember coming to church pregnant, although my son was christened in the church. We moved to Flushing and I think the distance and what I was going through was why I didn't return. It's funny I have always had a problem with the church regarding teenagers. They really did not have much for us to do to keep us connected. They only wanted us to do what they wanted us to do. It was not about exploring our interests. Any ideas that we had they would shut them down. You just got to the point where you didn't want to be there. After a while I felt the

This Walk Ain't Right! But, Help Is Along The Way

church wasn't serving us, they didn't care about us. Church just wasn't fun anymore. I was feisty back then. I remember writing a letter to the Pastor trying to get rid of one of the youth supervisors. She teases me about that to this day. I had to tell her, "Well mama you weren't doing your job and I had to tell it." But really I think that was a turning point for me. I felt we went from being cute to being in the way. I didn't have a connection to the church or God for that matter. I was armed with the religion I had learned, to pray at night, say your grace, and scriptures I memorized but no true connection or relationship. Even if I went to other churches I knew church etiquette, I knew good music, and I knew when people got the spirit. I don't think I understood it but I knew when it was happening. The sermons I never got. That was the time to go downstairs. When we were ushers, they would put the velvet rope across the center aisle. They would dim the lights. THAT'S NAP TIME YOU TELLIN PEOPLE! I remember as a little kid we would get in my mama's lap and go to sleep. When we got older if you were in the choir you were stuck. If you were ushering we would go to the store come back downstairs hang out and talk. We knew when we heard the organ playing a certain way it was time to go back up the stairs. Sermons, oh no! I cannot recall one sermon that stuck to me or can I recall now.

My friends on my block weren't in church. So I remember just wanting to have fun and I would hang out with the girls on my block. They were older than me they were my brother's age. They were two grades older than me in school. They had siblings who were older than them. The friends I was with were more developed than I. They also knew more because they had these older siblings. They were exposed to stuff that they should not have been but they were around them. I was always called the baby. They would always say she's the baby. She's the baby of the group. They had breasts and butts and I didn't have any of that. I was the cute one I was the baby. I got tired of being called the baby. I felt I ain't a baby. So I had to prove myself and I remember two of the girls were not virgins. At the time they were about 16 and they were talking about it. I remember thinking the first chance I got I would show them I'm not a baby. The funny thing is when I lost my virginity, they didn't believe me. Just like when I got pregnant, they didn't believe me. I was always energetic, laughing, silly and playful. Nobody believed me when I was pregnant. There was this guy who was 5 years older than me that liked me. He lived around the corner. He lived downstairs from my best friend's house. I knew the family really well. I went by his house by myself and nobody was home. So we did it! I was 15 and he was 20. It wasn't like anything I expected it to be, I mean it hurt a little bit but it wasn't anything! We did it a couple of times after that, and I got pregnant. We knew of birth control but I don't know what I was thinking. My mother didn't talk to me about it. She did talk to me about when my period comes and what to expect. It's funny at that time me and my girlfriends were hanging out with older women who were 10 and 12 years older than us. They were unintentionally influencing us, sitting there listening to these older women in their twenties talking drew us in. I used to wonder if I would have told one of them what I was doing would things be different. I didn't realize I was pregnant; my period just stop coming. My mother was into watching my period not me. I never really got sick. I worked at Elmcor that summer and I remember getting sick one time and didn't think much of it. By the time I went back to school on the first day I was so sick. I was on the train going to Manhattan to Fashion High School. This was my second year going. I got sick and my friend asked if I was alright? She said I turned white and my lips turned purple. So then it passed but when I got to school to pick up my schedule my head was pounding. We got back on the train to come home and I threw up in the train station. My mom made breakfast in the morning and all that bacon and eggs came up. I remember coming home and I got into my mother's bed. It's something about getting into your mother's bed. My head was pounding and those were the only two times I was sick. After that, I was never sick again. My mother had already taken me to the doctor. After that incident, she took me back to the doctor. The first time we went to the doctor he asked me in front of my mother if I was sexually active and I lied and said no. He said, "OK we won't worry about it she's young, it's summer, she's active. Take this prescription and it should bring her period down." It's funny I think there was a part of me that knew because I took those pills but I really didn't take them. Maybe that's why my son is so crazy now because I was taking those pills. No, let me stop. This time the doctor asked me again and I had to admit that I was. My mother could not believe it. I put my head down because I was so ashamed. I went to take a blood test and my mother called me in and they told me I was pregnant. They told us where I could go for an abortion. We got up in the morning and took a cab into the city and went to the place. The women examined me and came out and told my mother that they only do it up to 12 weeks and I was 14 weeks. They told her I could have an abortion but they could not do it there. They said I had to go into the hospital and it was going to cost like $800. They said I would have to stay in there a couple of days. My mother said, "Oh No! No! NO! If something happens to her it will be on me. She will have this baby!" Then we left. When we came home I remember my mother got on the phone with her sister and she said, "HELEN HELP ME!" She started screaming and she started crying. I felt like CRAP! I remember I was on the toilet. I was in the bathroom and my aunt wanted to talk to me. She said, "You just killed your mother! How could you! How could you! You killed her!" I just remember crying and not wanting to have a baby. I remember wanting to throw myself down the stairs. I remember punching myself in the stomach. I remember contemplating throwing myself down the stairs. I didn't feel like I was pregnant, nothing was changing nothing was happening. I wasn't sick, nothing was happening, as far as I knew I was the same Miss Understood. I didn't feel anything growing inside of me. Then I started showing at five months. Then one night he kicked and when I felt that kick that was it. To feel that movement everything else shut down. I remember thinking I'm going to be a mother and this is my baby and I love this baby. Everything else shut down there was no more thinking about trying to kill myself. I was like I hope it's a girl! I remember my friends on the block or even my high school friends didn't believe me. I wasn't showing but when I started showing they were like she is pregnant. I remember they felt the baby kick in school. They were devastated because I was the first one they knew who was so young and so pregnant. This was in the seventies when that whole teenage pregnancy thing started to pop. This was a real transition in my life. I was still a child and I was having a child. I didn't give up though.

Although my mom was hurt she was there for me. She continued to care for me and support me but I had to be a mother to my child. She made me take on the responsibility. I wanted to be a good mother to my child who turned out to be a boy. I put my child in the Boys Club and he got into basketball. He was a really good player too. I went to all his games I had to support him like mom supported me.

I remember my mother took me to dance school at Elmcor because I loved dancing since I was a small child, then I stopped and went back to dance as a teenager. The first time I remember being on stage dancing I remember having on a green & white costume. I think I was a horse or something; I had a little small part, everything seemed so big, when you're little everything seemed SO big; I must have been at P.S. 127—when you're little everything looked so big! The school is so small now when I go there.

As a young teenager I was part of a singing group with some of my girlfriends from the block, those childhood friends, called the "Frames of Soul" and we changed it to "Love Sensation" they were older than me. We would sing, go out to talent shows, we had outfits made for us, and we bought suits and stuff. Our parents came out and supported us. We called ourselves singing, you could not tell us we weren't singing. Ha, yeah we were singing! And that lasted for two years as teens and even after we had our kids. One of my friends always had a love for singing and we would play around and sing but it was just in my girlfriend's house at first. We just wanted to start a singing group, and we did. I wasn't one of the lead singers. I would choreograph our steps. We thought we were the female Temptations. Even back then I had a part speaking. We were doing something we called Ebony Princess. We had a part where this guy was coming over to us offering us jewelry to come to go with him and my part was to bop him on his head and say, "No I don't want or need your jewelry!" It was a dramatic part. It's funny I always got dramatic parts. Whenever there was a time to do speaking in our little act the speaking parts would always go to me. That's so odd when I think about that now; even when I was dancing with Miss Marilyn's Dance School. There was a piece that we danced to called Jesus is Love by the Commodores. There was an oratory part in the beginning before the dance started. I remember we did it at Rev.

This Walk Ain't Right! But, Help Is Along The Way

Ike's church up in Harlem. I remember it was a big stage. It's funny I don't even remember why we were there. The stage was huge and I just did my thing! I remember my friends saying yeah! This was in my early twenties and maybe my late teens. I remember I was at home on that big stage. I remember I was serious about my little part. I said my stuff! I almost forgot I was supposed to dance because I was so into my part. Wow, I remember that so clearly. You know I forgot all about, all this stuff. It's really funny. I was also in a play called For Colored Girls at the Library. I did this play about 1981 or 1982. I got this part because I was working at the Library and the programs we had were dance workshops and theater. I had to work because I had to support my son. I was really interested in the theater workshops. I loved the director John Barracuda. He was directing a lot of stuff outside so they had him doing the workshops. He would facilitate the workshops and then he would put on a production. I don't know what made me go and audition for it, can't remember. It might have been him who told me to do it. The funny thing is I didn't attend the workshops as a participant but I covered them because I was working. I was just there but I wasn't considered a participant. Then after I auditioned, I became a participant in the workshops. I remember he said to me that the way I recited my lines about watering the plant was excellent. He said I could never do it as good as I did it the first time. He said I did it good but I could not get it back as good as the first time. I remember my dance instructor gave me a card and said after seeing me in the play she felt like wow! Now I know where your true calling is. I was like, what are you saying I can't dance. Then I got more exposure to theater when John left. The new guy had a different twist to acting. I learned about the importance of what happens backstage and I learned about head shots. We had people who were older from the outside coming in for auditions so I got exposed to that side of things. I was exposed to holding auditions and looking at head shots. We knew who we were seeing and knew what we were looking for, some very specific things.

I got turned on to stage management where I assisted other plays that were being presented. At that point, I was the Assistant Director of the Cultural Arts Center at the library. Wow, this is how I got some of my training. I remember working on the stage and working with sets. I remember learning rules like you can't cross the stage once it's prepared for the performance. I learned that because I got in trouble with the director. All I remember was they were so annoyed with me. I tried to tell them that I needed something from the back but they were not trying to hear that, because this is not supposed to be done. They were trying to be as professional as possible so I learned that the hard way. But I was glad because now I know.

All of those experiences and the joy theater brought me led me to take theater in college. I was then asked to do little things in the neighborhood over the years. One of the ladies on Mount Horeb asked me to play a part in the *Women of the Bible* play. The woman was the chair of the committee and asked me to co-chair with her. She basically let me do what I wanted to do because she was getting older. I found parts for the women who wanted to participate but then again maybe I wrote them. Then again, I think I found those monologues and cut them down to make them work for what I was trying to do. I directed that play. It's funny I liked putting things together. I think part of my strength for directing came from teaching dance. My friend asked me to help her start a dance school. It's funny I had no clue about joining the administrative team of a dance school. I had no clue! We learned as we went along, we also had the foundation we got from our dance teacher. We choreographed pieces for her and that gave me help. It didn't come naturally to me and I was lost when it came to counting.

I was interested in working on *Women of the Bible* and I started to do research. The more research I did the more I developed an interest in *Women of the Bible* and wanted to write something and put my own little twist on things. I started to put my own spin on things. I started to think about how I would feel if I was in this woman's position and I came up with a play called *In the Name of Woman I*. The next thing I know I was teaching the women in my plays how to act. I didn't realize it then but I knew what I wanted so I worked with them to give it to me. I tried to do with them what worked for me. I would say to them put yourself in that position. Try to bring life to a character that you could step into yourself. You have to step into it. You have to try to feel it. Like if someone tells you to act like a prostitute. Sometimes you may not know what it feels like so you have to do the research so you can feel it. I can't just pick something up and read it or just write anything, I have to feel it, understand it, and know it.

When I was a kid, I always loved arts and crafts. I used to make costumes for my dolls and write one-act plays and have them act it out. Of course, my voice was all of the characters. I learned how to put written materials together at the Library as well. I learned how to put my name on stuff from a mentor at the Library. We used to buy sheets from Pecks and line them up. I use to do flyers for the library. I had a scrapbook of all my flyers. I wonder what I did with that. I would use paper and use sheets with different fonts. My mentor told me to put my name on whatever I worked on. Not that there would be compensation for it. He said it was good practice. He said later on down the line if there is credit to be gotten you would get it. A lot of stuff I continued to learn on my own. I use to play with the computer. I used to just practice on my own. I learned by doing.

You know I don't really know what told me to write my own play. I just started writing I don't know what made me say I am going to write and produce a play outside of the church. When I started writing the parts it was for the church but when I think about what happened when me and the Shepherd fell out, I don't think things would have turned out this way if we would not have had a parting of the ways. I found what the enemy means for evil God means for good.

It was after a committee meeting the Shepherd asked to speak to me. The night before this meeting, I sent an e-mail to the youth dept. supervisors stating that I wanted to join the youth dept. They asked me why I wanted to join. And I was like what do you mean why? One of them told me I had to speak to the Shepherd and I said OK. I couldn't understand that but I said I will. I didn't realize that they had spoken to him and that's why he called me in. He then asked me to tone it down a little and then I said what do you mean? What are you talking about? I left there very angry and hurt because I felt he was coming at me and had not heard my side and already made his mind up so I left angry and I wrote a letter. Then he sent me back a letter. I felt like people were lying to me. I felt I was being painted as a bad person. I didn't like how the Shepherd handled it. I expected better from him and more from him. Shoot he is my cousin! I felt he didn't even ask me what happened. He just started the conversation by saying I need to bring it down. I said bring what down? He said yelling at the kids and stuff, I felt unappreciated. I felt like I was doing something good and people were coming back and saying none of the positive stuff just all negative stuff. I was so hurt and I was so angry. It was almost like how I felt when we first started the conference and everybody bashed us and didn't want to come. I was mad and I decided I was leaving the church and no one could talk me out of it. I had my speech ready for each person who was ready to try and convince me otherwise. I was so dramatic about it. Oh yeah, I was so hurt. I didn't understand it. I felt people were so mean and wicked and all I wanted to do was do something with the kids. I wanted to teach the kids when you do something for God do it in excellence because He is so excellent. I also saw that these kids were talented and I wanted to bring it out of them. People were telling me they enjoyed it when I worked with the kids from Easter up until Black History. No one could say OK, yeah she yells at the kids but she is trying to get them to be the best that they can be. Nobody saw that. They just saw me as having a big mouth and just trying to damage the kids. I was angry. I was not trying to damage the kids. Each time I saw one of those people I wanted to take their heads off and I knew I had to leave. It's funny now I am like hey how you doing? I don't know what they were trying to do I guess they wanted to make me leave. But then again, I think that people were just being their mean selves and you are prepared for that in the street. I wasn't ready for that, not in the church, I was blown away when it happened in the church.

I came back to the church because I missed my Mount Horeb family. I missed church. I guess I should say I missed my church. I was going to church while I was out there and I tithed and fellowshipped with others. I enjoyed it but it wasn't the same. You know what? I realize this was a setup. God had been setting me up all my life. I got used to going to other churches then, but now I am the chair of the women's department. I have to go to other churches and I'm very comfortable with that. This was another setup. God is too much! It's nice and enjoyable but you feel sad about it because it's not where you belong. I never felt a connection to join another church. I was going to go back to the

This Walk Ain't Right! But, Help Is Along The Way

church I grew up in because my mother was there. Something stopped me from doing it. When I came back for the Women's Conference a prophetess told me she saw me on Mount Horeb leading people. I was not back yet and I could not tell her but she said she saw me in leadership there. I was like who? Me? And she said, yeah you. Look at me now I am leading the women. I wasn't there in my mind but God had another plan. Then the next thing I knew that Sunday I was back walking up the aisle. I had to let some stuff go and I did. When I came back everybody shouted and the Shepherd turned around to see why people were cheering and he smiled and hugged me. It's funny people welcomed me back that I never thought would. I guess people see that you are real and have to respect that even if they don't like it they respect it. I think that people do their dirt and don't think about pushing people out. When they see you leave they go oh I didn't mean for that to happen. It's twisted! It's a fractured fellowship practice they got going on. That's the next play I'm working on. It's all OK though because it all worked out. It was part of my setup.

It's funny; all the people that gave me such a hard time are still here. It's years later and they are all under me now that I am the chair of the Women's Department. Each of them holds key positions in carrying out the vision God has given me for the next year. It's funny how God, gets down! We are all forced to work together whether we like it or not. That's so funny to me. Wow, they are all under me. Wow, I didn't even realize that. They are footstools that helped me get to the next level. Wow!!! It's just like when you need to get to a higher shelf in the kitchen you break out the footstool or ladder to give you a little elevation. Wow, this whole thing has been a setup. It was all predestined. Wow, I can't believe it!

While I was gone, I finished *In The Name Of Woman I* and then I started to look for actresses and I got rehearsal space. When I was doing that play I learned how to deal with new people. I learned how to develop characters by coaching the actresses. I got to see how far I could push the women and see how dedicated they were. I said no experience was needed in my ads so I really got the chance to teach acting. I went to acting workshops and writing workshops which prepared me for this. Again, little did I know I would be doing this. I was interested in theater so if I saw something advertised and I would go because I enjoyed it.

I sent out flyers to different churches and my dancer came out to see another play I was in and I met her there. Then I ran into her again at a wedding and I told her I had a play and she joined the cast. It's funny I was now writing plays that were religious. I don't think they were relationship-focused yet. I would say they were religious. I think people felt they were watching a play. There were relationship moments but for the most part, it was religious. I added music to the play to make it more dramatic. I will sit for hours until I found the right music. After the first one, I started to work on the second one. I wanted to get more experience. I wanted to step out of the box. I added more music and I knew I wanted professionals. My self-worth wasn't so high because I felt like who am I to direct professionals. I had people send their resumes and I knew this would be a paid gig so I was intimidated by the people with professional experience and acting degrees. What I found was that people fluffed their resumes as well. I realized that no matter what experience they had they still needed to fulfill my vision. I realized that people are not as professional as they appear on paper. I realized that when I approach someone's work I approach it with a spirit of excellence and these women were not the same as me. I had to push and pull and work with them just as hard as the amateurs. One of the girls went to a school and she loved doing exercises. Everyone has their own style. I don't like to waste rehearsal time with too many exercises. I remember I was in a play and we had three weeks of rehearsals and all we did was exercise. I was wondering when we were going to get started. Then I had another guy come along and he did a couple of exercises and then he just started directing. When he started directing we didn't do the exercises. I think that's fine when you are taking acting classes and/ or workshops. I think that's cool but when we start working on a production and everybody knows they are in and knows their roles and their parts then we come to work. I'm sure that there are people who can argue against what I'm saying. Some people say exercises show more of what you can do and that is true. I used to do exercises with the first play but they were inexperienced. I wanted to see what we were working with, but experienced people oh no, I don't have time for that. My style is prayer, a little stretching then let's do it! Prayer becomes the exercise. I found that the rehearsals were really deep because we talked about God and what he meant to us. It wasn't long before you could see the difference between those who had a relationship with God and those who are not quite there yet but do believe in God. What I got from *In The Name of Woman II* was the experience of working with paid actresses and we were in an actual theater. Each play was at a different level and each one I would gain new skills. Now I was a producer. Who would have thought?

Prior to producing *In The Name of Woman II*, I started to work on producing my play *Dear Diary*. I was in the midst of the rehearsal and they weren't going right so I put the show on pause. In the meantime, a friend asked me to develop something for a fundraiser for her church. I had what I thought was a skit called *Dear Diary* that I was working on and decided to expand it and make it into a full-length play. This was a deep experience because the actresses "stuff" started getting kicked up as we rehearsed. I didn't know anyone's story. I used some of my own and different friends' experiences. I didn't know any of their "stuff." I was dropping them all off one night and the stories they told were amazing. As I am going through this I found myself trying to encourage them. At this point, I didn't realize that something was happening that was really different this time. In the first performance, people were clearly moved by the storyline and the music. The second time was at a conference and it was a performance. I noticed that people enjoyed it. The next time it was at the church and the women were moved and I added a dancer.

I wanted to incorporate the dancer more into the storyline. She was just a dancer in the beginning. Then I added her in as one of the main characters Spirit and you see her battle with the spirit and the flesh through dance. The next time we did the play people were so moved that they opened up the doors of the church. I realized then I was no longer doing performances, this is Ministry. It was all a Set-Up! This is how I learned to trust God because He knows the master plan. No matter how things appear He's got you!

So, I started to work on my new play *Fractured Fellowship*. I was so overwhelmed by that script it was over 400 pages. I looked at it and knew it was too much but didn't know where to cut. I had the pieces to the puzzle and no box top with the picture on it of what I was putting together. I realized I had to wait for God to give me the box top. The next day God told me not to start with the Shepherd's piece yet. Then I got a double confirmation because it is sequential. God does not want me to make it seem like *Fractured Fellowship* is Mount Horeb issues they are Kingdom issues. I read in a devotional *that* there is something only you can do. This is not the first time I heard this. This happened before these plays. I was at a church and this female preacher singled me out and said, "I don't know you but God has told me that you are the only one that can do what He has for you to do. Only you can do it!" This was back in 2006. All I know is I have to be patient and follow Him. My new play has been blowing my mind because it's so different. It just wasn't feeling right. I realize I can't move forward without Him. This time I have to be led from the beginning. I was in rehearsals but I shut them down until I hear from God and the direction to take. I am OK with that because I have learned trusting God is the only way to go. He will direct my path, right now I have to wait on Him. It's crazy because I have been getting so many requests for *Dear Diary*.

Miss Guided Reflects on Miss Understood Trust Walk

Wow! Look how God gave you an appreciation for dance and acting. He gave you the singing group and now the culmination; it all came together in *Dear Diary*. You were a stage manager and that's why you have no problem breaking down and putting together your sets. You were given opportunities to direct and do casting. That's what's so awesome and now I see why God brought you into my life. You are here to inspire me. Your story sets the stage for what's to come. It is a SET UP! That's why you had to shut down *Fractured Fellowship*. This play has to be all Him from beginning to end. In the past He allowed you to be in the forefront and He guided you from behind the scenes.

Everything happens for a reason. He shut you down because this was your time to reflect because all the messages' you were getting were His work, not your work. Do you remember when we watched Bishop Ellis and he talked about when God took His voice and that was his "shut down?" He said that he was doing what God told him to do but he had not checked in for his new assignment. You had to grow and develop which is what you did over the past few months. You are different now. Right after you put *Fractured Fellowship* down you went out to do *Dear Diary* and they opened the doors of the church. You have to rely on God because He clearly does not want this to be a performance. Everything about *Fractured Fellowship* must be Ministry. It's just so awesome how you have been prepared for what's to come. In the beginning, things just came naturally and you didn't realize that God was leading you through. Somewhere during the process, things changed. Miss Understood said, "Yeah, I don't just have religion anymore. I have a relationship with God." I told Miss Understood I would see her later because I had to go check on Pooh and Mama.

Wow! I remember when I got home, I felt so low. I was so inspired by Miss Understood but looked at my own life and wondered when was God going to set me up? I was feeling like my career that I worked so hard to build and meant so much to me was dwindling before my eyes. My pride really took a beating. Here I am working at this University I graduated from after years of practicing in the field of social work. I was a consultant known throughout the city for the work I had done over the years with young people. I am a trainer and a program consultant. I run groups with people who were facing heavy issues in their lives or on their jobs and parenting. I would go into service provider offices and talk to them, design a plan to make things run smoothly and productively, while at the same time giving the person I was working with hope. As I would go into an agency I made sure I prayed before I started my work. I would ask God to give me what he felt the people I would come in contact with needed. I remember walking away from meetings, trainings, and groups knowing it had to be God who took over because I couldn't even remember what I had said or done when the session was over. All I know is the people were uplifted, motivated, and at peace. It's funny now that I reflect on the process; I realize that before, during and after the sessions I was clear that things were in God's hands. But somewhere in between, I got pumped up on pride. I was MG. MG was "the woman" who could make things happen. My self-esteem and self-worth were so low that I was unable to focus on the one area of my life that was not tainted by wrong choices in my life.

I did the right things where my career was concerned. I went to high school, college, and graduate school. I made my parents proud. I got great jobs made really good money for the social work profession that is. I made a name for myself in New York and I was proud of that. The good thing about my director laying me off was that he knew I was valued in the field so he made it a point to tell top officials in the city administration that he laid me off for fiscal reasons. He knew that people would not buy that I did not know what I was doing. On top of being laid off, I was really missing my mother. During times like these, she would have been so supportive. I started to think about how she was before she got to where she is now.

Mama Was No Joke!

As I said earlier, I have had to deal with my mother's illness which has been one of the hardest things to deal with. I mean I am watching her deteriorate before my eyes. I keep asking myself what happened to that strong woman who was an excellent wife to her husband and mother to her children? This woman found a way to take care of herself, four kids and her husband, buy houses, cars, furniture, and food. She made sure we had what we needed for school, really nice clothes for church, and save money with an income that never exceeded $30,000 a year. My mom was remarkable and boy did she love her family, immediate and extended. When I look back, I realize she had a true relationship with God.

With the exception of my teenage years, my mother and I were extremely close. I mean that's normal for a teenager to think they know it all and their parents know nothing. I was so blessed to have her in my life. When I think back about how supportive she was to me in all my activities, projects, etc. She tried to expose me to so much. I think she tried to live vicariously through me. Her family didn't have much growing up in the south during segregation so she wanted so much for her family. Aside from taking me to church, she put me in dance classes where I performed in recitals with two left feet, and I still can't dance. She got me piano lessons which I took for six years and all I can play now is chopsticks. She paid for all of my costumes and travel expenses for all the choirs I was a part of from Jr. H. S. through college. I can carry a tune but I am by no means a singer. When I pledged my sorority in college and became a Fraternity Queen in college she paid those expenses as well even though she didn't have a clue what they were. All she knew was this was my child's interest and she supported me through.

When my marriage failed, she was right there praying and helping me through the pain, embarrassment, and feelings of failure. When I got pregnant, she was thrilled even though it was morally wrong. She thought I had waited so long that she would not live to see my child so she was so happy. When I was pregnant, she stepped right in to take care of me especially when I was put on bed rest. I remember when I had cravings she would say, "Let's go get it I don't want you to mark my grandbaby." That was one of those southern wives' tales. I think it meant if you craved for something and didn't get it you would leave a mark on the baby. How crazy was that! She was so awesome! I don't care what I wanted and it didn't matter what time it was we would jump into the car and go. She would not even get annoyed when we would get back and I would not eat what we bought because I didn't want it anymore. I had a problem while I was pregnant with gaining weight. I had lost so much weight before I got pregnant that I was so afraid of gaining it back. Each time I went to the doctor I would lose weight. I was also so depressed because of how Mr. Manhattan Slick (MMS) was acting.

Although I always acted as though I was not a church girl and had no religion I was so ashamed to be having this baby out of wedlock. Nobody knew how I really felt. Although Mr. Manhattan Slick was clearly a jerk I would have given anything to have him in our lives so my child could have what I had growing up. At least that's what I told myself. Let's face it; I should have known if he was a jerk while I was carrying his baby then he would have been a jerk if I were with him. But I enjoyed living in my own little fantasy world. I guess my reality was just too painful.

When I came home with the baby, my mama was in her glory. This was the first grandchild she said that she had in her home as an infant. This was also special because she was the mother of the mother. She said it is different when it's your daughter's first baby. Pooh, that's what I called the baby, had colic. She would scream and I mean scream every four hours when she got hungry. At first, the doctors thought she had an intestinal blockage. I remember I was so scared, but mama was there for me praying for my baby and encouraging me. I just loved them both so much. Boy did she love us. I got so close to my mother during this time because I finally got how much she loved me because I knew how much I love Pooh.

Even when Mr. Manhattan Slick came back on the scene she did not try to interfere. The only thing she did was have long talks with his mother and the two of them became fast friends. I remember we went south to visit family and MMS drove us down. It was me, him and the two grandmothers and Pooh in between the two of them for 16 hours. This was a memorable trip. MMS' mother, Mama C., was a real character. She was a comedian and she spoke her mind and if you didn't like it too bad. She had a heart of gold. Boy did I love her. Mama C. always had my back when MMS would get out of hand. That used to blow his mind. She would even get on his case if he was waiting too long to take me to get a Christmas tree. He would say I can't believe her, she is a Jehovah's Witness. She doesn't even believe in celebrating Christmas. She would tell him he was not practicing their faith so it didn't really matter. If I need help getting a tree, he should help me. He hated that. As I think back as long as she was alive, he didn't do the crazy stuff. He did all his dirt after she died.

Well, getting back to the trip down south. So we are in the car and all of a sudden the aroma of a bowel movement filled the car. We all thought Pooh needed to be changed she was in that potty training stage. When we checked her out we realized it wasn't her. Mama C. had a colostomy bag placed in during her surgery and somehow the bag was leaking. We had to pull into a rest stop so she could wash up and change her clothes. When we got there, she asked MMS, to get her some clothes out of her suitcase and I went with her into the bathroom. At first, she tried to wash up with me bringing the washcloth back and forth from one of the stalls. This was a difficult process and she got fed up. The next thing I knew she removed all her clothes came out of the stall and stood in front of the sink butt-naked. This was a busy time at the rest stop so lots of people were coming in and out of the bathroom. Now you know people were looking at her like she was crazy but she did not care. She said I can't be going through all of that, I need to wash myself up so we can get back on the road and I can't do it from inside there. Anybody got a problem with it too bad! I LOVED THAT WOMAN! I wish I was more like her. I would have been mortified or felt sorry for myself. She washed up and paid the spectators no mind. MMS came to the bathroom door to pass us the clothes for her to change into and he saw her in the state she was in out of his peripheral vision. By the look on MMS's face, he wanted to crawl under something. She cleaned herself up and we were back on the road.

When we got to Georgia, we dropped Mama C. off in Savannah and then we headed to Augusta where my family lives. On the way to Augusta, we took a wrong turn and ended up on a dark country road. I guess we were traveling too long because now my mother's memory problem kicked in. She was tired of riding and decided that she wanted to get out of the car. Now I don't mean she wanted to stretch her legs, she attempted to open the car door with the car moving. If that wasn't bad enough, she grabbed Pooh and said she's tired of riding too so she is coming with me. Luckily MMS has good reflexes. He stopped the car as she opened the door, thank God for child locks. We set the child lock on the back doors and continued to Augusta.

I remember when it became apparent that my mom was really out of control. One night I went to bed and the next morning I woke up to excessive banging on my front door. I got to the door and it was a police officer standing in the doorway. He was banging on the door with his nightstick. He asked me if I knew Mama D. I said yes, she was my mother. I said she is upstairs sleeping. He said no I don't want to alarm you but she is at the precinct. Apparently, she wandered out of the house. They found her six blocks away in a house dress in two different shoes and a hat. The officer said that the team that picked her up felt something was not right and they asked her if she was OK. She told them she wanted to go home but she didn't know where home was. She remembered her name and my name and they ran the names and found the address. I had to go pick her up. When I got to the precinct there she was chatting with the officers and when she saw me she said there's my baby, I got to go home now. I could not believe that she was there, I could not believe what she was wearing, and I could not believe her response. I was so scared but at the same time so grateful that she was found and not hurt. This was the beginning of a seven-year nightmare, mama got worse and worse.

MMS was not around during mama's decline. I remember the last time they saw each other. He stopped by the house on his way back from Family Court. Yes, we were back in court because I needed a custody order. One day he took Pooh for a weekend. I thought he was taking her to his apartment in Manhattan but he took her to his home in NJ. When it was time to bring her back, he didn't. I did not know where my child was for 24 hours. He would not answer the phone and I didn't know where to look. I went to the police station to file a complaint that she was missing and I was told I had a child support order and not a custody order. Maybe it's just me but if I have a child support order doesn't that mean that I have a child I'm caring for and he is giving me support. Geesh! My brother called me while I was at the police station to let me know that MMS had dropped Pooh off. After that incident, I wasted no time. The next day I went to court to file for custody. After about four no-show appearances, I was given custody. I can't believe the investigation they put me through to keep a child I was already caring for. This was a difficult process. It's funny though, each time he did not show up to court God would connect me with believers who were encouraging and uplifting. I guess I needed this because little did I know he was going to stop visiting her. At first, he would say he was coming and I would get her ready and he would not show. She was crushed. I remember her little face pressed against the window waiting. You had to pry her away screaming and crying. I stopped telling her when he was supposed to come so if he didn't show her little heart would not be broken. Sometimes I didn't know who was hurting more Pooh or my mom.

Mom got close to him when he took her to her doctor's appointments and when they would sit up late at night eating cherry vanilla ice cream together. Although I tried to protect Pooh, he would call her and tell her he was coming. That would burn me up because she was back at that window waiting. I called him and asked him not to do that but he just would not listen. I didn't know what to do. My money was really tight during the time when he was supposed to pick her up. I could not take her to a movie and it was too cold for the park so I would take her to Burger King because they had an indoor play park. We would leave when I realized he wasn't coming and wasn't just running late. It worked for a while but I didn't realize I created a bigger problem. From that point on Pooh would eat when she got nervous or upset.

As a social worker, I knew I had to get her away from that window. I forgot how comforting food can be. He then stopped visiting for about three years. I started working a lot to make more money to do more with and for her. The child support checks stopped. I had more bills now because I had to take over the house since mama was in the nursing home. I had to stop working the second job because it was a conflict of interest with my new job. I was still paying his tickets off as well. I got home most nights around 9 or 10 o'clock. I was so angry that he wasn't even a backup for her while I was working. Mama wasn't there to help anymore either. She would have been able to at least make dinner in the evening. It was easier to pick up fast food, bathe her, and put her down for the night because it was so late. Before I knew it Pooh and I gained a lot of weight in a short period of time. There was such a void in our lives. We both were miserable.

All I really wanted was for him to be a loving devoted father to my daughter. I really didn't want him. I wanted the kind of man God would send me. It was clear that I had made yet another bad choice in men. The guilt I felt was unbearable because now I was impacting my child by my Godless decisions.

We had to put mama in a nursing home. We were so blessed; thank God there was an opening at a new facility within walking distance from my home. I found comfort in knowing that before she went into the nursing home, she knew I was on Mount Horeb working on my relationship with God. Although I was going through what I was going through I was filled with gratitude. Mama was a woman of virtue. She was a woman who truly had a relationship with God. I know this because, when things got really bad and she did not know anyone in her family she knew God. She would say, "Lord have Mercy" or call out Jesus' name. This was really hard because she got to the point that she didn't know who I was. I can't even describe what it feels like to have your mom not know you.

By this point I was working on my relationship with God, I really had no choice, my job was bad, my finances were bad, my mom was doing bad, I had no man in my life. I was afraid to see anyone. I tried to date a guy and we were getting really cool even though he was a Moore, a derivative of the nation of Islam? Although I knew we were unequally yoked he was cool to talk to and hang out with. One day, he told me he was HIV positive. His ex-wife cheated on him to get crack money and she gave him the disease. The crazy thing about it was I was going to continue to see him but he was trying to see me and someone else. I wasn't that crazy I dropped him like a hot potato! Needless to say, I have not been in a relationship since. I'm going to wait for God to send me someone and if not, I'm OK. I came to the realization I can do bad by myself.

It was hard going to that nursing home. Pooh would break down every time we went. My brothers agreed to visit almost every day. I agreed to work with the administration to coordinate her care, do unannounced visits at different times to ensure quality care, visit the hospital whenever she was admitted in, and take her body to Georgia if she died. My brother Lee was still so traumatized from the two funerals from our dad that he said he could not do that trip again to bury her.

We had another women's conference and I was at a prayer and meditation workshop. One of the ministers who facilitated the group said that God told her to tell me that my mother was OK and I didn't need to worry. She told me that she wanted to see me. The conference was across the street from the nursing home so I went to see mama. Although I didn't want to miss the lunchtime speaker, I knew I had to leave. I was shocked because she knew who I was. She spoke to me. I told her where I was, what happened, and that I loved her. She told me she loved me too. I prayed with her and we visited for a while. I left her and went back to the conference. What blew my mind was the fact that I did not miss anything at the conference. It was as if God stopped time. I was so happy and so appreciative of this opportunity God gave me. I remember thinking look at what happens when you trust God.

Building Trust

Commissioner Mentor from the largest Child Welfare Agency in NY offered me a job. She knew my work and valued it. The great thing about her was she, too, was a Christian trying to walk this walk. She told me that someone once told her when a door closes God opens a window. I went to interview with her and it just felt right. It was unlike anything I had experienced before. I felt such a sense of peace. Although the interview was long, it didn't seem long. It was one of those great conversations that just stick with you. The reason I knew it went long was because I was left with 15 minutes to get from the bottom of Manhattan to the top in rush hour traffic. I was headed to my consulting job. Normally this would be impossible. But I believe it was God's will because I got on the parkway and it was clear. I remember thinking something must have been wrong like the parkway was closed and no one informed me because I got to my consulting job in 10 minutes. That was amazing. If you live in New York, you know what I mean. The hard part was the job took a while to materialize. Commissioner Mentor called one day while I was waiting and told me that she originally wanted to hire me for program design and development but she felt a need to have me do some staff development activities and supervise a number of people in the office.

She said they had skills and the potential to be great and thought I was the person to bring it out of them. Her only concern was that one of the people she wanted me to supervise was my friend Enlighten. She and I were very close. She thought this may present a problem. I informed her that the reason we were close was because she was my assistant on a previous job so this would not be a problem. Actually, I was very happy because Enlighten was my spiritual guide. I referred to her as my little big sister. Enlighten was like my little sister because I introduced her to program planning and she was younger in age. She's also my big sister because she introduced me to the Word, the Bible, and showed me how to begin to apply it to my life. I accepted the position, but NYC takes time to hire, so I had to wait. I remember during that time I was on unemployment and I had my two consulting gigs and guess what? No medical benefits. Guess what else, my daughter and I did not get sick during the three months I was unemployed. I decided if the job did not come through by January I was going to look for something else. The funny thing is I always prayed before the work I did. I did not pray for myself. Maybe what I call a rescue prayer here and there. That's when I would pray a reactive prayer for God to help me out of something. Again, why couldn't I trust, why couldn't I believe that God was going to work things out for me. I remember going to get the *New York Times* newspaper to look through the classified ads on the first Sunday in January. I could not believe it, there were fewer jobs than ever. The paper was so small that I went back to the newsstand to see if the paper I had was incomplete but it was not. There were no jobs in my field. I took that as a sign to trust that God will see me through. This was not based on my faith; this was based on the fact that I didn't have any other choices. The next day I got the call to start my new job. Again, why did I not trust that God would deliver? The funny part is I trusted that there would be a job waiting for me because they said so. Why? It's sad, I trusted a stranger's word but I did not trust God.

How Misguided I Was About Trust

I begin working on the new job and things were going wonderful. I am in my element again. I was responsible for so much. I had control over a lot of programs, services, and contracts. I was back. I was right where I wanted and needed to be. Remember, my self-worth was tied to my career. I still did not know "whose" I was. Commissioner Mentor was fantastic. She too prayed before and over her work. I was so content. After a month of working she promoted me. I was not given an increase in salary because it was too close to my start date, but it gave me additional authority. She promised that I would get my raise at my annual review. She said her boss had agreed to the raise but I would have to wait. It's funny how a job told me to wait and I had no problem with trusting and believing that this was going to come

This Walk Ain't Right! But, Help Is Along The Way

to pass, but when it came down to trusting God I hesitated and could not believe.

I was on top of the world. This new position came with additional responsibilities and three new staff. As time went on, I began to realize that my entire staff was believers. I attended church and Bible study at home as well as work. I was so content; I just knew that things were going to turn out well. I had a boss who loved my ideas, respected me, and taught me so much about being a good leader. Things could not have been better, everyone on my staff believed in God. I was so at peace.

As always, I had individual meetings with the new staff in order for us to get to know each other and look at goals and objectives. There was one woman named Conviction with who I made an unbelievable connection as soon as we met. It was weird I felt like I had known her all my life and we had just met. She too was a believer who truly had a relationship with God and looked to Him when she was making decisions. There was something about her that made me look at my responses to issues. I realized that I would respond to things in the flesh. Conviction would say things to me which left me feeling like I wasn't acting very Christ-like. When I would get on her case about how she made me feel she told me that was my own conviction. She explained that the Holy Spirit dwelled inside of me when I accepted God into my life. She told me that the Holy Spirit entered into me and now He needed to grow. She also explained that the bad feeling I would get was called conviction and He (the Holy Spirit) made me see I had to try a different approach. Enlighten also played a major part in my work life. Enlighten and Conviction both were actively involved in a lunchtime Bible study with another woman named Holiness who eventually became my administrative assistant. They also attended a lunchtime worship service called Wall Street Wednesdays. They invited me to join their little group which was like a breath of fresh air. The first worship service I attended with them focused on discovering your purpose, gifting, and assignment. I was left deep in thought because I now had a desire to find my purpose. It's funny everything I watched on TV or each sermon I was hearing dealt with purpose. I knew I had to find out what I should be doing with my spiritual gift of exhortation.

Trust

Now that I reflect back to Miss "Understood's" story, I realized and recognize this was part of my setup. I too was set up from the beginning. Reflecting on what Miss Understood went through in her trust walk, I began to think about my own trust walk. Believe it or not, I realized I had one. Sometimes you have to look back over your life and see things in reflection because when the events are happening you don't quite get it. Sometimes events seem so overwhelming that you are unable to sift out the good in a situation because the pain makes things so blurry that you can't see past the pain. Despite my getting through each painful situation, I was unable to leave it in the past. I am getting ahead of myself here. I guess that is an issue I will deal with later.

My trust in God was built brick by brick. It's unfortunate that each brick had to hit me upside the head. I was bruised before it got laid in the right place for my trust foundation. I was bruised somewhat broken but not unfixable. Now I realize that God had to do some serious work on me. I had issues with pride, control, and worry. Then Commissioner Mentor announced she was leaving. I was so sad. I knew I would miss her but I did not think it would affect my job. Why would it; I was MG. I was the person everyone knew, I was the person everyone respected and I was the person everyone liked. Hmm, how many times did I just say I? Nowhere in that statement did I bring God or Jesus into the sentence. That's because at that time I still did not get it. I realize now that I still had a lot to learn.

After Commissioner, Mentor left there was an acting Commissioner appointed named the Hit Man. This guy was unbelievable. The Hit Man was so mean to me and my staff. He tried to destroy me and the sad thing was I did not know why. We had strong differences just as I had with my boss at the university. I could not figure out what was going on. This man told me I was a poor manager and my staff did not work, they were lazy, unskilled, and played games. I thought I had entered into the twilight zone. I supervised over half the office, managed four consultant contracts, designed and developed six program components, developed training programs for the entire division, and was actively involved in its overall redesign. My staff had to work on these projects and they did exceptional work. I mean yes, we had problems with their time and leave and they would hand things in late but these issues I inherited from the previous administration. When I was hired, I was told to address these issues which are exactly what I was doing.

As I reflect, I can see how President Obama must feel. This accusation just did not make sense. I started to wonder if this man was on drugs. Each time I went to meet with him he would rip me apart. I was devastated. I could not get it together. I was so defeated. This just did not make sense. How was I supposed to motivate my staff when I was so empty? I became very withdrawn.

I did not know how much of a blessing it was to have a staff who all believed in God. This was interesting because the EEO office had a strict policy about religion in the workplace. It was a no-no. As I said before two of my staff were involved in a lunchtime Bible study and attended lunchtime services on Wednesdays called Wall Street Wednesday (WOW). I started to attend these activities with them. These services brought me so much peace and clarity. My co-workers, the other directors began to move away from me. I had no support from them. They acted as if they were glad this was happening to me. They had unresolved feelings about my relationship with the previous Commissioner. There was some jealousy. I guess they felt good for her, who does she think she is. I have no proof but I know there was backstabbing going on. I felt so lost. One day I was waiting outside his office preparing to go in for my weekly bashing session. His secretary, who was a wonderful person, was sitting at her desk looking at me. I did not know her that well but whenever our paths crossed her spirit touched me. There was something very special about her. She told me to keep my head up and to trust and believe that God will see me through. She told me to read the *Book of Psalms* in the Bible. She reminded me who I belonged to, that I was a child of the King. I went into his office with a new attitude. The Hit Man no longer was able to cut me down.

The *Hit man* said certain things that were not true and I confronted him on where he was getting his information. He was so frazzled by my response he began to spill the beans. His boss did not want to give me my promised raise. She needed to build a case not to give me what I was due so she "sicked" him on me and my staff. He also informed me that another director gave him some untrue information about me. Now I began to see what was going on. I was so pissed that I went on a mission to prove them all wrong. You see I was going to turn this around. Again I was going to change things. I did not go to God and ask him what he was trying to do in my life. I thought I had it all figured out. I figured I was going to show everyone who I was and who my staff was.

The next morning, I heard a sermon on excellence. I took notes and developed a strategic plan on how to demonstrate the work that my staff did in excellence. We developed a marketing tool, a book of programs that we were responsible for that listed our achievements. I think this really pissed people off because they did not like seeing the team progress and dispel the lies that were swarming around us.

Acting Commissioner, the Hit Man was replaced with a permanent Commissioner named Mr. Follower. It was funny because the Hit Man wanted to be appointed Commissioner over my division which would have given him a great deal of power over a number of programs. He thought coming after me would please his boss and would get him the division. Well, needless to say, it did not work for him.

I was the first to meet Mr. Follower at a meeting he attended prior to his official start date. I was a little leery because he lacked experience in this type of work but he was willing to learn. He was a lawyer. I really did not have a problem with this because teaching was something I did and I knew I was good at it. I felt things would be cool. At the meeting, we got off to a good start. I prepared all the necessary briefings for our first meeting to update him on my division. He also visited my division to meet the team and get his first impressions of us. I made sure every time he went to a meeting he was briefed and prepared to represent our department and what we were doing. I was constantly meeting with him and everything he asked me for I provided. He would email me at 2:00 o'clock in the morning and I would answer my blackberry and by the time I got to work the next morning I had everything he requested ready. I thought we worked well together. Little did we both know his supervisor, the one who jerked me out of my raise, and tried to act as though I didn't know what I was doing could not stand me. The funny thing was the feeling was mutual. You see I came from a background or if it's not written it didn't happen. I wrote a memo outlining all that I did at the agency and the lack of compensation I was receiving. This was prior to Mr. Follower joining the staff. The problem was I was one of her subordinates and she could "get me" whenever she wanted and she did.

Mr. Follower and I had a good working relationship which didn't sit well with his supervisor. That woman had an agenda and wanted to cloud his judgment of me with a lot of misinformation. You see the people who were above us were mostly lawyers and our perception of the work was different. These differences became a problem because those folks just didn't get it; and not getting "it," made it impossible to do the work that would best meet the needs of the youth we served. The situation, which my staff and I were going through, is where I truly learned that I had to trust God.

As I said earlier, I worked long hours at this job because it was almost impossible to get the work done. It was also because my self-esteem and self-worth were directly tied to the work I did. Don't get me wrong I found the work rewarding not only because I knew I was good at it, but because I loved making people feel good about themselves and helping people feel empowered. You see I truly believe that there is good in everyone. I think things fall apart for people due to a lack of resources when life circumstances become overwhelming. I guess that's why anyone who knows me knows my motto *is behavior is purposeful*. This means people do things for a reason. We may not like the reason but there is a reason. I came to this agency to try to make a difference in programming from the inside but I believe God had another plan. I was brought here for the staff, to develop, empower and encourage them through this part of their journey.

Things got really bad working at the agency. My staff and the youth were disrespected and mistreated. I was livid during this time period. I was ready to fight for the people I worked with. The harder I fought, it seem like the uglier things got. One day I was so angry, so defeated. I felt I was failing my staff because no matter what I did they were under attack. Miss Conviction and Miss Enlighten came to my office to see me and said maybe I needed to back off from the fight. They said they saw the toll it was taking on me. I told them that I felt like if I didn't defend the staff and youth who would. They both said God will. Miss Conviction asked me, "Did you ask God if you should fight for us or did you decide this for yourself?" Miss Enlighten said, "Although we appreciate it, you have to stop." You may be blocking our process. Maybe God wants us to go through this stuff to break something in us and you are getting in the way. You have to let go and let God." Miss Conviction said, "Either you believe in God and what he can do or you don't. God doesn't need your help." It was really difficult for me to give up the control, although in reality I really didn't have it, I decided to let go. Then the real tests began. When they saw I was distant and kept plugging away at my work no matter what they threw at me the attacks got worse. I was demoted from Director to Assistant Director, they took away half my staff, they replaced my staff after all the work they did with people who had less experience and were not as effective. Not only did they replace my staff, but the new staff were also doing their jobs at a higher title and more pay. I was livid. Miss Conviction told me that I was too angry and I needed to pray for these administrators. I remember thinking, is she crazy? I am not going to pray for these people I hate them. The fact that I really didn't like them is what made me know once I started praying I would be in trouble. I knew I would start off right but somewhere in the middle, I would ask God to get them. I knew that wasn't right.

Miss Conviction asked me to go to a Women's Conference with her at her church and I did. This conference truly changed my life. Every service and workshop I attended encouraged me to trust God. I learned that I had to forgive my enemies if I wanted God to forgive me for my sins. I learned that I had a purpose on this earth and God knew the master plan. I went into one of my workshops and I was so encouraged. The facilitator prayed at the end of the workshop and I bowed my head and closed my eyes. When I opened my eyes, I was crying and saying me, "Lord, you want me to do that." I felt really humbled and knew that God wanted me to do something but I wasn't sure what it was. You see I clearly had blacked out for a while because everyone in the room except a few people, me and Miss Conviction were the only remaining participants. I could not remember what God wanted me to do. All I knew was I was sure he wanted me to do something. Miss Conviction said she went to touch my back while I was in that trance like state to comfort me and something like a force pushed her off of me. She said the power she felt coming off of me was amazing. I left the workshop really disoriented, dazed, and feeling very vulnerable. I was clear on the fact that I was not in control. I was not used to that. Although the people were really nice I wanted to be back on my own Mountain where there were people I was used to worshipping with. When I left the workshop room, I ran into one of the ministers from my Mountain. I could not believe it. This was just what I was longing for. I talked to her for a while and I felt better. I saw the power of God that day. I also realized that God will send who and what you need when you really need it.

Later that evening we went into a worship service and the minister's sermon described exactly what I had been experiencing at work. She said all things work for good for those who love the Lord according to God's plan and his purpose. She told us that we had to pray for people who did evil things to us because they allow themselves to be used for evil and they will have to suffer the consequences for their choices. She also said those situations might not be God-sent, but they could be God-used. I started to see that God allowed this stuff to happen to me because there was a call on my life and I was just too committed to the work I was doing. I needed to have that kind of commitment to my purpose. At this point, I didn't hate those administrators as much anymore. Actually, I felt sorry for them and was happy because they were helping me get stronger. They were also part of my process of development. They were part of my "Set-Up." I had to learn to forgive. I was finally able to pray for them. It was amazing! I knew when I got back to work things would be different. I put my trust in God and knew he would work it all out. I was being set up for service.

When I got back to my division, I took advantage of the fact that my former staff was believers, Christians. We started to pray together again and attend WOW weekly church service held during our lunch hour. I grew stronger and stronger and I trusted that God had my back. The other thing I walked away from the conference knowing I was leaving that job. I didn't know where I was going but I walked around saying I'm leaving soon. People would say you got a job? I would say nope but ones coming. I trusted that God was going to remove me from that place.

Trust

When I got home from work tonight, I got a call from the nursing home. Mama was taken to the hospital. She had a cold and was having trouble breathing. I went to the hospital to see what was going on with her. When I got to the hospital, I realized how sick she was. I stayed with her for hours. I wasn't thrilled with the hospital care she received and tried to be there as much as possible. As the days went on she was getting sicker and sicker. I knew she was leaving us soon. I would go there and my ritual was to clean her up, the area around her, and brush and comb her hair. Although she could not talk to me, I would talk to her. I remember waking up one morning and feeling like my time was limited with my mom. At work, we were working on a major presentation and I knew I had to prepare my staff to do it without me. I told them that I did not think I would be present due to my mom's illness. We met and they got the presentation together and I left work to go see my mom.

As I drove to the hospital, I felt really strange. I got caught in traffic and it took me quite a while to get there. I remember getting off the parkway and feeling really off balance. I lost control of the car for a second. I just did not feel right. Something was very wrong with me but I could not put my finger on it. I got to the hospital and walked into my mom's room. I said hello to her and kissed her and proceeded to straighten up around her as I usually did. She was lying there with her eyes open and an oxygen mask on her face. I said to her, "Oh you are awake. I heard you were sleeping all day." I came over to do her hair and I noticed something seemed strange. I touched her face and she felt a little cool. I listened to her heart and I didn't hear a heartbeat. I knew something was wrong. I went to the nurse's station and asked for someone to come and help me. Everyone looked at me strangely. They just stood there. I said, "Didn't you hear me I need help." They said we will send you her nurse. The nurse came in and asked, "What's the matter?" I told her you tell me. There is something very wrong with my mother. She checked her vitals and ran out of the room. A few minutes later another nurse came to me and said oh my God! No one told you, your mother died about an hour ago. I could not believe it. I FOUND MY MOTHER DEAD! I left the floor and called my brother and was screaming mommy is gone and I found her that way.

My brother Lee was so upset I found her like that. He said they called him and told him but he knew I was driving and didn't want to give me the news while driving. He said he just knew they would tell me before I found her that way. He and my sister-in-law came to the hospital and we said our goodbyes. I just knew that I would never get rid of the image of finding my loving mama dead.

I went home and I planned her funeral. I was cleaning the house and listening to the gospel music channel, trying to figure out how I was going to get through burying my mom. A song came on that spoke to my spirit. It was called *My Help Cometh from the Lord*. The song was beautiful. I cried and the song ministered to me. I felt peace come over me and I believed and trusted that God was going to see me through all of it. I kept my end of the bargain with my brother and took mama to Georgia to be buried next to my daddy. Although this was the hardest thing I ever had to do I felt it was so much easier than I imagined. God made everything run smoothly; He comforted Pooh and I during the entire process. When I got on the plane to fly back home after the Georgia burial, I was aggravated because I was unable to sit with my daughter. I sat next to a woman on the plane that was a believer. We talked about how good God is and she asked me did I live in the south. I told her no I was coming back from burying my mother. I expected the usual response of offering up condolences. She didn't respond in that way at all. The lady said OK and now you have had this experience, you will be able to help someone else through their experience. Then she went to sleep. I remember feeling like wow. Yes, I will.

I got back on Monday and had to present on a panel of experts on adolescents aging out of the foster care system at a college. I remember thinking I don't feel like sounding smart. I don't feel like doing anything. I really don't feel like being around a lot of people; I just buried my mother and that image of finding her dead was still etched in my mind. But something said just do it and get it over with. I went to the college and the first person I saw was Miss Enlighten. The rest of my staff was standing around and when they saw me, they came over to receive me and offer words of comfort and support. Miss Enlighten saw that I wasn't really feeling this and said let's go for a walk. We went around the corner and found a park. We talked and I felt better and we went back to the conference. I ended up in that park a few times that day with people who encouraged me and ministered to me. During my last visit to the park, I was with a group of ladies and one was having trouble with her daughter. I ministered to her and we all prayed together and went back in.

So here I am sitting up on the stage on a panel with the top city and state officials. I remember people were saying things and I sat and listened for a while and waited for them to bring up a topic I felt like joining in on. All of a sudden, the moderator asked me a question. I answered and people clapped. As time went on, I realized that people were clapping and cheering about most things I said. During this question/answer and clapping/cheering exchange I was having, Commissioner Follower came in and witnessed the crowd's response to me. When it was all over he said, "Wow people love you." I said I don't know about that but I think they respect me and I think that's pretty cool. When we got back to the office Commissioner Follower held a staff debriefing meeting about the conference. He told the staff that he had to offer me an open apology. For so long he thought I didn't know what I was talking about because he didn't get it. He said he was amazed when coming into the auditorium, people were cheering. He said he wanted to hurry in to see what was going on. Much to his surprise people were cheering for MG. He said he had a newfound respect for me.

Commissioner Follower's boss left the agency and he was left to fend for himself. I told him one day he needed to watch his back because this was a cutthroat place. I said you may find yourself being used as a scapegoat. Sure enough, the other administrators took all his ideas he got from us beefed up their departments and found a way to make our department insignificant. Next, he was demoted from commissioner to trainer. I remember feeling so sorry for him. I also remember thinking wow God is no joke!

I started to send my resume out because I was so ready to leave this department if not the agency. I applied for a job within the agency that seemed to match my experience perfectly. I could not understand why I was not called for an interview. Then I started to think about it. Maybe God wanted me to leave this agency altogether. I decided to wait it out and interview outside the agency. In the meantime, I was asked to attend a conference in Atlanta, Georgia on working with youth. An old co-worker of mine moved to Atlanta. I decided to look her up when I got there. That night I called around and got her number. When I called Miss Hook Up, she told me that she was no longer in Georgia and had moved to Philadelphia. She was working for a consulting firm. She asked me how was I doing and I told her where I was working and hated it. She asked if I would be interested in working in Philadelphia. I told her I felt that was far and I was not willing to move. She said I would not have to. I could commute when needed and would be able to work from home. She said she would talk to her boss and get me an interview. I prayed and asked God to open doors for me. I knew it was time to leave. When I came back from Georgia, I was on a mission to leave the agency.

It was time for me to conduct staff evaluations. At this point, I learned that I needed to pray before I met with staff. I realized that my time there was limited and I knew God sent me there to encourage and support His children. So I would pray and allow God to reveal to me what the person should be doing career-wise. I had each staff member take the spiritual gift inventory and we would discuss possible things they could explore. It was really crazy because God would just drop things in my spirit about people to guide them to their purpose. This would blow my mind because they would always say this was confirmation for them.

The next day I went to work and was supposed to go to another worksite. Instead of getting off the exit to the worksite, I proceeded to my job. I was so into my gospel music that I missed my turn. I concluded it was no big deal they were conducting another workshop that afternoon so I will go later. When I got to the agency, going upstairs, I run into my administrative assistant. We started to talk about our Christian walk and what we were feeling God has been doing in our lives. As she was talking, God revealed to me exactly what her ministry was. I felt like something took over my body and I began to break it down to her in detail. When I finished telling her, I was shaking and crying. I didn't know where that came from. I was blown away. Then the plot thickened. She stood there staring at me. She asked me if I spoke to

Trust

Miss Conviction about this. I told her no, God just dropped that on me. She ran and got Miss Conviction and asked her to tell me what she told her about the dream she had. The dream was exactly what I told her. NOW I AM REALLY BUGGIN! I was amazed! I was crying and happy but at the same time wondering what was happening to me. I had to leave because I had to make it to the next training session since I missed the morning session. Walking out of the building, I thought to myself WOW! All of a sudden, I heard this audible voice say to me loud and clear YOU THINK THAT'S SOMETHING, THAT'S NOTHING. YOU KEEP SHOWING ME LITTLE BITS! AS LONG AS YOU KEEP SHOWING ME LITTLE BITS I'M GOING TO KEEP SHOWING YOU LITTLE BITS! I turned around to see who said that, who was speaking. There was no one around. I realized it was God. I was blown away and scared at the same time. I called the Shepherd and told him I had to see him ASAP.

I burst into his office and I told him what happened. He smiled and said can we pray first. I said oh yeah my bad, and we prayed. I also told him about what has been going on in my life. He asked me was I working on any projects for the Kingdom. I told him it's odd that he asked. I took a brochure I was working on out of my bag. I wanted to develop workshops on spiritual gifts and coping with life's changes. He looked at the brochure and said OK I want you to do the adult vacation Bible school using these workshops. I really thought the Shepherd had bumped his head. I explained to him, first of all, they are not workshops yet, and second, I ain't no minister! I can't do that. So he said OK develop a curriculum and give it to me to review. I developed the curriculum and gave it to him. I didn't hear anything back from him so I thought he changed his mind about wanting to use it. Then one day he said he wanted me to meet with him and the Christian Education Director to discuss the curriculum. We come together and he said are you ready to train this? I remember thinking, he is crazy. I'm not doing this. I told him I didn't know enough about the Bible to do it. He followed with, OK I'll do it. He chats with me about how he was going to do it. His vision was all wrong. I said, OK I'll do it, but you guys are going to have to help me. I divided the curriculum up into parts that I would do, what the Shepherd would do and what the Christian Education Director would do.

Today was the day to present the training I developed. I was so nervous. I was not my normal self because I came in with my entire flesh showing. There were people in the room who intimidated me. Although I knew this is what God gave me and the Shepherd was OK with it, I was still afraid of them. I was so nervous. I could not think about anything else but the fact that they were there. These were some of the people who didn't want us to have the conference. All my trust was out the window. I was so scared. You would have thought I never trained before. I prayed beforehand but I didn't believe. I felt I couldn't do it and that lack of confidence came through. We got through the training but I was so depressed. I had never trained like this before. I believed I should not have been doing it in the first place. The next day I spoke to Miss Enlighten. I told her what happened. She told me I have to trust that God knew what He was doing when He gave me this and to believe in myself. This was so weird to me. Any other training I had the confidence for but not this one. I spent the day praying and asking God to lead me through the rest of the training. I asked God to remove any barriers or obstacles I was experiencing. I went back in that evening and the women I was afraid of were not there. I proceeded to correct the wrongs from the day before and the rest of the training was amazing. People came up to me afterward and said this was the best training they had attended. I knew that it was God that made this happen. I felt like this was what I should be doing. The funny thing is the Shepherd said he prayed for God to send him someone to help with the Vacation Bible School and I walked in with this concept. I was blown away. I remember thinking; look what happens when you trust God.

I went to work the next day and I received a call from Commissioner Mentor. She asked me to come in for an interview at the new place she worked. I interviewed with Commissioner Mentor and her staff. I was prepared to take the position in her new agency. I was so happy because I was leaving. Then I got the call for the interview in Philadelphia. They brought me into Philly to have a lunch interview and offered me a job on the spot making $30,000 more a year than I was currently making. All my expenses would be included, travel, meals, supplies everything. I told myself this would be a good opportunity for me to write my book when I was in Philly overnight. I prayed over the offer and felt God said yes. I also walked away from that prayer knowing that I would only be there for a year. God had other plans for me although I didn't know what they were. I took the job and at first, I worked as a consultant during my final weeks at the city agency.

My staff gave me the most special send-off. They took me on a scavenger hunt revisiting all the places we visited together and each staff person was there to greet me with another clue to lead me to the next location. One took me to breakfast, one took me to the church we went to for Wall Street Wednesdays, another took me to a spa, and then back to the office. When we got back, friends and colleagues I worked with over the years came together. They put together a workshop based on my life and accomplishments in child welfare. It was so awesome because two of the people I trained on how to train led the workshop. I could do nothing but cry. This was one of the most precious moments of my life. After all of that, they took me to dinner and Pooh and MMS were there to surprise me as well. Yeah, he was back on the scene but as her father which is all I truly wanted. It was a wonderful send-off. I remember thanking God for allowing me to work with such wonderful people and allowing me to touch their lives in a way I could not have done without him.

When I started working in Philadelphia, I left the Mountain. I only returned on weekends and sometimes I was too tired to go to worship service. This was a totally different world. I was in a different state, doing different work although it was training it was a new subject matter. I was OK at first but as time progressed, I realized I was not happy. I missed my daughter so much. MMS was helpful. He stayed at my house and cared for her while I was gone. There were some highlights, I went to Virginia and Washington and trained people there and I loved it. What was great was this group was known to be challenging to train. I went with my little bag of tricks and the staff loved it. I reflected during my time of traveling, this is what I love about training. I love to help people get their second wind in the field as well as change their minds about training by showing them that it can be fun. But then it was back to

Philly doing paperwork and developing training programs on child protective work and computers. I HATED THIS! I knew this was not what I was called to do but the money was great, so I stayed. Calling friends at night, I cried about how badly I wanted to come home. I really should have been working on the book but I didn't.

During this same time, my ministry was preparing for the next conference. I worked with the committee indirectly. Planning the next conference was great because I felt like I was doing what I loved again. I knew this job wasn't for me and needed to leave. Again, I didn't leave according to schedule because the money was so good. One day I was asked to work on the development of a curriculum. We had two weeks to write it and I also had to first read a 500-page policy and procedure manual in order to have an understanding of what we were training. To prepare for the training, I stayed up day and night trying to write this thing. I slept about 10 hours in a two-week span. At one point, I stayed up all night writing then going to Philly, checked into my hotel, and never unpacked or slept. I just continued to write. After I took a shower, changed my clothes, and went to the office for a meeting. I then returned back to the Mountain. I had no time to sleep. This went on for days. One day I went to walk in my kitchen and my leg gave out. I thought it was asleep like your foot does, or at least my foot does but it wasn't. At the time, I figured it would be OK but it did not get better. I decided to go to the doctor to get it checked out. The doctor said I had to get an MRI, see a neurologist and do a Nero Scan. When the test results came back, I had disk bulges in my lower and upper back, arthritis in my spine, knees, arms, and neck and moderate nerve damage in my left leg and severe nerve damage in my right leg. I could not believe this. How did this happen? The next thing I know I am out on disability, in physical therapy, and no longer working in Philadelphia. I thought wow, be careful what you ask for. I was home now and had nothing but time to think. I thought about how I was supposed to be writing while I was away, and that didn't happen. I felt so bad about turning my back on what I was supposed to be doing. I need help. I started Reading my favorite scripture, *Psalm 121:1-8*. This scripture reminds me that my help comes from the Lord. I then decided to pray for guidance.

MG's Prayer:
Dear Lord: Please forgive me for my sins. Please forgive me for not trusting and believing in you. I have seen you bring me through so many storms in my life and yet I still act like a crazy person when the next time a storm arises. Jesus, I now see what you meant when you would repeatedly say to the disciples, "Oh Ye of Little Faith." Lord, I use to think how could they not get it; get you when they walked with you and witnessed your miraculous works. How judgmental of me. I am guilty of the same thing. You brought me through some tough situations when I knew You but would not acknowledge You. You brought me through the deaths of my brother, my parents, jobs, and relationships. Lord, you breathed life into those painful times that I thought I would never get Past. But each time Lord I cannot say that I was faithful that I knew You would bring me through, but You did anyway. Thank you for your Grace. Lord, I want to be a better child to you. I want to serve you better. I want to get closer to you. I don't want to wait until you pull me through and look back to acknowledge what You can do. I want to believe while I am going through a situation that You are with me and you will bring me through. I want to learn to hold on. I want my faith to be in a place where my complaints are replaced with praise. I thank you, Jesus, for being there for me and with me in spite of me . . . . In Jesus name I pray, Amen.

After praying I sat back and waited to hear from God. People were telling me that you must wait to hear from God. I went to the women's conference this year and the theme was *Women of Royalty*. At the conference, I learned that I am a child of the King and that I am royalty. I also learned that I had to make the time to hear from God. The facilitator said too often we run around doing all the things we think need to be done; living busy lives and not taking the time to sit quietly and hear from God. I used to say God brought me messages' from other people. What I learned was that was called confirmation, for something God has already laid on my heart.

The facilitator asked how many of us pray in the morning and then go jump in the shower. She explained that you can't have a conversation with God if you do all the talking. You can't get up when you finish and don't give him the opportunity to speak to you. She said sometimes you have to shut everything off to have your alone time with God. I knew I was guilty of this because I am always on the go. So I listened after I prayed and God said WRITE THE BOOK on my life and things that I'd been through. After hearing this, I remember feeling like wow! It works. It wasn't the audible voice I heard before. This was a quiet statement that was placed in my mind and I just knew it was God. I felt that there were things that I had been through that could help others through tough times. I also remember feeling as though God sat me down took my legs so I would do what he wanted me to do. I was ambivalent about this because I didn't want to share some of these details with my daughter. I called the Shepherd and told him what God told me and my concerns about my daughter. He asked what do you want, for her to learn from the streets or from you. I said from me and he said there you have it.

This was a very interesting time for me. It was a year later. I always knew I would only be on that job for a year but not like this. I received short-term disability which was awarded to me without a hitch. After three months of being out of work and seeing a neurologist, my primary physician, and a physical therapist, I was still not well enough to go back to work. I had to go on long-term disability. This process took forever. During this process, I learned to trust God but the waiting was driving me nuts. I had exhausted my savings account, child support was not coming in because MMS was not working and disability barely paid my bills. I was constantly in physical pain. I was at a really low point in my life. Since I was back on the Mountain on a full-time basis I went to worship services and I worked with the committee to plan the women conferences. I was in a dark and lonely place. I tried to rely on what the Shepherd was preaching and what I learned at numerous conferences and workshops over the years. Another thing I learned at this year's conference was that it's helpful to journal your thoughts and feelings when you are attempting to fulfill your God-given assignments and during those low points in your life. I knew that I had to trust God.

Miss Understood showed me that this walk is a Set Up. I have to trust that I am in the midst of my own Set Up. It's crazy though, it feels like God has given me puzzle pieces without the box with the picture on it. There is nothing to guide me or to reference. I have to believe that He will reveal it to me; I have to trust it will happen and I have to have faith that I can make it through the next step. What I didn't realize was that God does things in his own time which is very different from mine. I started to journal and realized I had to move on to the next step. The 4th step is to learn how to wait on God. I went to see the Shepherd and he encouraged me to trust the process.

> *The Shepherd Speaks On Trusting In God*
> *Trusting in God—Proverbs 3:5-6: Simple Navigation: You and I are on a journey. It's called life. Life is full of joys and sorrows. Life is full of ups and downs. Life is full of challenges. Because life can get really complicated, we need help navigating through our years here on earth. God has promised to give guidance to believers so we will be able to navigate through life.*
> *King Solomon was not wise because he was rich, but rather, he was rich because he was wise. Throughout the book of Proverbs, King Solomon guides the reader in practical and wise counsel to get a hold of life by trusting in God who is the Giver of life. Trust, like faith, is a matter of confidence. Faith is confidence in believing without seeing. Trust is confidence in believing based upon honesty and reliability. God is both honest and reliable.*
> *Oh how much easier life can be when we pull away from the danger of "SELF" and begin to wholly lean on God! Trust God even when you can't trace Him, because He will always be right there with you and for you. When you trust in God you are leaning on Him for help and strength. Our God is truly able to do all things but fail!*

Waiting

The Forth Set of Footprints:
Isaiah 40:31

Hey Lord I'm Over Here, Did You Forget Me!

MG's Prayer:
Good Morning God:
Thank you for waking me up this morning to have another opportunity to work on what You have put me on this earth to do. I now understand that there is a purpose for my life but I haven't figured it out yet. Yet, is the magic word because now I know everything I have been through is part of my set up. I looked at the road map the Shepherd gave me and it says my next step is to learn to wait. I am really going to need You to help me through this step Lord because I am so impatient. I am a little down about my back and my legs being messed up because I can't work. I have been out of work for a couple of months and I am getting 40% less than I am used to making. My finances are getting messy. Lord, please help me through this. Lord show me how to wait because I am getting nervous. I know I have to trust You but it's so hard. In Jesus' name, Amen.

After my prayer, I watched a television evangelist and he was talking about fasting. I heard about people fasting but I really did not know how it applied to the Christian walk. He explained that fasting is giving up something for a period of time so a person can focus on growing spiritually. It's a way to demonstrate to ourselves and God that we are serious about establishing and developing a relationship with Him. During this time you deny yourself of worldly things so you can go deeper in your prayer life and connect with God on a deeper level. It's funny I thought it had to be food you gave up in a fast but he said it can be food, drink, sex, television, the internet, it can be anything that feeds your flesh. He said it's not something that Jesus commanded but he did give scriptures that show people fasting in the Bible. I saw where people fasted before making important decisions, and people fasted and prayed. The Minister also said that the Bible says when you fast you should not make it public. Don't walk around looking solemn or telling everybody how you are suffering because you are fasting. This is something that should be between you and God. He said there will be times when denying yourself will become challenging but that's when you should pray, read your bible, and or journal. I want a deeper relationship with God. I am going to try this fasting. I am going to fast for the next week. I decided to fast watching TV during the day.

This fasting thing is harder than I thought. I don't know what to do with myself. Maybe I will work on my journal today. That will keep me busy and my mind on God and off the TV.

Journal Entry: Day One—The Beginning

It's morning and I feel inspired because Miss Understanding inspired me in her trust walk. She made me reflect on my own trust walk. The funny thing is I didn't know I had one until I heard her story. She taught me life's a setup and I have to go through it to get to where God is taking me. The Shepherd also supported me through my process and taught me about trusting in God. It's really hard because all I do is sit at home and go to doctors' appointments. At least, when I was running back and forth to Philly I had something to do. Check me out! I was so miserable at that job and now I am missing it. I know God must be like make up your mind crazy child.

Journal Entry: Day Two—I'm Waiting . . .

I feel like each day I am getting closer and I am moving to the next level. But it seems as though the hurdles that I am going through seem to be so much bigger. For the first time in my life, I think I have one dollar and some change in my pocket. I don't know where the next dollar is coming from. I mean I do know where God will bring it. But when? He will make it happen. I know he didn't bring me this far to leave me. I learned that in my trust walk. It will be coming, it's just that, I have to be patient and wait for stuff to happen. You know I have watched God do some miraculous things. I watched him do some stuff with Miss Understood, and then I watched her bounce back. But I guess that's what we all do. When we get off track we tend to bounce back. I say to myself you are never going to get into this situation again but it happens again. My friend Miss Taken said to me the other day sometimes when the Lord is trying to draw you nearer He comes through your health and your finances. For me, it's both right now. My health is crazy. It's crazy! My finances are crazy! A lot of it is because of this waiting. And it is a weight. It has become a W-E-I G-H-T! While I W-A-I-T on the Lord.

Journal Entry: Day Three—Now I'm Mad!

Why would God do this to me? I have not gotten a check since before Christmas. I am so angry! I know He can help me but He just won't. How could God be so mean to me? My back and legs hurt so badly. I have been off my job since November of last year. He did that! I was making fantastic money. More than I ever made in my life. I was paying my tithes until I became disabled. Is that it God? Am I supposed to keep tithing? Well, right now I have no check at all. So what do you expect me to do? They said they have to be sure I can't work. Can't You tell them? You put me here. Lord do you realize that they are going to come get my car, my home, how could you leave me like this. I know it doesn't matter but I am so angry! How could you do me like this! I spoke to Miss Understood today. She tried to help me see that I just needed to wait on You. I am going to tell You like I told her. You are taking too long! I am so angry, yes with You God! I can't do this! I can't figure this situation out by myself! I give it over to You God! I'm done!

Journal Entry: Day Four—I See the Light!

I went to a worship service today. The sermon was entitled *While Waiting on Your Deliverance.* How appropriate was that! The preacher told a story of a group of friends who went swimming. In the group, there was a champion, award-winning swimmer. The guys went out in the water without the champion and one of the guys was overtaken by the water and started to drown. The guys in the water with him went over to try to save him but he was panicking, kicking, and screaming. They could not help him because they feared they would go down in the water as well. The champion swimmer watched while sitting on the side making no effort to get in the water. Just as the swimmer stopped struggling and seem to give up and sink down the champion jumped in and brought him to safety. The other guys asked why he took so long to help and he said I waited for him to stop fighting and be willing to accept my help. The minister said that's what Jesus wants us to do. Stop fighting, surrender, and allow him to do what only He can do. The minister then talked about when Jesus was walking on water and one of the disciples wanted to do the same and come to the Lord and walk on the water as well. The disciple started to walk but fear overcame him in the middle of the process and he fell off. The preacher pointed out if he would have only kept his eye on Jesus he would not have fallen. The beauty of the situation was that Jesus still saved him anyway. Now I am feeling guilty again. I am so sorry God for my anger yesterday and for speaking to You in that manner. I know what You can do but for some reason, I don't always wait it out and understand that You do things in Your time, not mine. I believe You Lord, I will wait for You, and this time I won't throw a tantrum.

Journal Entry: Day Five—There's Help Along the Way!

I woke up this morning praising God. I am sooooo broke but I know I will be OK. So, I am on my way to church and I run into my bible study buddy and he hands me $50 and tells me that God said to give this to you. He said, "It's not a loan it's a gift. Praise God! "I took $5 of that $50 and put it back in church. I came home from church and Miss Understood hands me an envelope with a beautiful sisterhood card and $500 in it. I could not believe it. I was so grateful. I assured her that I was expecting a pension loan I applied for and I would pay her back as soon as it comes in. She said, "No! God told me to give this to you. It's not a loan, it's a gift!" I then start to cry and said well I will do the same for someone else who is in need the first time I get the opportunity.

Journal Entry: Day Six—Over Flow!

Wow my pension loan came through and my retroactive check for disability was approved and sent today. Thank you, Lord!! I am so happy. But don't I feel guilty for not waiting. I know guilt is not of you God it's just the devil trying to distract me from enjoying my blessing. I can catch up on my bills now. I just want to tell the world what God has done for me. I know I am going to go to church tomorrow and stand up and testify. I can't believe I'm going to really do it. I am going to get up in front of the congregation and tell my private business. Yes how can I not, it's not my story to keep? I got to tell it. Thank you, God.

Journal Entry: Day Seven—My First Testimony

I got up this morning really feeling sick. My body hurts so badly. I really need to take some pain medication and get back into bed but I can't. No, that's got to be Satan trying to hold me back. I have to testify today and sow a seed. There is no way I cannot tell how good God has been to me. I am so scared though, I really don't want people to know my business. There he goes again. This is not about me but it's about what God can and will do if you wait on him. I plead the blood of Jesus that's what I heard the ministers say to do. I am going to worship service. So I get to service, my legs and back are hurting so bad all I can do is sit. I start to think I can't get up there. I can't walk. I will do it next Sunday. I had made up my mind. That's what I was going to do. But then the Minister preached the sermon and she talked about how Jesus was in the boat with the disciples and a storm was raging and he was resting underneath. She said even when it feels like

He is far; He is not sleeping on us. In the most tumultuous times He will come through just wait on Him and He will say peace be still. I knew then I had to get up, and I got up and testified. I could not get all my thoughts and words right but I knew I had to say something about how good God was to me and how He brought me through. I did it! I am so happy. This fasting and journaling helped me through this process. I can't journal anymore though because I have to focus on writing the book. I got ready for bed that night and said my prayers.

MG's Prayer
Oh merciful Father. I come to you today first and foremost to tell you how awesome You are. You do such wonderful things even though I am not deserving of them. Lord I am so impatient and I know I need to change that. You have helped me through so much and I love You so much. Lord, I know I have a lot of growing to do and I just ask that You be patient with me. Lord could you help me to better understand how you operate and how to wait on You. Please forgive me Lord. In Jesus name, Amen!

God spoke to me and said that, "ALL THINGS WILL BE REVEALED IN TIME. He also told me that I have to live through each one of the steps on the road map they gave me. He said, "PAY ATTENTION TO WHAT IS CURRENTLY HAPPENING TO ME AND THOSE AROUND. THESE AND FUTURE EXPERIENCES WILL BE IN THE BOOK BEFORE I CAN COMPLETE IT. "I didn't quite understand because I thought the book was on my life story. I already lived it and I want to finish it as soon as possible. You see I had it in my mind this would be a good source of income for me while I'm out sick. That wasn't God's plan. That was my plan and we clearly had different time frames. I figured I could still speed up the process maybe when God wasn't looking. Ha! Well anyway that's exactly what I was going to do. If I waited on God this would take a couple of years. I figured I'll work it out. Although I was so grateful for all that God had done for me. In the back of my mind I still felt guilty for getting mad with God. I felt I was not worthy enough to write a book for God. I felt that I failed a test from God. I prayed and asked

God to forgive me. God revealed to me that I am not worthy. No one is. He is God. I have to remember that I am saved by Grace and God knew I was a knucklehead but he loved me and forgave me anyway.

In the meantime I went to the women's conference committee meeting. I got to the meeting early and I met Miss Lead (ML), a new committee member. We began to talk and get to know each other. I told her about how I got to this point and how I felt this walk is not easy. Before I knew it she was telling me her testimony. How weird was this? I just met this woman. It's funny people have always felt comfortable telling me their deepest darkest secrets, no matter how long I've known them.

Hey Lord I'm Over Here, Did You Forget Me!

Wow! This walk has not been easy for me either MG. It's funny I too was born a princess. My mom says my delivery was good, but I was put in the Intensive Care Unit. My father was sick but he still came to see me. He was an addict but still came although my mother was very upset. I was the baby girl of the family. I had three sisters who spoiled me. My father was in and out of the house so my mother was the head of the household. My oldest sister took on the mother role; she took on a lot of responsibility. I was pampered and cute, but not a cry baby. My family looked after me very closely, because of my early sickness.

The family was not a church going family, but it was a spiritual household. We knew who God was, doing our prayers at night and blessing the food before eating. No one actually talked about God specifically; we all knew innately that there was a God.

My sisters were very close even until today. My sisters always looked out for me from tying my shoes to doing my hair. Mom was remarkable then and now, but my father was in and out of jail, and on drugs. He would come home and then be gone for months. He was in and out. My father and mother divorced. Although they loved each other, my mother could not handle his addictions and incarcerations. I can honestly say my father and mother loved each other until he died.

Growing up the family was fun, loving and close. My father was a great father despite his addiction and he was well dressed. My dad

Waiting

loved his daughters and mother. Although I was unable to remember my sickness, I grew up as a daddy's girl, loved deeply. I have so many pictures and memories of birthdays. My father's death was a very sad memory. My mother says we had a connection since the first time he held me.

I can't remember going to church regularly, only the occasions like Easter and Christmas. I did not go to Sunday school until I got older. It's funny because we knew who God was. I was very close to both sides of my family maternal and paternal. We had a lot of family gatherings, dinners, etc. We were a very close knit family.

Both sides of my family are from the south. My mother is from North Carolina and my father's family is from North and South Carolina. As children we visited family in the south. I have memories of playing under the house, large beds and getting pickles from the pickle barrel. There are lots of southern traditions in my memory bank.

My grandmother did not go to church. She would watch a television evangelist. Grandmother died when I was 12 years old from cancer. She had cancer for many years. I remember my grandmother always in bed. She was a domestic worker, but no real memory of her going out too much, only to the store, family visits and sitting on her stoop. Grandmother would watch television a lot, specifically a television preacher who was always asking for money. Whenever she could she would send money. Grandmother read her bible and supported the ministry. No one really demanded or required that we go to church, but the spirituality of whom and what God was, was present in the household and family.

When we got older on Sundays we would go to Mt. Olivet where we attended Sunday school. Mother heard that they were having Sunday school and sent us. The Sunday school experience was forced; we did not enjoy it, and couldn't wait for the session to be over. We didn't argue with mother over going, but we were made to do it with no questions asked. I can't remember who the Sunday school teacher was, only that he was a man. I can't remember what was taught; only that I had to go and put the money in the basket. We did not have to go to church service, but went to Sunday school. Over time we stopped going to Sunday school and mother did not enforce it anymore.

Mother worked as a school aid and volunteer. My shyness lasted for the first two years of school; two of my sisters went to the same school for at least a year or two. The oldest had graduated to middle school. I remember the sixth grade and Jordache jeans. I was very popular and not shy anymore. I didn't hang out with the in group or bad kids. I was very small a stick, no shape, no boobs. I was buddies with the boys. My self-esteem was very high. I was popular and had lots of friends. I smoked reefer for the first time; smoked for about a year then stopped at about 13 or 14 years old. I only did because one of my sisters and a friend had only $2, but needed another $1 to get a tray-bag and I gave it to them. I had no intentions of smoking with them, but that was the introduction to my first drug. I figured since I chipped in, I might as well try it. I did it for a year and never tried it again. Two things made me stop, the first reason is my older sister. I feared her more than my mother. She knew that the other sisters were smoking, and I saw how she treated them. She was very disappointed in them. Because I am the baby and was put on a pedestal I didn't want to disappoint her for nothing in the world. The second reason was one day I was smoking refer and drinking pink or Golden Champale. I got this headache and I could not hold my head up. Something told me that this was something I should not be doing and this freaked me out and so I stopped smoking. I still hung out with people who smoked, but kept a distance when they were smoking. My introduction to drugs was to do it just to do it, but the experience of munchies, paranoia, etc. was a bunch of crap. I couldn't see using my money for that, I wanted other things. I guess I did not have an addictive personality. The same with cigarettes, tried a cigarette; did not know how to inhale, swallowed the smoke and I felt like it burned my lungs, so that wasn't for me either.

My father was an atheist. He did not believe. I hope when he died he changed his ways. My dad did not enforce his views on his children. Just like his addiction, that was his thing. Father admitted his atheism when I was a teenager. Being that I didn't know what I know now about God it was just his opinion. I didn't know all the wonderful things God does; I didn't want to have an argument with him. Now when I think about it I would've said, "How could you not believe

Waiting

in God, He created the earth." Yes, I knew who He was, but I didn't know a lot about Him.

I got saved in 2004 and I actually opened the Bible to read from the beginning and read that God made the earth; I heard that all my life but when I read it, I was like oh Wow! But I didn't know, heard it all my life (I've heard a lot of things about it) but never read the Bible for myself for the connection. When my father said that he was raised atheist, I just didn't believe. That's because I didn't know then what I know now. I could have said how can you not believe when God did this or God did that. . . . I never opened the Bible to read it like this.

I was a well disciplined kid; my mother never spanked me. I got one spanking by my father because I was beating up this one girl, yes little me, for whatever reason she was scared of me; this boy was egging me on, he liked me but didn't like the other girl. He couldn't hit on her because he couldn't fight a girl. This girl's mother saw my father one day and told my father can you tell your daughter to stop beating up my child. She knew my father, he was very popular, and he came home and he didn't beat me that night, that morning, before I went to school my father gave me the beating of my life. Standing up whipping me and telling me I better not do it again. When I went to school that day, that boy told me to beat up the girl, and me and that boy had a fight. I wasn't going to get a beating by my father no more. That was the only time my father ever beat me; I don't think that it hurt, but the idea that my father beat me hurt more. For the most part, when my mother said to do something, we did it. Besides smoking reefer, which she knows today because we talk. We had normal rules, don't have people in the house when she is not there, we barely broke them, me and my sisters were really goody two shoes. When we wanted to do something like the block parties or the jams in the park, we would wait until my mother fell asleep which was usually early. We knew when she sleeps you could ask her for anything, you couldn't get into trouble when she said yes.

As far as boyfriends, she didn't say we couldn't have boyfriends. I didn't have my first serious boyfriend until I was sixteen he and I are still the best of friends to this day. The petting and kissing went on for a while. I lost my virginity at seventeen; it was a wonderful experience, hurt like heck though. I was still little, even though he was a year younger than me, he was very developed for a young man and after that one time I didn't have sex again until about nineteen. It was very romantic though. He made me dinner and what not and we agreed to do it. It was just romantic for the first time, very patient, the whole thing even though we never had sex again. He wound up finding girls that were willing to have sex. I found this out later. We still stayed together, we did foreplay. He didn't try to push me, you know or try to force me, but that's how I remembered that. To me he was well endowed; I was little you know . . . that . . . I remember that my hymen was broken . . . the experience was beautiful despite the fact it hurt, but the act will be in my memory forever. We were together for two years, when I broke up with him I dated a guy in college and we were together but we didn't have sex. I went to Baruch College from 84 until 86 and I didn't have sex until then. So from 17 up until 19, I had my two experiences. I didn't have sex again until my sons father and I were together, I was 19. I graduated from high school which was a good experience. No, Let me back up because there was something bad going on in my house.

Sixteen . . . yeah at sixteen . . . me and all my sisters were no longer living with my mom. It was one of the lowest points in my life (and my sister's lives too). I have a younger brother, who is 13 years younger than me. His father was abusive (we didn't know it, for years we didn't know it) and to me he's a pedophile. He didn't do anything to me, but he made gestures to two of my sisters; one was 15 when it happened, but it really happened (my last year in high school) when it became evident to everybody. He was around since we were little, he lived up the block from us and he was just around (when my dad wasn't' there). He was like a friend who helped my mother out. I remember him babysitting us and Lord when it all came out what he use to try to do with my sisters. I was trying to think back to remember if he tried to do something to me, but I never came up with anything or remembered anything and hope I never do. When it came to light what he was really was doing I would sit and think and think until I gave myself a splitting headache because he babysat me when I was five. I would try to think if he touched me inappropriately, I have no recollection of anything happening. He was always around even more so of course

Waiting

when my father was incarcerated. Now when I think about him, he's such a leech. He sees this young woman with these little girls and he had to have been thinking it then. He would make gestures or say stuff to my older sister. She never said anything for a long time (I don't know how long it was going on), but she didn't say anything. He would make gestures when my mom was asleep. This one particular night . . . me and two of my sisters were always out,. we would go to house parties or the block parties, and we were always out. This particular sister would always be home and he would mess with her. On this particular day she couldn't take it anymore, that's when all hell broke loose; that's when we found out what he was doing or attempting to do. He never molested her, just the gestures and the verbal stuff. When it finally came to light my mother didn't leave him. We couldn't understand, my brother was born then and we couldn't understand why would you stay with him, when you see what he was attempting to do, why are you staying with him? We all left; me and my older sister went to stay with a cousin of ours, she was our first cousin. My second oldest sister lived with her children's father and another sister was dating this guy who lived in Manhattan or the Bronx so she stayed with his family. So we were all scattered at that time. My mother couldn't do anything. What we learned later was that he was also abusive to her. So she was scared. So she would rather us not be there, but what we found out later was that he threaten her; he told her, "I will kill them." So she let us go to protect us. And then . . . I don't know . . . we were apart for a long time, for months, almost a year. And I can't even imagine what my mother went through by herself. At the time I was very angry at her. You know, how you can put some man before your children. So I was angry because I didn't know. And then, like I said, I could only imagine the torture he put her through while no one else was there. I regret not being able to see that then, but eventually she left him.

    We were spread out for about a year and then something transpired one night. My mother's boyfriend went to work and my mother called my aunt, her best friend, she married my father's brother. She called and told her to come get her and my baby brother, come get us. I don't know what he did to my mother that night to make her say no more! She left, he stayed in the apartment, she moved to Jamaica to live with my aunt. She got an order of protection against him. One day she got off work, doing her normal routine and he met her in the staircase of her job. He almost killed my mom. He strangled her until her eyes were red. Someone happened to be coming down the steps and made him stop and that's what saved her life. If no one came, he could have . . . because the blood rushed to her eyes that's why they were was blood red . . . all the blood had rushed to her eyes. She had no oxygen. She said, "Whoever that person was who came down that stairwell at that time saved my life." I remember me and my sisters were angry at him, we wanted revenge against him. Uh, I think for about six months, I even put a hit out on him. But I just didn't follow through with it. I wanted to kill him, yes I wanted him dead. I knew where he worked. I knew where he lived. I knew a cop who said he would be able to help me out and I would be able to get away with it. He knew what I was going through; he was a friend of mine. He kept asking me, whenever you ready you let me know. We kept talking and something in me kept saying no, wait, wait, and wait. And I don't know what it was that made me not do it; well sort of. I think it was something to do with my brother, I loved him. I know how I felt about my father, he had nothing to do with what his father did, he was only two years old, three, no four at the most. You know eventually, I told my friend that I can't get into it. That I can't go through with it. And he is still living to this day.

 I wasn't praying at that point, but I wrote a poem about my mom. Of course I can't remember it now, but I wrote another poem. My first poem I want to say is when I was 13 called *Young Black Girl in Harlem* because my father would take me up to Harlem, when he went to go do whatever he went to do. Me and my three sisters would be on Lenox Avenue. The four of us just standing there together watching people. Words would just come to me; I think I remember a little, I *saw a prostitute, this young pretty young girl selling herself—sexy, sultry, stylish, slim, young black girl in Harlem. Turn to drugs, turn to tricks, turn to choices, turn to kicks, turned out mother and dealing father. No family life, just sin and dishonor.* That was my first poem about that girl, that one I remember. That was the very first poem that I ever wrote, that I could remember. So I guess that's how I dealt with stuff, my experiences

Waiting

(and all my poems are from something I've seen, something I've heard, something personal, feelings or whatever); all my poems are pretty much personal.

By that little glitch from 17-18 was one of the lowest points in our lives. During that time I was living with my cousin. My cousin went to church and I went with her a few times. During my teenage years, I visited churches. I would go with friends of mine who went to church and they would invite me. I was a visitor of churches throughout my teenage years, and my twenties, I was always visiting. Then I was actively going to churches. I guess because of other family members or friends that were into church or whatever. So I guess I could say by my teenage years I was going to churches on a regular basis. I went to pretty much all the churches that were nearby. It's so funny, when I was going to churches, never once have I gone to Mt. Horeb. My first boyfriends grandmother was a member of Mt. Horeb I would go to any particular church in Corona, never once did I go to Mt. Horeb. I passed it going to the park but never went up there.

I went in Queens, Manhattan; wherever my friends lived I would go. I know that I felt stuff, I was expecting, I was going, I knew I was searching. I knew that I wanted that in my life, I just didn't know how to incorporate or commit to it at that time. But I know that I would go and hear the Word, hear the message and I would get something out of it. I would feel the sermon and it would make me cry. I would feel something and it would touch me. But, it really didn't reel me in, it didn't reel me in. None of them would draw me down the aisle.

That's the one person in my life that I hate, truly hate. And just talking about him, makes me angry. This happened when I was 17 years old and for the longest I hated him. Unlike my mom and my sisters now, except for my sister that lives in Delaware, but my other sisters who he tried to do stuff with are friends with him. Well I'm not going to say friends, but speak to him and what not and my mom speaks to him. And for a good few years I think my mom sort of went back with him for a few moments when I was in my 20's. I couldn't understand that, you know. He knew I hated him and he was the type of person that plays too much. He rubbed you the wrong way, if he knows you don't like something. If I would go to my mom's house and he was there, I would turn around and leave. I couldn't be in the same room with him. He had that "evil spirit" or whatever. It was difficult I moved to D. C., my son's father was down there and I moved down there with him. I came back for a holiday and they invited him over for dinner and he came. I was already at my sister's house; he rang the bell. And I said it's either him or me. I said there is no way I'm breaking bread with him. I don't, I won't and I can't. He wound up leaving. My family was like, it happened so long ago, how could you not let it go? It's funny, you could do so much to me, but mess with somebody I love, and I am not that forgiving. I was holding a grudge and um . . . I just couldn't understand them being friends with him. Speaking to him! I still can't do it till this day. Really! Like I said, I hate him, still to this day, I've gotten better though. He could be at my mother's house and I could be there too, where as before, I couldn't. But all in all, the same animosity is still there and I know I have to let that go eventually, I ain't ready to yet. I love my brother to death . . . I love him, but not his father. So that was the one glitch in my childhood. I guess I try to block him out and not give any energy to hating him but to talk about him brings those feelings back.

    I met my son's father on the train. His line was I like your boots. And yeah, I can't remember what the heck those boots looked like I had on, but he said he liked them. When I was ready to get off at my stop he asked could he walk with me. I told him I didn't care. So he walked with me and he's talking and I was half listening. I was like; I don't care what his pitch is we are just talking. He gave me his phone number and asked me to call him. I was like yeah O.K. No sooner then he gave me his phone number I forgot all about him. He made no impression on me at that point. But like weeks later he remembered where I lived and he came to the block. I wasn't even outside. He asked someone on the stoop about me. They were like someone was out here to see you. So, I guess that impressed me that he would come back around after I didn't call. So I called him and we started talking and dating. We didn't even date long before Junior came along.

    When I think back to our relationship I never was in love with Junior's father. He just happened to be there, we dated, we enjoyed each other's company, you know, I didn't want to see anybody else. When I

Waiting

got pregnant, my ideals at 20, was you had the baby and you be with the baby's daddy. Marriage didn't come into the picture, because I was like, I don't want to marry you, but I want you to be there. We had a decent enough relationship let's just say, we had a friendship and that was good enough reason at the time for me to be with him. So I did. I felt he got me pregnant and however you want to look at it, I was having his baby and that made me want to be with him. So we stayed together and um....he was a good guy. He was really a good guy. He was there for me throughout the whole pregnancy, the whole nine. He was there, he wanted to be there at the hospital when Junior was born, but I had sent him home, because all I wanted was my mommy. Sure enough, he goes home and then I have Junior. He loved Junior. Oh My God, he loved Junior and he was a good provider, you know? When he was first born every pay day, he came and bought all his stuff. I still lived at home with my mother and he lived with his mother, we were 20 and 23.

I moved out and left home when I was 21. I left and moved to D.C., because Junior's father had moved there. We had broken up.

Like I said, he was a good father and loved his son. He was hands on, bathed him, fed him, changed him, played with him, the whole nine, he was there. I never knew that he was a drug addict. Never saw it; never saw the signs of it. Never saw it coming. He smoked reefer, but he never did it around me because he knew I didn't like it, it wasn't my thing. So every now and then I would stay over with him over at his mother's house, for the weekend with Junior. Junior and I would stay there and he would go and smoke and come back. So I never knew that he did more than that, you know. I didn't like the reefer thing, but he was always well mannered. As long as you didn't do it around me, then I was fine. I would tell the mother, you should make him stop . . . So Junior wasn't even a year . . . nine months maybe. He was about nine months old when I found out that he was doing cocaine. His brother told me, because he was mad because he wouldn't share with him. His brother saw him go into my pocketbook and steal my money. So when I got up that morning, his brother told on him. I was livid, one he stole from me and two he broke one of my three rules. When we started dating, I said three things that would cause us to break up . . . that was never hit me, never cheat on me and never use drugs or I'm out. So that morning I found out I confronted him. He admitted it and I left Junior with his mother and I got dressed real quick and I left. I came back and there was no discussion. There was no "baby, baby please, that was it." I never used that again in relationships, but I really should have. You need to end it right then and there. But anyway, we'll get to that later. I broke up with him and um; he kept getting high on and off. His mother got him to leave New York because the person who he did it with lived on his block across the street. So for a long time I was mad at that guy, but he was a grown man. For him, he did what he wanted to do. So he leaves and goes to D.C., he had family there. He must have been there for about a year and he started writing me ... He was saying I'm getting myself together .... and I want you back, blah, blah, blah blah. I was having some fun up here in New York and I was like nah, nah, nah, nah. But then I was like, maybe I should be with my baby's daddy. These were the ideals I had at 20, you know, he was off the drugs, maybe I'll give it another try and see if we could be a family. So I moved down there and we had a good life for a good while. That is as long as he wasn't on that stuff. When he is not using, there is nothing he wouldn't do for me or his son. There was nothing he wouldn't do for anybody. It's just when he's on that stuff, that's his whole life, his everything. So, I lived down there with him for two years, and then he started back with the drugs. So now I could see, you know there are traits in that stuff and when I first moved down there, he had a job; he worked for George Washington University. He worked for the college this was a good job. He got paid every week. He would get paid on a Friday. He wouldn't spend a dime of that money. He wouldn't even cash the check. He came home gave me his entire check and that's how we lived, I took care of everything. That's just how he was, he was there. He would take care of Junior and whatever else we needed to be taken care of. I would give him whatever he needed, give him a couple dollars. Everything else, I had control over. After a year, then it started to change. I knew then I wasn't really in love with him, because once I found out he was picking up again that was it for me. My father got sick and that sealed the deal for me to come back. I told him I was leaving because I don't want to be there anymore. There was no fight, no fuss. I came back to New York, and took my baby with me.

Daddy Where Are You?

We lived with my dad. No when I came back to New York, I lived with my sister for a little while until I could find my own apartment. When I couldn't find an apartment, I went to live with my dad and wound up taking care of him. My dad was diagnosed with AIDS. Junior and I lived with him in a one bedroom apartment. We had a futon and my father didn't like beds so he had a pallet on the floor.

Me and my father were hanging out together for that summer. And he was watching my son and I would go to work. My son is named after my father. It was just a coincidence that both my father and baby daddy have the same name. I tell people all the time his name could have been Joe Blow . . . anything . . . it just so happened his name happened to be the same; I didn't have a girl's name picked out. I knew I was having a boy. So, um, my father had AIDS and he was in and out the hospital a lot. My father was very vain, his appearance was always cool, dressed snappy, good looking but the illness took its toll on him. He started fading, lost a lot of weight, suffering. He started to pick back up using drugs. I was so angry. He tried kill to himself. He didn't want to live like that anymore, you know. He never had a steady job, He got SSI and medication for AIDS. I believe, he started picking back up because of that. I didn't know he was using until I saw him go into a drug den a couple of blocks away. I was looking for an apartment for me near my father's apartment house. There was a guy who owned a building, and I was inquiring about an apartment in his building. We were standing outside on the stoop and that block was a very active block. Directly across the street was a drug den and I'm standing there talking to the guy and I happened to be looking across the street and I see my dad going into the den. My heart hit the floor and I was so angry at my father. I never confronted him, which after my father died, I felt real guilty because I felt as a kid I couldn't confront my father about his addiction. I was a kid so there was a level of respect. Now I'm an adult and I felt I should have said something to let him know that I knew but I didn't. So, I saw him go in that building and shortly after that I moved. I didn't even want to be in the city anymore, I didn't want to be near him. I was so hurt and angry that he would pick back up. He didn't know that I knew. I moved but I would still check up on him, you know. I still had the keys to his apartment. And I would check on him, because I was the only link that other people had to him. My grandmother, his mom loved him with all her heart she knew that this is what he dealt with his entire life. That was still her baby, he was her first born, he's the oldest, he was her baby-boy, you know. So I would go and check on him.

From August all the way up to exactly December 14, I would have dreams about my father's death. Clear as day, where he was, where I would find him, everything. Every night, whether it was a dream sleep or day dream . . . I could be awake . . . I kept having the same premonitions about his death. I happened to be at my grandmother's house, his mother, one weekend visiting her. She was having her premonitions and she told me to go check on him, see how your father doing. And I said, I'll be going over there grandma, he didn't have a phone, but I said I'd better get over there ASAP. That was Friday. Friday night I didn't go because I didn't have a ride out there and didn't want to go out there by myself on the train. So I didn't go Friday night. Saturday, I asked a friend of mine who had a car to drive me into the City. So all the time we're driving there I'm sitting there looking out the window not saying much of anything.

Since I had the key to my father's apartment, I opened the door, smelled gas in there and I said Daddy. I kept calling him. He's not on his couch, because you can see the couch as soon as you open the door, you can see right into the apartment. He usually sat right there where the window was. The kitchen was around the bend and I kept calling out to him, Dad! Dad! But there was no answer. So first I am like he's just downstairs and I'm like Daddy and I'm looking down the path and I'm like Daddy . . . Daddy, he doesn't answer. I walk around the bend to go into the kitchen. My dad was laid back . . . and I said Dad . . . Dad and I'm like looking and calling him. Daddy . . . and I knew I knew he was dead. And the only thing that was different from my premonition was where I found him. I went down stairs and I said

Waiting

to the guy that drove me, I think my Dad is dead. And I didn't even lose it. Being that he didn't have a phone in the house, and I didn't have a cell phone, I don't even think cell phones were out, I think beepers were out. I had to go to a pay phone. I went to the corner dialed 911 told them about my father, that I thought he was dead. EMS is stupid. They asked was he breathing. I told them that I wasn't sure. I wasn't in the house; I was calling on a pay phone. I know that they have to go through their spiel, but . . . so I give them the address. I end up hanging up on the lady because, she was asking me all of these questions like did he have a pulse? I was like I don't have time for that. I gave them the address, to send the police . I got back up the block and waited outside the apartment for the cops to come. The cops come. I take them to the Apartment, Rigor Mortis had set in and they are asking me a few questions.

I had to break it to my mother, my sisters and his mother. And, uh my mom's reactions went through me. I know my mom loved him; they were together since she was 15 and what not. So I know she loved him but, I didn't realize how much she still loved him until I told her. She was asleep and I went to her house and woke her up and said Daddy is dead. My mother just cried . . . it came from the pit of her stomach and I couldn't console her. By that time I was like, my Daddy . . . and I just backed away from her . . . I went into the living room. It really hit me at that moment. She cried, I mean my mother poured her eyes out. When I called my oldest sister all I remembered is that scream at the other end of the phone. Like I said, I know that my sisters loved my father, but they didn't show it like I showed it. They had their own way of coping, because he was in and out of jail. They weren't attached to him like I was. I do realize they all loved him just as much as I did. I was just like a walking zombie. If I didn't have Junior, at that time, I think I would have committed suicide. Junior was my life that was my baby! I couldn't' leave him, but my father was my heart. That was the man in my life, you know. I can't even describe how much I loved him. It's funny at that moment all the people who spoiled and took care of me I was left to look after. Afterwards they got it together and we did things together. I mean we worked on the arrangements and everything. But that initial shock. It shook everybody. I think, now, those six weeks or whatever, however long it was that I started the dreams to finding him were signs. I know it was God preparing me for his death. Because any other way, I don't think I would have been able to handle it. I knew it was happening; I knew driving to his house that day that something wasn't right. But for whatever reason, it wasn't meant for me to go there that Friday night. I would have been by myself. I had somebody with me. I now know that was God's way of preparing me for that moment. I had experienced it already through my dreams. Like I said, after his death, I wished I said something to him, when I knew he was using, taking drugs. For a long time I blamed his death on me. I felt like if I had just said something maybe he wouldn't have kept using. Maybe he would've stopped; maybe I could have stopped him, maybe if I would have just talked to him. Maybe if I wasn't so mad at him. Maybe if I didn't move out. Maybe if I would've just stayed there with him or something. My mother was like Miss Lead, you know that's not true. But I didn't hear it then, I couldn't. I do know it now. My sister who lived in Delaware, she was away, she was in Germany, she had to come from Germany at the time. She wasn't around us a lot because she was in the service. She said, Daddy came and sat at the end of her bed. I prayed for him to come to visit me. But he never did. I wanted to say I was sorry. He never came. I think because she was away so much, he had to visit her. She said it freaked her out. I was like are you crazy, that was Daddy. She said that she was sleep and she felt the presence of somebody and she knew it was Daddy. She said she was scared, she told him to go. Daddy go on; you know she couldn't take it. I was like, come see me. He never did though. I actually said that one day, but like I said he had to go see her because she was always away from us. She made it to the funeral and stuff.

So my oldest sister grew up with the Shepherd. I did not know him. They were still friends and she called him. She said so you know Daddy died, can you come. And he was there at the wake. He said a prayer for my Dad. I will never forget because anybody who had a kind word to say about my Daddy or could do anything good for my father, you got my heart. He was there for us at a moment's notice. He came and said that prayer and I didn't see the Shepherd again for many years. Now he's my Shepherd here on Mount Horeb.

My Wants vs. My Needs

So after Junior's father there was relationships here and there. When I was in my 20's I was crazy, you know. I truly know now that God definitely had his hand on me, because I wasn't the most careful. To God be the glory I had no diseases. I wasn't thinking, I was just care free and having fun and enjoying being single and choosing to do whatever I wanted to do.

So now Diamond's father comes in. That's my baby girl. The signs were as clear as day, saying go the opposite way! But, um I saw him, I wanted him and that's all I knew. He was dating somebody, I didn't care. I saw him at a Tyson fight party. His sister had rented it on HBO and I was over there with my cousin and here he came. It was June, and I know that because it was his birthday. He came over to his sister's house but he wasn't staying. He breezed in and he breezed out. I didn't quite remember him when I saw him. I grew up with his sisters and him. He was seven years older than me so, I was hanging with his younger sisters and he was with the older guys. I didn't pay him any attention back then and he didn't pay me any attention either.

So I'm sitting there on the couch, and he was going out with his girlfriend to celebrate his birthday, but he stopped in real quick. I think he wanted to tape the fight. He came to hook-up the VCR so they could record it. I'm sitting there on the couch, my cousin sitting next to me and he walked in and I am like watching his every move. My cousin was also his cousin, but we are not related. I'm like who is that and my cousin said that's Joe and I was like what! So I saw him that day and I didn't see him again until that same cousin, who I was asking who he was passed away. I went to her funeral, which was, about a month later. She was 21. Then again I don't even think she was that old. I was 25 when my dad died. So she was about to turn 21, I think she was 20, because I had her by about five years. She was pregnant, I'm not really sure whether it was seven months or eight months, but she was pregnant though. The father of her child, I think he was into drugs, selling or whatever. She was at her mother's house one night, she wasn't living with her mother. That night they tried to convince her to spend the night because it was late. She didn't want to stay. She wound up going home and when she got on her block, a guy came up and shot her because of the boyfriend. He shot her right on her block. She died but they were able to save the baby . . . Yeah July 24, they shot her in the face the bullet ricocheted and she never recovered. She was in a coma on life support. They kept her long enough to get the baby out, but then she died, there was no oxygen getting to him for a good little while before they got him out of her, but he's fine. So during her wake and funeral, he was there at the house. This was really a sad time for me, we were really close, and we grew up together. We played together. You know what; I don't think the father of the baby really got to come around, because her father was very strict . . . He hated him. He blamed the boyfriend because of his dealings. The person that shot his daughter was retaliating, they felt I can't get you; I'm going to get the next closest thing to you. I don't think the baby's daddy had anything to do with the baby after it happened, I don't think he does. I never seen him over there and we don't talk about him or anything. So her mother raised him, he calls my aunt Ma. He knows about his mother, he's been told about her, sees pictures of her. So he knows of his mother.

During that time I ran into Diamond's father Joe again. So I'm at my aunt's house. Joe's mother and my aunt lived on the same block. So we're all at the funeral and stuff. There is so much sadness. He comes in and out again like I said I had an instant attraction to him. He just reminded me so much of my dad. He had the gift of gab, he was the cool type of guy and you know he just reminded me of my dad. I had to go to the store and he happened to be leaving the house. I am walking up the street to get to the store toward the Boulevard. His mother's house was close to the Boulevard. So I'm walking and he happened to be in his mother's yard, we talked a little bit. He was like, when you finish come back and talk to me. Girl, I couldn't get back from that store fast enough. I took whatever I bought back to the house. I go down the block and we sit in his mother's backyard. We are talking and what not. He tells me he had a girlfriend and I thought I seen the girl at the funeral. He said he sent her home. He said he got rid of her. Like I said, Joe was seven years older than me. Everybody is telling me that he got this reputation. I want to say like three kids, four kids, not

Waiting

really taking care of them. All the signs were there, you know, but oh well. We liked each other and we started seeing each other. I don't know if, it was love or what I thought was love. So we dated for a year and the following year I left him in New York and moved to Virginia. I was true to him, he wasn't true to me but I loved him. He was in pharmaceuticals, but I loved him. After a year of the on and off relationship and him doing his thing, finally, I was like you know what I can't do this with you. The thing is I didn't like dealers, because those are the ones that sold to my dad, but Joe was the exception to the rule. So we dated until I was just like, I can't. I saved up my money for a year and quit my job and took me and my son and we left. I had a girlfriend who I met when I lived in DC with Baby Daddy and we kept in contact. We had been talking and she was ready to move. She had twin daughters and I was like find a place and I'll be there. She found us a town house and we lived there together for a year. Then Junior and I moved out but for that whole year I was there I had no contact with Joe or nothing. Out of the blue he finds me. Like I said, we had mutual cousins. My guess is he talked to someone and asked where's Miss Lead? I can hear him. You let me get the number. I had not given him the house number to where I was. So one of my cousins had to have called my mom, got the number, and gave it to him. I'm laying down in bed and my girlfriend was like Miss Lead there is a Joe on the phone for you. I am like a who? She says there is a Joe on the phone for you. I get the phone and he hands me that hello. So here he comes again sweet talking me, and at that time I had started to look for apartments for me and my baby. So I am like, I'm looking for my own apartment and I need money for this and I need money for that, you know this and that. And he sent it. And I'm like O.K. I get the apartment and stuff and I'm thinking he's coming to stay with us. He comes down and stays for the weekend for his birthday. We get together, like I said I wasn't the most careful person back then, we get together and whatever. He decides that he doesn't want to move to Virginia. So I say alright, fine, no problem. I don't want you here if you don't want to be here. So after he leaves of course I realize that I'm pregnant. I'm 28 and going to have another baby. I'm thinking all these things. So I tell him and he's happy as can be. Oh my baby, this and my baby that.

So long story short, I decide to tell him, because he wasn't trying to commit and I know him by now and I told him I was going to get rid of her, the baby. It wasn't confirmed, but I knew that Diamond was a girl; well I felt it was a girl because the pregnancy was already so different and I just knew. I told him that I was going to terminate. So for a good while we weren't communicating. So he, shows up, bags and everything a month or so after I told him I wasn't keeping it. He must have found out that I was still pregnant. I am laying on the couch one night and hear the door turn and I am a few months, cause I'm out there now. His bag and stuff was at the door, he came back. I was happy as hell. So, we were together again. He moved on in. My son knows him and stuff and I'm thinking we are going to be fine. He's not working yet but that's OK I'm like, money was never important to me, just be productive. I don't care if you're bagging bags in the grocery store, just get a job, you know. So he moved down there from New York, but he's into this drug thing, the fast life. I guess it got the best of him, he couldn't take it or whatever and I am like you have to get something, as long as we can work together. Then I told him, you know if you don't want to be here, you don't have to be here, you really don't. I said if you want to do the long distance option that's fine, me and my compromising behind. You can stay in New York and come to VA, whatever. He said um . . . no, no, no, I'm fine; I'm, fine, blah, blah, blah. We come to New York for Thanksgiving, I go to my mom's house; he goes to his mother's house. And that was like a Wednesday. I don't hear from him Thursday, Friday, Saturday me and Junior go back home on Sunday. I didn't see him the whole time we were there. Sunday come, me and Junior are ready to go, I don't hear from him, I didn't see him. We go back home, don't hear from him, my phone was off, but anyway, I don't hear from him. He comes back, I think it was before Christmas, I can't really remember, but in the midst of him not coming home with us, I'm crying my eyes out. I packed up all his stuff. When he came back to VA his stuff was waiting by the door. When he did decide to come, I told him you need to leave. Simple as that, you need to go. He didn't put up a fight, his only words was . . . are you sure that this is what you want me to do. That was his only words to me, not, baby I love you, I made a mistake, you know, no nothing. It's are you

Waiting

sure this is what you want me to do. Yeah, you need to go, you really need to go and he left. I was seven or eight months pregnant, and he left. So, I said I'll let you know when the baby is born; you are more than welcome to come down here and be here when she's born. He spent the last night, I felt I can't be worried about a grown ass man, and I'm pregnant. I can't do it. I felt if you don't want to be here I'm not going to force you to be here. You want to be here for your baby, that's fine with me. He left and he didn't come back for her birth, which was in March. It was a scheduled birth, he knew she was coming, Diamond was a planned C-section. I gave him the information and I said it was March 10th, a Monday, you can come down here and my mom was there. His big excuse was I knew your mom was there and she didn't like me, so I didn't want to be there with your moms. Whatever, he didn't see Diamond until she was a month old cause we came to New York for Easter and he saw her for the first time then. He was all lovey, dovey with my baby and Junior. I was like give me my baby. He ran out to Jamaica Avenue and came back with a whole bunch of stuff. He didn't keep in touch until Thanksgiving, I came up for Thanksgiving and times were hard for me that year. It was a very low point. I lost my job, had Junior and Diamond to take care of, Junior was eight years old. After losing my job I got behind in my rent. I was forever calling my sisters and my mother for money. They were forever sending me money, trying to help me out. What I didn't know about, (because I had never been fired from a job.) I was living there, and was 28 or 29, and never knew about unemployment. I didn't know that was an option. I would have collected and stayed there. I was about three months back in my rent when I went home for thanksgiving. My mother and sister just sat me down and told me to come home. They said with us sending you money, we could help you better if you are here. I didn't want to hear that. I felt like I would come home with my tail between my legs, I had failed. I didn't want to but I decided to go back home. I thought about it and said I can't, I can't catch up. It was only a matter of time they were going to evict me. I didn't have the money to stop the eviction so I didn't pay at all. There was a hotel, the Quality Inn up the road from me. I put my stuff in storage, packed cloths for me, Junior and Diamond; I call it homeless because I was living out of a hotel for weeks. We stayed in that hotel from when we came back from the Thanksgiving break until the Christmas break. I didn't want to take Junior out of school until the Christmas break. I came home to NY a week before Christmas. You know I was depressed. To top it all off I had this bump right on the tip of my nose, that would keep getting scabbed up and I would pick it, and it just wouldn't go away. I was already little and I had lost a tremendous amount of weight. I felt like a failure. I was just so sad. I wasn't writing, I wasn't praying, it was just . . . it's funny at those two lowest points in my life, there was always anger behind it and I'd feed into it, I didn't reach out to nothing or anybody, you know. It was no one.

I left my stuff in Virginia, I couldn't bring it, and I had nowhere to keep it in New York. I came back and lived with my mom in December. I moved out in April to the apartment I'm in now. I was just like very low, I know I was depressed. I felt like I failed my kids. We had a good life down there in Virginia. I had a nice apartment, in a nice clean area. It felt good to come home and see it. It was a huge difference. I had maybe, $2,000 to my name, from the last two paychecks I received. When I came up here I still had to pay my storage down there. What I learned about Virginia was that piece of paper, was what mattered. It could be any type of degree, that meant a lot down there and I didn't have that. It was hard, even though I was doing the job, it didn't matter. I was trying to market myself but the jobs weren't coming. I got into a company, the Government Contracting Company. We bid on a job, it lasted for a period of time and then you rebid. I did well and they kept me and I'm the type of person, I try to learn a little bit of everything to make myself useful. I was doing a financial analyst position, making $25,000 a year, where the person who trained me was making $110k and I'm doing all the work. I was a financial analyst, but I didn't have the backing. If you teach me a job, I can do it. I had a nice little two bedroom apartment and it was just a beautiful life, I loved it down there. I've been trying to get back there ever since and I've been stuck here, I am not going to say stuck, but I've been here for 13 years. God knows the desires of my heart and if it is His will, He'll get me back there, you know. Just like me getting my degree, it's something within my reach; I just got to make it happen. Those are two things

Waiting

that I definitely want. And I hope that it is what God wants for me. So instead of asking for the desire to be taken away, I'm going to keep trying to move towards that.

Yeah so I came back here and when I came back, my heart was broken. I still loved Joe, but he had moved on. He had a girlfriend. I think he had her all along. When I came back, he admitted that he had a girlfriend now. I think he told me because I had moved back here. As long as I wasn't living in New York, I guess he kept us apart. So I remember the day, he said, "Look Miss Lead, I am with somebody now, but I want to be there for Diamond" and I was like that's fine. I said, "You know whatever goes on between me and you have nothing to do with Diamond. You want to be a part of her life, I welcome that wholeheartedly." It's sad because, he fell 100% short of that. I don't hate, I dislike him tremendously. I have no respect for him at all, whatsoever. I want to say I don't hate him, but I don't have the same feeling for him as I had for my son's father. This might be hate, because he is sick and I would have a problem helping him out. He has, I forget what it is he has, but I've always said that if he ever needed a blood transfusion or whatever and he had that rare blood type and only Diamond was the one who could save him, and she's a minor, I don't know if I would allow her to do it. If she's an adult, that's her choice, but I don't' know, so I don't know if its hate, anger, I don't know. I feel this way only because of how he has treated Diamond over the years and I wouldn't want her to help him now. I know it's not Godly and I know that, but for you to need her now when she needed you so much and you are not there for her and for me to make that decision, right now I am torn, I wouldn't know what I would do.

It's not even needing him financially, I am going to take care of Diamond the best way I can. She's not going to lack for anything. She's going to have her necessities; she's not going to lack for anything. I guess basically, I want the relationship I had with my father I want that for her. And like I said, Joe, I found him to be this huge jerk. I know another side of him too and I know he is capable of love, because when we were dating, his children were important to him. Um, I even provided for his children when he didn't have it. He would come to me and say oh little Joe is graduating and I need to get him this or that. So I know that he has that in him. Two summers ago, she spent the summer with him and he treated my daughter like garbage, like garbage. And I'll never forgive him for that. He had my baby in tears. He told my baby don't call him no more. I didn't find this out until afterwards. She wanted to come home and I didn't have the money to get to her at the time. She had to wait until he would bring her back. She never felt comfortable when she goes to his house, even before he moved to Virginia. Yes, where I wanted us to be originally, anyway he moved to Virginia. He has a house and when Diamond visits she's living out of her suitcase. There's no space for her. She's like a guest. He got married. He married the girl, his other daughter's mother. The girl he was with all the time, they wind up getting married. They have a house, I don't know if they own it or rent it or whatever, but they have a house down there in Richmond, Virginia. It was sad because when she went down there that year she was excited about it—seeing her father and him wanting her to come. Once she got down there I don't know what happened. He took her cell phone so we couldn't talk to me. Me and Diamond have to talk every day. He could go a week without speaking to Diamond, that's your relationship. I need to speak to my child daily. So he took her phone, she couldn't call me. I was pissed, because I didn't have the house phone number. I couldn't get to them, you know. When she was a baby up until a certain age he treated her like a daughter. I think that's because him and I had a relationship and friendship. When I stopped the friendship and really got fed up with his b. s. and wasn't compromising or as nice as I was, he took that out on her you know. So, she hasn't seen him in two years. Since the day she came back and he dropped her off. He didn't even get out the car, he didn't say goodbye, nothing. Yep, and he hasn't provided for her in any kind of way in two years. Throughout her life, he was only there off and on. We made agreements and he would break them. Everybody says she looks like me, but she favors his side of the family to me. I could show you a picture of her grandmother, his mother and her together they look just alike. It's so funny in that picture she stands like him. She has his mannerism more so. But anyway that love is definitely gone.

His wife loves Diamond. So her wanting to visit was I wanted to go over to Kim's house? It wasn't I want to go to Daddy's house; it was

Waiting

I want to go to Kim's house. Oh, I love her for loving my daughter. I'm not that type of female you know that's not me. I never was. I actually believed you can't help who you love. That's not a choice, so if you don't love me, I can't fault you for not loving me. I can't get upset behind it and wonder why. I'm not going to hold that against her. You can't help who you fall for, who your heart goes to or whatever. So when I found out about Kim, my whole thing was you treat my daughter right, and we will never have a problem. I don't know what he has told her. She and I never had a one on one, but they use to live in the Bronx and whenever I would call the house or whatever, I would give her respect. If she happened to answer the phone I would say, hi Kim how you doing, this is Miss Lead is Joe there. That's just not my makeup to be crazy, I'm not like that. And like I said Diamond loves her, so I know she was treating my daughter right. So, I never ever had a problem with her at all, you know. She calls Diamond to this day. She'll call Diamond out the blue, to ask how she is doing. She calls Diamond on her birthday and keeps the line of communication open. Joe doesn't. She loves Diamond, truly, I believe that, you know.

I think it gets to Diamond more so because Junior is not here. When Junior is around, you know he fills that gap. He was the man in her life. So I think it took its toll on her but she doesn't talk about it much. Well we have a running joke about her father, he is cousins with my cousin, and Diamond calls him my cousin daddy. So that's our running joke. Other than that we don't really talk about him. I don't bring him up to her. I don't sit and talk bad about him to her, never have. When she was younger, I use to try to make them keep their relationship. But when she got to a certain age, I took my hands off it. Because I am not going to chase you to be in her life, I'm not going to do it. His whole thing use to be "why doesn't she call me." That's how he use to be. She's your daughter, she's a child. Why should she . . . come on? So he, I don't know, he's, he's just strange. But, um, if Diamond wants a relationship with him, I am not going to fight it. I'm not going to tell her not to. I would love for her and him to have a relationship, but I'm not going to initiate it anymore. I'm not going to. When she gets older, if she wants to she can. She doesn't ask about him and every once in a while I'll say did your father call you. And she'll be like "no." If she calls him on her own, I don't know. I would love for him to act like a father and be there for her because I know how important that is.

I had to ask myself do I feel guilty about my selection. No. there's not too much that I do that I am really ashamed of. I know what I am doing; you know. I am fully aware of what I am doing. And as long as I am doing something that is not out to hurt somebody, I have to live with the choices that I made. If Joe wasn't Diamond's father, Diamond wouldn't be Diamond, if Baby Daddy wasn't Junior's father Junior would not be who he is. Like I said in my 20's I wasn't the most careful. I could have other problems.

Mommy Trying To Be Daddy

I always thought I could be mommy and daddy. I realize that I can't be mommy and daddy. I believe that now (a woman can't raise a man), but when Junior's father and I broke up he used to say, you know, when he gets a certain age, he needs to come with me, blah blah blah. And I was like, no he don't, I can raise my son, I know what I am doing . . . I don't need you to raise my son. But as Junior got older, there's just, how can I put it, I raised Junior . . . what is the right word, I don't want to say like a woman, I raised him, I am not going to say soft, it wasn't soft. There are things, as a woman I could teach Junior like how to treat a woman, manners, right from wrong. I am street smart, I told him about the streets. But you know, I had to teach him how to do the condom thing and talking to him about sex. But of course I am talking to him from a woman's point of view. Actually everything that I teach him, everything is coming from a woman's point of view. My first lesson on different points of view was the way my dad would talk to me and my sisters because my mom wasn't as open with us, for whatever reason. Don't get me wrong; when we went to her she would talk to us. But my dad was just the unconventional type. He would talk to us raw, completely and he was talking to us from a man's point of view. I think, as open as I am with Jr. I am not or I wasn't . . . how can I put this . . . it always just came from a feminine point of view., I mean some single mothers raised their sons and did a fabulous job

Waiting

doing it, but I just believe that at some point a man to man talk, that man view, that man opinion, that man's walk, is different from my walk as a black woman. It's is so different from a man's walk in this society and a woman can't relate that to a guy.

It's kind of like, I had a hard time explaining his father's or my father's addiction, because I was never addicted. But I can identify with someone who has been in a relationship with someone who is addicted. I can't teach Jr. some of the things that he needed to be taught. I feel that I fell short, but I did the best that I could, but I still feel that at some point, I think, whether a man is in the house or not, they need to be there at a certain point in a male's life to take them on that walk that they need to go on. There is a journey that a boy needs to go on and a woman can't do it. I truly believe that. I can't . . . when Diamond's out with the peer pressure from other girls . . . I can relate to that, but when a boy is telling you to go over and do something . . . . I can tell him you know better than to do that, but what is that worth when it's not hitting what you are feeling inside, only another man can tell you. When Junior would say, I ain't going to be no punk. From a woman's point of view, what the freak is a punk? You know.

Jr. has no uncles around either, Joe like I said when he came into Junior's life; he wasn't there for him like that. Junior did not know Joe was a dealer. What was he going to teach him? His godfather is my brother in law, Carl, but um, Carl was a good provider. He wasn't you know . . . l mean he was there for Junior, but no real male influence. My boyfriends were just my boyfriends. There was no one. If I'm just dating you, I'm not bringing you around my kids like that. I had that rule. I dated and I did my stuff, but Junior knows of his father, Diamond's father and a gentleman by the name of Derek. That went as far as us being engaged. That's all he knows. Diamond knows Derek; she knows who her father is. The only man she seen in our house is Derek. She knows my male friends, but there was never no uncle whoever. This is mommy's friend. She knows who friends are she sees them come at decent hours or whatever, what mommy do in the dark, they don't even know. They don't. So there was never anyone else.

I would say to any woman, if you had the outlet for a male child expose them to positive male role models. Listen, sitting down talking about sex with Junior was hard. He didn't want to hear that from me. You know, but I didn't give him a choice but to sit there. I didn't get any feedback from him. He would say, you told me this already. I would say so, well, Junior, this is our monthly talk, and you going to sit here and listen. But coming from a male, I know it would be different. Shoot just think about it; for starters we got different equipment.

Growing up Junior was the fattest little baby. He was so fat, he was jolly. He was the happiest little kid. He's my heart. He's my first born. We were thick as thieves. At one point it was just me and him for a good while. He was good in school, at least from elementary through junior high school.

Then, he started smelling himself. I don't think school was it for him. It's sad because he's very smart and personable. I feel like Junior has my father's name and also living part of my father's life. It's like, right now he's my father reincarnated, recreated. He has charm and appeal, and that smile of his will get him over more times than not, you know. But, once Junior got older, things got tough. In terms of discipline, I am not a spanker. I don't, I can't. I don't want my children to fear me; I want them to respect me. Just how I was raised, I tell you to do something you do it. I'm not going to hit you; I'm not going to beat you. That's just not me, I was a screamer and then I learned not to scream you know to talk to them. But I was a screamer for a while. But um I wasn't one to hit. But like I said, when Junior was little up until a good maybe 13, 14 it was do it and you did it. Around the age 15 I had to start repeating myself. It would get done; he was very respectful towards me. Minds me you know and all of that. But it was sucking of the lip, sucking the teeth thing. He was a good kid, good kid. Um, but them teenage years, he's a boy who thinks he can do whatever he wanted to do. I guess he thought I was soft, because I didn't hit him. But I was one for punishment; a hit lasts for five minutes, besides my hits didn't hurt him. I couldn't see hitting him to hurt him. So my thing was taking stuff away from you. Taking privileges away, so with that being said Junior stayed on punishment from semester to semester. He didn't get to go outside, he didn't get to watch TV, and he didn't get on his Play Station. I didn't take one thing, I took numerous things away. But he still didn't get it, he tried me and tried me and tried me. We

Waiting

battled with the school thing for dag on near two years. He was getting ready to go to Job Corp. I was like, if you don't want to go to school, I can't keep missing work, I would go up to the school to spot check and he never knew when I was coming. I would go to the school and Junior wasn't even there. He would be at another high school waiting for his friends to get out of school. This one really had me going. Your friends are at school getting an education and you are cutting your classes to wait for them to get out of school. You big dummy. I'm like, I don't get that, you know. But him and school, it just didn't click, it's not like he wasn't smart. He would get in there and he wouldn't have to study. He would get 80's and 90's, if he just went. At 16, Junior would come to me and say, Mom let me get my GED. I would say no, you're going to night school; you're getting your high school diploma. You got the two years. Just finish but he wouldn't. Finally, he went to take his GED at 17 and passed it the first time and graduated. The year he was going to graduate from high school he said I told you let me go and get my GED and this thing would have been over with Ma. So, um, he loved the street which is a trait of my father and like I said Junior is very personable. People gravitate towards him; they want to be around him. He has charisma and it draws people in. He was always the mediator of the group you know. Junior had friends in two gangs the Bloods and the Cripps. When they were at the Boys Clubs, and they both were there Junior was the one that kept the peace, you know. He grew up with these guys but, wasn't interested in joining the gangs. They were his friends from childhood.

After he got his GED, we were filling out applications to go to Queensboro College. I would say Junior pretty much hung out in Jamaica a lot. The Southside, you know that's where he hung out. That's where the Cripps was and they were into the rap thing. So, um one of the boys, this boy named Charles, he and Junior went to school together, they use to hang out quite a bit. Charles had been to my house quite a few times, but then this other group of boys who Junior hung with started really clicking with Junior's best friend Andre. That group of boys didn't really care for Charles. Junior sad it didn't matter to him. I think he get's that from me. I get along with anybody and everybody, you know. Anyway, being that he and Charles didn't hang out as much anymore, they still were friends. They did hang out occasionally because the other group of boys Junior was hanging with was into other things. Charles wound up hanging with these other boys. I believe it was the Bloods, that was what Charles liked. So it was Valentine's weekend. Junior and Dre, was hanging out, not with Charles, he was with his friend Andre. And, um there was something at church that weekend. So I was at church, that Saturday night, I think it was The Candle Light Ushers' thing. So I come in that night from the church but I didn't know the police left a message on my machine. I didn't retrieve my messages right away. The message said this is the police department and there was an incident but they would not say anything further. They said on the machine *"Junior we need to talk to you right away."* Junior had spent the night over at Dre's house. This was Sunday when I got the message, because when I got home it was late, so I hear cops on my machine. So I know where Junior is, so I call him on the phone and his mom, Dre's mom was on the phone. I asked if Junior was alright, is he over there. She said he was there and fine. So I was like OK I know where Junior was and he was OK. Then Sunday morning, I called and told Junior to take a cab home and I'll meet him downstairs and to come straight home. No I talk to him; I talked to Junior on the phone. I asked him Junior what happened last night. And he was like, what? Nothing! I was like something happened last night, Junior talk to me, what did you get into last night. He was like, nothing, me and Dre were here at his house, and we were helping his dad and such and such. And I was like well, I got this phone message something happened that you were involved in. What happened! He was like ma nothing! So I said get in a cab and I'll meet you downstairs. So he comes home and again I'm drilling him to tell me what is going on. The cops are not going to call my house for nothing. Tell me what is going on. He's like ma I don't know. Ain't nothing happen. So I asked did any of your friends get into a fight? Fighting, that's what I'm thinking. Junior was, like no ma, no ma nothing happen. So I call the Pct., tell them who I am, they don't want to give me any information. So, um I tell my family. I'm worried. I don't get this you know. So I go around to my mother's house. I tell Junior don't leave the house. He decides to leave the house anyway and visit his girlfriend who lives in Jamaica I'm so glad he did that, cause somehow throughout the day the police want Junior. They're hiding in my stairwells; they try to catch him coming in or whatever. They are in the back of the building asking people about him and what not. My uncle was living with me at the time and I was at my mother's house. He was going into the door and all these cops come out into the stairwell thinking that he is my son. Just getting home from work, my uncle calls me and says ML what's going on there's cops. So then I knew something was wrong. They were trying to grab up my son. I go to the Pct. inquiring. I told them I was his mother, told them I want to know what's going on. They still not giving me any information, we are just doing our job and you're hindering our case. And I said I'm doing my job, I'm his mother protecting my son and you don't want to give me any information. So I was like you know what I need to find Junior there is no way I'm going to lose him. So they were like bring him in we just want to talk to him. So I said why you hiding in my staircase when all you want to do is talk to him.

Somehow throughout the day, the word gets out that Charles and some of the other guys were arrested for hurting somebody. So I'm panicking and I'm like Junior are you involved in anything, whatsoever. Did you know that something happened, did you know, did you hear. If you did, you need to tell me what you know. He was like ma, no. I don't know why he would do something like that, I don't know. I wasn't with him. Me and Dre were together. So I'm looking at him and I'm like, I don't know who you was with, or what you would do, but I said I need to know the truth so I know how to focus. So you need to tell me. He looked at me and said ma I didn't do it. I'm not involved in anything. So it's the weekend, the holiday weekend, that Monday, its President's Day. I need to find a lawyer. So I'm calling around and someone told me about an 800 number for lawyers that someone gave them. So I called it and, they look up information for someone in my area and so forth. He gives me this man's phone number, he happens to be a police officer. I called him, told him my story and he wants us to come into his office that was Sunday. So for the night I'm like you can't come home. You're going to have stay at a friend's because they are looking for you and I'm not going to have them take you. So of course, I was going to try to have him hide out. Monday morning the lawyer has us come, so anyway, Monday morning we go to the lawyer and he takes Junior into another room, I can't hear the conversation. They talk and he calls the Pct. to find out exactly, what's what? They telling him he is wanted for questioning. He needs to turn himself in. I didn't think he was a suspect in a murder case. So he said he would bring him in, with his lawyer and I agreed. That's not what happened. Two of his paralegals went with Junior, not the lawyer. They had a warrant for his person, which is a warrant to get DNA from his body and they had a warrant for inside my apartment. So I go down and I see Junior at the Pct. I go into the room and I told Junior to talk about nothing, don't answer any questions. I go back down to my house with four cops; they go into Junior's room. They just take notebooks, old cell phones, and tee-shirts, clothes and everything, boots, sneakers and all his shoes and stuff. They are just taking, just gathering it into a bag so they could get the DNA. They took clippings of his hair, swabs of his mouth too. Later they come back and release him because none of his DNA could place him at the crime scene. Obviously they didn't know who they were looking for, but none of it was what Junior did. So they let him go. We leave thinking OK now they realize that Junior had nothing to do with it or the case. Little did I know they are still trying to build a case against Junior. So from February, I guess that was the 17th that we went into the police station, we left out there thinking that everything was done, and over with. We all realize that he had nothing to do with it, but from that day all the way up to July 15, 2005 they were still trying to build a case against him.

One of the Congressmen from the Asian community, in Flushing was really pushing to get these guys who killed a young boy. It became very political. He was out for blood, advocating for that family of the delivery man that was killed. It was him pushing the police. I guess when they first brought it out they claimed that there was three suspects in it. They had two; they needed to do whatever they needed to do to get that third. Because they had already arrested Junior, they went after him. They couldn't hold him because they had no evidence; to me it was a personal vendetta to get him. They didn't even look for anyone else, they didn't even try to look into other avenues, who else could

Waiting

this third person could have been to do this crime. They were just gung—ho against Junior and that was all there was to it, case closed.

So, we were going on about our business. Not thinking anything was wrong. My faith is getting stronger; I'm in the church now going to Mt. Horeb just about every Sunday. I'm there, I'm there, and I'm there. The day of my baptism, October 4, 2004, a Chinese woman gets robbed at gunpoint and who do they arrest for the robbery? So they come in my house about two o'clock in the morning, this was a Monday morning and they claim they had a warrant, I don't remember if they had given me a warrant, but that's what they said. I wish I could take all that had happened back and not have opened that door. So I open the door, they push in; they claim they had a warrant. They handcuff Junior, it was four or six of them, white cops. Uh, Junior is in his pajamas, they say you under arrest and Junior say, for what? This is like two o'clock in the morning and I was like where are you taking him. The cop said to the 110 on Corona Avenue, down Junction Boulevard, there's a Pct. I think it's 110. So they see a sweat shirt and throw it to Junior, which I think was rigged, purposely picked, because they just wrapped it around him . . . because the perp who robbed this woman had on a sweatshirt. So, of course, that's the mug shot that they take of him to show this woman, a picture of him in sweatshirt. So I get myself together you know. Junior said they drove him around for about an hour, asking him questions just trying to get him to talk. Then they finally take him to the Pct. I arrive and they let me see him. He says ma I can't understand, and he says the date and I say don't say nothing and I know where you were on that day don't worry. I'm not having it and we not thinking this is going to stick until they charged my son. He was on Riker's Island for a week before I could get the bail money together. They set a bail for him at $2,500 which took me a little bit of time. So I bailed him out. I didn't have any money for a lawyer and we wound up getting a public defender. Our first court date we went back for was November. We went back and forth from November up until July, for the robbery case. All the court dates was postponed because I truly believe they were still trying to build up a case for the murder. Every month he would have to go back to the court for the robbery. And all they would do is adjourn, adjourn, and adjourn. I think they did this so that they knew where he was, they knew where to get him. And when they arrested him for the murder, he was at a court appearance for the robbery, they adjourned it and the cop was right there and they arrested him right then and there. July 18, 2005 for the murder, they had an indictment and they arrested him on that day. He has been incarcerated since July 18, 2005. He was found guilty of murder in January of 2006, sentenced to 53 and 1/3 years to life. The other case came up later and he was found guilty of armed robbery and sentenced to 15 years to life. So he's serving a double life sentence for two crimes he didn't commit.

I'm doing, now I'm fine. I function; I had to keep a certain composure for Junior at his sentence. I had to do the same for my daughter saying he's going to be alright. You know I would go to church, and try and gain strength there you know.

I came to Mt. Horeb in January and from then on everything was happening around me. All while I was in services I was going through. The robbery and all the accusations, all the accusations in February and the robbery and I just, it just depletes you. I had not accepted God yet but I would go hear the Shepherd's sermons.

Like I said I always believed in God, I knew of Him, so those months of going and hearing, was like I guess a light bulb finally going off on what I was told. I was ready to accept God into my life. So it wasn't hard for me to believe to walk by faith, to believe to trust in God. It just clicked in then. At this point in my life I was searching for God, looking for God, looking for a church home for over a year. I was visiting in Manhattan, at Antioch in Brooklyn, I had been searching. This is where I was in my life. I wanted that relationship, so coming to Mt. Horeb was just the missing link and when I found it, oh, my goodness gracious. My sister asked me to come to church with her this particular Sunday. She said the Shepherd is the guy who grew up with us in the neighborhood. My sister had already been coming to Mt. Horeb for a while now. She was visiting; she had not given her life over either. People in the church thought that she was a member she was there so much. So I decided to go with her this particular Sunday. I don't remember the sermon, but all I know was when I walked through those doors and came pass the threshold, I had never felt that feeling

Waiting

before. I felt chills; I want to say the Holy Spirit. I had walked into Antioch, I had walked into Mt. Sinai, and I walked into all these other churches and never felt this way. I walked into Mt. Horeb, and it was just a whole out of body experience. I was whole, a sigh of relief, it was like a burden lifted off my shoulders, it was just like home, you know. I just started coming every Sunday. My sister wasn't coming anymore, but I was still coming. It was just like a matter of time and I was like this is where I want to be. Sunday, after Sunday, I would tell myself, sitting there waiting for the doors of the church to open. I'm getting up there; I'm going to get up. It was September 19, and I didn't talk to myself, I didn't discuss anything with myself as I usually do, we were standing up and the doors of the church were opened. My mom was there, she had just come back from Delaware. Diamond was with me, she was on one side and my mom was on the other side of me. And the doors of the church were open and I don't know something was speaking to me. Like I said, any other Sunday, I'm sitting there debating, mumbling, should I go up there and looking at who was going up there. This day, I was just crying and the next thing I know I said excuse me to Diamond and I was down the aisle. Boo hooing my eyes out, if you look at my form, you would think I couldn't write. You got to fill out your name; my eyes were blurry from the tears. The writing on the form was all crooked I would love to see that piece of paper right now. I couldn't write for nothing. It was an overwhelming feeling and it just happened. It came, like I said right on time for me to commit myself to God completely, turn my life over to God completely, cause He knew I needed Him for what I was getting ready to go through. Throughout the trial, you know, I prayed, the Shepherd kept me prayed up. The Shepherd was there with me when he could be there you know. That kept my strength up.

Oh, my goodness gracious, I was so excited about getting baptized, even the Shepherd saw how excited I was. I remember when I came out the water; the Shepherd said he never saw anybody come out the water like I did. He said Miss Lead you were just glowing. I have a picture of me with my eyes closed, and when he dunked me I remember when I came up I wish somebody would have taken a close up picture, because I came up smiling. I had a huge smile on my face when I came out that water. And I was just excited that whole day, it was just overwhelming to finally get baptized at age 37 it's like I'm finally here. After all I had been through the search for a church home and this and that. My mom, Diamond, Junior, my sisters everybody was with me that whole time. He and my nephews went out to the store for about an hour. Maybe an hour and a half and that is when they are trying to say he left my nephews, went over in Elmhurst, as a matter of fact he went got a bike, robbed a woman at gun point, beat her up, and came back all within an hour and a half and we all lied for him, and we all lied.

It's funny I never gave up on God. My being a mom got to me, because all through the trial, they were lying on my son. I was strong and I knew God is doing this, keeping me strong. I also knew there was a purpose for this, a reason for this you know. I didn't know what it was you know, but I kept saying we are going to get through this Junior. When they found him guilty, I was OK; I left the court, telling myself you going to be alright. It was at his sentencing that I lost it. I remember the Shepherd was there, when he got the guilty verdict, at his sentencing it was my mom, all three of my sisters and a friend of Junior's. We left the court room. Junior was 17 when he got incarcerated. After they gave him his sentence, me, my sisters and the girl, one of his friends, we went into the bathroom and I just lost it. I lost it. I decided that this was it for me. I completely lost it. I remember, I remember the walls, the stalls were right there, the doors are this way, but the walls was right there and we all was all walking to the bathroom and there was this stall and I kept walking and when I hit it, I just crumbled, I just couldn't believe it. My sisters, I just looked to them, I was crying but nothing was coming out of my mouth and my sisters was like let it go, let it go, just let it go. And I cried for a good while on that bathroom floor. After that I stopped coming to church. I think maybe for about two months. I was a mom that was in shock. I could not believe it that the lies outweighed the truth. I felt I was so mislead. I was mislead into thinking the truth would prevail. The Shepherd reached out to me and asked me to come see him. I went to see the Shepherd during that week after it happened, I remember sitting in his office. I guess he wanted to see what kind of shape I was in. He questioned me, he asked me, are you mad at God. I said no. It's not, I'm not mad at God

Waiting

and my faith is not wavering but all I know I told him I'm a mom and that's all. I'm not a Christian, I'm not a . . . I'm a mom right now who is feeling for her son and I just need time and I just needed time for myself. That's what that was. It wasn't that I didn't trust God anymore. It wasn't that I didn't believe in His word or none of that. As a parent to me you are supposed to protect your children. I couldn't protect him, I just couldn't protect him. It all just threw me for a loop and I just lost it and kept to myself.

I really got fed up with people. I hated for people to say to me you still got to take care of Diamond. That use to drive me crazy, you know. I would just sit there and listen to them. I didn't say anything bad, but in my head I was like I'm a mother to Junior and Diamond, I'm not just a mother to Diamond. I know I have to still take care of Diamond, I know I have to be there for Diamond. I know that, but every time somebody said that to me, you gotta take care of your daughter, which use to cut me to the core. I use to . . . oh my God . . . , I use to, I wanted to hit them, I really wanted to. My oldest sister just took Diamond under her wing and kept her on the weekends for me because she knew I needed time to whatever. She would say, we got Diamond, don't worry about it, or Diamond is going to spend the night with me tonight. I was like OK. I was just moving. I was functioning but I was really out of it. All his life I've been there for him. I got him out of stuff, in school when he got in trouble. I was able to go up there and talk with the teachers in the school or what have you. Being able to fight for him, speak on his behalf. I couldn't do it this time. I had to sit in that court room like everybody else. I couldn't stand up and say you know you got the wrong person. I couldn't defend him, you know. I know he was relying on me, I couldn't afford an attorney, who could really fight for him. I didn't get a paid attorney. I didn't, there are a lot of things that I didn't do during that trial. People would come up to me, friends, why didn't you let me know. I knew somebody this and I knew that. My faith was that strong that I didn't think that I needed outside intervention from anybody, you know. I was waiting, the truth was going to come through you know. So I just tried to let our legal system . . . the law do the right thing and it failed us. I was so naive. I was so mislead.

This Walk Ain't Right! But, Help Is Along The Way

Like I said when I lost it, I stayed away from church because I didn't want to be around anybody. I just needed to be by myself you know. I wasn't open, I wasn't accepting, and I was really shutting down, completely. I needed to be, go through, whatever I needed to go through. When I left the Shepherd's office that day he put his hand out to me he said come on let us pray. I wouldn't put my hands to his hands. I wasn't really open to this right now. I wasn't ready to receive that right now. I said, you pray for me. I knew I wouldn't receive it. I wasn't going to pray for the heck of it when I wasn't open to it. Like I said, I was sad, I was sad for Junior, I was so depressed. Every night, I crawled into bed and didn't know what was happening to my son. I was like is that TV show Oz for real? Is someone messing with my 18 year old son?

I was so messed up. I contemplated suicide, to the point I was in the tub with the knife in my hands. I know God was there with me, because I had run a nice hot bath, had the knife on the side of the tub, I got in the tub cause I read and saw it can be done this way on TV. I'm a punk I wanted it to be less painful. I told myself all I had to do was slit my wrists and the blood will slowly leak out and I could go to sleep and die painlessly. I had that knife right at my wrist. And my veins are very visible and I pressed it against my wrist and then I just had all thoughts of Junior was rushing to my mind, not even Diamond. All thoughts of Junior came in my head. I remembered when he was at Riker's, incarcerated before he got sentenced, every weekend I visited him you know. I was there. At that moment all types of thoughts of Junior came to my head. Who's going to visit him this weekend? Who's going to be there for him? Who's going to fight for him? We had to fight to right this wrong. Who's going to fight for him like you? Your mother will fight that battle like nobody else's business. His grandmamma loves him, his aunts love him, but they're not his mother who is going to fight that battle like nobody else's business but you. Then I prayed and I put the knife down and I didn't do it.

I still went to see Jr. even though I was all messed up inside, I went to see my son with great faith. Every time I went there he had a big old Kool-Aide smile on his face. When he wrote me he spoke about his sentence of 53 and 1/3 years to life. It's funny he is facing all that time

Waiting

and, every time I went to see him that same smile was there. This is five years later and that smile has never left him. From the time he was sentenced, his sprit has not been broken. Junior wrote me a letter and in that letter he said mom, we really got to pray hard, and Junior is not even saved. He's been exposed to God, he knows about God the way I knew from growing up, I wouldn't force him to go to church but he would go when I would go. So he wrote me that letter and he said we really got to pray now. Get down on your knees type of prayer. I was at church that next Sunday. I had stopped going to church and my mom would call me and ask are you going to church today, I would answer no I'm not going today. And I got that letter from Junior on a weekday and after he said what he said and I said pity party over. Junior's alright, you need to get it together and you going to be alright too. And ever since then I just keep getting stronger and stronger.

The Shepherd's watch night service was it for me. The turning point was, he had a coffin at the altar and he told us that people are walking around holding on to some stuff. We needed to bury it and let it die. He told us to write those things on paper and come up and place them in the coffin, for me that was my real breakthrough, that day, that night. I put my little piece of paper in that coffin and left it there at that altar. And I was like I believe, I believe. That was the pinnacle for me moving forward from this point on. There is a reason, a purpose for Junior to being there. My thoughts were, like I said; I can't teach him everything he needs to know as a man. The reality was Junior was out in the streets, some of his friends are involved in gangs. I know that there are things now that Junior tried to indulge in and God felt that, if he continued on his path worse can happen. God allowed this situation to show him that this is not the place where he wants to be. Even for the little bit of stuff that he was in, or what you think you may want to get involved in, it equates to jail, it's not where you want to be. So I'm a let you get into something that you didn't do and this is where you going to be. I don't know what Junior's purpose is going to be when he comes home, but I believe that he is going to come home and use this experience for good. His friends look up to him so I don't know if he's going to make an impact on their lives in some kind of way or what, you know. But God is using Junior for some reason and

This Walk Ain't Right! But, Help Is Along The Way

I'll see it when he comes home. He's also using me for some reason. I wish it was just me though, for a sacrifice but not my child. I'd rather me than him, I'd rather me than my sisters, I'd rather He use me. The first question people asked me after Junior got sentenced is, how are you doing, how can you deal? My answer is always its God, that's all that is. My strength comes from Him. Nothing else and nobody else, you know. They say I don't know if I could do it, I say if you believe yes you could, if you believe yes you could.

From the time I got baptized the one thing that stuck in my head that the Shepherd said, was "just because you turned your life over, doesn't mean that bad things are not going to happen. Hard times, you are not immune to them. When you turn your life over to God bad things still happen to you." I remember that clearly when he talked to us. The bad stuff that I'm going through and what Junior is going through and what Diamond is going through I look at it as it gets easier. I'm not going to say that I still don't get upset. I mean plenty of times I cried, and still cry, which is evident right now, you know. The tears are not hopelessness tears, it's just when I think about Junior and where he is, even though I believe with all my heart that he is coming home when God sees fit for him to come home, you know. But to think about him there, yeah I might still get sad, and yeah I'm going to cry, and feel bad you know, because of where my son is and because of what he is going through. Regardless of what the devil meant I know God is going to turn this situation around. There are days at church when the spirit hits me and I am a blubbering fool. Those tears are good tears because I feel His comfort. It's just overwhelming, you know. It's great, just to see him move, and then there are times, what I'm learning now, is that God will be there step by step by step and you can't shake him. This is what I am going through right now. The appeals are starting to go through for Junior, and I'm about to watch God move it's like blowing me the freak away. He's been here but never like this to me before. Like I said something will happen and I'll be like, thank you God and He would have come and gone and I'm blown away with my afterthoughts. People said that appeals take five years; Junior's appeal has taken three years so far. If he's going to do all this time, it'd be five years before something happens. Appeals are

Waiting

in the mix right now. Hasn't even been a complete three years yet. So when people say it takes usually five years, it ain't happening. So I'm like overwhelmed; I'm like trying to fix my mind in case this isn't the time. I'm not going to get too high up there and God's like no it's not time for him to come home yet. But I'm watching Him work right now and it's just like, it's just blowing me away. The case they built against my son is falling apart brick by brick.

People said it wasn't going to happen for years, and they are bugging out by what's going on and what not. God's working on Junior, and God's working on me, because my walk is stronger. I'm trying to be so much more obedient, to God's will, to God's way, to His word. I study more, you know, my talks with Him are more, when before it wasn't. I have Bible study at the church, every Wednesday. I have Bible study three days a week at my job. There is a group of us, we are on *Exodus* now. I'm trying to be a true tither and the Shepherd's sermon last week on the bailout providing for the Kingdom, it's so where I am right now, you know. Tithing is like each year, I talk to God, I say I'm going to be a good tither and I want to, and I do know that I want to; I'm a giving person period you know. So each year we have this talk, and each year I fall short. And I told myself that this year, so far, praise God, I've been a true tither.

But, I said I don't care if my Con Ed is about to be cut off, I got candles, I don't care I believe. So, I'm like, as much as I have seen Him put His hand on me in so many different ways how can I not., I'm just so overwhelmed by God's goodness. When people see me now in church, before the tears was sad tears certain sermons the Shepherd would preach, or the dance ministry would be ministering, just the song would touch me in a way, it was just . . . But now, my tears are happy, thankful to God, it's just not sadness, it's just not that anymore you know. I'm just like; I'm going to praise You. Its tears of excitement, it's overwhelming. It's just so many positive emotions.

I gave it up to God. I said here take Junior, take Diamond, just here. A lot of what I went through with Junior I didn't share with my mom, with my sisters, cause watching my mom being sad, I can't take that. I could understand her sadness because you don't want to see your children suffer or hurt. So a lot of stuff I wouldn't share I just held it all in. I acted like, like I'm OK. I knew for me to cry on my mom's shoulders would just bring her down. I just didn't want to be a burden to anybody by putting all my stuff on somebody else. That's just how I am, I just carry it, and carry it, and carry it. I'm independent like that, and then I gotta ask God.

It's hard sometimes. It's not that I don't think it's going to happen, it's just He does things in His own time. He puts you through stuff just to show you who He is. So I'm like, I'm excited that things are happening sooner than they are supposed to. And that's Him telling me that if I say it's going to be five years, it going to be five years. If I say things are going to happen in three years, then it's going to be three years. That's how I do, it's not according to the courts, and it's not according to me. So I am not getting caught up saying, oh what if the appeals don't start coming back. I already know that if it doesn't come back the way it is we just got to fight another battle. It wasn't His will to let it happen right now, but it's just His way of saying I Am God, and I am here and I can move things and let things happen. So that's why I mean I'm not trying to get too excited, cause it might not be His will right now, but I know His will, will l be done eventually. I know something is going to happen, I just don't know when. So all while this is taking place, I'm watching Him move. I'm getting excited you know. I see You doing stuff God that other people say it ain't the norm but He ain't the norm. So I'm watching and I know He will show, He will reveal Himself to me. That's why, I try to hold tight and not get too excited, before He knocks me down a few pegs. Let me just do what I'm doing. So that's where I am. My sisters know that the appeal is in the works, now. I have my prayer warriors who know, there are a hand full of people who know. My best friends don't know and I'm not like broadcasting it. I'm letting God do it. Like I said I asked certain people to be my prayer warriors, pray with me. I've been fasting; this is how I wait on the Lord, sit back. It started with prayer and . . . I know my walk is different from others but we all have to learn to wait on God. Anytime you think it's just you going through stuff all you have to do is talk to someone. Like my Bible study group that I have at work. We sit and we talk and you know we have gotten closer and we share stuff and we learn stuff about each other. To look at them, you wouldn't

Waiting

think that they go through with what they go through. Hearing their story may not be the same as my story, but it's a story in itself. And it's like they've gotten through it. And you think it's just you, but God is everywhere with everyone. It's just like WOW! Like that song, *"He's Got the Whole World in His Hands"* and it's so true.

I'm beginning to understand my purpose. I really don't know what exactly I'm supposed to do. I know what I would like to do, I would like to help people, with what I am going through, that's my avenue to speak to women, or help mothers who have sons who are incarcerated, or anyone who has someone who is incarcerated go through that journey. It wasn't easy going up to Riker's Island to see my 17 year old child. Riker's is one of the worse institutions out there. It was hard going up there and being searched and being treated like you are a criminal and being looked down on because you have a loved one incarcerated because they don't know the true story, you don't know my story. So it's that whole experience, even when I had to travel to different facilities when my baby was sent to a prison. My day would start at 2 o'clock in the morning to get to the destination to catch a bus to go see him. To go to a facility at 8 o'clock in the morning, having to stand outside waiting for the doors to open, rain or shine, cold or hot, you know. And seeing other women like me older than me, my age, with kids, with little babies, you know. So I don't know if I'm supposed to be an encouragement for somebody, or supposed to help somebody get through it. I don't know, I mean when my father was incarcerated, I never went to visit him. My mother never took us to visit him. But I wrote him constantly. I still have the letters from my father. My father, each bid he did, I did it with him. I've had friends who have been incarcerated. I've did bids with them too sending packages, you know writing the letters. I have pen pals with people who are incarcerated, who I have never met. We've lost contact since then, but I've never, ever looked down on someone who has been incarcerated. I've tried to be there for people who have been incarcerated. So I guess now, God is blessing me, because I've been a blessing for someone else. So, He is protecting Junior you know, unless Junior is a very good actor. He's hasn't been hurt, his spirit hasn't been broken. None of the negative things that could happen; maybe all of those years I have been there for others who were incarcerated, my blessing is coming now, that my son has been incarcerated. He's being protected and taking care of, avoiding stuff that could go wrong, and what not.

A Born Encourager

I've been a closet poet, I don't even want to say a poet, and I would say a writer. I like to write. When I think of a poet, I thing of Nikki Giovanni, Maya Angelou, Langston Hughes, Phyllis Wheatley, you know, people of that caliber and that's not me, I call my poetry fluff. I'm real hard on myself; I mean the piece I did for Black History Month was not fluff, that's not fluff. But the majority of my stuff, it's not like Maya Angelou, not that I am belittling what I do, but I just don't see it up there with them. That's just not what I'm supposed to be, it's just not the poetry that I'm supposed to write. I'm supposed to write the poetry that I'm writing for whoever it's supposed to fit. The first poem I ever wrote was supposed to be my stepping stone. That's just my personality. I'm a, when I see a stray dog, I help a stray dog. It's just me, if I am able to help; I'm going to help you.

In the late 90,'s, me and four of my girlfriends, we started a women's group called Star Rise, and we had a big old mission. Star Rise stands for Sisters Together and Rising in Self-Empowerment. We had this desire to encourage women, some of us were single mothers, we were that lower middle class type and we wanted to be an encouragement to young teens and talk to them and guide them. We all had different things that were going on and the group stopped. We were doing empowerment seminars, we were going into groups, and we were motivated. One member was leaving New York and it was put on hold, I was out numbered. I remember crying that day. I said if we stop now, we ain't going to get it back together, we never got back together in the end. I was left with wanting to help people. When I went to Baruch, my major then was computer information system, cause that was the biggest thing coming up. I don't know why but I just put my major down. Did my little two years, had Junior, left college and wind up getting into the work force. I worked in the finance department, accounts receivables, accounts payable, financial analyst, so I was into

Waiting

accounting and that was my field for years. I wanted to go back to school for accounting. I got a certificate for bookkeeping and started doing things to build towards that. When I go back to Baruch, which I plan on doing, sometime, my major would be sociology that is what I'm going for. And at first, I just wanted like the easiest thing that I could get. I just want my degree. Then I started looking in the book at the majors, and I was like I could do something with this you know, sociology or something in that field. Maybe that's where I'm headed.

It's funny in all I been through I never said why me. I know Junior has said, not like, why me. He'd question, "Why God is" . . . how he put it? He's questioned it but not in a negative way. He's said I don't know why God is putting me through this. But you know from the time it all started I said God is not putting you through this, God is letting you go through this for a reason. And the reason why we don't know yet because God thoughts are not our thoughts and His ways are not our ways. Like I said, since he's been incarcerated one of his friends has been murdered, one of his friends has been shot, and I know if he was home he would have been with them in those situations or with them at that party, at that event Junior is a protector. Junior won't start a fight, but you get him into a fight, he will fight, he will fight for you. His friends always came to get him, they needed him. This use to drive me mad; I would say tell your friends to walk away, don't come get you.

Right now Junior is in a maximum state facility with harden criminals. I thank God for his persona. Junior doesn't have this bravado, macho thing. He's kind hearted and he shares, Junior doesn't want for nothing while he is incarcerated. Now I have learned to stop doing without because, me and Diamond, we was struggling because I didn't want his account to have a negative balance. He's got food there. We were going to my mother's house because I was at a point when I felt he shouldn't be there and while he's there I'm going to make him as comfortable as I can regardless. We did without, went without, my sisters made sure Diamond had. They would always say bring Diamond over for dinner; they just picked up on what I was doing. My whole mind set had definitely changed, and I now realize that I was dealing with some guilt for not being able to stop him from going there. It took a lot for me to realize that it's not about me you know. It was nothing that I could have done differently. It was already mapped out what was going to happen. We could have still had a paid lawyer and Junior would have had to go through whatever, he just needed to go through. I have heard this same sermon preached throughout this time. God will remove you from families, from friends, from situations. He will remove you for whatever reason. It comes back to the question of can a woman raise a son; I couldn't at that point in his life. I believe the only way God can help Junior out or make me see is to take Junior away from me. I could not keep him from the streets. Granted he was able to avoid getting caught up into the gangs. I used to tell him who's to say that one of them won't say, hey roll with us and then you get caught up in something. He would say I know mommy, I put him on punishment for two weeks at a time. That was not enough. I guess you gotta be harder on a guy. I wasn't that hard. Yeah I demanded respect; you listen to what I say. But when he walks out that door, Junior was on his own. He had to learn whatever it was to being a man when he walked out that door; it was what mommy couldn't teach him. To me God was like alright, I got to take the reins cause daddy is not doing, he's on drugs. That's the way I see it was part of my process my growth. I had to come to terms with why he's there. It was the streets, death, gangs, drugs or prison. I'll take prison for 100 ALEX! But he's been safer there than Southside Jamaica. So you know I'll take that, that's my faith. That's what I believe, that's what I'll tell anybody that's in my heart, that's in my walk, in my everything. When I read the Bible that's what I see, this is my living proof of what I've been reading so far. I'm learning and growing through what the Shepherd is teaching, preaching, my Bible studies at my job, the Bible studies on Wednesdays, conferences, women's revival, women's ministry, this is it and that's it for me. I've evolved from 2004 you know, that's where I've evolved from. It's not mine to fight, God gave these kids to me to love, to nurture, to take care of the best way I can and everything else God will do.

Now I'm a pure water head at church. But for the longest, I would, hold it in because I thought crying is a sign of weakness. I thought you just can't, you gotta be strong. All that just festered in me. I now know in your walk it's OK to cry. I also know we are not supposed to have a spirit of fear and I'm not, I'm not afraid, it's OK to have mixed

Waiting

emotions, you are still human. I'm not going to pretend to be holier than thou, but I'll shout out about the goodness of God. But if I'm weak, if I'm sad or all these other emotions, I'm not going to be scared to let it out. I'm not going to put on a front. Well you know God is this and God is that. Yes, I believe that wholeheartedly, but if I need to cry my eyes out and release, it's OK to cry your eyes out and release. He already knows what's in your heart period. So you don't have to put on this, what I call a Christian front. God is this to you, and God is that you know. I'm not going to be that way; I don't wanna be that person you know. It's OK to let it out because you are human. Jesus let it out so you gonna question Him, you gonna question God. I'm watching Him do His thing and after it's all said and done whatever His decision may be, I'm going to say, well alright. My thing is your walk is going to take you through some stuff! God is going to pick you back up no matter what you go through; He's going to see you through. I believe that wholeheartedly. I believe that there will be times of sadness, and you will cry and you will get that way depending on your situation. Yes, but I am a Christian and yes, I'm God's child, but I am Junior and Diamond's mother too. I'm flesh, I'm not perfect. If I was, I'd be Him and I'm not that. I'm working towards being as close as I can be to what he wants me to be.

My children's disappointments are going to hurt me you know, and their joys are going to excite me because I'm their mother. God made me that way. So regarding your walk, your faith, believe what you read, believe what the Bible says wholeheartedly. I would say take baby steps, move at your own pace. Don't move at anyone else's pace. Don't try to be what someone else is in their walk. So I'm moving at a tortoise's pace. I'm fine with that. I'm in my two little ministries and I am fine with that you know. I'll be a cleanup crew, a cooking crew; I would sit in any other ministry God wants me to. But I'm not going to overwhelm myself with so much stuff that it's taking away from my walk. I think I'm in the areas where I'm supposed to be. Caretaker, I'm with women, helping to motivate women. If I'm being an inspiration to others, that's great. I'm with Miss Understood in the drama ministry that's where my creative juices are flowing and you know Miss Understood is an inspiration to me. So I'm in the two places where I'm supposed to be and I'm fine with that. I am so good while I wait for deliverance.

Wow! What a story. Now don't I feel like a whiny brat? Miss Lead your story is so deep. You are so strong and you have been through so much. I understand what you mean about helping and/or inspiring people gives you strength. You inspire me in so many ways. If you can walk around with your head up with all that you are dealing with then so can I. You never know what a person is facing until you sit down and talk to them. Miss Lead really understands that Jesus is love. No matter what she is going through she tries to express and show love. When you read the Bible you see that is what Jesus did. Although he knew his purpose and knew he had rough times ahead he walked around showing love and kindness. He encouraged, He inspired. You are so right, I can wait on God because I know what he has done in my life. In the meantime I know I have to trust him and draw from what I have learned from Him and you. Our time is not His time and I can wait because He is in the process of working things out. I believe that and now I have to work on me. Miss Lead told me don't worry Miss Guided, God will help you through.

While I'm Waiting, I Guess I Will Check Me Out

After the meeting I went back home to truly reflect on Miss Leads story. I don't remember anything we discussed in the meeting because I was so taken back by Miss Leads story. I was led to go to the dictionary to look up the word wait. It stated, *do nothing; a period of time spent while expecting something to happen.* I realized at that moment I was misguided by how I perceived waiting. I thought waiting was being dismissed, left on hold, forgotten, in limbo, others first me second. I realized I was so wrong. To wait is to pause and let God work out the plan He has developed for me. He needs time to work things out and prepare me for what's next. So I had to develop some in the meantime self-exploration activities. I decided that starting tomorrow I will have a lengthy devotion in the morning spending quality time with God. I will wait to hear from Him now. I also have to do a lot of self exploration to ensure that I am operating in love. I have to ask myself:

Waiting

1. Have I ever shunned anyone, wounded anyone?
2. Have I ever looked at people the wrong way in a worship service?
3. Have I ever made someone feel lesser than me because they had a disability or addiction?
4. Did I ever decide I would not connect with a person based on how they were dressed not knowing their circumstances?
5. Have I judged people's praise because they praised differently than I do?
6. Have I passed judgment on someone based on someone else's opinion?
7. Have I ever said or done something to make a person want to leave the service?

Then I asked God, if I have done this or anything else to hurt someone to please forgive me, and show me what I could do to make people feel comfortable, to uplift and encourage them to deepen their relationship with You. His answer was then and continues to be work on the Women's Conference and you will continue to grow and develop. I also learned that my child is always watching just as I was when I was little. I have to teach her about relationship not religion. I have to teach her about compassion not compromise, I have to teach her about love. I have to teach her that the first commandment is you should love the Lord your God with all your might, your heart and soul and the second most important commandment is you shall love your neighbor as yourself. That means that you have to love yourself. I really think if you don't get the Jesus relationship right then all your relationships are going to be problematic. Jesus is love and if you know that then you will treat yourself and others with love. Therefore you just can't go around hurting people's feelings. This is the beginning of a beautiful relationship. I was so busy trying to be religious that I didn't make the Jesus connection. I truly found the missing link. When I met the Shepherd he exposed me to a sermon that brought me back. This was the sermon that made me truly understand who Jesus truly is. Can you imagine I was going through life without connecting with Jesus? I realized that I believed in God but I was not familiar with Jesus, His purpose and what He did for me. The next morning I ran into the Shepherd and he dropped these words of wisdom on me.

The Shepherd Speaks On Waiting on God
Waiting on God—Isaiah 40:31: So many times throughout the course of life we get spiritually weak along the way. We won't pray. We won't attend service regularly. We just won't when it comes down to the things of God. We must understand our strength is in God, and when we won't, God will!
The eagle eye Prophet Isaiah had a keen insight on the things of God based upon his experience with God. In Isaiah Chapter 6, we see the Prophet at a low point in his life after the death of King Uzziah. Once Isaiah experienced the transforming power of God in his life, he then realized that God is often waiting on us to see Him for who He is. He is God and God alone.
It is important for the believer to stay close to God. In spite of what you may be going through in your life, don't get discouraged to a point where you want to give up! God wants you to soar . . . "mount up with wings as eagles." God wants you to have stamina for the race . . . "run and not be weary." God wants you to be steady . . . "walk and not faint." "Wait I say on the Lord!"

Deliverance

The Fifth Set of Footprints:
2 Timothy 4:18

Hey Lord I'm Drowning,
Throw Me a Life Preserver!

Wow that Shepherd really knows how to sum things up. I was ready to start my day with a new attitude. I took my daughter to dance school today at the children's cultural center. I am trying to keep her occupied because she is really missing her father. She believes it's her fault that he is not around. Pooh has always loved to dance and this is something that I felt she could get into to make her feel better about herself. I have found that bad things happen in life which we don't always understand. This can result in diminished self-esteem. I figured she will feel better about herself when she gets on stage and the audience is applauding her efforts. In my trainings I try to tell people all the time that good self-esteem can't be taught in a classroom. It's not lost in a class room unless something bad happened in class therefore it can't be corrected in a classroom.

I went outside to smoke a cigarette and I ran into my friend I met here at the dance school, Miss Taken. There is something about her that I was drawn to the moment I met her. We were outside smoking one day and she told me she worked in a rehab and I thought she would be great as a women's conference committee member. She joined the committee and we have been cool ever since. We work well together; she's a lot like me. Although we connected we never had time to get to know each other. We felt this was a good time to talk since we had to wait for our daughters. I asked her how she got into rehabilitation work and she said wow that's a long story. Then she said well we've got the time so she began telling me her story.

Taken

I was a happy baby. Honestly my mother and I never really talked about my birth. I know my cousin Stuart and I were really close, before he died and his mother and my mother went into the hospital at the same time to have us. I came three days before him. It was always him and me and then my sister came, 11 months later. I was always happy we were always together. Most of the time in my life I stayed with my grandmother; I don't remember my mother talking about what labor was like or how long it took to have me or those things, we really never talked about that. I mean, we talked about me, I was a happy baby, I was always around everybody and I always wanted to be on the go, but we really never sat down and talked labor and delivery.

We lived with my maternal grandmother and grandfather, at first and then my mother and father got their own place. My father was an entertainer, my mother was too, she was a singer. When I was about five, this is my most vivid remembrance, about my parents; I remember they were having a fight and some woman, well I know now my step-brother's mother, came to the window for my father. My mother and father had a big fight, and I remember my father hit her and my mother called my Uncle Junior and told him about it. She said this is it, she's going back home, she wasn't staying with him anymore and she wanted him to leave. I remember my Uncle Junior coming there and hitting my father. I remember him going over the other side of the couch and I remember thinking, not knowing which one to go to, my mother or my father. Since I didn't know which one to run to, I just cried. I just stood there and cried. I remember holding on to my sister Monica, Nancy wasn't born yet. I remember it was just yesterday, like I've never forgotten that memory. And then we went to live with my grandmother. So that's like the one memory I have and I think I was about five or six years old.

I've always protected my sister, Monica, since birth, since she came into this world. My sister, Monica, was born its funny . . . we never

Deliverance

talked about my birth. But I always knew that my birth was this happy occasion and my father came into the hospital. You know little things they would tell me here and there; I've always known that my birth was a happy occasion. It was a happy time for my parents and a happy time for my grandparents. I was the first. My Aunt Gail, she couldn't have kids and she wanted me. She use to try and tell my mother to let her have me. You know, the kid that everybody loved and I got love from everybody. My sister Monica on the other hand, I was only eleven months old when my mother had my sister. So she got pregnant right away. My father always wanted a boy so he called down to the hospital and asked them what it was. When he found out that it was a girl, he wouldn't come. I always knew that story, I don't know who told it to me or where I got it from, but I know it to be true because I always heard other people say it, I always felt like for some reason, it was just me and her against the world. I always protected her since she was born; ever since I was old enough to even know what it was to take care of somebody. She has always been the person I have to make sure was alright.

My grandparents, at that time, they were very well off. We lived in Bermuda and my grandfather took care of all of us. So we had this really, really large house up on a hill. The whole family kind of lived there. I guess my grandfather was one of those men who was kind of like over his family and told everybody what to do. He seemed like he was a very powerful man, but I don't really remember him cause he died right after I was born. But I know he was definitely one of those head of the family kind of men. So, like, everybody moved. Most of the family still came back for like Sunday dinners, at my grandmother's house, it was like that kind of thing. Yeah, we lived in Bermuda until I was ten. Me and my father were very close, he would come and get me and Monica and he would take us places. I just remember him taking us around a whole bunch of different women, cause my father was like really a womanizer. We had other siblings from him. My brother Darryl and my sister Gia. He would get all of us as kids; we would all hang around each other and stuff like that. Gia is, I think like maybe a year younger than me and Darryl is about two years younger, about Nancy's age.

We started going to St. John's Church about I guess when we were like seven or eight maybe. I began to go to church with my grandmother. My grandmother has always been there in every memory I have as long as I can remember. I remember her waking up in the morning, putting her legs on the side of the bed and reaching for her Bible, before she got out the bed, before she went to the bathroom, before she did anything, she would wake up, her legs would swing over the side of the bed. She would sit there and read her Bible, that was the first thing she did every single day. I definitely always remembered her doing that before she did anything. She was Baptist; her church was St. John's Baptist Church in Bermuda.

I don't even remember my mother going to church until we were like older, until we got much older. I don't remember even going to church with my mother. That was something she did, we didn't talk about it.

We were like really happy, really happy kids. We never wore shoes, we came home, I mean we wore shoes to school, but you came home from school and kicked off your flip flops. It was never, really cold outside or anything. All the kids would say meet me down, let's go jump off the cliff. We would you know go home drop off our books, and like run, go run to the water, like the water was like five minutes from my grandmother's house and we would run to the river, jump off the cliff and run back, what we use to call "a coming back up the road," we'd run back up the road. My grandmother lived on top of the hill too, she lived further up from us and we would run up the hill to her house, run down the hill to get soda Pop, like we basically had a real childhood. It was just all of us, me, Harry, Samantha, and my sister Monica. My mother and her brother were the only two who had kids. My Aunt Joy and Aunt Bell didn't have kids. So my Uncle Junior had my cousin Harry and Samantha and my mother had me, Monica and Nancy at that time. Nancy came like when I was about six, yeah cause I'm six years older than her. My mother brought her home; I never connected with Nancy when she was a baby. I don't remember, I mean now, of course, she's my best friend, but when we were kids we never really had that real connection with her. I always say it's because me and Monica remind my mother of too much pain. You know, my father put my mother through a lot of stuff. I always remember my mother kept crying over my father. I never really remember her smiling because there was always something he did. All I ever remember him bringing my mother was pain and he was the light of my life. Monica also felt he could do no wrong. As for my mother, I always remember her crying over something; like he was with other women. He was an entertainer. My father and his father were the biggest thing going on in Bermuda when I was a kid. When you came off the plane they were signing autographs at the airport, you know, all of the girls would come down there and all they wanted to do is be with my father and grandfather, and my Uncle Gus. They made that song "*This is Bermuda*." They were famous. Everything he did, everything they touched, people wanted to be with them. And I didn't find out until later that my father was getting high. I was sure that was a large part of what was going on with my parents too. My mother never used drugs, I mean my mother never used drugs!

So, when I was nine, between eight and nine, my mother met this man, his name was John. Now as I look back, part of my mother's problem was that she just loved my father, she just loved him so much, she just loved him. So in order to get away from the pain, she tried to start new relationships. She met Nancy's father and that didn't work out. She had my sister and she was still in love with my father, it was just that simple. So she couldn't move on down there. So she met this man, John and was with him for like a year. She was already ready to marry him, come to New York and live with him. Me and my mother fought about this for a very long time, because she stripped us. Ma took us away from everything we knew. We didn't have no say so in it; she brought us to New York and she changed our last name and she had no right to do that. So our name was Smith in order for her to bring us up here, to get that green card, we had to have the same last name as her because she married him. She asked my father to let him adopt us, so we ended up getting his name. She brought us up here; we came up here, and moved to Corona. I remember coming to the U. S., and leaving Bermuda, I was very, very hurt, we didn't want to leave our friends and our family and stuff. We came up here to nobody; we had no cousins, no nothing. I was also a little like excited too. New York was a big place; I had never been off that island. Bermuda is . . . , you

This Walk Ain't Right! But, Help Is Along The Way

could probably fit Bermuda inside of Manhattan and probably have room left, that's how little our island is.

I remember being in the fourth grade and coming up here and seeing snow for the first time, you know sitting in the classroom and it started to snow. I ran to find my sister and the teacher was saying you can't leave the classroom. I remember, I flew out the classroom and telling Monica it's coming out the sky. We ran outside and we started screaming. It was the first time we had ever seen snow. We really never believed that it came out the sky. We would say it don't really come out the sky. We never really understood as kids that you all had the same sky as us, so how come our sky didn't have snow falling out of it. In Bermuda TV came on at 11 a.m. and it went off at 11 p.m. and you got two stations. We are a British Colony, so we talk like people from England. So anyway, when we came up here and TV came on and stayed on, I was like wow and I didn't want to go to sleep. I didn't do anything wrong, I was this good little kid cause all I wanted to do was watch TV, just stay in the house and watch TV all the time. Then my parents, well John bought a house in Bayside. We were living in Corona for a year when we moved to Bayside, I was ten and just turning eleven. We had this really nice house. Me, Monica and Nancy, we never really paid John no mind, like I don't even remember them even getting married, I don't even remember anything about their wedding or going to a wedding or nothing like that. I don't talk to my mother about him cause that's just a whole another story. I think we was in that house six months and one day he came home early, my mother was working two jobs, and I caught him trying to do something to my sister Monica. She was crying and she was telling me she didn't want to sleep outside on the bed because he was going to come and take her and all this stuff. So I took her, we had bunk beds in our room, so I put her in the bed behind me in the bottom bunk. He came in the room one night and he told me to come here and I went in the room and started crying that he better leave us alone. He started to tell me if I start telling my mother he would kill my mother if I didn't listen to him. I did what he told me to do. I went into the room and he started touching me. It's really weird cause I always wondered what a penis would really look like. I never knew because every time he would bother us it would be

Deliverance

dark, so we really couldn't see him. But, you know, he would make us hold his penis, like literally hold it. So I always wondered, like, what is that thing what does it really look like. I remember thinking that, it's funny the stuff you think about when you are so afraid. I mean I was so afraid of that man. I was so, so really afraid of him and it's funny because as afraid of him as I was, I was more worried that he would do something to my sisters. He was messing with my sister six months before I even knew about it, my sister Monica. So you know, that's when I had the attitude, you are NOT bothering my sister man. I don't care what you do to me, but you are not going to bother her anymore. My sister was very, very afraid of him, it was horrible watching her. I had to protect her.

I remember one time, me and him got into an argument and I told him that you are not bothering me no more. You are going to leave me alone; I ran downstairs to call my mother and went in the kitchen to pick up the phone to call my mother and the lady had me on hold to get my mother to the phone. He came into the kitchen and he had a knife. He came up behind me and he put the knife to my throat and he told me to put the phone down and he told me if I call my mother and told my mother, that he was going to kill my sisters. Then he said whatever I'm doing to you, I'll do to Nancy. She was only like five years old at that time. So you know I was really worried that he would do something to them. That was all I really worried about that he was going to hurt them; I was eleven. By then it was like a whole year of just . . . I was so angry; I've come a long way because I never use to even be able to talk about John without crying. I'm never going to say that I forgave him, cause I don't think I've ever forgiven him, but I've let go, I'm not as angry anymore. I understand that he was a man who had a sickness. I would like to say that was part of my character building process, but you know to some people they would say, "Get out of here!, but the truth of the matter is I got a lot of um, I guess I would say, I got a lot of my strength, like that would never happen to me now. Nobody would be able to do whatever they want to do to me. Part of that comes from what he did and the care taking thing comes from that too. So, you know, some good, some pros and some cons from that. I really hated that man, like I really hated him. The only reason he stopped messing with us is because this girl, my mother's friend in Bermuda's, daughter was 18, and she wanted to send her away to school. This was my mother's good friend and she asked her could she come and stay with us. My mother has these lifelong friends, people she's been friends with since she was five, six, seven years old. The lady came up here to stay with us. And he got into a relationship with her. That's the only reason he stopped bothering you. Once this lady, girl came to stay with us he just started having sex with her. So my mother came home early one day, and she caught them together. She called her mother and told her mother what happened. Then my mother told John to get out. The girl ended up being pregnant. I think she had a baby with him. But he left and he moved to California and we never told my mother what really happened until like years later, I must have been like 34 when I told my mother about that.

My grandmother came to stay with us after that. The lady had moved and my grandmother moved up here and she stayed with us. My grandmother always knew, from the day she came back up here. First of all, we spent every summer with her. So in the summer time she would always ask me what was wrong with me cause I never let my sisters out my sight. Like, they couldn't sit in no man's lap. Like my uncles and stuff would try to come and hug us or kiss us and I would tell them get off her, leave her alone. My uncle, he would be like Miss Taken what's wrong with you? I would be like nothing. Just like why you got to be hugging on us and everything. We said hi and then I would remove them. So my grandmother always knew. Then we talked about it, I think I was about sixteen and me and my grandmother actively talked about it. But I never told anybody else.

Keep It Moving!

A year and half after John left, my mother met Pop. I never even called him my stepfather. No, but me and him went through a lot, Oh my God. I refused to go to their wedding. I wouldn't. Now, he's gone and she met Pop. My grandmother came to live with us and my grandmother was taking care of us; my mother was working two jobs and I am like twelve now, twelve or thirteen. I met Mr. T and she

Deliverance

meets Pop at the same time both of us met these two men. Pop started coming over and taking us out, trying to talk to us. I met Mr. T; he is my oldest son's father, when I was thirteen. My mother was like bugging out cause I was talking to a boy.

There were only two families in Bayside that was on welfare, the Nathan family and they had seven boys and three girls and the Roberts, who had like twelve kids in their family. Honestly, they were the two families, that everybody's family would be like I better not catch you with those Nathans, I better not catch you with those Roberts. They had so many of them, like older brothers and they did drugs. I liked Mr. T's brother, I didn't like him, his sister and I were real good friends, Wendy. She would say listen you can't be going with Billy cause he ain't really ready for no girls yet and all of this stuff. You need to talk to Mr. T he likes you, that's who you should be talking to. Mr. T was two years older than me. So he was like fifteen when I met him, he was one of the bad boys of Bayside. I think the first time I ever kissed him I was about fourteen or something. I never did nothing with him until I was like sixteen. The first time I had sex with him I got pregnant. So POP was there and we use to fight a lot. I think that's the reason why Mr. T and I got together cause it was always so much fighting in my house. It was sad, but I couldn't, nobody really understands the feelings you hold on to when you go through something like what John put me through. I wasn't really worried about me, but the fear that John or any man could put his hands between either of my sister's legs was just too much for me. Whatever he did to me, I felt like I could handle it, whatever came my way I was supposed to handle it. I was the one who had to take care of us. I really never believed that my mother was strong enough to take care of us. No, I always felt like I had to be the person to have to take care of us; I have to be the person to wipe my mother's tears when my father would hurt her. I felt like I always had to be the person to put a smile back on her face to make everything alright. It was all on me to make it OK. I always felt that's my life. There was a part of me that could see that Pop, could be really good for my mother, but I just couldn't, I couldn't take the chance. Like if he would pick up my sister and put her on his lap, she would cry and I would go crazy; I would be like what are you doing, why are you touching my sister, put my sister down, we don't need no father. I told him that from the first time I met him; we don't need no father, like Keep It Going!

I realize I was mad at my, mother, angry at her for not knowing and the not seeing. Then I would think did she know and did she see and not want to see, all of that kind of stuff. I don't even know how my mother looked at all of that and didn't know nothing was wrong. Just the anger I felt at that man. Like I just, I never gave him a chance, I never gave Pop a chance. From the very beginning I had a sign up that said KEEP IT MOVING STUPID! We were not trying to feel it. I didn't let my sisters like him you know what I'm saying. I always felt like Nancy, betrayed us by liking him, cause that's the only father she knew. She didn't even know what was going on. She don't have no memories; I don't think anybody from the past even really knew that me and Nancy have different fathers. When they speak of being a Smith they always included her. So I don't really know about the story, but we all have the same father, but we don't. So I always felt like the reason my mother could deal more with my sister is because, she looks more like her. Nancy's father is light skin, we know him. She looks at my father, when she looks at us, especially me, cause I look just like my father, we have the same hook nose and everything, and I mean everything. My son, Andy is the spitting image of my father. So I always think that that's why she wouldn't, couldn't ever be really sure of what was going on or didn't want to see it. Maybe she couldn't handle it; it was too much for her. Yeah, you know like it was too painful for her; she's just one of those women, me I am so different, you know I've become such a different woman. I don't have no time or space for no man and I know it's because of that. Like, I know it's the pain that I carry. But me and Pop we use to battle. I mean like one time he hit me in my face. He only hit me one time, he back slapped me with a ring he had on and like I wanted to kill him. I went off on him, like who do you think, you are? I didn't tell my father, because I was angry at him too, how could you let her, make some idiot adopt us what was you thinking about? So I think that's why I ended up wanting stuff, cause I think I just needed something. I needed, I just needed something you know, I don't know what it was, but just in that house, I just always felt like somebody needed to pay attention to me. I don't know.

Deliverance

    Me and Mr. T wound up really getting together when I was sixteen. I got drunk off some Southern Comfort in the bathroom in the gas station across the street from White Castle. Me and my girlfriend were babysitting for this lady that lived on the corner of our street and he came down there. I don't even remember the whole thing, all I remember, was that song *Let's Get It On*. We were singing that song and I don't remember nothing else, cause I was so drunk. I know I got pregnant after that. I remember for the whole time I was pregnant I would lie in the bed. Mr. T. had started smoking weed and I had never tried drugs; I was sixteen and I had not tried anything. He was smoking weed in my room one day and he was blowing it in the bird cage. The bird got out of the cage and started flying around the room like he was crazy. He let the bird fly out the window; I was like you let the bird fly out the damn window! I loved that bird, I really loved that bird. The bird was high; he definitely got the bird high. I was crying, cause you know I really loved that bird and I had the bird for like a year. I was crying, and said you let my bird run away and I'm pregnant. He was like you're what? I hadn't really told anybody yet. My mother never told me about pregnancies and your period and life. She never really told us any of that. I really kept thinking that if I just didn't pay my stomach any mind, the baby would just go away you know, I wouldn't be pregnant. I just kept thinking it was gonna go away, it was gonna go away. And then. I went outside that night and I was telling Joy about the bird and she said if you don't tell your mother that you are pregnant I'm gonna go and tell her myself. It's been too long and you are gonna end up in trouble or whatever. So I went in the house and I was crying and I told my mother that I was pregnant. I remember she turned around and she looked at me. She took me into the bathroom we had downstairs by the kitchen and she beat the crap out of me, like she kicked my ass. I think my mother always had all these dreams for me, but they were her dreams. I wanted to go to Spellman and I was a A+ student, and I was getting scholarships, I was gonna be really something, life was gonna be what she thought would be good for me.

    Anyway she took me to Jamaica Hospital and she made me have an abortion, but I was one week over the time limit I guess to have one of those regular abortions. I had to go into the hospital and stay in there. I had to walk up and down the hallway in pain, in agonizing pain. It was October 20 and I would never forget that crap. October 20, 1974 cause I walked up and down those hallways and up and down those hallways and I was so sick, like I was in so much pain and I was crying and I was crying; and I never even told Mr. T that I was having an abortion. This little old black lady was in there with this white dress with me and when the baby came out she took the baby. I remember that baby like I have never forgotten that, cause it was this, this little; and it had little beginnings of little toes which I guess it was really the beginnings of little feet cause I was four months pregnant. She took it and she swung it in my face and said look, look what you did. And she took it and dropped it into this white bucket. Even to this day, I could hear her drop it, drop this baby into that bucket. Like that really messed me up and I was like crying and crying. I didn't tell my mother about that. Like I never, I never felt that I could really tell her. I never felt like I could really go and talk to my mother about anything. My grandmother was my rock my whole entire life, that's who I told everything to, I talked about everything with her. So, after I had the abortion, my mother put me on birth control pills. I couldn't sleep, I couldn't eat, and I got mad skinny. I had no desire to eat anything. I didn't want to be with people, like I cried all the time. I always knew that I had done something that God would never forgive me for and that's what I used to always tell my grandmother. I did something that God would never, ever forgive me for and it wasn't even my fault because I didn't have any say so. My mother never asked me if I wanted that baby you know what I'm saying. There wasn't even a question, it wasn't no you're having it, it was you're not having it, you know. She never asked me what do you want to do? We did not have that discussion. OK, she beat the crap out me in that bathroom and she beat the crap out of me the next day again. Every time she saw me she was like ready to kill my ass. And then she told me, you have an appointment and this is when the appointment is, and this is where we are going. She took me to the hospital, she made the appointment for the abortion, and she wouldn't let the doctor even talk to me about it. Back then, kids didn't have a choice. It wasn't like now where we have these clinics where you can go and do things on your own or you can become emancipated.

Deliverance

There wasn't anything. I was very sheltered in Bayside so I didn't know nothing about it even if there was. It might have been like a year later and Mr. T was over my house and we was in my room talking and I cried over everything and he was like what is wrong with you, like what is wrong with you? I was like, I just can't stop thinking about that baby, I always thought about that baby. He got up and took my birth control pills and threw them all down in the toilet, then said so we'll just have another baby. Every time we would have sex we just knew we were going to make another baby and we were not saying anything to anybody and we never did. I told my mother I was pregnant with Baby T in March, I mean in February, yeah in February . . . March, April, May, yeah in February and I had my son in May.

She got mad; we had a real big wedding and everything. This time when I told her, I said, you could do whatever you want to do to me but I'm not getting rid of it, I'm having my kid. I had got a scholarship to Hunter College and to Spellman. I missed six months of school by being pregnant and having my son. Once I told my mother, I wasn't even going to school. She just, did the wedding thing and I moved into my apartment and she was like you need to finish school. So I went back to school, soon as I had Baby T. I started studying and I waited until September and I went to the people and told them I wanted to graduate with my friends. It was really important to me that I graduated on time. They was like you are just gonna really have to make up, take classes all day and, that's what I did, I did all of that. My grandmother was living with us in Bayside and had my son from the day he was born; like she took care of him and she let me finish school. My parents, my mother did, financially. My mother always had my back. My mother did know how to make things OK, as long as she can make it OK with money. That was her way of providing me with support, like with emotional support she never knew how to do that, until now. But when I was younger she didn't know how.

It's really funny, my sister Nancy got into . . . , like I always knew God from my grandmother.. My sister, Nancy, was like 11 and she use to go to church with this girl down the block. She met this girl and she was going to church and she got real into this church, it was a Pentecostal church. She got real, real into this church. She started wearing skirts, she wouldn't wear pants. She would go to church with this girl all the time. Nancy wouldn't lie, she wouldn't do nothing. So one day, Mr. T was there and this boy I had met, lived in Astoria Projects. We met them in school and one of them liked me so I gave him my phone number. And he called me one day. I said Nancy, tell him I'm not here and she starts crying and saying I can't lie. I was like I will kill you in this house, cause Mr. T was there, and I said Mr. T is gonna kill me. This was around the time, the first time Mr. T ever hit me. It was just before we started having sex. He hit me for the first time and that was because of a guy. He found out about. This other guy I was talking to and he hit me. I was like oh no this relationship is over. I broke up with him.

He went around and told everybody in Bayside that I cheated on him and whatever. We were a close knit group, all the kids out there hung out together; so they were all like you can't do this to him, he loves you and all of this crap and so I just forgave him and I went back to him. Then, it became like a normal thing, you know whenever he would get mad, he would just hit me, you know what I'm saying. I was a kid and I loved him so much, I really loved Mr. T and I knew his family was very, very poor. I already knew about his father. I think that could be what brought us together, that I knew that his father weighed like 450. pounds, he was a gigantic man and he was big and he was black, like real, real dark and he had big bubble eyes and I was scared of him. He would always treat me nice whenever I went there, but I was always afraid of him. I loved his mother, she was like one of those ladies that you grew up with that she never finished school; one of those ladies like who only went to the fourth grade or something. It was like she was really ignorant, but I loved that lady. I knew her husband beat her. She didn't know any better, she didn't really take care of her children either. She didn't take care of them at all. I knew that the father beat on her and I knew that all their sons beat their girlfriends. Mr. T's sister, Val got beat on a regular basis, Herb beat her up. His other sister, Roz got beat up on a regular basis, and the third sister, Gerri, boyfriend was always beating her up. So it was a regular thing for the girls to be getting beat up by their boyfriends. Most of their boyfriends were friends of their brothers you know what I mean?

All the brothers beat their girlfriends and all of us were friends. All of us would come together and all of us got beat up; it was a regular, normal thing to me; that we all got beat up. So, I never really thought about it. I also knew that the father had sex with every one of his daughters. I knew that he was sexually abusing his daughters because I just knew what was happening to them. I think that was part of why I got so close to them, even though they would never come out and tell me, I always knew. I don't know, I always say that women who have been abused just know one another, I always say that. I think that was one of the reasons why we always was close with one another.

Mr. T use to beat me on a regular basis. In the beginning it was just once in a while and then, after we got married, like after I moved out of my mother's house, it was just crazy. We would just fight. He would just kick my ass, it was no other way to put it. He would just beat me and sometimes it would be for what he thought, sometimes it would be for absolutely nothing. One time I was eight months pregnant, he was getting ready to beat me up and I was scared that I was going to lose my son and I remember that it was this little, little window in the bathroom. I remember praying and saying God please, please I got to get out of here. The only way out of that bathroom was through that window and to this day I laugh because cause I tell it to my trauma mammas. God made that window big enough for me to get out of and then closed it back. I couldn't get back in after I got out of it. I was out on the fire escape.

Ok Now I'm Afraid

My sister Nancy, by going to this Pentecostal church would talk to us about God when she got back into the house. I use to always think, you know God, I knew God from my grandmother and I knew that I could never curse Him and I don't think I got angry at God. I never think I ever blamed God. I think somewhere along the line I might have, in the back of my mind, but I don't ever remember thinking, well where is your God? when he was molesting me or whatever. Nancy use to say things to me and she scared me, I always felt scared of God. The day she wouldn't lie for me she went into the closet. She forgot she started flipping through the Bible. I told her I was going to beat her ass. I put her in the closet I locked her in the closet, Yes I locked her up in the closet. I was like how dare you not lie for me. Are you stupid you could have gotten me beat up. She started going in the Bible reading passages to me from *Revelations* telling me that the world was going to end and I was going to hell. I was like it don't say that in that book; let me see that little book you are reading. Nancy was like oh my God don't' touch the Bible it's gonna burn if you touch it, you are going to hell. Me and Monica beat her up and put her in the closet took the Bible from her and sat down and started reading it. I started crying and calling my mother. I was like oh my God I'm going to hell! So that was my first experience with the Bible. I wasn't pregnant then, cause I hadn't had sex yet when that happened cause I was only fifteen. So Mr. T and I, you know, were getting there but I hadn't officially done it yet. She started saying to me, oh you lie to mommy, you bring boys in the house when she's not home, she start talking about all the things I'm doing, she said I'm sinning. She was like you are going to hell, let me show you in this book. I was like what's that book, give me that book and on and on. She went into the Bible and showed me all these places I'm sinning and stuff. But I couldn't believe she said I was going to hell and I called my mother, I was so scared. I didn't understand because I always heard, my grandmother say to us that no matter what God was going to take care of you. God was gonna make it alright. Even when we left Bermuda and we was so scared, she said God would never leave us by ourselves. I've always believed everything that my grandmother said, if grandma said it, it was always true no matter what. I guess that was my first real encounter with the Bible. I never thought about where I got it from. I always knew that God was here. That's one of the things to this day that if I could really do my whole life over, there is nothing really in my life that I would change. I know that everything that I went through was just for me to be who I am. The one thing in my life that I would never, never not regret is that abortion. I would always regret that because I always have thought about that. I've always thought about that baby, I always wondered what he would be like if he was here. You know what I mean? I've always thought about what I would have named him and everything. And more importantly I sometimes think about my son Baby T and wonder what it would have been like if I had him and he had his brother who would have been two years older, so he would have had some guidance. I always remember that and believe things always happen for a reason, like everything is supposed to happen, it's supposed to happen, then I guess he was never supposed to be here. You know that's the one thing in my life that I will always regret.

Sisterly Love

If somebody would say do you know everything about Monica I would say yes and not even think twice, because I know. I don't think she and I had any secrets at all. I don't think that there is anything in this world that she doesn't know about me and I believe that there isn't anything in this world I don't know about her. So, she knows everything that has happened to me. If you are ever in a room with the two of us and you watch us you might wonder if we are not one person. Like we really look alike, we are a lot alike, and we are both caretakers. She's a lot like me, so even with things that were going on, she was trying to do her own thing and she was just as lost as me. I need to tell you the truth cause my sister still hasn't found herself. My sister is very violent, she is very angry with God. She still hasn't addressed the stuff with John. I know just by the way she lives her life, I could tell that she's just very angry. She wants to, like she's tried to go to church, she's tried to have a connection with God. She always asks me after everything that He has did, after everything, He let you guys down so much how do you hold on to all this faith? How do you know that He is gonna always show up? I'm like, I just do, I can't explain it to her. So I told myself I had to make a commitment to get back to like going to church every Sunday and really try to get involved more. I don't want the answers for myself anymore. I want the answers for my sister. I don't want my sister to die without knowing God. I know she knows deep down. If it's in me than I know that it's in her. My grandmother left that kind of desire, that kind of faith. If she passed it on to me she would have to have passed it on to my sister. Me and my sister have always been together, especially when we were in Bermuda. We never were apart, we slept in the same bed; everything with us has always been Miss Taken and Monica. We always dressed alike, you know. My sister was a twin, and her twin died. My mother got into a car accident when she was pregnant with them, she was 8 ½ months.. Monica's twin sister died and her twins' teeth and her hair ended up in Monica's breast. They didn't even find that until Monica was like two years old, she use to always have pain. Losing her twin and only having me may be the reason why we have this connection that we have. I don't know but she's the only person I talk to about anything and everything. I never really talked to anybody else about anything and everything. I never talked to Mr. T.

Grandma....And Then there were Drugs!

I think from going to church with my grandmother as a little girl I always kinda of knew for some reason, God had me. I just always knew that God was there and it was going to be alright. Whatever I was going through, I don't think that I was ever angry at God. I always hated my mother for what she did and I think it took me a long time to forgive her. I told you before I never had that connection with my mother. I mean I love my mother, I really love my mother and to this day, we have a good relationship but I didn't think we would ever have that special mother daughter thing. I don't think that we will ever have that, but I know what we do have is very special and I'm so blessed. I don't feel short changed because I know I had that with my grandmother. I can't tell you how much I loved my grandmother. My grandmother was like everything to me. Grandma would not lie to me. I remember being in the hospital, I even remember walking up and down the corridors. I was thinking God let me be alright. I knew I would be. I remember thinking that I don't know where it was coming from. Now I know because Grandma said so and she doesn't lie.

We use to play this game in Bermuda it was called spinning tops. I don't' know if they played it in New York. They had this thing that was wide up top and had this metal piece at the bottom and you use to pull the string off and it use to spin. My sister Monica pulled it off and the thing hit the ground and the thing hit me in the head and I almost died. The Drs said that if it was a quarter of an inch in any direction then I would have been a vegetable forever. It's funny; I don't remember a lot of things, like a part of life before that. I remember being in church with my grandmother, maybe she took us more than I'm remembering think she took us. Maybe we was in church more, I remember us being in that church all the time you know what I'm saying. So my mother got married again when I was thirteen. I didn't want to go; I refused to get dressed but my father's sister, my aunt Molina was out here, she came and she talked to me. I ran away the night before and I ran away to her house. She talked to me and she told me that my mother deserved some happiness and that she loved Pop. I shouldn't stand in her way. She said what was going to happen to my mother when all of us got old enough to leave her and leave home and that my mother would be alone. Would I want my mother to be alone? I said no then she said that I should really not stand in her way; so I went to the wedding and I was miserable as hell when they got married. I just knew that meant another man was going to mess with us.

I had baby T as time went on. Mr. T beat me up all that time, he cheated on me, he slept with my friends. Mr. T had too many issues, I just couldn't make life OK for him no matter how hard I tried. Pop got him a job at the union. He had this really good job, but my parents still paid our rent. My mother and my grandmother still went shopping for us; they came every Friday with these bags and bags of groceries. They never let him, they never forced him to grow up and be a man so he never felt like he had to. Now I know that was a problem, but at the time, to be honest with you, I always felt that my mother owed me something. So whatever she did I've always felt that she was paying off a debt. Mr. T was making money and he had no bills, paying nothing. To top it all off every time I turn around he's beating me up. Everybody knew that. Pop had to come and pick me up at least two times a week. In the beginning he would come and I would pack everything up at like three o'clock in the morning. He would make five trips back and forth to pick up all my stuff right, then, he was moving it all back. That's why I now say Pop is a good man, because it took about six months for him to realize that he was moving me back and forth every week.. He started saying no, just you and the baby that's it. You are moving back tomorrow anyway. So he wasn't moving my stuff anymore. Even

then it was you can do for me but I don't like you. I was so mean to him. Deep down inside I liked him, I always liked him but we always battled because of my fear. Because my son was the first everything, now my same aunt who wanted me wanted my son. My grandmother was raising my son; she moved up here and stayed in my mother's house. My mother never had a boy, all she had was us. So Baby T is the only boy, he's the big time guy in everybody's life. So I'm in college, I'm working two jobs, my aunt who is living where I am living at now she moves. Pop talk to the landlord and the landlord says that me and Mr. T could have the apartment on the first floor of the house that we are living in right now. So I'm nineteen years old by now, Mr. T is now twenty two and we are living over there and just when we move in the lights went out in New York. Mr. T gets arrested and goes to jail. He and his boys stole a limousine. Mr. T was using drugs by now. Before I left the last apartment I walk in the bathroom and I had never seen drugs in my life. I was nineteen and I had never seen no drugs. I knew he smoked weed but whatever, you know that's on him he smoke weed. I walk in the bathroom and he and these two guys are in the bathroom got this big white bag with this white powder in it. I seen needles and I start crying and grab the white bags and I then throw them out the window and they are screaming you know, for the drugs. Mr. T is punching me in my face I'm standing there crying the guys run downstairs. I call my girlfriend who lives upstairs, me and her been friends the whole time we been living there. I call upstairs to her and tell her I found these big white bags and put them out the window. She tells me she would call me right back. I didn't know she and her man was getting high too. Her man went running downstairs to get Mr. T's dope. At that time it was quarters of dope. All of them go back upstairs to her house to get high and I'm downstairs in the house by myself crying my heart out. So then it became a regular thing, they would all go upstairs to her house to get high. I never got high with them. I never got into drugs when I was with Mr. T. I don't' think he would ever let me get high. But um so then we moved over here, and we are over here for six months or something and Mr. T gets arrested and he gets a year. So he goes to jail for a year. While he's in jail, I'm in college. I'm still at Hunter and
I'm doing this paper for my psyche class. We got to the zoo and we

Deliverance

have to watch these gorillas for six hours to right this paper. We get to the zoo, the whole class is at the zoo and we are observing. This white guy pulls out a joint and he says come on this will make this more fun, we'll smoke. Remember I never got high before; so I started smoking and I said this stuff is great.

Every summer my grandmother would go back to Bermuda and she took Baby T with her, cause they would do things like that, I would say mommy what time is Baby T coming home and she would say well Baby T went to Bermuda with your grandmother. They would just take my son wherever and I wouldn't even know where he was. Now here I am like this nineteen year old girl in this apartment by herself, never been on her own, never used or nothing. I'm still in college and Mr. T is in jail and like for the first time in my life I could do whatever I wanted to do. Mr. T. kept me from a lot of stuff; he didn't let me do anything. If my mother wouldn't have took him, it might have been different.

So here I am now, it's hot outside, its summer time and my friend, Chrissie starts telling me to come on lets go to the club. She starts taking me to a club in the neighborhood. So now I meet Padre and he's in the club and he starts passing me this bill with this white stuff. I'm like Oh My God, I ain't never used anything. I didn't even know how to find my nose without a mirror. Padre is Abraham and Andy's father; actually I started hanging out with Big Boy first, he gave me blow, not Padre, but Padre was a big dealer in the neighborhood. I started hanging out with dealers. I'm the new girl on the block and like you know all of them were trying to talk to me. Big Boy teaches me how to sniff and all of that stuff, and I started using. So now, I've been on my own for about four months. For the whole summer I've been on my own and here we go. I get to the jail to see Mr. T and I didn't realize that he was pissed with me about something. He tries to beat me up right there in the visiting room. So the police come and everything. But I'm growing up now and I'm finding out that the world doesn't revolve around Mr. T. He's not what I thought he was. I thought he was the hottest thing in the world and you're not. There are a lot of men in the world like you, like guys that know stuff and everything. So he comes home and we're walking down the street, he's only been home for like two weeks and we're walking, I'm pushing the stroller

This Walk Ain't Right! But, Help Is Along The Way

and he's talking to me. So, we're just hanging out and this guy walks by and says hi. So he's like how you know Herb and duh, duh, duh. So I said what are you talking about, so he takes the umbrella and just starts beating my ass with this umbrella, just busting me all in my head, my mouth is bleeding. So I don't know what had come over me, but I just looked at him. I said you know what Mr. T just kill me, just go ahead and kill me cause I'm done! I'm just done. Yeah I said that out of fear, but you might as well kill me cause I'm not coming back no more. I've had enough now and really, like I don't want to do this no more. And I don't even want the house. By now; my parents had already bought the house that I'm living in. So I went back around the corner to my mother's house and I told her that I wanted to leave and she was so happy. I'm not going to have him living in the street, so you guys are going to have to let him live there and I'll go get my own apartment. So I left him, living there and I went to Flushing. I went back to the first place where he and I was living but on the other side of the street. I just started working; I dropped out of school and started working. I started like really getting high now, not being with him I really did anything I wanted. I really started using a lot, like getting high all the time and then I met this guy named W in the interim. He was this gorgeous guy. He was so good to me and good to my son. He wasn't interested in getting high all the time and having thugs in his house all the time. He wanted us to live like some kind of semi normal lives instead of just sniffing cocaine all the time and going to the clubs. By now I just wanna hang out all the time, I felt like I missed a whole bunch of stuff by being with Mr. T. So, now I'm like really at Padre's house a lot more and him and I start messing around. I really fell in love with him. I think I fell in love with him from the first minute I met him. I think I'll love him until I die. Yeah, I just loved him. Like I really felt that God gave me him. He knew everything about me and I have never met anybody that treated me that well; no lie. I felt like he really treated me like a person. I, never had nobody ever pay any attention to me, I felt like nobody ever really listened to me and then he and I started seeing each other regularly.

My roommate left and I had my own two bedroom apartment, I was living with Baby T and I was still working and still doing everything.

Deliverance

One day Padre showed up at my apartment and he had his bags and everything. He said that Louise his girl found out about us and she put him out. So, he moved in and then we were together from then on. The next year crack came out and we all started smoking and we lost the apartment. Padre has this really, really good drug business and we would make a lot of money. In the beginning when everybody was just doing heroin it was one thing but once crack came in and everybody started smoking, it was a whole different story. We lost the apartment; my parents had paid my rent like three times by then. So when we lost the apartment, we moved, we went to stay at the Martinique Hotel. That's when the Martinique was in the news, they had these big rats. By now I had Abraham, and Abraham was about ten months old and my parents had taken Baby T from me, actually she had never really given him to me. Since the hospital I didn't really have him. Abraham and Padre and I were staying at the hotel by then. I went out and found an apartment in the Bronx. The building was empty; the man had just renovated it. I took everybody from the shelter. I went back and told everybody at the Martinique about the building. So the building turned into like an apartment kinda shelter place. Everybody in that building now is using cause everybody in that hotel was using. He liked everybody, and let them pick out their own apartments and everything, like it was crazy. So we all moved in there and then I started smoking crack. And by now Baby T is about nine and my mother is like uh, oh.

Oh I skipped this part, when my mother found out that she was pregnant with my brother. Pop takes me outside and says these mean things to me because my mother is telling me to leave my son there for the night, but she's pregnant with her son. He's letting me know that things are getting ready to change. She's gonna have his son, and now they are going to be their own little family. My mother had her own plans cause she never gave me back my son. You know what I'm saying? But, you know him and I have always gone through it. Baby T and I, never really had that constant bonding time. Padre always felt that, the first five years of a kid's life are the most important and whatever they get in the first five years is what really molds them, really makes them who they are. Padre always felt like if my parents got their hands on my sons, they would not turn out to be anything. He always felt like that.

This Walk Ain't Right! But, Help Is Along The Way

So Baby T is nine now and they always had him out there in Bayside. He's always had this great life, you know going to Bermuda, my aunts taking him to the Canal, and he's been to Rome. Baby T has been to beautiful places and seen many things. He's always been exposed to this. Every weekend he would go skiing, they had this house in the Pocono's by then. He would be in the Pocono's skiing. He had this whole other life going. Then he had this insanity that he came to every other weekend when he came to me. You see he always wanted to be with me. Baby T and I had that thing, I don't know what it is between the two of us, but we always had this thing. I was my mother's first born, but it wasn't like that. My son is a grown man now MG but days don't pass that he doesn't' call me. If my mother didn't call me, I wouldn't talk to my mother for a month; you know what I'm saying. She might go through my mind or somebody else might bring her up, I love my mother, but that isn't our relationship, we don't have that. Like my sister Nancy will speak to my parents every single day at 7:10 a.m.; She gets on the phone with Pop and talks with him, and my mother. We don't have that but I don't want that. Baby T and me, we always had this bond. So either he was coming to stay with me or he was not. So I was smoking, I started smoking crack. And I get sick and it's on his birthday and he's turning ten this date. Now he already had been coming to the Bronx to stay, it's the summer time now. He had been coming to the Bronx for about a week and he was meeting all these boys. He's hanging out with them, he's going to Yankee Stadium, and they are stealing the tickets to sell to the people outside. So he's already getting into the street and he's ten. I say to him, what do you want for your birthday? He looks me in my face and says what I want is for you to stop smoking that stuff and he turns around and walks out. Now I had already left a hundred dollar bill for him on the dresser. Padre still selling weed, he always been dealing. So I leave the money and he wouldn't even take it. He said I have money, I make my own money. And turned around and he walks out. So we all get dressed my aunt and family is having this little party for him right over here in the Bronx. And we get there and all of sudden I get sick. MG I stayed sick for three months. My mother took me to every specialist. I went to Beth Israel, going through tests. I couldn't sleep at night. At night I couldn't

Deliverance

take any light; I had to sit somewhere in a dark room. I couldn't eat any food; I could barely keep water down. I was in the hospital for two weeks they could not find anything wrong with me. I was so sick. I could not take that; my head did not stop hurting. I mean it was just like my head was about to burst open. They ran all kinds of test on my head and they couldn't find anything wrong. For three months, I was like a stick by that time, I could not eat I was so skinny right. So all of sudden one day I look up and whatever was wrong with me was gone. Just as fast as it came it was gone. I got up and I felt better. My head wasn't hurting me no more. Remember people were still coming smoking, buying crack and all of that. And everybody was in the back room and everything. So that afternoon I feel better, so I can smoke again. So I go and try some crack and I put it in the stem and started hitting it and my head feels like it's going to bust open, my heart starts palpitating and I'm thinking that I'm gonna die. I am going to die. So I'm screaming and I'm crying I'm gonna die. And my friends and them they coming running in and they take all of this dope they hadn't cut yet and they are shoveling it up my nose. And everybody is talking to me they saying Miss Taken just calm down, just calm down. And Joy she's there and she says easy, just easy. So I'm breathing, breathing and I finally get myself to a point where I say I'm gonna be OK and I go back into the room where I've been for three months and sit and I lay back down and I say God I swear I will never smoke again. If I live through this night I will never smoke again. And I woke up the next day and I never smoked crack again. I never smoked crack again. And I say that to this day it poisoned my system, maybe it was just the drug that I wasn't gonna be able to get into me. I don't know, maybe that was what was wrong with me for those three months, you know the poison. You know that was when what's his name got burned up . . . . Richard Pryor. That's when you had the ether and everything. So it may have been something in the production, into making it into crack that got me sick. It was poison for my body, but I never ever smoked after then. And then I just stayed in the Bronx.

We never paid rent. Actually we wouldn't lose the apartment for not paying rent; that's about the only place where rent got paid. That's, cause welfare would pay the rent. But um the guy we was renting from,

This Walk Ain't Right! But, Help Is Along The Way

that apartment building that I was staying in started getting raided a lot because it was a dust block and these weird people started coming around there. Baby T and his friends went down by tracks to play where the water and stuff was. While they were down there, this man started chasing them and they all started running, it was five of them. This man got one of them; he got one of Baby T's friends. And this is like a year after I got sick, so Baby T had to be ten or eleven. The man caught him, he raped him and he killed him. Baby T could never get over that. He felt like he left his friend, but I always tell him what was you gonna do. The man was chasing you and it could have or would have been you. Baby T felt like it should have been him. So he just, he couldn't stay up there anymore. Like he was, it was just bad for him. You know really I don't think he was ever the same after then. Like until this day we never talked about it. He kept saying I shouldn't have left my friend; I shouldn't have left my friend. I think he always blamed himself cause they were running so fast that they never turned around to look back to make sure that everybody got away. It was in the newspaper and everything. It was late at night MG; little kids should not have been out that late. A lot of things that went on with Baby T I feel a lot of guilt about. I feel like if my mother would have just kept him. I know that that's part of what I go through with her; she knew what kind of life I was leading. I'm not like that with my grandkids. Like if I knew that my grand's mothers are not taking care of them, they would have to send me my babies. One of them knows that he is not my grandson, but he knows that I am the only grandmother that the three of them know. So she would have to pack them babies up and send them all to me; I wouldn't leave my grandkids to go through all that crap. I always wondered, she saw how I was living, knew what I was doing so why would she keep sending him back to me. Why would you keep letting him come back to me, like it made no sense to me? Lil Pop was two years or three years younger than him, so it was Lil Pop and Baby T together for most of the time, cause Abraham didn't leave until we moved to Brooklyn. So she had him, so why didn't she just keep him with her son. But I found out later it was because Pop's mother didn't want my son around. You know what I'm saying. My parents always lived in Bayside, but my stepfather, Pop's mother never wanted him

Deliverance

to marry my mother. She felt like she already had three kids, a ready made family. Once little Pop came then that became her whole world. That's the only grandkid. So he was her world and she really didn't want anything to do with my sons, unless it was after school. My sons would walk Lil Pop to his grandmother's house and my sons would have to come to my house after school. They didn't want to go to her house, cause she would make them sit on the porch until my mother came home. She wouldn't even let them in her house. I found out later that's why Baby T would keep coming to me cause he wouldn't want to keep going through that.

So we leave the Bronx. We come to Queens first. So we stay there for a while and we find all this cocaine in the house and we went crazy with that for a while. We had all this money; we started delivering stuff to Bermuda and all this crazy stuff. Then we move to Brooklyn. My parents owned an apartment building in Brooklyn and they put us in there. Abraham's like seven and we are living together, Padre's dealing. A friend of his did something to these Italians and they come into our house shooting everything up. Abraham and Baby T are here. They are coming into our house and they are not really looking for me and Padre, but they will kill us if they have to get this guy they want. Baby T hears them and he takes Abraham who is like seven now and they jump out the back window and they are holding on to like the side of the house. So these guys are like shooting up the house the person that they are looking for is not there. So Padre being the person that he is talks them into believing that he's not there and they leave. Baby T and Abraham come back into the window and Abraham is like real real shook up and I'm not really paying too much attention cause I'm getting ready to get high now, I need to re-sniff another bag. My mother comes the next day and she picks up Abraham and she Baby T, I'm not paying any attention to my sons. I'm using so I'm not really paying attention to what is going on with Abraham. I'm not paying attention to the fact that he's leaving with a bigger bag than normal, I don't pay attention to his clothes or anything cause all I'm doing is getting high. But I'm working; I'm still working at the rental car place, now I'm working at National instead of Avis. I'm just using, I'm working and I'm using. Padre's working and he's using. Abraham leaves with a big bag, so come

This Walk Ain't Right! But, Help Is Along The Way

Sunday my mother doesn't bring them back. So I'm saying to myself Abraham got to go to school. I call and she tells me oh he's just staying an extra day. So he comes back that Monday, maybe it was Thursday, I'm out in the street, Padre's out in the street. Padre's actually selling drugs and I'm out in the street coping. Abraham's really in the house by himself, and when I come back home, Abraham's gone. I really didn't pay attention to the fact that he's gone cause I just thought he was in the street somewhere until about midnight. I'm like where the hell is Abraham. That's when Padre comes home, Padre would never forget the kids. Whatever is going on Padre would pay attention to his kids. So he's like where's Abraham and I'm like I thought he was in the wind, he's like you are unbelievable. Of course we went through what kind of mother are you and all this and that. I was high, I didn't pay attention. So he call my moms and my mother says that my father came here while we weren't there and Abraham was there by himself, he was hungry, he hadn't eaten all day and Pop took him. So Abraham's not coming back no more. I'm alright with that. So he's gone he went to my mother's house to stay and now both him and Baby T are living at my mother's house and me and Padre are still in Brooklyn.

    I think I'm pregnant and I go to the doctor and tell them I think I'm pregnant and want an abortion. I know that I've been using and never used when I was pregnant with my kids and didn't want to bring no addict baby into the world. The lady tells me that I am like two months pregnant, so she schedules the abortion for April 8, 1988. So I go to the hospital to have the abortion and I'm lying in the bed and she tells me that I'm not pregnant, right? This lady comes in to put this thing in my arm and she says oh Miss Taken what are you doing here? You are not even pregnant so you know it don't make any sense for you to be here. So I'm like what are you talking about? You took the test and said that I was pregnant and she says no, no, no you're not pregnant; it was a mistake, so go home. So it's my check day. Me and my girlfriend Linda we are in a hurry now. Linda is dead now, God bless the dead. We are in a hurry now we are trying to get out of there, its check day. So the check cashing place is right across the street from the hospital and we already scoop that up cause we gonna use as soon as we leave the hospital. Three months pass, no period, my breast are blowing up like crazy, I've been using every single day. I go to Flushing Hospital and I find out that I'm four months pregnant. So there is no way in the world now that I'm gonna have this abortion now. I'm not gonna do what I did before ever again. So I am like I guess I'm gonna have this baby. Two more months pass, I wake up one morning and my whole throat, the side of my face is all blown up. They rush me to the hospital, now I know that this was Sarcoid but I didn't know I had **Sarcoid** back then. So they tell me I got the mumps. So now the Dr. and everybody is in the room, my parents are in the room and telling everybody I need to have an abortion because something is going to be wrong with the baby. Not only am I on the methadone program, cause I was on heroin for the first four months, right after I found out I was pregnant I went to the methadone program and said to detox my ass. It's NYS Law that you cannot detox a pregnant woman; she would have to be maintained on 40 mgs of heroin until I had him. The hospital is not allowed to detox you, it's against the law because the baby could die kicking, you know, detoxing off the methadone. So I had to stay on the program, my son is addicted to methadone, I have the mumps and they are telling me that he may probably be born blind or retarded or something.

So again I call on God. I'm downstairs in the basement of my parent's apartment building and I am talking to God. We lived on the first floor and my parents had bought me a washer machine and dryer for Christmas and it was in the basement of their apartment building. So I'm down there washing my cloths and my mother comes down and she's talking to me, telling me that I have to have this abortion. I'm saying to myself where did I even know to have faith in God? I don't even know where I found out that there was a God but I know that methadone kept me high I never could get off that high, 40 mg kept me high. I don't know if I was hallucinating but I swear to everything that I love that in that basement God told me just like I'm talking to you right now, God told me that my son was gonna be fine, and that I had to have him and that nothing was gonna be wrong with him. My mother had come down the steps while I was praying and she said you have to go and have this abortion and I told her mommy I'm never having an abortion like that again. I will never ever, ever kill anything of mine ever again. I know it's bad enough when you have one of those quickies, you know those quick abortions when you are only like two months pregnant maybe there is nothing there, I don't know, but that's what they tell you. But at six months, there is a baby inside of me, I feel him, he's kicking, he's breathing. You know what I mean. I can remember that conversation with my mother like it was yesterday. I was too determined about what I was going to do. He determined what I was going to eat. There's been times while I was pregnant, I've gotten up and I went to Wendy's, and started eating Wendy's and then something inside of me says what are you doing dummy, you don't want Wendy's you want White Castle not Wendy's. And I'm like, dead serious, we leave Wendy's and go to White Castle and I would eat again. I was like you're not going to tell me what's going inside of me. I know that this baby inside of me is alright. For whatever reason, mom, I'm not going to tell you that God told me that he's not going to be blind. God didn't tell me that he was not gonna be retarded. God told me that whatever he was, that he was gonna give me what I needed to take care of him. I knew it, I just knew it. She was like how do you know that and I said I'm telling you. God! Like whatever it is God is gonna make it alright, I know God is gonna make it alright; I just know. And I kept telling her in that basement. I remember when I had Andy until this day; I always call him my miracle baby. I tell everybody that cause he wasn't supposed to be here because of everything that could possibly have happened. To try to get rid of him and God said no, this is your baby. It's funny to this day there is something that goes on between me and my son Andy, that I can't deny anything. When I had him my mother was standing in the window where they have the babies and of course my son was addicted to methadone so as soon as I had him they incubate him., They incubate the babies' right after they are born then they call Children's Services (CS) on you; to get a CS case. I already had a CS case on me cause the program already told them. So the lady is telling me that he is kicking and that he is really sick and he might die and I'm looking at him and I'm crying. And I just looked at her and I was like no he's not. And she's looking at me like I'm crazy you know. This baby has been taking 40 mgs of methadone and 40 mgs Phenobarbital. He's gonna be kicking for a week or two; then when

Deliverance

you get him home he's gonna be a mess. He's not gonna be sleeping all night. I said no he's not. I just knew that Andy was gonna be alright. I told my mother that, I said God said that he was gonna be alright. I even talked to my grandmother, and that was what really made it real for me. I said gram I'm telling you I don't know if I'm going crazy or if it's the methadone or it's the drugs but I know that Andy is gonna be alright and she said if you know in your heart that he's gonna be alright then he's gonna be alright. Sure enough I had my son and they gave him Phenobarbital for three days and my baby was off that Phenobarbital and he went through it in those three days. You could see he'd be in that little incubator and his fist would be balled up so tight. He would just be shaking, his whole body would be just shaking and he kicked that Phenol, he kicked that methadone and three days later they took him out of that incubator. Two days later the CS lady came to my house to make sure I had pampers and everything else I was supposed to have. I went to that hospital and I told that lady to pack up my son and give me my baby. I got release papers from that lady from CS and she said Miss you should probably leave him in the hospital cause he's gonna go through some stuff. I said he's gonna be OK, give me my son. She gave me Andy and I took him home and that boy ain't ever missed a beat. He ain't ever gone through what she said he would go through. None of that, none of that. She told me I would be staying up all night, him crying and stuff. That boy been sleeping from the day he came home until now. Sleeping ain't ever been a problem for that boy.

We have a saying in Narcotics Anonymous that we all have this emergency God that we call on. To make sure this is dope; to make sure that this ain't beat, make sure you know, oh God make sure that I get a bang. I know I always had that; I always had that emergency thing going on. And for some reason I always knew that, I've always known that God was there, even the darkness of that room with my hands wrapped around that man's penis, in the midst of that knife being put to my throat, my father walking out on my mother and walking out on me, cause that was what he really did. With everything, with everything, with everything that Mr. T did Mr. T has beaten me, Mr. T has beat me for hours, I mean one time I was beat for an hour and half straight. Through everything I always knew that God was gonna make a way, always. With every one of my kids, in the midst of my addiction, every one of my kids, I stopped long enough to get them Christened. Even though I was using and my mother use to always say what's that about? Every one of my kids, I'd be high, I'd be so messed up, but I would make sure that I would take time to get them Christened. All three of them was Christened at a Baptist Church. That's where their father got christened; I mean that's where Baby T's father got buried when he died. So I really don't know what the connection is, I don't know. But I always knew that Spunky was gonna be alright. When I had him I knew he was gonna be alright.

When Andy came home, about a week later, I got on a program. I was going to my program. After two months, no Andy had to be about six months old cause he was starting to do little things. He was about six months old and I was starting to come off the program. And then when he was almost a year, Abraham was at the house and Padre told me that he was gonna keep them and I went to my program. My counselor at my program knew Padre's cousin. The cousin calls my counselor and said that Padre had got picked up, he was selling dope in the street and he got arrested. I was totally, totally devastated that Padre got arrested. Andy and Abraham were with this lady that lived in our building. I went to Padre's cousin's house and everybody was in there; my counselor from the methadone program walked in there. Her and her man was in there and they were using. It bugged me out that she was using. All of them were in the room shooting dope. I was the only one sniffing, everybody else was putting it in the cooker and I was sniffing. I was devastated because of Padre. Without him I just, I never felt like I was whole without him. Like whenever he went to jail whether it was six months or a year, the whole time he was there I felt like I wasn't a whole person. Padre never hit me, one time he threw a box of cereal at me; I remember it was a box of Super Sugar Crisp.

We sniffed, but I couldn't get high. I was on my second bag, I sniffed a whole bag and I couldn't get high. Padre's cousin, Joy, she says to me put the stuff in the cooker, what are you wasting it for. And I said are you crazy, I ain't shooting no dope; I ain't no addict. So they took my dope and they put it in the cooker like that's where you can use a spoon or a soda bottle cap, you could use a lot of things but at that time we were using a spoon. You would pour the dope in the spoon with water and you would mix it up with a piece of cotton. Then you would draw the drug off the cotton and then you would shoot up. Because I wasn't shooting up I just knew I wasn't an addict. So they took my dope and they put it in there and then that's the first time I ever shot some dope. And from that moment on . . . no he shot, he shot me, somebody shot me up. Somebody shot me up for almost six months. Until it got to the point where I knew that this girl was giving me all water and I knew that she was taking all the dope. I said this is bull. This chick is sitting here totally nodded out and I ain't feeling a thing. You ain't giving me the same thing you giving yourself. So I just took that needle that day and started shooting myself. I started getting high in my bathroom. I would take Abraham with me, and he would be sitting in the bathroom while I would shot off. Padre didn't know that I was shooting. I decided Abraham could come in the bathroom with me cause he always did everything to try and protect me; this time he was trying to protect me so Padre wouldn't find out.

My girlfriend and her man, who was the head of all the court officers in one of the court houses; you know the ones that wear the white shirt, he was a white guy and every time he would come to our house, he would OD. Every Friday, every damn Friday, he would use too much and OD. So he came in there, into the bathroom and I knew they were getting ready to shoot up in there. I did not want to put myself in a position to be in there, like I didn't want to sniff it. Like once I started shooting I never wanted to go back to any sniffing ever again. So I told Padre, I don't know, I'm not wasting my stuff. He tried to kill me that day, chasing me around the house with that hammer. I knew he wanted to hit me with that hammer. But I wasn't really worried that he would, he never wanted to hurt me, it was that he was so disappointed. So then I was like, I'm gonna stop, I'm gonna sniff. Like I could only remember two times that I really saw that man cry and that was that day and the day his father died. I was like Padre I'm a stop, I'm a stop. I didn't stop. It just got worse and worse and worse. I started getting track marks everywhere and I would be shooting all the time. I stopped working. I started stealing strong medicine (heroin). I started selling drugs in Brooklyn it was ridiculous like seriously; I was seriously in the

This Walk Ain't Right! But, Help Is Along The Way

street selling drugs. Padre was selling drugs and he got arrested. And then I took this guy's package and I was using, I used up all the drugs. I didn't save enough to cut up and sell to make his money back. I went the next day to get my check and I didn't get it. The guy seen me in the street and he beat me up so bad in the street. He was kicking me all in my stomach and in my head. The whole time I was on the ground and the whole time he was beating me up, all I could think about was please don't take my money, please don't take my money. I had money in my pocket to go cop and all I could think about was I don't care if you beat me up as long as I could get away from here and go cop. The guy really liked me; he didn't beat me as bad as he could have. He let me go and I went and copped. You know, I just stayed out there and started selling until I got arrested.

The first time I got arrested they put me in a program and I stayed in the program for about six months. When I left the program, I came back to Brooklyn. We left Brooklyn, we left out of that apartment and we moved to Queens, cause my Uncle had died. So my mother was like, keep changing boroughs; she was thinking that it would keep me from . . . it would be better for me, but it never got better. It wasn't the boroughs; I was doing a lot of stuff. I was doing so much to Pop in those buildings. He had six apartments in that building, right, and my parents was crazy, cause they never knew nothing about drugs or nothing like that, so you know I was running his building for him. I was collecting his rent and everything. For like three years, he always thought that none of his tenants was paying him rent. So every now and then I would give him the rent money. Then I would take the rent money, one for me and one for him; one for me and one for him. They knew I was on drugs but they didn't know nothing about drugs so they did not put it together. I had sixteen apartments rented out in that building. There were only six apartments in the building. I had sixteen people in the building paying rent. I was taking welfare from them. All my friends who was using I had them all living in the building. I was renting out apartments to them and the welfare was paying all this money. That poor man wasn't getting a dime, you hear me. Then when he finally figured out . . . I forget what happened he got a letter or something and he found out. He came there and I left. I moved out and I went to Queens. So he started coming there collecting the rent. He started getting all geared up to go there and really go off on these people and the people still live in the building. To this day they still live there. He went to one lady's apartment and he knocked and he said you know I really need to . . . before he could even get the words out of his mouth she said oh Mr. Pop . . . hi where's Miss Taken, she was so excited. Here's your rent money. That girl used to pay her rent a week in advance. Before it was even time for the rent she would be paying her rent. So then he found out that everybody in the building was paying rent. He had no problems after I left everybody in that building paid their rent. He had the best tenants I ever seen in my life. I left and he had his building back. Then I moved to Queens. It was time for me to do something because the first program that I had just left out of they had a warrant out on me for 2 ½ to 4 years for getting busted for selling strong medicine.

I went to the precinct and the next day they took me to court to see the judge. The judge let me go under my own recognizance. He told me that I needed to go into a program. I went into Su Casa and I stayed there for seven months. I got into a relationship in there and it really bothered me that I was messing around on Padre so I just left. Everybody in there was messing around and they wanted me to tell them and I wouldn't. I came home. I stayed on the streets for a year and a half. It's funny there goes God again because they did not issue a warrant for me when I left the program. I was mandated to that program by Brooklyn TASCs. That stands for The Treatment Alternative To Street Crimes. They are the people who put you in programs. They work with the judges and the courts. They are like an overseer. They get your urine; they follow up with the programs to ensure that you are still in the programs and all of that. I don't know what happened with Su Casa. I left there. I got clean June 24th. Su Casa was from methadone to maintenance. They give you a blind detox. You never know if you are taking methadone or orange juice. For the whole time I was there for the first six months I felt sick in the beginning but you never really feel real real sick because they are bringing you down real slow. So you don't even know you are coming off the methadone until you are off of it. So when they told me I was clean I was all happy

This Walk Ain't Right! But, Help Is Along The Way

and everything, but then two months later I left. I went right back to getting high. I don't even think I was home like three days. I was back in Queens shooting dope. When I first went into detox it was '92 and my son stayed home with his father, Padre. When we were in Queens, Padre got busted. He went outside with this dude and they got in the car and they were about to pull off and the police pulled up. They were looking for the guy Padre got into the car with. The guy had a whole trunk full of counterfeit money. Padre had drugs on him. The guy went to jail for the money and Padre went to jail for the drugs. The money was in the trunk of the car and it wasn't Padre's so they could not put that on him. So Padre got sent up for 2 years. He got 2 to 4 years plus he had a warrant from Brooklyn but he never had got caught until now. When he got busted maybe about a month later, we were all sitting in the house me and Andy were sitting on the bed watching *Urkel* on TV and I had just came back. Two guys my friends came over to my house. Remember I am not in an apartment anymore. I was in a two story house. We were living there for about 2 years before we burned it down. It was my uncle's house who died and there was an old lady living there that we would look out for her. So we are sitting in the house and we had just cleaned up the whole house and somebody came to the door. It was two male friends of mine and they went into the bathroom. They had 2 ounces of cocaine. I didn't know because I was in my room shooting up. So I'm in my room and I always kept 4 syringes full of drugs. So I'm hitting my friend Dave and I'm getting ready to shoot up myself and I have like this syringe hanging out my arm. All of a sudden the police come in and raid my house. I had all these people in my house. One thing about me I never let anybody in Corona be homeless. Everybody knew that they could come to my house and stay there. By the time the police finished collecting people in that house, in the basement and in the attic, there was 17 people in that house. One time I was so full that I didn't have no place else for anybody to sleep so I just let this guy sleep at the kitchen table. I just couldn't see people in the street. I just couldn't do it. Then we had pit bulls everywhere. I had three different pit bulls and two of my pit bulls had just had puppies so that house . . . it was a disaster. The police raided the house they ran in the door and the cop came in and saw

Deliverance

Andy laying there watching TV right, he was 4. He used to be outside at 10 at night riding his bike up and down the street. This night he happened to be in at 7:30 at night. He is sitting on the bed with me while I'm getting high and he's watching. Andy used to watch me nod out. He would take the cap put it on my syringe take all my drugs and everything and hide them. You see I would fall asleep because I would be up for 2 and 3 days and then I would just fall out. He would take the syringe out of my arm, untie the belt, and take my drugs. He would put everything away for me. It's crazy like the stuff I did with my kids. So when the cop came in he looked right at Andy and he looked at me with such disgust, he was a white guy I will never forget that cop. He looked at me with disgust, he took all my syringes and put them on top of the closet, I had a big brown closet in my room. He said you know what bitch that's just how he said it. He said I'm gonna leave these right here for you. He said I hope you get out and I hope you come back here for this and I hope you kill yourself. Then he scooped Andy up and he said do you have somebody that can come get your son. Andy was screaming and crying for me. He called my mother and she came. Actually the lady from across the street she loved Andy. She use to always come and get him. God gave each one of my sons an angel when they were little. Each one had someone that could give them some normal stuff in their life. That woman would come and get Andy all the time. She was an older women living alone. She had grandkids and every time they would come to spend the night she would come get Andy. In the daytime sometimes she would be going to the store and she would come up the block and ask me if Andy could go with her. Her name was Barbara; that lady she treated him so well. She came and took him from the police and my mother came and got him from her. Then they took all of us to jail. I stayed on Riker's for six days and the warrants from Brooklyn for leaving the program never popped on me. They gave me a bail. They gave me a $2,500 bail but it was Thanksgiving. My mother told me I had to wait. I was calling my sister, now I remember Nancy had got clean. She got busted too. Wait a minute I didn't tell you about my sisters and how they were caught up too. Me and my two sisters were getting high together. When I first met Padre, we were in bed one night and my sister Monica came in and asked for some coke. He told her to go ahead in his pants and get it. He forgot that he had two packages in his pants; one that we had been getting high out of and it was cut. The other was pure uncut. She got that one and almost died that night. She never got high after that. A year later she left and went to Bermuda. She has never gotten high since then. Nancy on the other hand started smoking crack and she really got crazy. My sister was really out there. She got arrested in Brooklyn we all kinda started together. I was already sniffing dope. She started coming to my house and she met Jamel and they started sniffing coke together and they went together for about 4 years. They were around the same age. She was cool with the coke, she was doing her thing. She was in school but once she started with that crack she was done. When she got arrested they put her in a program and when she came out of Samaritan Village she stayed clean after that and she never looked back either. She has over 20 years now.

So we were all getting high together. We was living in Corona I came home from jail because Nancy came to bail me out. I took a cab home, I will never forget, there were people waiting for me. They were all in my house getting high. I went straight into my room and I said I know that cop didn't really leave that there. Do you know that that cop left that there? All those syringes with heroin, as a matter of fact it was speed balling, heroin and coke in there. I never even stopped to think how you know he didn't put something in there. I grabbed that stuff and started getting high. I had been on Riker's Island for six days. I didn't detox because they had me on 20 mg because I was real sick in there. When they had me in the bull pen my girlfriend that was with me she was 4 months pregnant. She was real sick because she was pregnant. She was throwing up and I was too but she was throwing up more because she was pregnant. I had so many abscesses and so many tracks up and down my arms; I mean I have track marks everywhere on me. I mean I have track marks on my legs all the way to the bottom of my feet, my hands, everywhere. It was crazy. As soon as they looked at me they knew they had to do something with me. I was so sick that I just laid there on the floor. I was so sick that I was too sick to get up. That's why when I seen the judge and he put a bail on me I didn't even care. I just wanted to sit back down. So when they took me to

Riker's they gave me 20 mg. 20 mg is not going to do anything for me I have a $100 a day habit. All 20 mg did for me was take the edge off and make it like I could focus a little bit. I was kind of like kicking cold turkey but it wasn't enough. Everything that happened just wasn't enough. I never had a desire to not get high. I never had a desire to be me. I never wanted to be who I am and just be in my own skin and just be me. I always wanted to be outside of myself or something like that. I came home and I got high and I kept getting high. Remember now the first thing that that man did was took my baby from me. I thought everything was gonna be alright because I thought he was going to be with my mom. I figure everything was OK. All three of my sons are with her. I figure I will see them when I feel like it. I will just keep getting high. I'll keep getting the food stamps and the money, I'll cash in the stamps and I'll just use. But my mother would not let me see my kids. You see Nancy had already been in Samaritan and my mother had been going to those damn family groups and found out about enabling and all of this other stuff now. Remember she wasn't up on this stuff before but now she knows. She started talking this you got to get better stuff. I was like what you talking bout get better, chick please, you better give me my son. She was like you will not be coming to my house; all of a sudden she had all these rules. I was like she done fell and bumped her head coming at me with rules. Give me my kids!!! She was like I am dead serious. You are going to a program. Yes! You are going to a program. I will call the police on you myself.

I was blown away. I was thinking I'm gonna paint up the house and I'm gonna get myself together and just get high from time to time. I was like whatever OK I will go to a program I ain't got nothing else to do.

So I said I will sign up for a program to make you happy I will go to a program. I was supposed to leave to go to the program on December 10th. I didn't go. I felt like I wanted to be out here getting high for the holidays and I will see them after Christmas. So I changed the date to January 10th. On December 26th my house burned to the ground. We all sitting in the house getting high one of the girls runs outside screaming my name and I'm like why is she buggin? What do you want? She's screaming and everybody is running to the front. The house is on fire. All I'm thinking is she done fell and bumped her head. Now I'm sitting there with all my syringes, my food stamps and my welfare card. I'm sitting there. Everybody else is scrambling to get out the house. They are all screaming for me, Dave is like this is not a game. The fire is on the steps. In order for me to get out I have to get down those steps. The fire is coming down the steps from the top floors already. I'm like alright alright I'm coming I'm coming. I finished getting high and I can't find my keys and Dave is screaming for me to come on and I'm like I'm coming I'm coming at this point they have all left me. I am the only one in the house. The fire comes all the way down the steps. The fire is like right here and I have to run past it to get out. I could feel the heat from that fire. All I can feel is the heat coming to consume me. I'm stuck now. Two people done jumped out the top window one of them was pregnant, the old lady on the second floor they done got her out of there. Everybody is up from down in the basement, everybody is gone. The only person in that house was me. I cannot move. I'm just standing there staring at the fire. I was so stuck, I was just stuck. I don't know if it was fear, I don't know what it was but I couldn't move. I just kept looking at the fire like just thinking I'm gonna die? It was crazy. The whole back of the house was on fire. So I can't go back to the kitchen and go out the back door to the back yard. The Fire Department and everybody is coming but they are hearing from the neighbors that it's a crack house and they should let it burn down. So I'm standing there and Dave runs back in the house and literally picks me up lays me on top of him and runs out the door. As soon as we came out, the ceiling just collapses in a matter of seconds. We just made it out the door. We are standing out front and I'm standing there crying. Honestly part of me was thinking like why didn't you just leave me there. I was thinking this could be over for me. I guess there has always been that part that was just tired. Another part of me was like thank you so much for saving me. But then, I was like, what are we gonna do? So we went to the Red Cross and they gave us money and then we went to welfare and they housed us in the Westway Motel. We stayed there for two weeks. Then my son and his friends got into a big fight in there, when I went to pick up the checks they were giving me because they said I could stay in the motel until they got me a home I was told I had to leave because I had too many people. So I went and stayed at my girlfriend's house for like two weeks and I called the program and the man told me I needed to get there right now. So I don't even have a choice now. It's not about if I want to go or not. I'm homeless now for the first time in my life. I've been in a place before where I didn't have an apartment but I never had been in a place before where I was homeless on the street and I have nowhere to go. Padre is not here. I don't know what to do because of course he's locked up. He was locked up before the house got raided. He's in jail he's got two years and now I'm like out in the street with no place to go. I am trying to stay at my girlfriend's house but I don't know anything about staying from place to place, person to person. I really don't know how to do that. So I say forget it God is in charge and I guess what I'm supposed to do is go to this program. So I figure let me go do this program thing and get it over with. So of course, now I know the devil was mad at work because a week before its time for me to go to the program I'm sitting at the welfare. I am there with my girlfriend. I'm not supposed to be there. I went with her. I m sitting there we have been waiting all day for them to call her name for her check. They finally call her name, the first name they call after hers is my name. She was like you know they just called your name for your check. I was like get out of here it's probably some other Miss Taken. She said how many Miss Taken's do you think there are. Just go up to the window, give them your card and see if it's you. I was like come on how does that work you are sitting in the welfare for somebody else and they call you for a check? I had already been there to get my check before from the house burning down. So unbeknown to me they still had another check for me that had been there for two weeks and I'm sitting there that day and the lady is still calling off my name. I go up there and she gives me a check for $362. I get the check, I get the money, I go back to my friend's house and of course I'm getting high. So now that I have the money I'm thinking I can stay out a little longer I don't have to go to the program right now because I have money. I had already gave my friend $100 to hold for me so I would not spend it. But that friend left me and went out and spent my hundred dollars. So alright, I guess I am going to the program because I'm broke again. So I called the program and he's says you have to be there on time and

This Walk Ain't Right! But, Help Is Along The Way

I'm like OK whatever. I was at the program January 10th and all of a sudden it's January 31st and the man is telling me that I have to go before the judge. The judge says, "What are you crazy. I am not leaving this chick in no program on the Lower East Side of Manhattan. Look at her; she's like a dope fiend. She is totally a drug addict. She not staying down here. You better find her a program upstate somewhere or I'm sending her back to Ricker's Island." So I go back to the program and I tell everybody that the judge said I can't stay there. So they tell me you are gonna go back to jail when you go back to court so you should just go home and be with your family or whatever. So I don't tell them that I don't have no family to be with because I'm thinking I will just go back to my friends house and hang out for a little bit more. So I leave and my sister and her husband, well in the process of all this we had this business where we were sending drugs back and forth to Bermuda in Campbell's cans. There was one guy who kept the business. We had stopped doing the business. He didn't because everybody else that was involved was in jail or programs or whatever. He kept the business, so he still has this whole big business going on so he came up here. When I get back to Corona, I hear he is up here and looking for me. So I go stay in a hotel with him for a week. While I'm in the hotel the program calls me and tells me, actually they leave a message with my mother to tell me that I can come into the program on February 8th. So I'm thinking shoot, he's up here and I want to keep getting high. But then I think I better go into a program because I'm running out of money. So I tell my mother don't worry, don't worry I'm going to the program. So my brother-in-law says he's leaving, he's going back. He says he would stay up here another week so I would have a place to stay but he has to leave because he's buying boat parts so he could put the drugs in to get them back onto the island.

I go to the Post Office to check my mail and the bail money that I put on Padre, remember a year ago I bailed him out and he got sentenced and went back in jail. So the bail money is here now, I have my bail money back. I'm thinking I am gonna have $2,500. Oh My God. I am gonna kill myself. I mean I almost killed myself anyway. Oh yeah I skipped that part too. Padre had got hit by a car so he got like $50,000. I like spent that in about three months. That's how I got all these marks all over my body. I have so many like track marks. Look at my arm; this was like open when I went into the program. It wasn't even closed. It was an abscess. All these marks you see all up and down my arms this was all from shooting up. I even have them up and down my legs. My girlfriend used to shoot up in her breasts. I only did that one time and I didn't like that at all. I even went into my feet but that hurts too much. But all these marks you see all over my body are track marks. It just started clearing up. I mean it took 15 years. But anyway, so I'm thinking OK so what am I gonna do. I'm like battling with myself in this hotel room. I'm like, so I'm going to get this money and I'm gonna use. What's gonna happen to me? I don't want to be in the street. Like what's gonna happen to me. I just can't, I was too afraid to be in the street like that. Even with all the things I have done like the house burglaries in Nassau County. I mean I have done so much but, there was this part of me that was like this is not how my grandmother raised me. I had to live right. I had to take showers every day. I had to . . . I couldn't just live in the street and I said I'm just gonna go to the program. So I went and got high of course. I went and took my friend in the cab with me and we went and got the check. Then we went and bought like 4 bundles and I sniffed like 4 bags of dope in the cab on my way there. I gave him one of the bundles and I gave him a couple of hundred dollars. I always looked out for my friends, so I gave him a couple of hundred dollars to take care of himself. I sent Dave and them some money so that they would be alright. Then I went into Samaritan with about $1,700 left. The guy looked at me and it's funny because he and I work in this field together now. He said you can't come in here with that money. We don't hold that kind of money for people. Immediately I am like this is a wonderful thing let me call him back? I had bought a whole bunch of pills to take in there with me cause I knew I was gonna get sick, they don't stop you from being sick but they help you from getting as sick. I knew I wasn't gonna be that sick because it was only a week and a half that I had been shooting dope again so I knew I would be sick but not that sick. So I said I'm gonna take the pills with me. Now I'm thinking I don't need these pills because I'm leaving. It's not my fault that the man wouldn't let me in the program. I might as well just go and stay in the hotel room and just shoot some dope. But there was this other part of me that said I'm tired. I was really tired. So I called my mother. I said mommy I gotta come there because this man is telling me that I can't stay with this money. My mother said I'm coming and literally hung up the phone and I'm telling you it wasn't even 10 minutes, we looked up and my mother was standing there. She lives at least a half an hour away. She was at the door in 10 minutes. So I gave her all the money. Then she let me keep $100. They sent me up state after about 2 weeks. But before I went up I was down state for orientation. I was real sick while I was down there. The third day, I remember saying I can't do this. I can't be sick, I never could do sick. I never, ever made it through that. This guy was sitting there and he heard me saying I couldn't do this. He and I are still friends till this day. He turned to me and he was in orientation too, he said come on man we can do this together, I said naa, I can't, I don't know how to make it through sick. I have never been able to make it through a day. I said I would do anything to not be sick. I'm not going to make it I'm telling you. He was like alright. You can leave but NA just came in the building. Why don't you go with me to NA first? You can listen to them speak and if you still want to leave then leave. I said alright. Now I'm mandated anyway. I am facing 2 to 4 in Brooklyn and 2 to 4 in Queens's because the damn judge wouldn't put it together. So I would have went to jail for who knows how long, but I didn't care. I just didn't care I just couldn't be sick. So I went to NA and I'm listening. So this woman named Sharon came in there and she starts sharing. She said my name is Sharon how you living. She starts talking and I was just mesmerized by her, really mesmerized. I was just listening to her story and the things she did and the drugs she shot and how she had like let me see I have 15 years now, so she must have had like 8 or 9 years back then. I was just like listening to her and looking at her, she's lying. All I kept thinking to myself was she's lying. She's gotta be lying about all of this stuff, she went to jail, did bids and now she's sitting here looking all clean with some gold. I was like get out of here. So Ron went over to her and got her because he told her I was leaving. I was like, I can't do this and I was crying. I was like I'm really sick, I'm really sick. She told me could you just look at your arms. She was like have you really looked at yourself. She said I'm serious, have you really really looked at yourself. I was mad skinny; I had 3 teeth in my mouth. All my teeth were gone and I was like so thin and I was just like so sick. I had all these open blisters all over me. I was just nasty, just nasty. She was like is this what you want? Is this really what you want? I started listening to her and was like alright I'll try it, I'll try it. You know in Samaritan when you get ready to go upstate they don't tell you when you're going. They come to you that morning so you won't run. The next morning I feel like God didn't even give me time to make a decision. I had told Sharon I would stay tonight and I would try to make it through the night. I took one of the anti sick pills and I had two pills left. The next morning they came and told me to pack up I was going upstate to Ellenville. I didn't even think about it, I just like put some stuff in a bag. I got all my stuff and put it all in the bag. I remember I was in the van and I remember getting up there. All the way up there I was crying. All the way up there I was asking God to just help me. I was saying I don't want to be sick no more. I was really disgusted with myself. I was like I really don't want to do this no more. I was like just help me. If You just help me a little bit I will help the rest of the way. Sharon told me something that night before I left. She told me always remember and I put this on my message at home for the first 10 years I was clean. She said if you take one step God will take 10. So all the way up there on the van I kept thinking if you just take this one step God will help you. I kept talking to myself right? I got out the van and in Ellenville it was freezing up there. It was cold up there. Now this is the crazy thing. I was down state and I got $1,700 and $59 at my mothers' house right. I mean $1,600 and $59 at my mother's house right and $100 that they left there for me. All this stuff I bought at the store, this is new stuff. I stayed at Downstate from the 8th to the 19th. They are taking me upstate to Ellenville on the 20th and tomorrow's my birthday. The whole time I'm sitting at the table talking and I'm thinking it's going to be my birthday in two days; I m out of here. Are you stupid I'm out of here. Then I meet her and she makes me really look at myself. Nobody never told me what I looked like. You know what I mean. The whole time nobody ever said to me have you looked at yourself. I really had to look at myself. I mean I had 3 whole teeth and 6 pieces of teeth. In my mouth, I had 3 whole teeth

This Walk Ain't Right! But, Help Is Along The Way

left; my face was all drawn in. I must have weighed like 120 lbs. My arm was cut wide open. I had legions all over me and my leg hurt so badly because I had an abscess on my leg that was about 6 inches long. Padre had taken care of it and he had Abraham take all the poison out of it but it never healed right. So it was like open and it always hurt me. She just like made me see because she used her own story on me. She made me really really look at myself. I was just like crying all the way up there on that van and I was thinking if you take one step God, I will take 10. Over and over in my mind if you take one step God I will take 10. I got up there and I said to myself if you are going to do this, you really have to do this right. You can't do this wrong and I took the pills that I had left. I took one pill and I took the other one and I threw it in the snow. I remember that last pill was green and I threw it on top of the snow and I just looked at it. You see I wasn't supposed to have these pills. They never knew I had them. This is why I said if you are going to do it, you have to do it right. You can't go in here trying to sneak in stuff. So I left the pill in the snow and I walked inside. I went in there and I stayed up on that mountain for 10 months. For the first 3 months that I was up on that mountain I didn't think I was going to stay clean. I figured when I got out I would use, get high on the weekends. I would just get high a little. I wasn't really committed to getting clean. Then the next three months I was like maybe I just might get clean for good. I mean I had like 8 months on that mountain. They put me in what's called Ready Re and that meant that I could go down state and spend the night at my friend's house. I had no family where I could stay at their house. My baby sister was in a program just getting ready to come out. My mother wasn't having me in her house. Not because of me but because of my kids. She knew that if I was caught at her house they would have taken my kids from her. So I really had nowhere to go except my friend and she's gay. The whole time I did treatment that's who supported me her and her girlfriend. So I'm at her house and I'm messing with this dude that I met in Samaritan named John and he came over there. We are listening to music and we are playing around and he's getting ready to leave. My friend has this other friend who likes me. Now I have never been in a relationship with a woman or have I had a desire to. I never even thought of being in a relationship with a woman. Up to this point I had never touched or kissed a woman. The thought of being with women never entered my mind in my whole life. This girl I knew she liked me. I could tell she liked me. So John leaves and she stays. She is standing there. She worked at a Police Department, she was a cop. So we all leave and go to this club a gay club. So I'm not drinking, I always didn't like alcohol. I would have maybe 1 beer here and there the whole time I was clean, but the alcohol was never my thing. The question of whether or not I drink alcohol never came up for me because I can't drink. I may drink a half a drink and I'm done. So I decided to have a beer that's it. So we get back to the house at four in the morning. I will never forget this girl she kissed me. I remember thinking like when she kissed me I remember thinking like . . . . I always had a problem with ministers when they said being gay ain't right but I never really thought about it. I mean I always thought it wasn't fair. But for some reason when she kissed me I FELT SO SICK!!!! Like something wasn't right it was like so not natural. I couldn't believe she kissed me. That was the only thing going through my mind. I could really hear my grandmother's voice like telling me damnation and thinking about Nancy shaking her Bible at me it was so crazy!! I called her, she had just moved out the program. I called her at like four in the morning. So I said you know this girl just kissed me. So she started doing the same thing she had been doing 15 years ago. She starts yelling OH WHAT ARE YOU DOING.!!! But something's different in the way she was talking to me. So I said Nancy what's the matter. She was like don't worry. I was like I have been here all day and you haven't come to see me something's wrong. She's like don't worry don't worry. I hung up the phone. The girl had left and I'm going to lie down and John comes back so he says I just came back I'm gonna spend the night with you. So the next day Nancy comes and I kept looking at her and I knew something is wrong. I looked at her all day and I knew something was wrong. So John was still there and we were having fun laughing and joking and talking; we're cooking making pancakes with strawberries on them and everything. They are all laughing at me. I don't even know why they are laughing at me and I don't even know what they are laughing at but it was the kiss. So I was the joke, we had a great time. So I get back

This Walk Ain't Right! But, Help Is Along The Way

to Ellenville. When I get off the van two of my closest friends are standing there Marilyn and this other girl. They say you have to go back to the staff office. I'm like oh my God they found out about me and John. But I could automatically see by the look on Marilyn's face that it's a whole lot deeper. So I'm thinking something happened to my son Baby T. In the meantime he's staying in the streets. He was staying at his dad's house then he would argue with them and he would have nowhere to go. He had been through so much stuff during this time. So I go and the counselor gives me the phone and it's my grandmother on the phone and she tells me that my cousin Stuart died. My cousin Stuart was born at the same time as me, I told you that, like so we are two days apart. So through our whole lives we were always there for each other. I mean the drugs we did together, the selling drugs we did together. We brought the drugs to Bermuda together. We went to Amsterdam to get drugs together. The trafficking, we did everything together. So when I got clean, when I really decided that I was really tired and I really decided that I was going to do this I called him. So I'm talking to him and I'm like you know Stuart we really should do this thing. I mean really let's just do this thing because he had got arrested and he had went to jail for bringing drugs to Bermuda, it was getting crazy. I was like why don't we just get it together. He was like you know what I'm not gonna use no more. He said I promise if you go in the program and you get yourself together I'm gonna get clean and I'm not gonna use anymore either. He actually stopped getting high. Both of us was clean, but he thought he could deal drugs. So he bought this package in the night before, his partner was in the back yard burying it where they would keep their stash. He took out a couple of bags and he put it in a baggy and then he decided to try it. So he was doing some of it. So he came to Stuart to tell him this is good stuff. He said we had never gotten nothing like this, nothing this good. So he must have forgot Stuart had been clean for like 11 months. So the partner has him try the dope. So Stuart puts his 5 year old daughter on his lap and he's feeding her some ice cream. He starts sniffing the dope with his daughter on his lap and he's not thinking about he's not use to this stuff anymore. So he goes into a nod right away. He drops the ice-cream on the floor and she starts crying and runs to get her

Deliverance

mother. He just died right there with his daughter on his lap. All the thinking that I was doing on that mountain, I didn't know what to do. That's the only time I could truly say I was so angry with God. I was so angry. I went into my room and I was sleeping and I was angry and I kept thinking about all that I did. The houses I robbed, the people I hurt, the things that I did. All the things that I had did to my kids. I felt how could God leave me here and take my cousin. Even with the stuff he did he never hurt nobody. So I was like really mad and I went to sleep. I remember falling asleep and I remember waking up that morning. My friend woke me up and asked me was I gonna come downstairs with her. I remember I said I will be down there in a minute. I was just laying there talking to her and the next thing I know my cousin was standing there and he was reaching out his hand. It was like I was still sleep and he was telling me to come and go with him and he was scared and he didn't want to go by himself. He was telling me like come and go with me please I don't wanna go by myself I am scared. I was reaching for him and it was like in a second I was going to be touching his fingers and my girlfriend came in the room and she woke me up. So I couldn't grab his hand. I woke up so mad at her, we still laugh at that, she was like girl please that was that damn Heroin making you dream. I was like I have 9 months I don't have no Heroin dreams. Stuart came to get me and you stopped it. Me and her still laugh about that. She is like Miss Taken that boy did not come to get you. I'm like listen my cousin came to get me; I know he came to get me. I woke up for some reason from that moment on I really knew he was at peace. I was telling my grandmother you know granny he is really at peace. They wouldn't let me leave and go to Bermuda to the funeral. That's one of the first things I did when I got clean I went to his grave. Well by the time I got clean it was time for me to bury my grandmother and we buried her right on top of him. I went to his grave and even to this day when I go to Bermuda I go to his grave and I just laugh and I'm like you were trying to take me with you. I know you came for me and I would just laugh, I don't care what nobody says I know that boy came for me.

I left the program after that. I made a promise to him. I think right up to that minute I wasn't really really serious. But when he died I promised him that I would never ever ever shoot another bag of dope. He would never have to worry about that. After that I just got clean. After that I went to get my Certified Alcohol Substance Abuse Counselor (CASAC) papers and met Larry and I went and got certified as a mental health counselor and then Larry and I got together and I moved in with him. The whole time I was getting clean, Padre was in jail. When Padre came home I had already met Larry. I was already seeing him and I really think to this day that I got with Larry because Padre and I are no good together. To this day I never stopped loving Padre but we are no good together. Soon as Padre came home I got back with him right away. I was still in Reentry and he didn't have an apartment yet. He was staying at his sister's. I found myself hanging out with him and our old friends walking around the house with bags of dope and I had my sons with me. I looked up and I was clean. I was like what are you doing here. Everybody here is drinking and getting high. Passing bags of dope to everybody and Andy it didn't bother because he was only like 5 or 6. Abraham was looking at me and the look he gave me was like what are we doing here mommy? What are we doing here? Remember I've been gone like a year and change. They haven't been part of the insanity; you know what I'm saying. They were like living a normal life, although they didn't want to be at my mother's house life was normal. Abraham had been at my mother's house for like 4 years and Andy a year and three months. I said Andy I don't think it bothered. But Abraham was like what are we doing here? I looked around the room and I said to Padre I can't live like this anymore. I said I don't even fit in here anymore. I came here with you because I really thought I could be clean and still be a part of all this. But I can't. I don't fit anymore. The things that these people are talking about I don't want to talk about anymore. I don't want to be talking about whose going back and forth to jail, who slept with who, who killed who, what bag of dope is better. Who got the good dope, who got the crack? How much money . . . I don't want to talk about this. I want to talk about some mental health stuff. I want to talk about substance abuse. I want to talk about finishing school getting my CASAC and studying. That's all the stuff I was doing at Larry's house. He was already working in the field. The time when I met him, he had 4 years clean and he was already going somewhere. He was just getting ready to sign up for school again so he could get his masters. When I met him I used to laugh at him because he was crazy as hell. He would say all I want out of life is for someone to call me doctor. I'm gonna get my PhD and he had all these dreams so the conversations I was having with him was so inspiring to me. When I looked up and saw myself sitting in that house I was like I can't. I love you but I can't. I will never love anybody like I loved him. Padre became my best friend. To this day Padre is my best friend. It just would not have worked. He just wasn't ready. If he was ready we would probably die together, if he would have been ready. At that time and that place he was still sniffing dope and I was just too afraid of using again.

I moved in with Lawrence and I ended up getting pregnant with Ana and we went and got married. Before my grandmother died we got married. She wanted to see us get married. She went with us to City Hall. She called me when I was pregnant with Ana and she asked me to please not have another baby out of wedlock. She was like please don't do this again. Mr. T and me were already married when I had Baby T but Abraham and Andy I had with Padre and we never got married. She was like could you not have another baby out of wedlock. So Larry and I we went and got married, more for her than us. I did that for her and we had Ana.

Maybe a year and a half after I had her I went to the doctor and I found out that something was wrong with my liver and I got sick. As soon as I got clean I started going back to church. I was going every once and a while. When I was in Re-Entry, that's the last days of the program, I needed to make a meeting. I made this meeting and this woman was sharing and it turned out that the woman was the same Sharon that had gotten me to stay. So I met her back that night and I asked her to be my sponsor. So she became my sponsor and she hooked me up with all these women, wonderful wonderful women who had like mad time. I became a part of this whole blood line of women and stuff. We used to go and meet at each other's house every other weekend. I really always say that my first few years of recovery was such a gift from her because she really helped me to become like grounded. We went to my mother's summer house and we gave some things to God and she taught me. Everything that Sharon did was surrounded by God. She taught me, when we did the third step turning your will and your life over to the care of God as you know Him. She told me if you don't get the spiritual part of who you are in this fellowship you are not going to be able to stay clean. You can't do it on your own.

Although Narcotics Anonymous is a spiritual program, not a religious program, it really is based on God. This man sued Narcotic Anonymous because he said we have the word God in our literature 52 times, so how could it not be a religious program. All we talk about is God, but she really helped me with that. I really believe that that third step is what got me to reality. I really wanted a relationship with God. I wanted to believe in Him and have some faith. I was half stepping I would go to church sometimes but then when I got sick, when God blessed me with Ana and I got sick and I went into the doctor's office and he told me that I was really sick . . . My liver was not doing good at that point and I had to go on all this medication and I remember just sitting in my car and crying. I was like God please; they say its three stages till death or whatever. I was at the let's make a deal stage. I was like listen God just let me be around to give her some stuff. I'll stay clean I will do what I have to do I just want to stay around her. I want to tell her some stuff; I just want to see her go off to college. I don't have to see her get married none of that. I just want to give her and Andy some stuff. Up until I got sick I think I was taking time for granted. I was like oh I have plenty of time to tell my kids some stuff but when I got sick I realized how precious time was. When I lived in the hospital for that month; I got sick and I had 105 temperatures. I was in the hospital for 4 weeks and 2 days. I laid in that hospital and there were so many times in that hospital I just thought that this was it. I was so sick. The whole time I was in that hospital I prayed so much. Padre's brother who was a shepherd came and prayed over me. The Shepherd of his church came and prayed over me. Our Shepherd, he came and prayed over me. I was at the hospital and the making a deal stage was over for me. I was at the surrender stage; I was like you know what God if you don't give me more time it's OK, it was like this peace I had. It was like I knew I had spent the first seven years of my daughter's life I knew I was sick for 5. I knew that sitting in that car and promising

Deliverance

God asking God for time I knew I had given enough and said enough to Ana and Andy because God gave me that extra time. I knew I had told them the things I wanted. When I first was sitting in that car and she was only two years old I was so afraid because honestly I wouldn't want nobody in my family to have my kids. I love my sister Monica to death but she's very sick so I don't know how long she would be around and my daughter loves my sister so much. At that time they told my sister she had 5 years to live. I would not have wanted to give my daughter to my sister for her to die after I die and go through that. I had to tell my husband how I didn't think he could raise my daughter. I was really really sick so I had to think about what I was going to do with my kids. The only person in my life that I knew I would want to have my daughter was my son Abraham's wife. I knew she was going to be the person to care for her.

    I thought my daughter wasn't going to change. She was this sweet little kid. I didn't want her to become angry and bitter. But she changed and she is angry and bitter. She had a lot of issues and I knew she would be angry and I knew they would be the people who could help her through the tough times. My husband agreed and said he would get her on the weekends because he knew he would not be able to give her what she would need emotionally. He knew what I was saying was the right thing. Then I told it to my mother and sisters. I didn't say why I just said I have my own reasons. I would want Andy to stay at home with Larry so he could be in his own house. He has always been independent and able to take care of himself. He was pushing chairs to stoves cooking food for himself when he was four years old. He would always come to Mount Horeb for food at the Soup Kitchen and Pantry. At 4 he would get the shopping cart stand on line get the cans of food and pull them back home. He would take bottles and cans and cash them in. I knew he would be alright. Ana changed a lot after I got sick so I knew it would be hard taking care of her. Even the school said they didn't understand why she is so angry. She still is not the way she was. I guess she won't get back. When I get sick it really scares her. I try to take her to church. I try to keep her involved in the church and have her talking to people in church. This way she will understand more things. I don't get sick as much as I used to anymore. I changed a lot of my life and my habits. Now when things start happening with my heart and stuff I don't even tell her. I don't tell anybody in my house. I don't think that they need to know. I think I'm at a point where I get sick and go to the doctor get meds and I'm OK. I handle it, because they can't handle it, especially her. It just makes her more and more bitter and she's just now coming around like a normal little kid. I can cough now and she don't come running to see what's going on with me. I can lay around in the bed. Today's the first day in a long time that I actually slept late and she didn't come in the room and say are you sick. It's OK I can just rest without her getting concerned. I don't want them worrying about me. When I first got sick I was on another mountain. I didn't feel like I was home. I just didn't feel it there. I always felt like when people would see me I was my mother's daughter. It wasn't for me it wasn't the place for me. The Shepherd preached one day about forgiveness and connecting to your kids. I must have stood up for 5 minutes standing up in front of that man. All I could think about was my son Baby T and all the stuff I've done and all I put him through. So I gave my life over that day. When Ana started dance I was talking to someone who asked if I went to church and I said yes every Sunday but I didn't feel connected. I didn't feel like I was supposed to be there. She told me about Mount Horeb and invited me to worship. I came that Sunday and the Shepherd was preaching and I had a totally different feeling. I came there and felt like I arrived. The fourth time I came; a female minister was preaching about gratitude and being thankful for some stuff. I started like thinking about everything. I thought about the jail cells, times I should have died, the different places I have been in when people were shooting and just everything. My life was just like flashing and so much stuff. I was like God has brought me through so many things. I felt like this is where I belong. I had been there about 4 or 5 times and I didn't put it together until that day that this was the same place that fed my family when I was out there. I started to remember standing on the side by the gate and I said I'm climbing Mount Horeb. When I first went to Mount Horeb I wanted to do so much. My life has gone full circle. My mother met my step-father in the house I live in now. I lived there when I was 18 years old. Then me and Padre came back there when I was 25 and I came back in there when I was 32. I

Deliverance

moved back here and my church is who fed my kids. The circle of life is weird. You know the walk is not easy it's hard. Sometimes I think like what's it all for? Do you really need to go to church? Or can you just be like I know there is a God and that's that? I will go to church and the Shepherd will preach and I will get encouraged. Like one time the Shepherd preached and he was connecting Psalms in the Bible to songs and he would start singing songs. I have never forgotten that sermon. As a matter of fact that sermon has been on my heart for like a month now. It was so moving and you can't get that sitting at home.

God gives me a lot of angels. Since I got clean God has done nothing but put angels in the midst. Like my boss, Carl, I had a year clean and then a year later I was talking to him on the phone about trauma group. That's the group for women who have been molested. He asked me to run a group with him because his co-leader was leaving. I was surprised he asked me because he never saw me in a group but he said he saw how I talked to the trauma mamas, on an individual basis. That's what we call them. I started to run the group but it was deep because up to that point I had not dealt with my own trauma. I could not really talk about being molested. Prior to running the group I would see the girls coming out of group and they would be crying and come to me and talk about the things that had happened to them. It's funny I always knew what to say to them. Doing that group and then me and Carl leaving there on Tuesday nights together and sometimes it would be 11 at night. We would like sit in his car talking until like 2 or 3 in the morning. We would talk about my trauma. That's how I got to be OK after 7 or 8 years of these talks. I mean later I ran the group alone when he got his promotion but I worked through my stuff with him. And then like I said Sharon, Dorinda, all the people God brought in my life when I first got clean. They taught me like how to have women friends and trusting. They taught me how to take care of my sons and be a mother. They taught me how to say no to my kids. I didn't know how to do that either. To know the part that a mother plays, I mean I had that from my mother. I mean I knew I was supposed to guide my kids but never really knew how. They all came into my life and taught me. I mean like my friends. He brought some awesome women into my life. I mean like every year in February we all go away together.

It's so funny because I'm the person that they will call up and talk to about God. They will say things like I want to have faith but I don't know about this faith thing. They call me and they are talking to me and I don't really know nothing either but to them they are like just ask Miss Taken she knows everything. I have to laugh at that cause I feel like I don't know anything.

I got onto Mount Horeb and even now for whatever reason God put it on my heart to come and be a part of the women's conference committee and I met all of you women. I started befriending you and you women started sharing your lives with me and that is really what this is all about. It's just about people sharing their lives with you. That's how God showed me other people. Then I meet this guy Mo who I have talked to on the phone. We have never physically met. He saw me in the hospital when that thing happened to my kidney and I had to have that new path put in there. He came to see me but I was out of it. If I passed him on the street then I wouldn't know him. But yet I can talk to him about anything and everything. I can get on the phone with him and I feel free to say all kinds of stuff. It's really weird. When I was coming up as a little girl I felt like God shortchanged me. I didn't have anybody to talk to about none of my stuff. Like everything in my life was just mine. The only person I ever really dumped it on was my sister Monica. I never felt like anybody cared enough to listen. Then I grow up and God gives me all these people that I have to dump everything on and I don't hold onto anything. I mean like my whole life is like one big open book, especially at my job. I tell my clients everything and anything. I share everything with them because I want them to know that I did the same things you did. I slept in abandoned buildings, I had no place to go, I did house burglaries in Nassau County, and I've been in jail. I've done all that.

The first time I shared was in Narcotics Anonymous. Every time I shared my story there was one thing I never shared with my sister. This story I shared in Narcotics Anonymous was about the couple of times when Padre went to jail. When I was using I never had to prostitute right, so Padre was always there so somehow or another we made money. We did burglaries and I never was a woman who could think that I could sleep with somebody to make money. Not for nothing I'm real scary you know. I'm a real scary person so I can't be jumping in and out of strangers' cars. I'm the person that is thinking like you getting ready to kill me or something. I remember one time there was this old man and I knew he liked me and Padre had got arrested. I was so sick and I was always afraid to be sick. I always worried about that. I was so sick this morning. It was mad early in the morning. I saw him and I knew that I could just go to his house and just be with him. I shared this story in NA one time. I was talking about what it felt like to lay there. I knew the man but he was still a stranger as far as I'm concerned. I had this stranger who was on top of me doing whatever the hell he was doing, I was as stiff as a board just laying there holding on and just clutching that damn $20 bill like it was $500 waiting for him to finish so I could hurry up and go. I was just laying there not understanding that with a man it takes nothing away from him. Only the outside of his body is touched and he moves on. When a women has sex with somebody, or every time you have sex with somebody a piece of your soul, you are giving of yourself, that's the most precious part of us that God gave us and to just give it away. I remembered thinking I can't. This was at the very very end of my addiction. I remember thinking to myself while I got clean and I was doing my 4th Step and I remember writing about that. Maybe that happened so I could have a glimmer into what life was getting ready to be like. That's not something I ever had to worry about the whole 17 years that I got high. If I would have continued to use that was definitely gonna be my future. I knew that I wasn't the person to do that because those little stupid things, and to me they were stupid things, I would worry about. But it would have been only a matter of time that someone who was using would have said Miss Taken shut up, close your eyes and just think about what you can do with the money. I couldn't get past that. I shared about that in that meeting and I shared about the pain and I shared about what that felt like and the degradation and all the things that we do that comes along with being in the street and using and not knowing from one moment from the next. You know people hear that people get arrested and they go to jail and people say well they should not have done what they did. People don't think about what happens to you. You go to jail and you get these cold silver bracelets put on your arms. You get treated like nothing. You get taken to a jailhouse and somebody puts you in a cell. Then you are strip searched, take off all your clothes. They have to look under your arms lift up your breasts, they look between your legs, you have to bend over hold your behind open for somebody. You have to squat down on the ground and open up your vagina so they can make sure there is nothing up there. Nobody really thinks about the degradation you go through when you get arrested. If you really don't incorporate that part and you are the type of person that just tells yourself it was nothing then you have no problem going through it again and again. Or you could be like me and really have a problem with it. That was too much for me. I hated that. When I hear about people going to jail that's what I think about. I don't necessarily think about what they did to get there I think about what they go through when they get there. I pray that it is really hurtful to them and that they will see the degradation that it is and don't want to go back and they don't wanna do anything to have to go back. It's so much to it and you just know that God . . . There's got to be a reason you got all these people waiting on Jesus and one woman touches his gown and He didn't say somebody touched me like wait a minute somebody touched my hand. He said like wait a minute somebody touched my robe, like He felt it in his gut. It's gotta be a reason why that women, at that time and Jesus was at that place at that time. That's how I look at all of our lives. There's a reason why we are all where we are supposed to be at those specific times and at those times in our lives God sends somebody there that's gonna tell us something and it's for a reason. But if we don't really see it for what it really is we will miss it. We might not take it for what it's supposed to mean, we might just miss it. I talk to Mo all the time about this. I listen to people when they say I wonder if I'm doing what I'm supposed to be doing or what am I supposed to be doing. He was talking to me about evangelism and He asked if I have a vic.—that's people you bring to the Lord and they allow themselves to get saved. I told Him I have a lot of "vics." I have a whole program full of people. I got some guys who have murdered people, I got some pedophiles, let's keep it real there are some people who are coming across my path who have done things to children, people who have hurt their own children, people who have been hurt, I have sat in rooms with women who have told me that their mother's held them down while they sold them to their first trick. I have all these people that God brings in my path and every single one of them at no time do I miss the opportunity tell them about God. Like anytime I get the opportunity to tell them about God I tell them about God. No matter what they talk to me about, no matter what my boss may say or think about it, my thing is oh well they will be fine. I feel this is the chance I have to tell this person. You got to be able to see this for what it is. You can't minimize it. You have to know that God put me here for you. You have to know that I'm your angel today, and you know what? Watch out for your angels, look out for them, and take advantage of them. Then pray that God puts angels in your children's lives so when they are ready to hear something that there will be an angel there to tell it to them. I really believe it. I guess that's why I do the work that I do. When I'm not doing what I'm supposed to do, I feel it. When I'm not going to church and I'm not getting up and putting in the effort. I honestly feel it, it's like I know I'm doing wrong. God lets me know I'm doing wrong. I would say that I'm evangelizing all the time. If that's what the meaning is. I'm telling people about God and telling them my story and letting them know about grace and mercy. I'm always telling people about that then I guess that's what I'm doing. I mean I tell clients all the time that Mr. F It always travels in 3's. He never travels alone. As soon as you say F It, he brings pain and misery everywhere he goes and the only way to combat it is to bring Jesus and grace and mercy with you. That's the only way we can do it. That's the only way we can combat it. There is nothing else. I don't care how you try to do it, it ain't never gonna work because as soon as you get ready to say I don't care here comes Mr. F**k It, the next thing you know you look through the peep hole and there is Mr. Pain and you open the door and Mr. Misery is standing there; and you have let all three of them in and you are back standing there. Before you know it you are caught up in all of that stuff all over again. When you look for Jesus you will find him and then grace and mercy come along with Him. You know then that you are all balanced. I hope I explained what I am trying to say. It's like you know you are balanced out and you know you are gonna be alright.

This Walk Ain't Right! But, Help Is Along The Way

Everything I've done in this world let me tell you Miss Guided, I've done some stuff, and I've hurt some people in this world and I think about it. Some of them I don't know their names and I don't know what they look like but one time my car got robbed when I was in Target a couple of years ago. When I got in my car and I saw that my car was robbed, I know how I felt. I left my pocketbook under the seat and they had took a bracelet and all these coins I had been saving for Ana since the day she was born. I thought about it and was thinking about all the different things they took. At first I was getting so angry and then all of a sudden a peaceful thing came over me and I said OK God. I was alright because everything you do in this world you have to some way pay for it and you have to make amends for it. In that moment I knew exactly what the people felt in Babylon, Riverhead, Mineola, all those people out on that island for like a three year run. I was going up in those people's houses stealing their stuff. I know exactly how they felt then. They must have felt horrible when they realized that I had been rummaging through their stuff. There's some things that I stole from those people that was so sentimental. It was stuff that didn't even get me any money. It was sentimental value to them; it was worth thousands of dollars. That's how I felt about those little lousy couple of coins that they took from me when they robbed my car. I was thinking wow it is exactly how those people were feeling when they came home and found that I had been in their house. I just believe that everything you do has to come full circle. I said OK this is my day to find out what it felt like. I let it go. Whatever had come over me ready to complain I let it go. I thank God for the experience. I thank God for allowing me to feel what I felt and then forgive myself for what I had done to those people. I really hurt some people.

My son Baby T, I taught everything he knows. All the wrong things I taught him. How do you go through life knowing you taught your kids all the wrong things? My mother didn't teach me how to be hungry and take things from people to eat. My mother didn't teach me to get on a corner and sell some drugs just to get a new pair of sneakers. My mother didn't teach me how to buff a razor blade up my behind because I'm on my way to the penitentiary and how to take from people and hurt people. I taught my son all of that and I take full responsibility for that. You see when I was using I wasn't who I am. I was somebody else, I didn't care. I taught him everything wrong. Now he is paying for everything I taught him. He is paying for all the mistakes I made. My middle son has always been like lost. He has always been this kid that never thought he was where he was supposed to be. He left my house because he didn't want to be there. Now I look at our relationship and we are so close. We have the most awesome friendship. I don't know if that's what a mother and son is supposed to have. What I do know is that God has placed something special on our relationship and it's great. I get to share in his son, I get to help in raising his son and I get to give him the things I was never able to give his father. I look at Andy and I don't know how much he remembers. I look at him sometime and I wonder how much of that life does he really remember. I know he remembers being at my mother's house because he talks about it a lot. He doesn't have a relationship with my parents at all. None! He loves them but he has no relationship, he has nothing with them. The whole time he was there a lot of things went on that he didn't agree with. He saw things happen to his older brothers and he feels that they do some stuff sometimes that's not right. He has the ability to remove himself like his feelings set them aside take a look at it later and then move on. He has always been able to do that. That's what he does with them. I watch him and we've talked about my addiction. I mean we have all talked about it. There is a girl who lives out here and she drives a school bus. She use to get off the bus come to my door and the window and bang until I came to the door and gave her Andy. If it wasn't for her, my son would have never went to school. This was another angel that God put right there. I was like she was a bus driver for God's sake. Why don't you mind your business? What part of not answering you don't get. She would get off the bus to come get my son. Boy would she bang on that door. I would be like what do you want and she would say I'll wait. Get him dressed I'll wait. She would look at me like she knew I was a drug addict. I would be looking like what is her problem? Padre would say why you don't try sending that boy to school. It's so funny when I got clean I was making a meeting at Elmcor out here. Who walks in there but her. I found out the whole time I was using she was in recovery. She had like five years clean and she was coming to the steps to get him because her thing was I wish somebody would have come and got my son. So she was doing for my son what nobody ever did for her and what she couldn't do for hers. I was like wow. I was amazed by that. So I've caused a lot of people a lot of pain and I just try to live my life I mean even when I was using I tried to live my life where I never wanted to leave anybody homeless. I took in animals. When my house burned down I had three pit bulls, like 20 puppies, a big turtle, a cat, a rabbit and an iguana. We had so many animals the ASPCA raided the house and took them all. We got them back though. I was always the person who took in all the strays so it was never really hard for me to open up my heart. I always knew that God gave me this gigantic heart. My heart was too big. I had all this love and I just needed to find something to do with it when I got clean. I give it to my clients I give it to people I come in contact with. I went and got my CASAC because I wanted to help people get clean man. I don't want anybody to be crying and using against their will anymore. I watched my children be hungry and had to choose between a bag of dope so I could be straight or food. The dope won every time. I would have to get the dope first, get straight and then get money to feed them and wash clothes. Remember I couldn't be sick. I remembered all that and that's why I went and got my CASAC. I really, really wanted to help people get their kids' back, to become real mothers to their children, to take care of their families. I push all my clients to go to church. I always tell them to go and find a God of their understanding. Some people get clean and they just are angry. They don't even realize that they are angry. When they start realizing they are angry they just say I don't have to worry about this part of my life. It doesn't have to be the God I know it could be good orderly direction. I don't care what you get you have to get a God of your understanding so you can have a higher power, something higher than yourself to believe in. Then once they start getting themselves together and they start seeing it they all usually go out and start finding churches. I fight with them on my job about things like the clients can't go to church on New Year's Eve. That's crazy and then they say OK, OK I'm not going through this with you and they let them out for church. When they come back they have all these stories to tell about how good it felt to come to church on New Year's Eve. Normally they are getting high or on top of roofs shooting off guns or whatever.

I've seen so much. Baby T started telling me all the stuff that he did. My son's role model was this guy I introduced him to. He got with my son when he was 15 years old. He gave him a bike, gave him $200 and took him shopping. He told my son to open up 6th Street for him and that's what he did. This guy went to jail and got natural life plus 200 years. That's crazy to me because once you're dead your dead. Um his father was a detective. When his house got raided they found bodies in the walls, he was building his house. When he killed the people he put them inside the walls. Someone told the police so they knew where to look. He used to have Kilo's of heroin in his car and bricks of cocaine, crack and stuff. He used to keep a lot of his stuff in my house on 6th Street. He would be in his car driving and the cops would stop him but he was OK with the cops. He would flash a badge and they would let him go. So they have to have had a reason to go up in his house. Somebody told on him. Apparently he killed a girl from out here and that's what he went to jail for, murdering her. I think one of her brothers told. You think you can just be killing people. You can't be killing somebody's sister I mean come on. They buried her in one of the rooms in that house. I don't know what they were doing to the bodies; I guess it was some sort of embalming because there was no odor. It's crazy you could live there knowing that there were a bunch of dead bodies around you like its nothing. My son was watching the History Channel, and they did a whole story on this guy. He called me up and he was laughing and saying mommy I want you to look at this. These are my role models; he never knew how much that bothered me. He was laughing saying these are the role models you gave me. He didn't even understand the seriousness of what he was saying to me. You know what I mean I thought about it and was like these are the role models I gave you. This is what I showed you a man is supposed to be like. But we don't be thinking about all of that when we are getting high. Now when I look at my kids, l look at Ana and I tell her totally different things. I tell Andy totally different things. It's funny and I am raising my grandson and my son will call me at like 10:00 and ask me where his son is. I will be like Baby T, little T is 8 years old. For 8 years he has been going to bed at 8 and 9 o clock at night, when you gonna get it. He cracked up laughing, and says mommy I still can't believe you put some kid to bed at 9:00 at night. He was like 9:00 at night; Andy was just coming home when he was 4. I'm like ahh excuse me I'm not living like that no more. We can laugh about it but the reality of it all is that it was 9:00 at night and I didn't try to do something different. It's all about making amends; you can't make amends with some people you hurt but you can definitely make amends by doing things differently with other people.

I had a lot of amends to make. I wanted the whole world to be OK and I know that's not possible but at least all the people that God brings into my life; I could try and touch their lives. I could try and tell them that they don't have to live like that no more. They can try something different. It's funny I keep bringing all my clients to all the meetings I would go to. The problem is, once I bring them there I can't go to that meeting anymore. I keep losing my meetings. The other day I was laughing and I was saying you not bringing nobody to Mount Horeb, I gave up my meetings but I'm not giving up my church. I remember I walked in and they were there on New Year's Eve and I was like you gots to go!! No I'm kidding. I love to hear their response to the church. They say Ma I love it there. It's so nice your church. You know God just be WORKIN IT OUT!!!

It's like the other day a client was moving out and we took him shopping and stuff. He's not really into God yet. He's getting there but has gotta lot of stuff to get pass. So we took him shopping because he never ever in his life had his own apartment. He was 40 years old and never had nothing, never had a job, never had his own apartment, nothing. So we get in BJ's and he buys a TV and we're buying sheets and Tide and stuff like that. So we get to the sheets and he says oh my God I don't have any sheets for my bed. So we get to the sheets and I say get this one its 420 thread count and it's on sale this will be good. So he's just standing there and I said come on. So he's staring at the comforters and he's like but Ma I'm gonna have to get a comforter. He said it's gonna be cold right, it's a basement apartment, a studio. So then he says oh I can't get that. I said why that's a nice comforter set, he said no that's not for me it must be for girls because it says it comes with shams and skirt to it. I don't need no skirt that must be for girls. I cracked up laughing. I was like look at this guy. The little things that people don't even know; he doesn't even understand what it means to have a skirt that comes with a comforter set. Me and my co-workers were laughing so hard tears were rolling down our faces. So we explained to him the skirt concept.

You know it's really a joy to watch them come in like little kids and when they leave they are men and women. I look at some of them and I'm like wow. There is this man who is 68 years old and I call him Mr. When the clients come in I always see them as kids they are my babies. I feel a little weird because he's like 68 years old and I'm telling him what to do. He looks at me and he's like what you talking about I'm an old man. I know what I'm doing. I look at him and I'm like wow he's grown, he's 68 and the drugs got him too. But God, Oh my God, I look at them like if you only knew or could get what God can do, you all would be alright. They don't understand that all you have to do is ask God for forgiveness for everything that you've done. For hurting people, for everything, it's all you have to do. You don't have to pay nothing and you don't have to beg. There is nothing in the Bible that gives you a list of 100 things to do and then God will forgive you. All you have to do is come to Him, accept Him and just ask. All you have to do is know that there is a God and just ask Him and He will forgive you. Then just begin from right there. Once you ask God to forgive you and you recognize that God has forgiven you then forgiving yourself comes so much easier and you can just breath and move on with the rest of your life. They just be looking at me when I'm talking to them. I say to them, I don't even know if I'm saying it right, I just know and I don't know how I know, I just know.

That's my conflict with my middle sister. I want her to know God so bad. I want her to know. I know if I just could go to Bible studies and if I could understand a little bit more then I will be able to explain it to her. Then she'll get it. My mother keeps saying that's not how it works I just have to keep praying. My only prayer for my sister is that God will touch her heart and let her know him like I know him. Then others tell me keep walking your walk and she will see. Show them the Jesus in you and they will see and say hey I want some of that. I'm just

This Walk Ain't Right! But, Help Is Along The Way

like I hope so I really hope so. I just feel like she will be incomplete if she doesn't get it. She just has this yearning for it. Then again sometimes I wonder if maybe she is yearning for something she's already got. You know how you want something and you can't see it and its standing right there in your face. I say you know what? Maybe you already have it. God's been there all the time and maybe He didn't leave you maybe you left Him. Maybe if you start thinking about all the things that happened to you. Go back to that night when you thought you were going to die, go back to the time when you stole my medication took it and went out of the house and the man hit you with his car and you laid up in the hospital in a full cast for a year. Go back to all of that and remember all of that. Remember the fear you went through. Then think about how there isn't anything else but God that has brought you through all of that. How could you have survived all of that? Nothing else but God could have brought you through all of that with some sanity. I always tell her that and I'm going to keep talking to her. I reminded her of the time when she went to the doctor and she weighed a hundred pounds soak and wet. I said your feet were really bad and your hands were so dark that they were black in the inside. Your liver was hardly working at all. The doctor told you that you had 5 years to live and put you on some medication. The meds were not 100% but they started to help your liver to heal itself. Here we are and those 5 years have turned into 10. That's something to believe in. Do you think the doctor has the last say so? He doesn't and it's not about him. You die in God's time not the doctor's time. I know people that the doctor writes you off and 10 years later you are still sitting there. It's not his journey, when God says so it's so. It's just that simple. I thank God for everything. I thank Him for you. I will even say where did that come from I will say that had to be God because I'm just not that deep. He gives it to you to help others. Just like that day you walked up to me MG and said you are supposed to do something really special in rehab. You said you did not come in thinking that but when you saw me it just came to you. He just dropped it on you, and then you dropped it on me. I ain't going to lie I was like yeah OK. But you know this walk ain't easy but I would not have it any other way.

Deliverance

Wow I am amazed by your story. You have been through so much. I am stunned. I forgot about that day I walked into service and saw you and I was driven to tell you that you would be doing something special in rehab. I didn't know it then but I realize that there is discernment that comes with my gift of exhortation. I am not trying to act like I can predict the future or anything but God drops things in my spirit, directions to guide people. It blows me away when that happens. I used to say where did that come from? But ever since I had that incident when I heard His voice clear as day I realized it is part of my gift He has given me. You are so amazing and I thank God that He has brought you into my life. I have learned so much from you about struggle and having a relationship with God that's not broken even when you are in the midst of addiction. You see my husband and brothers were addicts but they were taught religion not relationship. I think that's why they had such a difficult time getting pass the drugs. Once my husband got the relationship part he was able to get off the drugs and start a renewed life.

I guess it's the social worker in me but your story really speaks to me about how dysfunctional relationships and functional relationships can chart the course of your life for years to come. MT asked what I meant by that. I mean, your step-father violated you and robbed you of your innocence. He took something from you that you spent years trying to get back through drugs. On the other hand your grandmother taught you the importance of having a relationship with God by demonstrating her relationship. Grandma prayed, worshiped, talked to him and loved Him dearly. What she showed you was so strong and so believable that you relied on her relationship until you developed one of your own. You believed that He would see you through some of the most difficult times in your life. MT said this is why I have so much gratitude for Him. He is awesome; He looked out for me when I was too strung out to look out for myself.

Wow where did the time go? We better get back inside and pick up our daughters, plus its getting cold out here. Are you cold MG? It's beautiful out here. I think it's this cold I haven't been able to shake. My daughter got a bad cold and she slept in the bed with me and of course I got sick. You aren't cold MT? No I told you it's beautiful out here, you better check that out.

I went inside and got Pooh and went home to get some rest. I felt horrible. I figured I would take some cold medicine and try to sweat this cold out once and for all. When I got home I took the medicine but it wasn't working. As a matter of fact I was having difficulty breathing, I had a 102 temperature and felt so week. Pooh came into my room and said mommy I think you should go to the hospital you don't look good. I was too weak to drive and too weak to even call the ambulance, so Pooh did.

After multiple Asthma treatments and a fever that would not stay down they decided to keep me for observation. This was the beginning of a journey that I never expected. So it's Friday and I call my family and ask them to bring me some of my personal items I'm going to need to stay here. I had a feeling since it was so close to the weekend I wasn't going anywhere until Monday. I felt so lousy that I didn't really care. As long as I had my Bible, CDs, a TV and my gospel music, I was OK. The biggest thing was I had to leave Pooh but my family and Mr. Manhattan Slick looked out for her. When I first got into the room I didn't have a roommate. This was cool because I got to choose the bed by the window which was close to the bathroom. I was so weak that I needed to be close because walking was difficult.

The doctor comes in and tells me that they want to run tests because the medication they were giving me didn't seem to be working. He told me that I will be seeing a Lung Specialist and he would be here in the afternoon. While I was talking to the doctor my roommate came in; this woman walked in the room and did not appear to be ill. The doctor left and we introduced ourselves. The woman's name was Sister Mary Kate, she was a Nun. She said she was here for a special test and she was only going to be here overnight. It was funny because she and I connected immediately. She was such a nice lady. We talked for hours about our families and especially about God. I asked her when she went into the convent and she said she was 18. I didn't ask her age but I would guess that she was in her 60's early 70's. I was so impressed by the fact that she has given her entire life to serving God. Here I am teeter tottering back and forth between total commitment and holding on to my past, present and worrying about my future and this lady has unselfishly given her entire life over to God. We talked about Jesus and what He did for us by giving His life. This conversation was awesome because I never sat and spoke with someone who was Catholic about God before, at this level of detail. I realized that we may be from different denominations but we were connected through Christ. I told her how much I wanted to be fully committed but something was stopping me and I didn't know what it was. She told me to pray and just say yes to God no matter what He asks of me. This lady was so nice and warm and encouraging. It's funny she was only supposed to be there over night but she was there for days. I was in and out of it though, much sicker than I realized. When I was in the bathroom, or testing or sleeping, she would make sure I had what I needed. She made sure they came to bring me fresh, linen, supplies, meals or whatever.

My cousin called me today just to see how I was. She was not aware that I was in the hospital. When I told her she said I was on her mind and now she knows why. She came to see me. She and I talked for a while and she is such an inspiration. She lost her mother, aunt and youngest daughter in a fatal car accident a couple of years ago. I remember she came into her 12 year old daughter's funeral rejoicing. She said she knew she was in heaven and she was OK with that. I told her that day, when I grow up in this walk I wanted to be just like her. She and I talked and she prayed with me and we had such a nice visit. She showed me a book she was reading called *What Happens When a Woman Says Yes to God*. I couldn't believe it. This is what I had been talking to the nun about. My cousin gave me the book and I was so happy and eager to read it. She also told me about some financial problems she was having. She said she was behind in her rent and needed $500 to catch up but she knew the Lord would provide. It was at that moment God said to me help her. I thought about what Miss Understood did for me and I took out my check book and wrote her a check for $500. I told her she did not have to pay me back just do it for someone else one day. My cousin left and I showed the book to Sister Mary. She said wow this is exactly what we were discussing. She said God really wants you to focus on Him. I told her I agreed and immediately began reading the book. It was amazing. It was what

I needed to read and talked about how I felt. Little did I know the wisdom I would gain from this book would change my life? The next morning after 5 days the nun left to go home. The funny thing is she called me every day on the room phone. I could not understand how she was able to get through to me because I didn't have the phone on because I had a cell phone. Anyone else who tried to call me could only get through to my cell phone. God made a way for her to get through to me. Each time she called I was growing tired of being there but the sound of her voice gave me a sense of peace.

The doctors said I have an infection in my lungs. I have been here a week now and they don't know what the infection is. They want to run more tests so they can figure out the right antibiotic to give me. I feel so sick, I want to go home but I want to feel better. At this point all I can do is pray. I wonder who they are going to put in my room next. I put my headphones on and listened to my James Fortune and FIYA CD I will Trust you.

MG's Prayer
Dear God,
I come to you tonight sick and very tired. First I would like to thank you for giving me such a lovely roommate who touched my life in ways I can't explain. I feel You sent her to me to watch over me and encourage me and she did. I love you God for that. I don't know what is going on and why the doctors can't find what's wrong with me but I thank you for the wonderful nurses and the doctors who are doing the best they can. I know that you will deliver me from this situation when you see fit. I pray for strength to endure what's to come. I thank you for my cousin and her encouragement and the book that is helping me so much. I pray for deliverance Lord. I thank you for the people who are looking out for my little girl and please continue to have them take care of her. These things I thank you for and ask in Jesus name, Amen.

In the middle of the night they moved a new roommate in my room. It is a little old lady who is 104 years old and looks 80. I know this because her daughter came in this morning to sit with her. Her

Deliverance

daughter is 85 and looks 60. She said her mother hurt her leg in the nursing home she was in and they brought her here for observation. Apparently the pain is raising her blood pressure. This is something I'm familiar with because my back pain causes my pressure to elevate. The little old lady was so sweet. She thought I was someone she knew from church and she kept talking to me as if I were that person. She reminded me so much of my mom when she was in the second stage of Alzheimer's.

I went into the bathroom to freshen up for the morning. While I was in the bathroom I was bombarded with thoughts, messages, about this hospital experience. God told me that I would be here for a while. I remember thinking I have already been here for a week how much longer do I have to stay. It's funny I didn't get upset I just said yes to God. I felt that He wanted me to learn some stuff while I was here. I was a little concerned because Pooh's 14th birthday was this week. I have never missed her birthday. Although I knew this would not be a great thing for me to be in the hospital on her birthday I knew it would work out. God told me I won't be home for her birthday so I arranged to celebrate it here. I came out the bathroom and called Mr. Manhattan Slick and Wisdom and told them that they had to help me make this work for her and they agreed. The Lung Specialist came to see me and said he would like to keep me here for a few more days. He said he still doesn't know what's wrong but now I have been coughing up blood and he is alarmed. At first he thought it was from straining but the tests indicate that there is an infection and blood in my lungs. He said he was going to run a few more tests and hopefully we will know something soon. I was OK with what he was saying because God already told me I would be here. That night the little old lady had a rough night. She was in a lot of pain. I called the nurses to tend to her. They gave her medicine but she was so disoriented. The thing that blew my mind was she kept calling Jesus. I remember thinking wow. She's just like mama; she may be dazed and confused but no matter what she still knows Jesus. I said my prayers:

Dear God:
You clearly brought me here for a reason. I am so humbled by this experience. I am so weak and each day they tell me something else is wrong but don't know what's wrong with me. I am not afraid and I know that's because of You. You are keeping me through this. I am not even upset about not being home for Pooh's birthday. Only You could put me at ease like this. I thank you God. I pray that the little old lady sleeps peacefully tonight. Lord, have mercy on her and take away her pain. I love you Lord and thank you again for everything, in Jesus name, Amen.

The next morning I woke up and the little old lady was leaving. She was feeling better and taken back to the nursing home. It's funny I learned from her again the importance of having a relationship with God. Even when your memory goes if you have a true connection a true relationship you will never be detached in and out of consciousness. Wow God is no Joke! I went into the bathroom and God spoke to me again. He said I need you to let go of some stuff. You want to be delivered from your past but you won't let go. I can't just take it away from you; your will is too strong. You are going to get some more news today about your health but trust me you will be OK. When I came out the bathroom the nurse was there. She said my sugar levels were really high because of the amount of steroids I was receiving. She said I have to take insulin shots three times a day. My IV kept failing because my veins were collapsing and I had to get the port changed daily. Again I was OK with what they were saying because again God had already told me. I just said so do what you have to do. I started craving sweets like crazy though. I asked Mr. Manhattan Slick to bring me some candy and fruit and he did. Wow he is really stepping up to the plate. I felt maybe I shouldn't speak too quickly because he may stop. My doctor came in and said that he really didn't want to send me home because he still is not clear on what's happening. He said if my insurance company gives them a hard time he will send me home with a nurse because I was too weak to function alone. I told him that I was not going home in this condition and God has blessed me with good insurance so that should not be a problem.

Deliverance

As I was sitting on my bed and listening to music I kept hearing in my head 18 years, 18 years. I was trying to figure out what was that about. Then I kept hearing 18 years while reading my Bible. OK now I was bugging out. I did not know what that meant. I called Miss Understood and asked her did she know of anyone in the Bible who went through something for 18 years? She said kinda but I can't tell you who that might be off hand.

I called the Shepherd and asked him if there was a woman who went through some stuff for 18 years. I was familiar with the women with the issue of Blood and that lasted for 12 years but I kept hearing the number 18. He said yes the crippled women. In *Luke 13:11,* she was bent over and had led a sin filled life for 18 years. I read the passage and started to think about what I have been dealing with for the past 18 years. So I took out a pad and wrote down the word dates and listed 18 years in chronological order. Then God told me to write down what event happened during that year that really bothered me and I didn't realize it but I never got over these issues. So then I wrote down the word weight which is what He gave me next. He said these things have been weighing me down for years and I need to let them go. Then He said something awesome. He reminded me that I lived through them; I survived each of those stormy times in my life. He said not only did you survive you gained something each time. You must become aware of the things you gained. You should no longer allow theses weights to weigh you down; these are things that are standing in the way of having an intimate relationship with Me. You must see that these things have given you the ability to fly over troubled waters; these events become your wings. You went from dates to weights to wings. When I finished the list it looked like this.

Dates	Weights	Wings
The Year It Happened	What Weighed Me Down	Knowing This Allowed Me To Fly Above It
1991	Daddy's Death	No More Suffering
1992	Husband's Addiction	He Got Help
1993	My Divorce	I Was Set Free

1994	1st Brake Up With Mr. Manhattan Slick	Diminished My Sin Life
1995	Became a Single Parent	A Special Bond Developed
1996	Mama C. Has Cancer	A Closer Relationship
1997	Mama Has Alzheimer's	Cherished Time
1998	Pooh Had Surgery	Avoiding Hearing Loss
1999	Failing Relationship With MMS	Discovered Who I Am

Dates	**Weights**	**Wings**
The Year It Happened	What Weighed Me Down	Knowing This Allowed Me To Fly Above It
2000	Mama C. Died/Manhattan Slick Gets Married	No More Pain/I Found God
2001	Garnish My Paycheck	Consulting Experience
2002	Mama's Health Declines	Received Help Caring For Her
2003	Got Laid Off	Got a Better Job
2004	Mama Didn't Know Me	Mama Didn't Know My Pain
2005	Dis-Ease Death	He Was Saved & Drug Free
2006	Severe Problems at Work	Learned To Trust God
2007	Mommy's Death	She's At Peace
2008	Disabled	Found My Purpose

Wow God is blowing my mind. I learned so much about myself; all this time I thought I had put all this stuff behind me but I didn't. God has reframed my experiences from negatives to positives. I guess this is what it means in the Bible where it says And we know that in all things God works for the good of those who love, him, who love him who have been called according to His purpose. (*Romans 8:28-KJV*). I feel like someone just lifted a building off of me. Wow. Then God said to me use this activity in the future to help someone else shed their weights. I put my headphones on and prayed before I went to sleep.

Deliverance

My Dear God,

WOW! Thank you for the revelation You showed me today. I feel so free. I feel like I have been walking around with plugs in my body and you gave me the ability to remove them. I mean the plugs served a purpose. They were there so I would not bleed all over the place because I was walking around wounded. Somehow I found a way to plug up my wounds but that did not work for me and You knew that. You made me remove the plugs and although there are still holes the plugs became more uncomfortable than the initial injuries. Thank you God for allowing me to see what was blocking me from You. I ask that You continue to work on me so I can be who You are calling me to be. I love you Lord. Good night.

I got my third roommate this one was a real doozy. She was a little old lady. This lady reminded me of Estelle Getty from the *Golden Girls*. This lady was very nice to me but so mean to the nurses and doctors. She was a religious women she said she was Catholic. The reason why I say she was religious was because she prayed, talked about her involvement in church and, the importance of receiving Communion. She had a fit when she thought they were not going to bring her Communion. She complained about everything. She said she was worried about her daughter and she cried. She said she was worried about the food they were going to give her and she cried. She paced the floor and said she was worried about her sister and she was worried about worrying. I thought this was a joke like I was on the show *Punked*. This woman was unbelievable. She would talk about God one minute and then worry about everything under the sun the next. This lady was driving me crazy. God has me in a place of peace, I'm not worried about anything, but this lady is truly testing my patience. She started in again about the laundry list of things she was worried about. I could not take it anymore. I told her in the nicest way I could that someone once shared something with me that I wanted to share with her. I told her if you are going to pray don't worry, and if you are going to worry don't pray, you can't have it both ways, it doesn't make sense. She looked at me in bewilderment. She did not say another word until it was time for her to leave. She came over hugged and kissed me goodbye. Then the golden girl said to me you know what young lady, what you said made a lot of sense. I am going to try and remember that. I told her that I hope things work out for her and her family. She was getting ready to complain, I could feel it. Then she stopped herself and laughed. She said they will because I'm gonna pray and not worry. I said Praise God! And she left.

No sooner than the *Golden Girl* left another roommate was brought in. This time it was a Korean woman. I was a little leery about this roommate, I usually get along with everyone but I have been a victim of being followed around Korean stores. It was my experience that they didn't have good experiences with some black people. I wondered if she would have a problem rooming with me. I was just grateful I didn't have to spend another night with the worry wart. The women came in with her husband, she spoke very little English and he spoke a little more than she but not much. They both came in and spoke to me and smiled. I was happy that they were friendly.

Today is Pooh's birthday and I was happy because Wisdom arranged for us to celebrate it in the hospital. Mr. Manhattan Slick brought Wisdom, Pooh, and my niece Kindness with her son up for the celebration. Pooh wanted a camera like my niece Kindness had. They brought a cake, balloons and the camera. She was so happy. I was so grateful I was able to celebrate with her. I was sad in the morning because I wasn't there when she woke up because I have always been with her when she woke up on her birthday. I called her and woke her up on the phone and then Wisdom took her to breakfast. Mr. Manhattan Slick picked her up and they hung out at family day in the park until they came to see me. We enjoyed each other's company and I walked them to the elevator. I laid down put my headphones on and prayed.

Dear Heavenly Father,
Did I tell you how awesome You are today? This day was amazing! I am so grateful that you are there for me in spite of me. You have showed me so many lessons and resolved so many issues in such a short period of time. Today I learned that worrying just takes too much energy and does not make sense if a person truly trusts you. I learned that it's important to be patient with people who are

trying to figure out this relationship process. Just because a person is not where you may think they should be you must still try to encourage them, even if they get on your nerves. Lord I am also so grateful for the time I was able to spend with my baby girl on her special day. I thank you for my friends and family that made this happen. Lord what I am really blown away about is the fact that you know how much it hurt me that Mr. Manhattan Slick was not at the hospital the day she was born. Here we are 14 years later in a hospital with him celebrating her. This meant so much to me. I have always felt cheated by him not being there and You worked it out where he showed how much he loves her. That's all I ever wanted was my child's father to truly acknowledge her and love her enough to show up. He showed up today and that meant the world to me. Thank you God! You have brought new meaning to better late than never. As matter of fact I know what they mean by you are an on time God! In Jesus name, Amen!

I woke up this morning feeling sick and my throat was hurting so badly. When I urinated I could see particles coming out of me. My first reaction was to get worried but I remembered to pray. I said God I don't know what this is but I am not gonna be scared. I'm just gonna tell the doctors what's going on and I am in the right place to get help. God then told me that I was really sick but he was going to heal me. He gave me a vision I saw that I was in what appeared to be an operating room. I was with doctors and nurses and they were about to put me under anesthesia, God then told me it would not be surgery it would be a procedure that I needed and I would be fine. I came out the room and the lung specialist was waiting for me. He explained that I would be undergoing a procedure tomorrow. He explained that there is fluid in my lungs and he wanted to extract some and have it tested to see what type of infection I have. He said they would take me into an operating room and perform the procedure. I started smiling. I know this doctor thought I was crazy. I was smiling because God had just told me this in the bathroom. I said OK do what you need to do. He said first I need to do an MRI test and some x-rays but I will schedule the procedure for the morning. He also said that they think they know what I have and the infectious disease team would be down to see me. Now if this would have been any other point in my life prior to coming to the hospital I think I would have panicked, but I didn't. The infectious disease team came in to see me next. Those guys were kind of scary. It was four of them. I felt like I was an alien from out of space. It was the way they were looking at me and talking to me. By this time Mr. Manhattan Slick was back to visit. He questioned the doctors and wondered why I didn't question them. I could not explain it because God told me I was going to be OK and I knew I would be. I said OK and thanked them and enjoyed my visitors.

The transporters came to get me to take me for my MRI test. I remember I had this test before for my back. I remember I didn't like it because it was so closed in. At first I was OK but as I was in there for a while I started to get a little antsy. I started to repeat the *23rd Psalm* and I was OK but if I was in there another minute I would have freaked. So here I am again. This time they say I have to go in twice with contrast and without, that's a fancy way of saying they are going to do a test with dye and one without.

So I get to the room where they are doing the MRIs and there is a lady ahead of me. She tells the technician that she is claustrophobic. She says she is going to try to go in but she's not sure. So she goes in and flips out. She starts screaming and yelling and totally loses it. The tech got her out of there. So now I'm lying on my stretcher thinking this is great. I was trying to build up my nerve and this lady freaks out before me. So the tech wheels her out the room and puts her in the hallway. She was so freaked out that she doesn't even want to be in the room with the machine waiting for her transport. Now it was my turn. The tech told me he could pipe in music if I liked. I ask if he had Gospel stations and he said no they don't come through in the basement. I said well give me what you got.

I said a prayer. Jesus I need you right now, I am so scared but I need this test. Please calm my nerves and come in here with me so I won't be scared.

No sooner than I finished that prayer I felt what felt like arms wrap around me as if I were being hugged and peace and warmth came over me. I said JESUS! I know that was Jesus. I said to the tech I am

Deliverance

ready now. I was so calm, as a matter of fact he had to tell me to stop moving because they were playing an old school song that I knew and I was singing and bobbing my head to it. He pulled me out injected the die and said one more time. He said I'll try to be quick. I said take your time I'm fine. As he rolled me back in I said come on Jesus and we went back in. Before I knew it the test was over.

So my new roommate was also a Christian. Her place of worship family came to see her and prayed by her bedside. They sang hymns in their language which I thought was really nice. I knew how important that was because I loved when the sisters from my house of worship came to see me and called. The Shepherd visited and prayed with me and encouraged me. He also called on the phone and I called him. The deacons came to see me and brought prayer and communion as well. My worship family made this experience bearable through their encouragement and support.

My roommate's husband left the hospital and his wife's doctor came to see her. The doctor was Chinese and did not speak Korean. She was trying to get my roommate to understand she wanted her to go through chemotherapy as soon as possible. The roommate tried to use the few words in English she knew telling her she wanted to wait and pray on this decision and talk to her Pastor. The doctor started yelling as if she were deaf and said in the most insensitive way.

You don't have time to wait for God. You are going to die! Then she walked out the room. I got so angry. I was so hurt for the lady. She looked so hurt and had no one to talk to. I called the nurse and told them that I wanted to file a complaint on the lady's behalf. That was so wrong, so hurtful, and they agreed. The lady did not understand much English but she understood that. I felt so bad. I asked God what I could do to make her feel better. He told me to read the Bible with her. This was an amazing experience. I walked over to her and held her hand and said that was mean and you will be OK, she was wrong. I asked her if she had a Bible. She understood me and took hers out. I didn't know what to read but I knew we had to read something to take her mind off what had just happened. We fumbled for a minute or two because my Bible was in English and hers was in Korean. We both realized that they may be in different languages but they were in the same order. Somehow we managed to signal that 1 meant the *Old Testament* and 2 meant the *New Testament*. Once we figured out what testament we wanted to read we would count the books out on our fingers. Once we knew we were reading the same thing we laid in our beds with the curtain opened and read the Bible together silently. A sense of peace came over our room. It was so beautiful, so amazing so peaceful. Later her son came in and he spoke fluent English and he translated for us. I told him what the doctor said and how she said it and he thanked me for looking out for his mother. It was late and he stayed a while and left. After he left, my roommate started talking to me. She was speaking clear English. I could not believe it. We were talking, communicating. It was amazing. All I can say is there is no other explanation other than but God! After we talked for a while I put my headphones on and prayed:

Dear God:
You did it again! Another awesome day! You taught me so many lessons today. My day started off with You telling me exactly what was going to happen. Thank you God you prepared me so I wasn't afraid of the doctors or the procedure. Then you sent me for a test and I felt the arms of Jesus wrap around me and console me when I needed it the most. Then You allowed me to encourage my roommate. Then You showed us how to read the Bible together without speaking each other's language. Then You miraculous You!!!! You made it so we could understand each other and have a conversation. I am in awe of You. Thank You for the experience, thank You for being You. I love You. In Jesus name, Amen.

OK today is my procedure. I have to get up and go to the bathroom and talk to God before they come to get me. I could not get in right away because my roommate also has a morning ritual. Her Pastor and husband come in every morning for prayer. They also do some kind of healing ritual I am not familiar with. She would get up at 6 every morning take a shower get ready and lay in bed until they came. They would pray for healing. She believed she was being healed and I have to say she looked better and better each day.

So it was my turn to go in the bathroom. I had my talk with God. I looked in the mirror and saw how sick I was. I also saw how much weight I had gained over the years. I saw myself differently than before. God said to me don't worry, You will be beautiful again just trust me through your process. To be honest I didn't know what that meant but I will trust Him. He said everything would be fine so I was ready. They take me down and my veins were not cooperating. They could not give me the anesthesia because they could not find a vein that would not collapse. The nurse was very nice. She was so warm so friendly. The Anesthesiologist grew impatient and said he was going to go into my jugular. The nice nurse said no let me try one more time. I said wait give me a minute. I said a quiet prayer asking Jesus to show her which vein. She said I got it. I said of course you did. She said what you mean. I said I had a little talk with Jesus. She said Oh you're right. Why didn't you do that to begin with? And we both laughed. I was out in a matter of seconds. I came out fine. The doctor got the fluid he needed.

I had to stay for a few more days until the results came back. They said I had a rare infection and gave me some super expensive medication. They also told me after all my years of smoking I had no traces of lung cancer or emphysema, no nothing. After 21 days I was allowed to go home. The last night I was there I just reflected on all that I experienced. This was the most amazing experience of my life. I will never forget what transpired in that hospital.

Miss Guided Deliverance

Wow deliverance is a difficult step. You would think by now I would come to realize that there isn't anything about this walk that is easy. It's funny as you begin to recognize that this walk is a process you begin to see that the way you see things initially are not how they actually are. I mean they are real but you are looking at things through the lens that you currently have. As you grow through God's process you begin to realize that you need help, you can't fight your battles alone. You need help, and that help doesn't come from friends or family. Too often we reach out to them and it's funny during those times you just can't seem to connect with them. Either they are not home, not answering the phone or just not available. I know there are people who don't have family or friends or a support network and they too feel alone. No matter who you are or how much family you have or support you all wind up in the same place alone and searching for answers and peace. That peace you can only get from God. My first understanding of deliverance is that God is powerful and can do anything. All I have to do is ask Him to take it from me and I will be delivered.

I move further along in my process and I begin to realize that God has given us free will. He wants us to come to him freely not forcefully. Along with this is the development of a willingness to relinquish control of all aspects of our lives. It's kind of like driving a car from the passenger seat. You know there is a driver who is behind the steering wheel but you feel a need to take charge, take control. Although you know you should stay in your seat and let the driver drive you still find the need to look both ways when approaching an intersection, simulate putting the brakes on when you feel something is coming your way and danger is near. Although you know and supposedly trust the driver you still feel the need to take control, stop the car, take the wheel or give directions. Somewhere deep inside you know that you should sit back relax and enjoy the ride. We have to be willing to give up our stuff or stop holding on to things. I think what happens is for so long we have these coping mechanisms that we are accustomed to. They are a part of us whether they are healthy or not. It's just that these are the things that help us to continue to function so we are not willing to let go. Then we find God and He says I got you. We don't automatically believe that he will make it better. So we keep holding on to what we know. In order to be delivered I have to be willing to try God.

I think the third part of deliverance is understanding what you are truly being delivered from. Too often we want to be delivered from some of our destructive coping mechanisms. We think that's the problem but these things are usually a symptom of a bigger problem. It's kind of like taking a *Tylenol* when you have a fever but when the *Tylenol* wears off the fever comes right back. That's usually because you were treating the symptom and not the root of the problem. It's like if you have an infection you must treat it with an antibiotic not a fever reducer. Most times we have blocked consciousness of the true core of the problem, so we can't allow God to remove it and we can't give it up because we are not aware of the true problem.

The Shepherd called to see how I was doing after returning from the hospital. I told him I was OK physically but mentally a little off balanced. I admitted to feeling so guilty. I had this beautiful spiritual journey in the hospital and then I lose it in the car with MMS on the way home. I was so angry and I found myself bringing up old stuff. Things he has done in the past that I thought I had gotten over. The Shepherd said so I guess you have not forgiven him. I said I thought I did but I guess I haven't. He told me that I have to let go of what I am feeling to truly experience deliverance. He also told me that the bible says we can't expect God to forgive us for our sins if we can't forgive others who sin against us. He said I really needed to work on that.

I told the Shepherd that it must have something to do with all the stuff he's done to me. It's like his forgiveness credit reached its maximum limit. Maybe that's why I am having a hard time. I asked does the bible say a person gets to keep doing stuff to you over and over. He said no people are not supposed to keep doing stuff to you, but you have to remember that's between them and God. You on the other hand are supposed to keep forgiving them. I said oh yeah I remember reading something about forgiving 70 times or something. The Shepherd laughed and said yeah kind of, sort of like that. He found that so funny but I was like that's crazy. He said look at how much stuff you have done and God shows you Forgiveness, Mercy and Grace. I said I guess you have a point. He also said I would be surprised how good I will feel if I just let that stuff go. I was like yeah right, but I agreed to work on it. He then spoke about deliverance.

The Shepherd Speaks On Deliverance by God

2 Timothy 4:18: If there is any one person in the Bible who knows firsthand about the delivering power of God, it's the Apostle Paul. Paul was delivered both spiritually and physically by God. Paul makes it clear that he wasn't always on the Lord's side. There was a time when he persecuted the church and rejoiced in the persecution of the Saints. But God delivered Paul from a wrong way of thinking and living in Acts 9.

Once Paul decided to live his life to the preaching and teaching of our Lord and Savior Jesus Christ, he experienced the same type of physical threats and dangers that he was use to inflicting. Paul had been lynched, rioted upon, ridiculed, almost stoned to death and ship wrecked. So if anybody knows anything about the delivering power of God, surely Paul does.

In his letters to his spiritual son Timothy, Paul encourages him to be a good leader and to be a warrior. Knowing full well the ability of God, Paul assures us that "God will." That's the good news. In times of trouble; in times of sorrow; in times of sickness; and the list goes on. We must come to know God the deliverer. He not only will deliver physically, but spiritually as well. Even after salvation, the deliverance should be the prayer of the believer. "Know that God is willing to stand by you, to strengthen you and preserve you for His Heavenly Kingdom." To God be the glory, Amen."

Healing

The Sixth Set of Footprints:
Luke 13:11-13

Lord You Took it Away, But I'm Still Hurting!

My Friend, Miss Story, came to my house to see me after I got out the hospital. She asked me how I was doing. I told her I was so happy to be home. I also told her I had a meltdown when Mr. Manhattan Slick picked me up from the Hospital today. I think I really have to do some work on myself regarding forgiveness. I thought I had forgiven him for all the mean, horrible things he had done in the past. I know the bible says I have to forgive in order for God to forgive me but it's easier said than done. I really thought I had but I guess I didn't.

While I was in the hospital I was on a lot of steroids to improve my condition. Steroids can change your personality, they are mind altering. I really was not my normal patient self. MMS said something to me and I don't even remember what it was but I was ready to take his head off. I was so angry. The next thing I know everything I WAS FEELING THAT I HAD BURIED CAME OUT. It came out very nasty too. I could not believe how angry I was. Miss Story said that's not like you. I said I know right but being who he is he could not just let me have my moment. I've been drugged up for the last three weeks and finally leaving the hospital. Oh no he had to argue back with the crazy person. How crazy is that? I felt rage like I never felt before. I was so angry that I wanted to jump out the car on the highway. I think I tried but he stopped me. I was totally irrational. Later I thought about what went down and although I was angry that he would not let me have my moment I knew something was very wrong. That rage came from somewhere; the meds lit the flame but all the stuff I was feeling was sitting inside of me. I was just waiting I guess for the flame to be lit and I exploded. This is what I mean about This Walk Ain't Easy. I have to forgive him and that's all there is to it no matter how hard it is. I have to work at it. I told myself I forgave him since I let him back into my life as a friend and co-parent. What I realize now is that I gave him *A Pass* not forgiveness just *A Pass*. She asked what I meant by that. I said I am going to define *A Pass* as when you let the incidents or occurrences go but you don't let the feelings associated with the betrayal go. Although I was delivered from feeling bad about his lack of participation in Pooh's life I guess things are still unresolved, my feelings that is. I feel so much better since he's involved but I still have open wounds regarding what initially went down. I guess I haven't healed from that yet. Miss Story said Girl please! Healing is so challenging. It's not easy; it's a process in itself. Let me tell you my story.

Well unfortunately I have no knowledge of me as a baby. Never talked about it, never been discussed. I know my mother loves me, but no baby pictures of me. We just never talked about it. I don't have any idea of what I looked like when I was a baby; not at one, two or three years old. I think I may have maybe one or two pictures when I was six or seven, maybe two or three pictures. It bothered me a little that there were no pictures. She never talked about me as a baby, nothing no discussion. I think Mom almost died with my brother, it was a decision that had to be made, and it was the child or the mother. But God prevailed; it turned out good. And, you know, she didn't have pictures of my brother either. I just have one brother.

I remember as I got older my mother always made me be a lady. Every day, my hair was combed. I mean my mother made sure I was immaculate when I was a child. I was dressed to the tee, the little dresses, and when I got older she would put a little perfume on my neck, things like that. I got lots of dresses as I got older. I can even visualize the picture of me when I was younger; at that point I had to be, like I said I had to be either five or six, or something like that, but as an infant I don't have any knowledge of what I looked like or anything.

I think my mom always went to church. Well the sad part is that I found out really recently that I was never christened so that kinda upset

Healing

me a little bit. I didn't know that. I remember making a joke about it, how can I not be christened. She said nothing really. If I didn't realize how much my mother loved me, I would take it personally. I think it was based on her struggle. You know about her raising two kids. My mother was divorced early you know. And I think they stayed together when I was little but I just think that she struggled a lot you know. She said she would sell her jewelry for milk. She had two kids and she was working, so I didn't take it personally. I think it was just about survival.

There weren't too many pictures of my brother either. Maybe a few, maybe some of him on a bike, in my grandmother's yard but not a lot. My father's mother, lived in New York, but my mother's mother lived in North Carolina. From what I understand that relationship was good when the parents were together, but when they broke up my mother was sort of on her own. That's why I don't look at it as something bad, because I know my mother worked hard for her kids. It's no doubt.

My dad and I were really close. I can't believe I'm crying. It's hard still for me to talk about him; he was always involved in my life even though he wasn't living with us. My best memory was when my dad would pick us up every weekend, every single weekend. My mother was coping with my father. He was so upset when he found out I was a girl and my grandmother would say what do you want us to do shove her back in there. He didn't want a girl, he wanted another boy. It was funny we became so close, he use to uh like I said pick us up every single Sunday and um, we just became friends. When I went to school I would work for him at his company after school. He was the one who sent me to charm school, taught me how to do my nails. I remember when we use to walk to charm school and he was the one that taught me about loving myself as a woman. My mother took up the same role, but she was the mother in the house. She was the one that disciplined us, got me ready, and made me feel that I had to always be immaculate. Which is an issue now, and was always and my father was that way too. He wouldn't let me come outside without my nails done, whether he was there or not. I had to have them all freshly polished. He said either they are done or you are not going outside.

My first church memories were Easter Sundays. I remember when we use to get all dressed up and of course go to church on Easter

Sunday, but um other than . . . my mother would go to church, my father and mother was divorced at that time but um, I don't have any strong memories about church. I have some memory of walking to church on Sundays, you know, especially on Easter Sunday. My mother would have to work so much she would go to church when she could. I remember us as kids, getting the dog during the week when she had to work until ten o'clock at night, walking him to the bus stop to meet her and walking back home. Uh, I think I was in Junior High School.

My mom, she was always faithful I mean trusting and believing in God. I knew that. I would remember her saying just little things, like just trust in God, just trust in the Lord, you know, trust in the Lord. And being around my extended family when they shipped us to North Carolina every summer; it was about praise God and I remember the big hats. Services weren't every Sunday down there. But I remember when we would go it would be the big hats. I remember my aunts, every aunt always talked about God. So that was instilled in us you know and that was my concept of Him when we were young.

The Shepherd would come to the house for dinner and there was the picture of Jesus with the blue eyes. I said my prayers, "Now I lay me down to sleep . . ." the standard prayer and bless my food. I don't know at what age I started, maybe five or six. The whole family, all the aunts talked about it you know, trusting God, and you know you really didn't question it, to me it was just agreed. I wasn't like some of the kids that were five or six or seven that get up there and make announcements and do a little singing in the church choir you know, it wasn't like that, but He was there. God was important.

I never remember my father living with us. So, he would, we would talk to him every day on the phone and uh he was strict, very strict. Then he would pick us up every weekend. We knew the color of his car and got excited when we saw him coming. I was so wild in my teenage years; I went to Fashion Industries High School in the city. I use to go to my dad's office, he owned his own company. I use to work for him. For two years I use to make $15 a week. My father use to take five as soon as I got paid and walk me to the bank with that $5, yeah the old school mentality. I use to ride over to my girls, I don't know where it was, somewhere in Brooklyn, hanging out with the wrong crowd.

Healing

I was dating guys I shouldn't be dating, guys that were drug dealers, drug dealers! That was until my father found out. My friend and I were going out with theses drug dealers you know. We didn't date little drug dealers, it was the ship load type of drug dealer. So I hung out with this guy, left the house around 9 o'clock at night, lied said we were going to this party. We were all coming from an afterhours spots at about 12 in the afternoon. Then it happened one day my friend's mother was waiting on the #5 Bus and here we come walking down the street with our little dresses on, our high heels. She started questioning us, she couldn't find out where we were coming from and she beat us both in the street. I was in high school and she told my father's mother. I wasn't living in that neighborhood, we lived in Flushing and they were waiting for us when we got home.

My brother and I were close, played a lot. We are just a few years apart, three years apart I think. Yeah, I think we were friends for the most part. I know that my brother and I both struggled with my father's death. He cooks and every time there's an event he tells a story something my father said to him, I think it's something about the man he is. There are some aspects about my father that I didn't like; one of them was he didn't want to apologize for stuff. I think that there is more that he did we block and I think that both of us have issues with his death. For me, I have serious issues. Yeah, I have issues with it uh, well just in terms of I miss him you know, just had great times with him. He died from cancer, it was so quick.

I was 24 when my dad died. I remember because it haunted me and that stayed with me for a long time. I had spoken to him on the phone. I couldn't remember whether he was in the hospital at the time or he was home, I think he was home. He told me, to tell him that I loved him. Which I always said that I loved you and he promised me, he said I promise you that I am not going to die. And then he died that night. So I think it took a toll on all of us, but for me I just couldn't come to terms with it.

At the time we didn't live together and at that time we didn't see him . . . I talked to him a lot, but I really didn't see him a lot. I don't really remember how it happened. I think I found out when my mother mentioned it. I just miss talking with him MG. I remember when I got my heart broken he was there. It was my first close relationship I had when I was in college. He left me, he dumped me. My father came over and we walk the streets in Flushing until 12 or 1 o'clock in the morning and he walked with me and talked with me. We went to a diner; he just came and got me. He rescued me from my pain.

I waited until in my 20's to get into a real relationship and I had thought this guy was a nice guy. He was introduced to me by someone at my job. We started going out and of course like I said he was older than me. He was in the same business my father was in which was insurance and he was mature. I liked him, he met my family. After we were intimate I started hearing less and less from him. I guess he was engaged prior to meeting me and they broke up for a little while. He went back to her. The funny thing is I knew something was up because I saw a picture of her. The girl looked like me, her name was Miss Story. That was a clear sign. After that I called my dad, I was crying and of course we talked about everything. He use to always say, you're my girlfriend, we could talk about anything. People use to see us together like three days a week. That's why we were so close.

He taught me about a lot of things, like I got to trust myself and him of course. I remember he use to lie on my bed; he believed in the subconscious mind, he would say you are so beautiful, you know you're beautiful inside right? We were pretty close. My grandmother would say you know you are too close. She didn't like it. You need to let it go a little bit. That wasn't happening because I truly was a daddy's girl.

My brother and mother were pretty close. I think that's because my father didn't live with us. We had our ups and downs. Like every time I would run to daddy because he didn't live there, it would always be but she's my baby and things like that. I personally believe my mother had a little conflict there, but there was little she could do.

As a teen I was hanging out, trying to get into stuff, smoking and things. Like I said lying about where I was and um I could tell you the one day that it changed. Honest, to God, because it was right near here. We went to a party, hanging out with this girl; I went to the party. I thought it was one of those hole in the wall places, but it was a nice spot, with only one entrance on Northern Boulevard, I'll never forget. The girl's sister came in and said that her boyfriend was out

Healing

there arguing with someone and they were shooting. I started freaking out, I need to get out of here and I knew I needed to leave at that very moment. When I went out side, I said I gotta go home. So, I was outside watching the commotion. I didn't want to get shot; there was only one way in or out. MG, I started walking down Northern Boulevard and at that time there's no car, no cell phones, nothing like that. So I'm walking down Northern Boulevard and I look for one of those dollar cabs or whatever because Flushing wasn't that far, couldn't find one. So I keep walking and this guy was walking towards me and I say to him don't go down there because they are shooting. So he says well there is a party down this way, from where I'm coming from, they shootin down there too so don't go down in that direction. So I doubled back and I'm freaking out because I don't know how I'm gonna get home. I see a pay phone, I have to call my mother; there is blood around the pay phone. I called my mother and told her the situation and I stood there on that corner and I said to myself, I made a promise to God, I said God if you get me out of this alive, if I get home safely, I promise you that I will change my ways and I'll change the people that I hang around with. I promised, I just prayed and prayed. All of a sudden I see this little red car zooming down the street. It was like it stopped and my mother yelled Miss Story and I yelled mom? I ran over there and my mother was like in her nightgown no robe on top, nothing, it was summer time. She must have just put on some slippers and bolted out the house. We ran into this other girl, who was at the party and took her to the train station she was going to Brooklyn.

I tell you the honest truth I did not break that promise to God. After that my friend would call, and I cut off everyone, everyone. I cut them all off. I wasn't playin; I cut off every one, MG. I said no more hanging out in Brooklyn with those people that I was hanging out with, I said no more hanging out in Flushing with those people I was hanging out with, and I said no more hanging out. I didn't hang out with any of them. I hung out with my mother, my family and by myself. I was a loner. I was in high school; I felt so good that I didn't break that promise. It scared me so bad. I promised and I did it. For years I was by myself, yeah. God saved me because I was headed down the wrong path.

This Walk Ain't Right! But, Help Is Along The Way

After the first guy, I dated this guy from Brooklyn that was the drug dealer. Then it was like a four year period after, it was no one. He was pretty cool; you know a young guy and stuff like that. I would hang out with him in Brooklyn; he was fine. When I got beat down in the street by my friend's mother, I couldn't hang out with the same people anymore. He was part of the whole group. She was dating his friend and stuff. Her mother, the one that we got beat down by, yeah we were close, yeah we became close friends. And also, my drug dealer boyfriend, he hit me one time and I thought it was because he loved me. I got smart with him in front of the stairs and he hit me. He was cool, I was so into Brooklyn and then he started punching me and you know the drugs were his thing. I always stayed in school, I don't know when things started to change, but I didn't want to be with him. I didn't know but my mother was praying for me. I just didn't want that anymore. I started going into the city and just started seeing new things you know. I wanted more, you know. I started hanging out with girls, just hanging out. One of the girls I was hanging out with went to jail, got caught with drugs. And I think it was then that God really saved me. I was just hanging out with the wrong crowd.

When we moved to Flushing that's when mom started going up to Mount Horeb, I think one of her friends was going there. I would go every once in a while with her. Even though I gave up those friends, the friend who we got beat down by her mother, we went out from time to time. But still, it wasn't me still doing crazy things anymore. One of the favorite things we would do was buy Cosmopolitan magazines. I loved the cloths, the designs, the styles. I loved that look. You know, stuff like that. At the time we weren't too much into Essence. But anyway my mom introduced me to Mount Horeb you know.

One day I said to one of my girlfriends, I said I want to be baptized, I want to be baptized. Out of the blue, it kept bothering me and I said it once in a blue moon. I think it was because I was getting older. I wanted to be baptized. I kept going to Mount Horeb with my mother. She said do you want to join? I wanted to join but I was too afraid to get up there. I said I wanted to be baptized; I don't know I just wanted to be baptized. I went to worship services one day, and you know, they did altar call and my mother said come on, come on and I just went

Healing

up there. And you know it's so funny I realize now the reason why I kept feeling that I wanted to be baptized. After I got baptized I got diagnosed. I don't know exactly how long, I don't know whether it was two years or anything like that. But I think it was within a year.

Um, I don't know. I had to be in my 30's. Yeah. I had to be in my 30's, because I was diagnosed in 2002. So that was seven years ago. I had to be 39 because it was in . . . . yeah 39.

I was going to church, there were no consecutive Sundays. I was going there during holidays, special holidays prior. Once I got baptized I started going regularly. Um, I just went, there was no real understanding. I just had a yearning to go. I ignored the people. I thought they were mean; when you first go to worship some people just say things that aren't nice to you. After a while, I would come home crying. Not everyone, but some people. I am a very sensitive person. So it was like little things that they may say. One time, these women said to me, oh would you like some cake; they were serving in the dining room. And I said no. Most people would say OK. She said, oh look at her, who does she think she is, she don't want any cake. You think you're better, you don't want any cake. And um, I wasn't involved in any kind of ministry, you know.

You know it's so funny the first person who approached me about getting involved with something was Miss Understood; it was a part in a Christmas play. The role of a little angel and she gave me a little card with my role on it. I really didn't know then but she would turn out to be my friend.

My mother was a Trustee at that time. I think the first ministry I joined; I think it was the Body and Soul. Yeah because I wanted, I started to feel like I wanted to help people. After that I think I got involved working with the youth, then the Campaign for Christ, and then the The Shepherds helpers.

I came out of all them when I got diagnosed; I think it was 2002. It was good, because my only friend I really hung out with was Angela who had just gotten baptized too. I loved being in the ministries. It was great! I was diagnosed by accident. I use to go to this Dr. and my neck was fat and that was one of the symptoms. So, I went for breasts examine and I think the doctor said we should get your thyroid checked.

This Walk Ain't Right! But, Help Is Along The Way

They took a blood test or whatever. I didn't think anything else about it for a while. So I had problems with my breast, there was something with my breasts. They thought it may be breast cancer. And you know they were checking me out and the Dr. I don't know why but she said something about my blood test. She said it's something inside the blood, so she started examining around my neck and I think they took a little, a little incision or something. She recommended that I see a specialist. I asked her what was going on? She didn't respond. So she had me see the specialist and she examined me. I don't remember I think they took . . . they had to take blood. I think they took a sonogram also. I remember when the Dr. told me. I was at home; I had just come from getting my hair done. The Dr. asked me if I was home by myself. I was thinking that's an interesting question. So I said yeah, but she told me anyway. She said well they are very concerned. She said that they fear that I may have cancer. She didn't say that they think they were almost positive. But we can't say that, I don't remember the exact words, but it threw me for a loop. I cried, because when you think of cancer you think of death. And I cried and cried and she talked to me on the phone for a little while and I cried and cried. So when I got off the phone, the first person I called was my sister-in-law. I didn't call my mother. I couldn't do that to her. By that time my mom and I were tight. We were so close and I couldn't do that to her and so I went to the doctor without her, I took my best friend with me someone I had dated for a time. The Dr. talked about surgery and other things scheduled for the next week. Finally I told my mother, she was so upset, she didn't believe it. She's in denial at this point. We went back to the surgeon, got together, talked about it, she was still in denial. I mean just totally upset about it, mad. My mom had told me after the surgery that the Dr. came and said that it was malignant. They said that it was three kinds of cancer, and if I had any kind of thyroid cancer that would be the best one. I never forget, and it's so funny what you remember. I don't remember my childhood but I remember the day they rolled me upstairs to that room. I had stuff wrapped around my legs and oxygen mask stuck around my nose, my chest is stuck with tubes around my arms. I was tore up, but I didn't feel that way. I never forget, they rolled me into the room and I looked at my mother and I asked her if it was cancer and she said yes. I wasn't really upset at that point because my dad always said that you must always lift yourself up, you can't feel sorry for yourself. So they said to me Miss Story we are gonna pull the bar down and we are gonna slide you over, pull you onto the bed from the stretcher. So I put my hand back and I said wait, I'll do it myself. I had to lift myself up; I just had to do it myself. They said OK you want to do it yourself and I motioned yes. I had to start from the beginning. So I slid myself off, it may not seem like much to anybody else, but I did it myself or God allowed me. And then um, the very next day . . . , Wow God has been so good to me! I went home the next day. Before my mother and the doctor came in I sat up and I brushed my hair back. I guess that was coming from being vain. I brushed my hair back and I think I had my lip gloss. She came and um you know she talked to me and stuff like that and uh I went home the next day.

Initially they said I had cancer based on my blood tests. Just the blood showed that there were levels of cancer there. They decided to go in and do a biopsy and they told me that they were extremely positive that it was cancer. They took the thyroid out. Yeah, when you have thyroid cancer that is in the lymphoid that's fine, I mean it's not fine, but it's not deadly like some cancers. After that they waited for a month or so. I had to go back into the hospital for a couple of days for radioactive iodine treatment. No visitors, you had a room that was isolated. Everything was covered with plastic and um, my mom would call and the doctors' would come in for five minutes or less. The doors were closed 24 hours a day. You were just by yourself in isolation. It's so funny because at the time I had these two big bay windows, in my room and the view was beautiful, the fleet show was in town. I was so messed up from the medication and nauseous. But I got through that, so I'm out for like five, six days. You are actually radioactive. You take this little bar and it makes a noise that shows you that you are radioactive, you can't be around people, and it's contagious. You are not suppose to be around children, nobody. Yeah like when I went home I had to eat out of paper plates, anytime I went to the bathroom I had to line it. It was just . . . I couldn't be around any of my nieces or nephews; I couldn't go to church or nothing. So I would spray the bathroom and would have to go back to my room.

This Walk Ain't Right! But, Help Is Along The Way

I was so sick MG when I was in isolation. I think for two days, I couldn't, I couldn't, do anything. I could pray to God, I didn't even pick up the Bible; I just had it near me. But even the books, everything I took in there had to be destroyed. So whatever I took, at least most of the things, 90% of the stuff I couldn't take back home, because it was contaminated. When I go to the bathroom, I had to be careful of what I touched, I walk around the room and on the floor were towels and I had to use plastic gloves. So um but most of the time I was in bed, barely ate you know.

I watched TV, I slept, and I just laid there. The medication wasn't that bad that where I was throwing up all the time. Just the way, your stomach is upset constantly so I would eat a little bit at a time. I could have sworn the food was moving without me even touching it. Then at the same time my mother had to get me a lot of oranges, a lot of solid candy because you have to keep that saliva moving. Drinking a lot of water, and I had to constantly drink water, even though I was nauseous. All I could eat were oranges, solid candy and drink water. You know to keep the glands. This was not a good time. I could not express it because you can sometimes get a little down and I didn't want to worry my mom I was concerned about how she was feeling.

So after I wasn't radioactive anymore I was happy. I was still going to church, still establishing a relationship with God, I wasn't where I should have been, but I depended on Him. I made one mistake. I went to church and I testified too soon before God told me it was time. And I testified and talked about my situation, just basically and God had delivered me and now I'm cancer free. And that wasn't the case. I had to go back for more tests and um, they had to do a body scan. The test was scarier than the surgery, because I'm claustrophobic. Then I got the phone call about the blood test results, then the test they give you has iodine in it which goes through your body and it scans the body. It picked up more of the cancer and they called me, the second time they called me, I cried, because it wasn't that far apart, you know. I sat there and I cried and cried, I cried right there on the phone with my doctor. This meant more surgery and I couldn't really stand it by this point. I would always tell my mom, and she would go with me to all my

Healing

tests and I would say I feel it, I feel it, this is it mom, I think it's gonna work this time. I went back into the hospital, into another surgery.

I went into the surgery, had the surgery and remember they are going into an area that they went into before. So you had to sign a paper because they are near your vocal cords and everything else. With that, you have to be very careful, they already messed it up the first time when you didn't get it all. Went back in had the surgery, went home the next day. They go in, see the cancer and remove it. Then you go back into the hospital again for treatment, a higher dosage of radioactive iodine treatment that's supposed to kill off all the cells that may be remaining. So I go back in, uh, this time the dosages were I guess higher than I really expected them to go. OK I was alive this is what I told myself. I was asleep, this time a bigger toll on my body. I was so sick and, I was in the hospital. This time I had stayed longer because I wasn't drinking or eating. I think I didn't eat until like two days after I was there. I couldn't because the dosage was so high that I was sick constantly. I drank water and I would throw it up. I just couldn't keep it down. Then doctors came in and they said we have to give you another dose. I cried . . . cause you're in there another day, you gotta get another IV because I wasn't eating or drinking to get it out of my system. So, um, my mom calmed me down she would call me and talk to me. I wasn't in a relationship then, my dad wasn't' alive, he wasn't alive to see me go through this. I relaxed and finally after that my mom and brother came and got me, my brother was always willing to come and get me and they took me home. I got through that, and then, because it was the second time I was depressed and I was depressed for a while, I couldn't get over this one. I kept saying well where are you? Remember I'm establishing a relationship with God. I would cry and come to church. I would come to church and then I would cry. Then I couldn't understand, I couldn't understand God's words at that time and one day I broke down in the house by myself. One day I just said I should just commit suicide; I just should jump off the terrace. I couldn't take it anymore. I said to myself, just do it, just do it, I know now that was the devil and just as I was convincing myself my mother came in. Later when I was by myself again, I started crying again and I started yelling and screaming and banging on the

This Walk Ain't Right! But, Help Is Along The Way

floor. I said . . . . I told God . . . . , you can't possibly love me because I wouldn't go through all this and I'm no longer your child. Cause you wouldn't do this to your child. And I cried and cried, and I just cried because I was by myself. I felt so alone. You know how you cry until you got a headache. I just couldn't understand it, because the devil was getting the best of me. So, I got through that night and I was depressed for awhile.

Well, then this is the situation; there are all kinds of physicals that I had to go through, The GYN, all of that stuff. One day I went to my primary Dr. and he could not detect what it was. But he felt something was abnormal. So he . . . he wrote up his information and he said, he told my GYN. I guess what he recommended or what he saw. It was a Friday that Monday I knew something was wrong. They called me first thing Monday morning. The girl said to me you have to go to a specialist. So I said what are you talking about, why? Why? What is it? Well, you have to see the specialist. I said this is my life. Is it cancer? So she said yes, in the ovaries. Yeah, the ovaries! So I said that's crazy. That was a Monday. I went to the specialist later that week I think it might have been that Tuesday. We talked, I didn't cry, the nurse said I can't believe that you're so strong. So I started joking around, making a joke, that's how I got through it. So we talked about surgery, scheduling the surgery and things like that. He told me I had two options, either to do a full blown surgery, cut me up to see if it's really cancer and I would have to be in the hospital for days or do like an Iscopic which is a frozen biopsy. In order to do that they would have to remove the ovaries and test it while you are under. If it's cancerous then they would have to open me up and remove the cancer. So, I decided to get the Iscopic, because based on what they were saying it was probably the best thing. So I talked to the Dr. about that, he decided to talk about surgery for that coming February.

That Friday, of that same week, after I saw the Dr. and decided to have the surgery, I went to my surgeon to get my test results for my thyroid. When I got to the Dr.'s office, she said, oh didn't the oncologist tell you. I said tell me what, she said your thyroid cancer has reoccurred. I said are you serious, I just came from another hospital. So I cried a little bit, and um by the time I got downstairs, my relationship with

Healing

God had changed. I didn't cry, and I said that's it. Now I know what they mean when they say to you turn it over to God. That's when I said, whatever is going to happen, I said to God is going to happen, and I said I'm just leaving it up to You. I didn't cry anymore, I went back and told my mother and went back to work.

And then there was test, after test. Went to the New York Cornell Hospital, had the test done, the entire test done. And then um got the surgery, there was no cancer in my ovaries. After that, which was in February 2007, and then I came home, took a week off. Couldn't get up or move too much the day I came home from the hospital. The next day after that surgery, I was on the phone with my oncologist planning the thyroid surgery. He said it couldn't wait, so you know, I'm scheduling the test, and all the while I was home. When I went back to work, I uh started getting tested for the thyroid surgery which would be in May. When May came my mom went with me for the test and stuff like that. They wanted to make sure the biopsy indicated that it was cancer from the neck. I went into the hospital, no more radioactive iodine, because it's not working. They can't understand why, because usually with this type of cancer they go in, they get it and that's it. But they can't understand why it's not taking and so, your blood level has to be at a zero to indicate that the cancer is gone. When I first got out the hospital it was twelve, then it went down a little bit to like a seven or eight. They told me the only way it goes down is through surgery. And I said are you sure, it can't just go down gradually? And they were like not really, it doesn't usually do that. So you know I did thyroid surgery after that I was like I can't do this anymore. Then my relationship with God was so much stronger you know and during those two surgeries I was in a real relationship with God, yeah.

At this point I had been through so much. The vanity stuff didn't seem so important anymore. Don't get me wrong I still kept it together but I saw things differently. The hardest thing for me to have done in my life was to have to be with someone and be in sweatshirts and just have a tacky date. I just wanted to have someone I could share my life with and just be comfortable. I want to be able to let myself be free sometimes, you know, and I think that's what's important to me right now. And that's hard for me to just be myself because of my upbringing.

When I was younger, I use to say I want a boyfriend, I want a boyfriend. I had so many dates; I left all that stuff behind. So every summer I would be sitting on the terrace, just sitting there, beautiful summer, just sitting there on summer nights, no boyfriend, no friends, no nothing. I use to hang out with me. Cause my girlfriend, my best friend at that time got married and moved to California. So I really didn't have any friends. And I was, you know, so down about not having any friends. Yeah I wanted one. I didn't have any friends at that time and then I met you know, my friend Debra and we would go out from time to time. I met and dated this guy who turned out to be a jerk. You know, after him, I didn't date for a while. And when I say awhile, I'm not talking about for six months or something like that, I mean for like two years. Sometimes, I wouldn't go out for four years. I was just going to school; you know doing my thing, going to church. I finally started dating someone.

Then I met this guy on Mount Horeb. He's you know, kind and good and stuff like that. We exchange numbers, and started a friendship because I had been dating someone. We became friends; I didn't want to get serious. I was just in and out of small dating relationships at that time. I wasn't looking for anything serious. We just started talking. He is the most wonderful person to talk to on the phone. I enjoyed the conversations and I started relating . . . I always relate a man by his actions and how he is, his character against my father which is not good. My father was very intelligent. If someone I was dating couldn't hold a conversation with me for hours, if a man couldn't sound intelligent, couldn't talk to me, couldn't hold a conversation that was it. I didn't look beyond what it was. We talked about things; the first time we talked for about an hour. I think um over five . . . six months. No, I think we went out on a date. I didn't think much of it because there was no way I was gonna get involved with a preacher. Oh Yeah I didn't tell you he was a preacher.

Not that they are boring, but they are preachers . . . yeah. They're different . . . so we would go out to dinner here and there. I mean really, not that they are boring, but they are preachers. And it was like . . . they are different. I felt I had to always be on my best behavior, we would go out to dinner here and there. And I would say all in all you know

Healing

we didn't have a relationship, we were friends. But I think my head wasn't open to it at that time, I wasn't ready at that time.

No, I just didn't want to, because he was a preacher, so as I got to know him, it was like wait a minute you're a preacher and we would talk about normal things. You know, because, I am not going to lie what I thought from the very beginning, and this is not to be conceited, but I think he sort of adored me, but not in a conceited way. I don't know how to put it. I felt a since of comfort you know. I loved it, I loved it. I would wear jeans and sandals. I felt so comfortable with him. I felt that way from the very beginning. I think because, this is what God wants, you know. I was scared to commit. I loved the way he made me feel. So . . . this was a bad risk, I was use to being all alone. I knew he liked me for me, but I wasn't sure where I was going. I had been hurt you know; like I said I didn't know, I didn't know where I was going in this "relationship."

Well, we gradually went through stuff, I thought he was wonderful before, but the surgery with the uh, ovaries, yeah, yeah. With him I felt so much stronger. And maybe because I felt he was a preacher, I held him at a higher level, which you should not, which is what he told me. One day I was so depressed, I just wanted to cry, he said what's wrong and I said I don't know, I'm just, I wish I was dead. He was sitting in my living room and he said go get the Bible. Every week he started giving me scriptures to read, the scriptures helped me feel strong. I felt that I needed him to get me through. At one point, I wouldn't get up and go to the doctor's without him. And even though my mother was there for me, she took care of me, I could not open up to her because I didn't think it was fair. I would never cry in front of my mother, I just cried when I was by myself. I couldn't really tell her how I was feeling. Once in a while, I would tell her, I'm just tired. I couldn't really tell her that I had enough and I couldn't do this anymore. I felt like, she was just looking at faith. It was like, I'm trying to be a child of God, but sometimes I can't. I did not want her to go through that. I just couldn't do that. But with him, he was my sounding board; I could cry and tell him how without feeling remorseful to him you know. We really started talking, I just liked talking to him, I liked him as a person, and he was always polite. I said OK all men do that in the beginning, and MG, after a while he just kept being a gentleman, opening the car door, etc. I'm thinking he's really like this; he is really nice. We were talking, just hanging out more.

After I had the surgery with the ovaries, we were pretty tight then. We were boyfriend and girlfriend, and it was pretty hard for me to tell him because you know. . . . I am a woman; he said he has no fears, so I said I have no fears. I beat myself up about it, because I said, I should I have checked, I should have done more research. Now that one of my ovaries is gone. I beat myself up for awhile, but I got through it because of my relationship with God. I had become so strong, you know. I was becoming happier about who I was. It was still hard, you know, you want to produce for a man if you can in your life. But he was cool about it, he was by my side, he didn't flinch. He became close to my mom, check on her every day, stuff like that. She liked him; he was very nice you know . . . they were comfortable with each other. Then the thyroid surgery came up and he went with me through that. He would pray in the hospital before the surgery; we found a little corner, called family members on the speaker phone; my uncle my, brother came with me. We would all pray in a little room and stuff like that. He would or maybe my sister-in-law's father led prayers. My sister-in-law's father was a preacher. He would call people from the Dominican Republic and they were praying for me too. I mean everybody was praying because it was yet another surgery after a couple of the previous one.

And, so at that point I was like OK, it's gonna happen, it's gonna happen. A little tired, a little weary, but uh I was getting through it you know. I seriously think that my relationship with God was changing because I trusted Him more. When I first testified, I didn't; I never used the word trust. I kept saying I had faith, but this is what I believed through my experience. I believe you could have faith, and not trust God. And someone said that this is impossible, but this is how I feel. I believe that you . . . I believe that God can make miracles, I have faith that He can heal the sick, I have faith that He can move mountains, but do I trust that he would do it for me, I didn't trust that he would do it for me. After reading certain things in the Bible about trust in God and the preacher bought me a study bible where it focused on the women. I think it took me, I would say, two years to learn that. I started

Healing

talking to God and praying and telling Him that I trusted in Him, but I had to believe it. And you know when He brings you through certain things, there is a reason I started wanting to help people more and more. I was just happier. Things started changing. I was happier, there were times when I was sad but I learned to turn it over to God not that I didn't cry and worry sometimes, I did. But I would say prayers until there was nothing else to say. I would cry sometimes and get a little bit depressed and I would pray for His grace and His mercy. I started trusting Him. The Shepherd's counseling and his sermons changed my understanding of trusting in God. Every time I heard a sermon it was on something that I needed. Between the Shepherd and the preacher I was straight. I remember something the Shepherd said, I think it was in 2007, I typed it out and put it on my wall and that's where it stayed he was preaching about watching what God will see you through. I typed it up in big bold black letters and I put up a picture of a boxer with his hands up in the air and every time I would get discouraged it was right in front of me. I started ministering to other people. People started coming to me about their cancer and other problems. I developed a friendship with a woman, um, who is now a vender of ours. I bought her a Bible and to this day we talk about her situation, I tried to boost her ego up, you know, to teach her that God can do all things. I don't push her, but now she calls me and she just tells me about her day at the hospital and her sickness and stuff like that so, my whole life has changed.

And you know what MG, I wrote in my diary one time that I would never want to go through this again and if I had to write that in my diary again, I couldn't. I can't say I would not have wanted to go through all the surgeries, the stress that I went through because I am a better person. I like who I am now and I have come to realize that I have God in my life. I went to the doctor two weeks ago and the level was at zero to indicate that there is no cancer. The last time I had a surgery was in 2007 and every time I go back it gets better, the levels go down on its own, but with God. Last Thursday or the Thursday before last, I went to the doctor and he said that the level was 1.4. I was like yeah it was one that's still good. So he said to me I still believe that there might me something wrong that this is here or it's the thyroids, everything else is cleared up at this time. So it is God working through him. And you know what, MG after I had the surgery for the ovaries, I had the surgery for the thyroids, um they told me when I went back for the test for the ovaries and thyroids and everything, they said they found a mass in the uterus. This is after I had just had the surgery. I said . . . it was in the same time frame, what is going on. So the radiologist recommended a full hysterectomy. And I am like oh my gosh, that's not right, I don't understand it but that's OK I'm just gonna trust in God. So he recommended the hysterectomy. Thank God when I went back to the doctor he said I want to test you first. Well he said, I don't think you need the hysterectomy. They were giving me so many mixed messages. I thought do these doctors know what they are doing. They should... they are from Cornell; Cornell is supposed to be one of the top hospitals. So I went for the test, turned out to be a bunch of cysts, funny shaped cysts. So I was just going through so many changes. I kept saying what is going on; I was going to the doctor at this hospital, that hospital, this test, that test. It was two different hospitals and then when you go for the test sometimes you don't go to the hospital, you have to go somewhere else outside the hospital. Every time I go to the hospital for a test is when I'm having surgery, other than that I would be going to two and three doctors in one week. You know trying to schedule it with my job and this and that, you know. So as it stands, it's at a 1.4, I just leave it to God, whatever is going to happen is going to happen.

Ministry was a good distraction from it but not a lot because there is so much going on in my head. I would have to say the last two surgeries I was so grateful for the people around me. I think I started testifying about some of it. I was grateful people were feeling me. I got to know Miss Understood, Wisdom, Miss Taken and you. That helped me out to come here and hang out cause I felt like I had friends that I could just lean on. Of course being busy in the ministries, they are distractions; you are busy. I remember when I use to come to church and cry all the time. Sometimes because I couldn't understand, and the last couple of years are because I was real sick, sickly.

Every time I would go to Mount Horeb, if I started crying, it was because of my cancer. I'm thinking about it now, I always picture myself lying on that bed and I start crying about it. I'm like, because God got

Healing

me through it. I am so grateful because I've known people who have had the same cancer and have died within a year. I am grateful you know? I think that it helps because I developed friendships on Mount Horeb. After everything I've been through, I testified how good God has been and a lot of people will come up to me and start talking to me and say I prayed for you and start hugging me. They wouldn't pity me; they would say I prayed for you.

My Preacher, he would talk about the future, if we were married you know. I was glad he would say things like that. He was such an important part of my life. I could not imagine how I would feel if we broke up. I depended on talking to him everyday. Every single day, uh unless like I'm mad at him or something; for the most we lean on each other. We have gotten closer and closer. We know each other's ways and likes and dislikes, you know. We try being up front and honest about what we feel so we won't have disagreements. It's hard for me to think of myself without him because I feel like I depend on him, and I don't mean financially or nothing like that. He's just someone to talk to; he picks me up, he lifts me up. You know, I'm just excited about him. So I mean I'm not saying that there aren't some days when you don't want to be bothered, but he's still there. It's funny, we would go to the mall and look around, and look for rings. I kind of figured something was going on because he would ask questions about it. Settings and cuts, you like that, and sizes you know. I would say that one was really nice. Then nothing would ever happen. So I figured that maybe one day down the road, because we been looking at rings whenever we would go to the mall, but nothing would ever really happen. Then one day we were looking at a ring and he asked me did I like it, and I said yes, it was very nice. Do you like this band and that band, and I said yeah I liked it. We went to a bar-b-cue one time, I couldn't understand why he kept saying well tell your mother, brother and them to come. They had a family bar-b-cue with his family. He thanked everybody for coming and there were a lot of people. He said um, I asked God to send me the right woman in my life and I believe Miss Story is the right woman and I want to spend the rest of my life with her. So I kinda knew right then, he was about ready. You know, you know, I want to spend the rest of my life with you . . . and so. I was looking for it then. But he didn't ask. And still didn't know what was going on. Then Christmas came and, I think it was Christmas Eve. He . . . well actually he just handed me the ring in the box. For me to take on the role as his wife, his line of work, his position in life, you have to feel, really know, she's the one. Not having the right person for that role it can build you up or tear your down. So, I don't think that I am fully, really taking it all in; maybe because I'm not there yet. At this point I'm still here. I am a little nervous about handling things. I want to be a wife, MG. I want God to come first; I want my holiness to come after that. I don't want to put the church activities before my husband. I don't want to exhaust myself doing so many things within the church, that I neglect my husband. I see a lot of woman do that, they get so caught up in the life whether you are a first lady or what. You get so involved in going here, being invited here and there that you have separate lives. I don't want that. So I don't know how I'm gonna handle that, just by communicating and talking about it. I guess my whole life after God has to be the next priority, before the church itself because I realize now that it's a building. All these manmade ministries are wonderful, but I can't allow it to tear me and us apart. Hopefully people will understand, because when I was introduced as the woman in his life you know people come up to you and they hug you and they were very nice. When you meet them again, sometimes you can't remember everyone, you don't know whether people find that offensive or not. You can't remember everyone's names, so they would say well I met you before you know, and I'm coming into their family. Hopefully, it will come to a nice middle of the road and all of us will understand each other. But I guess trial and error. This is something new for me. I know God will make it all good because he brought us together.

You know, it is easy to tell a woman, a Christian woman to trust God, to have faith. I haven't, I mean, I'm not one to judge when you go through stuff what's more important or what's heavier, what weighs more than the other. But to say to someone who hasn't experienced loss, sickness to trust God, I can tell them that. I don't really expect them to just get it because I said it, it's hard for them to grasp. It's easier for someone who has been through some stuff and healed because they relied on God. I think they might find it easier to understand. Let me make myself clear though I said easier by no means am I'm trying to suggest that it's easy; it's a lot easier when you have walked through some stuff with Him. I have learned the best way to experience God's healing power is to establish a true relationship with Him so you will know and believe for yourself. I think that's the most important thing. You have to pray, I believe prayer is the answer. That's how you communicate with God. Everybody experiences turmoil in their lives, but to what degree. Do you understand what I'm talking about? So, I would say my life has changed because of God and a helpful thing to do is to listen to people's testimony. I found hearing what they've been through helps you understand how powerful God really is. You start to see if he did it for them; he can do it for me. If you haven't been through some major changes, that have devastated your life, I applaud you, that's a blessing. I have to say that it's also a good thing to some degree to go through it and to be victorious, that's a wonderful thing too.

So again, I can't say it enough the only thing I would say to someone who was looking to God for healing is establish your relationship with Him, pray. If you go through the things that are devastating, pray on it. You may have lost a loved one and it affects you like it did me when I lost my father, it devastated me to go through that but I didn't have a relationship with God back then. Yes with the cancer it was different because my emotions were out of control, my body was out of control and it was year after year after year. It's not like a one year thing or two or three, I've been going through the cancer experience since 2002. It's a process where my whole life was changing. The only way I didn't give up was because I knew I still had God and he was my Doctor. You know, building a relationship with God it's like a developmental process. It doesn't work overnight, it comes gradually. It's funny I envisioned myself speaking for the American Cancer Society. That is what I envisioned myself doing one day. I see it, I see myself doing things like that. And now that this whole situation with the First Lady has come into play, you know that boggles my mind; I don't know where that's leading me. I do know God is setting me up for something. I do know I would like to speak to an audience of people. I don't want to speak where everyone is crying because they are sad; oh that's a sad story. I don't want to do a sad story. I want to give a story of faith and hope and power and strength, you know and stuff like that. I want to encourage and inspire people and let them know about this Healer I know named Jesus who will also uplift you. I wish and hope for that. I envision that. It's a vision that pops into my head all the time. I know that I would like to work with the kids. But I know by the time that I get there by 7 or 7:30 the kids are in bed. So, maybe on a Saturday, hopefully, and you know, MG, there are so many people out there who are just hurting. When I went through my situation in the beginning, I feel that I had nobody to just cry on their shoulder. I didn't have my friends; none of them were there for me to just talk. One of my friends would always look at me and say, you are so strong; little did she know I wanted to just cry in her arms. I didn't want to do it to my mother, didn't do it to my brother because I didn't think they could handle it. So I would cry by myself. I didn't want to do it, you know, not in front of you or in front of Wisdom or anybody. I knew you guys were dealing with your own stuff. Later I was able to come, come over to vent. I had nobody, I felt, I felt alone. The most powerful thing about isolation and constantly being in and out of hospitals is that God is right there in that room with you. God is an awesome God. You really get to know him in the alone time. I have a whole new attitude; I know how to pick myself up when I'm down. I'm not saying that I'm not down for a while, but not that long, I take my time-out. I pick myself up and I am good because now I know where to turn. Then one day when you least expect it you are looking up saying it's God's time you find yourself smiling and saying by his stripes I am healed!

Wow Miss Story I can't believe you have been going through all of this for so many years. You truly have never looked like your circumstances. Miss Story said girl please. It was all those years of my mother and father making sure I never went without, having the outside together. It was such a part of me that I kept that up without trying. If it wasn't so embedded in me I would have never been able to keep up that front. Yes Miss Story it was part of your set-up like Miss Understood talks about. God prepared you all your life to be the person He has made You to be. Wow I know you are about to blow up because you are so inspiring, so caring so compassionate and just downright beautiful. I am so glad God brought you into my life. You have truly given me

Healing

hope; I know it may not be today and it may not be tomorrow but I too will be healed. I Believe! Miss Story left my house and I settled in for the night. I started to reflect on all that she said.

MG's Reflection on Miss Story's Healing Walk

Miss Story begins her story with no pictures or memories of her as a baby. Then she talks about the loss of her father and the pain she felt, her promise to God about hanging out before she even knew Him, had a relationship with Him. Miss Story blew me away with her story. She talked about learning to truly trust God. She talked about the difference between having faith in God doing for other people but truly trusting what God can do for you.

She also talked about waiting on God and how she jumped the gun and testified before God told her to. Then after her premature testimony she experienced so much more to bring her to the place where God needed her to be.

Miss Story then talked about deliverance and how she got so frustrated that she wanted to take her life. She was angry and felt God did not love her. She didn't feel like she was His child anymore. She also stated that she got to a point where she learned to be delivered she had to let go of her worries and put it all in God's hands. When she relinquished control and truly let go is when God started to deliver her and rebuild her life. Most importantly she talked about how God is a healer and when she truly believed and let Him do what He does she began to heal physically and mentally.

I find it ironic that she was groomed to be a first lady through her parents and life experiences. She also shows you how you can look at a person and they appear to have it all together but you don't know what is going on with them and God. She also says as horrible as it was she is happy she went through it because it changed her life.

MG's Reflections on Her Own Healing Walk

Where do I begin I think first I need to make sure I truly understand this step. I have heard some people say healing and then deliverance and then others say deliverance and then healing and then I hear people use them interchangeably. Then I want to know how restoration is different from healing. I am going to have to pray and see what God reveals to me on this one.

Father God:
I know that you are not a God of confusion. I really need to understand what you are showing me. Please reveal to me what each of these steps mean and what the differences are. In Jesus name I pray, Amen.

No sooner than I finish praying a small still voice explained it to me this way. Say you fall into a rose bush, when you get up your body is covered with thorns stuck in your skin. You are experiencing a lot of pain because of these things piercing into your flesh. All you know is if these thorns can be removed you will be released from this excruciating pain. So you call on a loved one to come and help you remove the thorns. Each thorn is removed and you are **delivered** from that excruciating pain. You go into the house and you sit down and you realize that although the thorns have been removed and you have been **delivered** from the excruciating pain, you are not back to your normal state of being. You feel discomfort from the open wounds (sores) because they still hurt. They are a constant reminder of the incident because they hurt when you move, they hurt when your clothing touches them, they hurt when you bathe. The sores are a constant reminder of the initial trauma of falling because they have not **healed**. There are still residual effects that will remain bothersome until the wound closes and the **healing** process concludes. Once the wounds on your skin are completely closed free of any sores, infection, scabs, and sensitive to touch the skin is **restored** and the **healing** process is complete. **Restoration** of the skin is complete. No more pain, no more discomfort. The trauma is behind you. You are free to resume life as you knew it before the fall.

Thank you God now I get it. Healing is really recovery. When I think of the word recovery there are three things that come to mind. I think of somebody who recovers from a surgery, or recovers from an

Healing

accident, or recovers from an addiction. There is a process that you go through and within this process there are ups and downs.

Initially it may be physically painful. It is usually accompanied by mental pain which is the hardest to get past. It's hard to get past this stuff because sometimes you want to deny that you have a mental health issue regarding your trauma. Sometimes you think you let it go but it has rented space in your head or your heart. You are left wondering or people are asking why you are sad all the time or mad, destructive or just numb and unfeeling. After a while if it's not treated it consumes you. You have to deal with what is dealing with you.

Miss Story clearly shows you that you have to understand that you have been undergoing a process that God is the author of and finisher. The destination is to have faith that God will see you through. Then you must pray and believe that what you are praying for God is hearing you and will come through for you. Then You must trust that God is aware of what you are experiencing. Lastly you must have faith and know that God's ways are not our ways and He is working it out but He has not let you in on the plan yet.

Miss Story also demonstrates that along with your faith you have to do your part. She suggests that we pray and read the Bible for strength. I think this is an excellent point. I read in the Bible faith without works is dead *(James 2:14)*. I have come to realize that you have to do your part and work it out. Working it out could be many things in many ways. It could be the examples MissStory used-prayer and reading the Bible or from my Social Work training seeking counseling through a Shepherd, therapist, rehab, or at least talk it out with a friend. Do what you got to do to get rid of it. People underestimate the damage that can be done when you hold it in. In your mind you tend to relive the trauma. You are plagued with so many what ifs. What if I did this or what if I didn't do that? You focus on wishing that the trauma didn't happen and tend to feel sorry for yourself, feel guilty, especially if you feel it was self inflicted or someone else was hurt during your process. This especially happens if you are living with secrets that may be eating you alive. Unresolved issues can play out in so many ways, such as anger, guilt, fear, promiscuity, depression, and the list goes on and on.

Sometimes you got to dig deep; sometimes you have it buried for so long that it may take a minute to find. All I know is you have to get rid of it! If you don't it will hold you down, hold you back. I have some stuff I still need to deal with. If I don't get to the root I will not be able to truly fulfill my purpose. I cannot allow that to happen because God has been too good to me. I have to allow myself to heal.

I was having trouble figuring out why I still felt like I had sores even though I did the Weights to Wings activity and felt delivered. I went back 18 years and I realized that those were weights that I picked up and I needed to reframe those weights and look at how beneficial those occurrences were in my life. That was good, but that was only a start. I now know that there is some other stuff I need to address. There were symptoms that demonstrated there was a bigger problem. I had to really go deep and find out what it was. I had to keep asking myself what was it? What was it? I think that's when I went back to the door. To the guy who tried to molest me. I started to look back and I truly began my healing process. I dug really deep and I came up with some wounds with picked off scabs. Ooh that sounds really nasty but this is some nasty stuff I am recalling here. I needed that scab to be picked off because I had issues that were never buried. I then started to realize that this is the reason why I have approached relationships, and dealt with men in the way I dealt with them. I realized that I had a sick set of standards. I realize that the whole pedophile incident somehow shaped my thinking. It made me feel if I open up a door to something then it meant it was OK, I allowed it to happen therefore I deserve what I get. Although I know my mom was angry and afraid of the thought of what could have happened;. she handled that wrong. I was left with an open wound because of that. I was never told it's not your fault. I was told you should not have opened the door. What I saw was everyone angry ready to fight and it was my fault. I walked around all these years blaming myself. The reality is, I made a mistake and mistakes are part of growing but when I made that mistake I felt like you deserve what happened because you opened the door. You made your bed and now you have to lie in it.

Now as I develop this relationship with God I understand that Jesus paid it all. I realized I did not deserve that! I also understand that

Healing

I need to forgive myself. As I learn and I read the Word and I learn about God and forgiveness, I have to understand and learn that I was a child. Even if I wasn't a child by no means in any shape or form was that incident my fault. I mean that was a dark place that I really did not want to revisit. I know in order to heal I had to reflect. I had to go back there. Now that I have gone back there I realize that as a small child my innocence was robbed. I was welcomed when I came into this world. I had this wonderful family, this wonderful life; we went to church and did all the things we needed to do.

I see there was some kind of disconnect between what was happening in my world and what was happening when we were in church on Sundays. I realize now that my parents had a relationship and accessed strength and endurance when we went to church. They came out stronger and I came out the same. My introduction was clearly about religion.

So there I was, didn't know about sex but someone tries to molest me. I didn't understand drug abuse but everybody's big brother and sister in my neighborhood were dying from overdosing on drugs. There was a lot of stealing going on in my house. My middle big brother had a drug addiction and I always feared he was going to die. You couldn't just leave money lying around in the house. Piggy banks were a no-no. I remember my banks were stolen and all the money was taken just gone. They didn't even leave my banks.

My brother next to me was falsely accused of rape and went to trial and was facing jail. Thank God he was cleared of all charges; the girl lied and confessed to lying. I think about it and I feel for him because just as that took a piece out of me, I can't even imagine what it took from him. I felt my innocence was robbed, I couldn't even imagine what he felt. So I couldn't have been more than 8 years old and I knew what rape was, child molestation, drug addiction, and theft. These were the things I was exposed to. At no point was I taught to take these things to God in prayer. I guess they felt I was too young to understand that. The funny thing is I wasn't too young to face the issues. Now I know I should not have been exposed to any of that. But the fact remains that I was. Paula White always says the bad things that happen in our lives may not be God sent but they will be God used. Therefore I am closing the doors that I left open and finally moving on. At this point I heard a voice say go write in your journal. This is what I wrote:

I was misguided when I opened the door to a pedophile. He was older, smarter and more calculating than me. I was a child therefore it was not my fault. I forgive myself and him. I am closing that door that led to a lifetime of insanity and open the door to abusive relationships.

By His stripes I am healed. I didn't realize it then. I just realized it as I am going through this healing experience—how I continually open the door to abuse. I close the door to feeling that my innocence was lost. I decree in the name of Jesus that it's time to close all those open doors once and for all. I was misguided when I open the door for the Contender and I gave myself to someone too early, out of wedlock and then suffered in silence. I made some bad decisions but I was young and didn't realize I was in over my head. No matter what I did he did not have a right to hit me. I forgive myself and I forgive him because I don't have to contend with that any longer. I choose to close the door to my domestic violence filled teenage years. By His stripes I am healed.

I was misguided when I opened the door to marrying a man without consulting God. I knew he was doing drugs. I made some bad choices regarding this man and I forgive myself and I forgive him for everything he took from me. I close the door to Dis-ease. By His stripes I am healed.

I was misguided when I opened the door to another unhealthy relationship. My self esteem was so low at this point in my life that I settled for less than I deserved. I made a bad choice in remaining with someone I was not happy with and I beat myself up about it. I finally stood up for myself and I forgive myself and I forgive him for the way he treated me. I close the door to low self esteem. By His stripes I am healed.

I was misguided when I opened the door to a sin filled life of forbidden fruit. My flesh was so weak and I know it was wrong. I forgive myself and I forgive him and I close the door to condemnation. By His stripes I am healed.

I was misguided when I opened the door to selfishness as a means to becoming whole. I thought I was in control of my life and I now

Healing

know I was wrong. I forgive myself for being so self absorbed. I close that door and relinquish control to God. By His stripes I am healed.

I was misguided when I opened the door to idolatry by making a relationship with a man more important than developing a relationship with God. I forgive myself and I forgive him for all he took from me. I close the door to ignorance. By His stripes I am healed.

I get that now. I came to the conclusion that I don't have to suffer in silence when I make mistakes by opening doors, I just need to be prayerful about the decisions I make. What has happened to me during this healing process is that I have put a lot of effort into seeking God. I want to know more about who God is and determining what God wants me to do. I have looked at my experiences and circumstances. I am trying to gain insight and learn lessons from them. I don't have to live like that anymore. I am learning now about believing and trusting in God. Before, it was not possible. I had not entered into a relationship with Him. You can't trust a stranger. God is no longer a stranger to me He is my friend. I still have a lot of growing to do but I get it. I now understand that He has to direct my path. One time I heard Joel Osteen say that God is like a GPS system. When you start on a journey God maps out what we are supposed to do and where we are supposed to go. Our free will tends to make wrong turns on the journey believing we know the best way to go. We tend to think we can do it without God's assistance. The beautiful thing about God is He knows we are going to mess up. He doesn't just count us out; we are not lost forever. He recalibrates and configures out another route for you. He shows you a whole different direction you can go in. I think that's the other piece I learned about healing. I learned no matter what you go through God is there whether it's something God takes you through, satan leads you to or self inflicted. God said He will never leave you or forsake "you." Each time you come through a test pass or fail there is a story. These stories become your testimony. Your testimony has been developed for you to help someone else through their mess.

I needed to write these things down; I praise God for leading me to it. I thank Him for encouraging me to write because it is healing me. It has made me realize some real deep rooted stuff that I needed to deal with. There is a song that says every round goes higher and higher (*Jacob's Ladder*). I found that to be so true. Every round does go higher and higher in this walk. I really understand that this is a process. I know I have a long way to go in terms of getting to know things and understanding. But that's OK because the more I learn the stronger I get. I am also realizing that I have to give back. I have to let people in and share my stories so it can help them. It's important that I tell my story. For a long time I didn't want to tell my story. I felt like I didn't want my business out there and didn't want my daughter to know. Now that I am healed I am starting to realize that maybe she needs to hear. I feel maybe she needs to get a clear understanding of what I went through, what not having a relationship with God can lead you to. I'm just so thankful. I also learned that God is not like the people I have been dealing with. When you have a misguided relationship with God all the other relationships in your life fall short.

Oh MY GOD!!! I feel so free! Thank you, God, You are so awesome! I have been carrying this stuff for so long and didn't realize it was part of me. I have let go of it and I am free.

I am developing a relationship with God and I see how God views me, I see how God treats me and I see what our interaction is. I understand how I should to be treated, how I want to be treated, how I need to be treated. I understand what I shouldn't put up with. I understand my faults and I am OK with them because God is going to help me with them. I understand that God loves and understands me and I don't have to beat myself up about my short comings.

Don't get me wrong, I am not at a place where I won't go off or I won't get mad or I won't lose it from time to time. I am striving to be like Jesus. I am very clear on the fact that I am not Jesus. I would love to be as much like Him as possible but I know that I'm not there. I also know I have come a long way from when I got out that car. I used to hold grudges for long periods of time. I still do from time to time but I feel so convicted about it. Before I really didn't care, but now it eats me up inside to hold a grudge. I pray to God that one day I get to the point where I don't hold grudges, and that I will be able to just let things go right away. I have to admit that this healing step is deep. Shoot all of these steps are deep. Every time I approach a new step I am still finishing up the previous step. It's like they are all so closely linked.

Healing

I think that you begin to see glimpses of what that next step is. They are not isolated they overlap. I really thought that developing awareness was restoration. I think I got caught up in the overlap. I jumped into pockets of restoration and felt the comfort there and figured I was there and I had arrived, but before you are healed you have to go through healing. This means that you are getting better but you are going to have some days where you relapse and you don't feel so great and that's OK. A nun once told me the sin is not in falling down its lying there.

Now as I get healthy I realize I don't want to be fat anymore. I don't want to be connected to these negative coping mechanisms. When I was in the hospital God told me I was going to be beautiful again. I BELIEVE GOD! But most of all I have to get my health together so I can do what God wants me to do. I have to be able to move around, I have to be able to get to people and help people. The devil is a liar. I will be healed physically. You know it's starting to bother me more and more that people I love aren't saved. Maybe if they see what He has done for me they will get it. I realize that it's about your personal relationship. I need to know what's right and promote what's right. I want to make sure the message is clear. Wow this has been an awesome day. I better try and get some sleep now. Let me say my prayer first.

My Dear Heavenly Father:

I thank you Father for the opportunity to serve. I ask you Father that you make it so I represent you in the best way possible. I understand that you have been preparing me. I ask for discernment to understand that once I go through something I get the lesson I needed to learn. And when I learn give me the ability to share that lesson. I just thank you Lord. I understand that restoration is about to come. I see things are being restored. I get it! I get it! I get it! Thank you, God. *I really understand. I'm at a new place. I am ready to go to the next step. I know I am not fully restored but I know I have to live through restoration and know it's also a gradual process. I think that I was starting to look at restoration like bam you are restored. I now know there were things you allowed to happen to draw me closer to You and again I thank you. In Jesus name, Amen.*

Just as I finished praying the Shepherd called me to see how I was doing. He said he had not seen me in a while. You see I knew he was a stalker. No, let me stop. We talked for a while. I told him what had transpired. He summed up healing so beautifully.

The Shepherd Speaks on Healing

Healing from God—Luke 13:10-17: It is such a blessing to have a Savior who can not only heal us of our soul diseases, but has the power to heal us our physical diseases as well. By faith, we should always go to God in prayer for our healing whether it's one who has been sick for 38 yrs (John 5), 12 yrs (Luke 8) or 18 yrs as we see in our key text in Luke 13, Jesus is able to rid us of our diseases. He is a Savior that not only makes us well but also makes us whole. Jesus goes down in history as being a "wounded healer." Isaiah 53:5 lets us know that Jesus shall be "wounded, bruised and chastised." Based upon the affliction that was placed upon Him, we can be "healed" as well as "whole." The blessing of healing lies in the fact that we serve a risen Savior who has proven to be victorious. There are times when we have seen in the lives of family and friends that there was no deliverance or healing for their dilemmas. It is not that God is not able; it is we have to trust the will of God for our lives. When God heals us, it is important for us to glorify God in our bodies. We must not only give Him the praise, but also allow our lives to reflect His presence. We must be witnesses of His wonder working power, by telling the world of His healing power. Our testimony should be, when you're looking at me, you're looking at a miracle.

Thank you so much Shepherd that was so deep. He laughed and told me to have a good night and sleep well. I said I will. I took out my MP3 player and listened to my girl Yolanda Adams. She was singing *I'm Gonna be Ready!*

Restoration

The Seventh Set of Footprints:
Job: 42:10-17

Lord I'm Free! Jesus Paid the Price
I Believe! At last I'm Free!

MG's Prayer:
Good Morning God:
You are so AWESOME!!! I can't believe how well I slept. Yes I can, it's because you showed me once again how much you love me in spite of me. You healed my soul and I thank you. I am so grateful to finally have a relationship with you, I truly know what that song means that says I was blind but now I see. Lord you are amazing! You have granted me such peace. I thank you for all you are doing in my life and what you will do in the future. Thank you God for being you! I love you! I give you the entire honor and all the praise. This journey has been a trip but I am so grateful that you allowed me to go down this path to renewal. I'm ready Lord. I know the next step is restoration. So let's do this! I'm looking forward to my lesson. Order my steps today Lord. In Jesus name I pray, Amen.

Miss Understood called earlier and asked me to come out to Bible study tonight. So I went and it was such a powerful lesson. The Bible Study was about name changes and becoming a new person in Christ Jesus. We reviewed the following passages in the Bible: *John 1:41, 42; Matthew 16:16-18; Luke 22:31; Mark 14:37; John 21:15-17 and—Acts 9:1-4; Acts 13:9.*

We learned about how a spiritual transformation should take place and the person becomes a new person in Christ. This newly created person receives a new life separated from the previous worldly life plagued with darkness and no direction. When Jesus calls us to step into our purpose, we become changed and begin our journey. It was really interesting to learn about how in the Bible God gave people new names. The Shepherd showed us real life examples of this written in the Bible. This guy named Abram became Abraham, and his wife Sarai became Sarah. A man named Jacob became Israel. They were all from the Old Testament. Simon-Cephas became Peter and Saul of Tarsus became the Apostle Paul, they were from the New Testament. This is really a deep concept. The Shepherd said that Peter's old ways before he walked with Christ was really weak. The Lord changed his name and the new name meant strength. The Shepherd then showed us incidences in the Bible when Peter would slip up and show signs of his old ways. I know what that feels like. Sometimes people just take you there. When Peter would mess up Jesus called him by his old name. The one that really blew my mind was this dude Saul. He was walking around or riding around with his Posse beating up and killing folks. The crazy part was he did this because they were followers of Jesus and God still used him. Wow, this showed me God can and will use anybody. One day he was on his way to go mess with some more people and he heard Jesus voice speaking to him through a vision, asking him why he persecutes Him. That would have bugged me out. I mean I heard God's voice before but I would have been tripping if I heard someone talking to me that I didn't believe existed, especially if I was doing people in for believing. But God is so awesome and forgiving that he decided to use him and changed his life and name to Paul of Nazarenes. To top it all off this dude wrote a great deal of the New Testament. God is no joke! He can change anybody. I found this fascinating."

One of the lessons I have learned is that we are called to follow Jesus. It's not just a coincidence. It wasn't like we decided that this was something we just want to do. I mean, yes we do have free will so we have a choice but I also realize that it is all part of this master plan. During this time period we go through changes, if we truly surrender and are obedient and go with the flow. The change makes us a new person in Christ. This kind of reminds me of how in the world you hear people say they have an altar ego and give themselves an alternative name that's usually connected to certain personality traits or an alternate "them." A better example may be cartoon characters or super heroes. They always have an alter ego or another name for themselves when they transform to a "Do Gooder." Two familiar examples for this may be how the Millionaire Bruce Wayne transforms into Batman. The Newspaper reporter Clark Kent transforms into Superman. Although these characters are fictitious I think this demonstrates the point of how a transformation takes place and a new person immerges and a new name is acquired. I can't believe I used the super heroes as an example. I guess all those years my brothers forced me to watch that stuff on TV stuck with me. I guess it's hard to shed some things.

After the Bible Study I came back home. I was in deep thought. I was fascinated by the whole name change concept. I asked myself, Restoration? What does it really mean? To me it means you are ready for a fresh start. You have renewed strength. You have a change in the way you view yourself. For me, based on what I have been through its moving from inferiority to superiority. I am a victor not a victim, not in a prideful way, in a way of understanding who I am. I have learned I am a descendent of the King. I am royalty! I am ready to accept my rightful place within the Kingdom. I don't have to be weighed down anymore with pain, guilt or shame. It's great! It's like the old you is dead and you get a new you. I understand what I have been through and it's just that. I have gone through it. It's over! It's done! I can move on! I feel so free! I feel so at peace! I could just go to bed and sleep as well as I did last night. I think that's exactly what I'm going to do. But I have to say my prayers first.

MG's Prayer:
Dear Heavenly Father,
I come to you tonight first and foremost to thank you for all you have done for me. I continue to be at peace. I feel like a building has been lifted off me. I know it's because of you. I carried so much stuff from my past into every relationship and even let it get in the way of my relationship with You. I'm so sorry Lord. Please forgive me. I ask you Lord to reveal to me what you want me to do with the rest of my life. I know all the things that I have been

through have not all been sent by You but I know that You used those things to build me up and I thank You. I know that You have been setting me up for something. I know that because I'M STILL STANDING! I owe You so much and I know I could never repay you but I just want to do what I can for you. Lord I want to be real for You. I don't want to be one of those a fake Christians, double minded Christians or the person who wants to keep taking from You and not give back. I want to continue to develop a long lasting relationship with You. Use me Lord to help build Your Kingdom. Use me Lord to help people who have been through painful situations and to show them if you did it for me You can do it for them. These things I ask of You and thank You for. In Jesus name I pray, Amen.

He Called Me Out My Name!

The next morning I woke up and I slept so well, I felt disoriented. I really did not know where I was. I looked around the room because I felt like I was in another place. I immediately realized that I had a dream that just seemed so real. God was speaking to me while I was asleep. I woke up with a message on my heart and I just knew it was from God. The dream which I remembered clearly was about God talking to me about name changes. So at first I wondered if I dreamt this because of the Bible Study I attended. As the memory of the dream became clearer and clearer I knew it was God. He told me that each of the ladies that I met shared their stories with me but they were not just stories they were their testimonies.

Each woman including myself has undergone a transformation. He said he had new names for each of us. He explained that Miss Understood had to learn to trust God, because she misunderstood who was in control of her life. She had to realize that she could not go through life doing as she pleased with whom she pleased. She had to realize and recognize that God was setting her up for service and she just needed to trust the process. He was putting before her. God said, "Miss Understood now understands that she is being used to show people through dramatic presentations, who God is and how He operates. She understands that He will come through no matter what things appear to be. She also understands that she loses her temper about things that she is passionate about. These situations are allowed to happen so she could grow and develop as well as use the issues as materials for her plays. The plays are her ministry. She now understands and people understand where she is coming from. So God said, "I'm changing her name from Miss Understood to Understand." God said, "SHE IS RESTORED!" She now approaches life understanding that God has a purpose for everything that happens. She understands that she must trust the process. She now approaches the Christian Walk with a clear understanding of *The Set-Up*.

Miss Lead spent most of her life seeking the truth because she was constantly misled by people who deceived her. So many people mislead her down the wrong path. So many people told her lies and made her think things were what they were not. Miss Lead settled for less than she deserved by following misleaders. As a result she was she forced to approach life in a reactive way, which resulted in misdirection and going through some trying times. Now Miss Lead knows to take a proactive approach to life by seeking God for direction and waiting on Him to answer before she makes her moves. God said, "I'm changing her name from Miss Lead to Lead." God said, "SHE IS RESTORED! Her life is changed." She learned that God will bring you to and through things in his time. God is showing her that you have to wait for Him to set things in motion and then He will allow you to take charge of things. In the waiting process He builds her up, has her assist women in need. He showed her while waiting for Him that she can move forward and become the leader and role model that He has developed her to be.

Then God said, "Miss Taken lived a mistaken life where she had so much taken from her as a small child. It took her a while to bounce back from the robbery she suffered in losing her innocence. She attempted to gain peace through the use of drugs but she was mistaken. That didn't work because the drugs took from her as well. Miss Taken knew that God was present because her grandma prayed and had a relationship with God. Miss Taken in her darkest times muscled up the strength to believe that God could be there, even for her, in all her pain and all her madness. God said, "No one will ever take away from you again I am here. You have been set free to take charge of your life. I deliver you from the pain, the bondage and the hurt. Your are free to live a joyful life, you are free to love yourself, you are free to forgive all who hurt you and you are free to forgive yourself.: God said, "I'm changing her name from Miss Taken to *Takin Charge. God said,* "SHE *IS RESTORED! You are* commissioned to restore your life and help others become restored."

Then God said that Miss Story has lived a mysterious life. She does not look like her circumstances. She represents those who walk around looking together on the outside but sick and torn apart in the inside. Miss Story was in so much pain, experienced loss, and suffered in silence to the point where she was about to give up and take her life." God said I'm changing her name from Miss Story to Story To Tell. God said SHE *IS RESTORED!* God stepped in and showed her that He was there although her life felt like a suspenseful mystery to the end. God showed up and showed her that He works in mysterious ways. By His stripes she was healed. He turned her life around. She is no longer Miss Story, she is restored. She became Story and her life became a Fairytale; no more voids, she found her Prince.

God said, "And you my daughter, you have lived such a misguided life. You were taught religion and although you have been able to draw from memorization to help you through some tough times, you had to develop a relationship with me. Without your connection to me you were searching to find the one. You felt the void of a relationship you did not have and did not know. You lost family members, you lost yourself but you never completely gave up, you came to me. Not only did you come to me for help you continued to help others in some of your own darkest times. So my daughter I am about to take you from ruins to restoration, from victim to victor, I want to use you to guide some of my wounded, depressed, hurt, and down trodden. You are no longer Miss Guided you are restored. Your new name is Guide. Go now and be a Guide to my people, write the vision, teach them what you have learned, help them through their struggles."

Oh my God! I thank you for this Word. I thank you for choosing me Lord. I am ready. I am restored. I am redeemed. I am repaired. I went to get my Bible and meditate on my favorite scripture—*Psalm*

121. I know I can do all that God wants me to do because my help comes from the Lord.

MG's Morning Prayer
Good Morning Lord,
This is the day that You have made and I will rejoice and be glad in it. I am so excited! I thank You, Lord for waking me up this morning and giving me the opportunity to do what I should have done yesterday for You and didn't. Lord can I do it today? I can't wait to get started on what You want me to do. I ask You, God to order my steps. I don't want to step out on my own; I want to follow your lead. I know that You have been there for me all along. I know You were there when I did not acknowledge You and I am so sorry. I know you were there waiting for me to come to You of my own free will. I also understand that Your permissive will drew me closer to You when I did not follow your perfect will I thank You for being the God of many chances. In Jesus name I pray, Amen.

Developing My Testimony: Understanding My Journey

This walk has not been easy, but there was help along the way. It has been and continues to be a journey. I now know how necessary the journey was and still is. I have lived and learned so much from reflecting on my circumstances as well as the women God allowed to intercept my path. I recognize that adversity was the vehicle God used to set us up for His service, success and inner peace.

Although I accepted the Plan Of Salvation when I was a small child I really had no clue as to what I was accepting. But thanks to God I was reeled in. I had to cry out to God and ask for help. I would not and could not do it on my own. I was stripped of everything I was depending on that which was not of Him. You see I had a hunger for love, security and protection. Although I didn't always make the right choices for myself, I have this awesome God who didn't give up on me. Instead He demonstrated His love by becoming my personal GPS system. He put me back on track directed my path and patiently waited for ME to answer His call and complete the work He started in me. What a Mighty God I serve!

Truly Understanding the Walk-Thru Model

I am so grateful to God for ordering my steps. I now understand that chart they gave me in the New Climbers' class. So far I have taken seven steps in the right direction. I am almost at the top of the Mountain. Now these steps were not baby steps. Each step was a process in itself covering a lot of ground and distance. Those seven steps that I took (exposure, acceptance, trusting, waiting, deliverance, healing, and now restoration) have guided me down a path of spiritual growth and development, self discovery, self love, self worth and selflessness.

Being introduced to the "Walk Thru Model" is what defined the processes that molded me and established my foundation. I have learned that I can utilize these steps each time God needs me to change something, or get rid of something that does not fall in line with where He is taking me or needs me to be. When I am *exposed* to a situation, I must remember that God is present throughout. I must *accept* God's help, guidance and wisdom in the situation. I must be obedient and *trust* where He is leading me even if it doesn't make sense to me. I must be patient and *wait* for God to resolve the situation. I must be willing to give up some stuff in order for God to *deliver* me. I must allow myself to reflect on what God has taken me through and participate in the *healing* process. I must remember to hold on because after the process, God will *restore* my soul and make me into a whole, healthy, loving and productive state of being. Lastly, I must share what God has given to me through *ministry* with my brothers and sisters.

While on this journey, I feel like I have gained so much more than I lost. One of the things I was known for when I was working in the world was the development of Acronyms, and Desk Aids. These tools were creative visual reminders of crucial concepts covered in trainings. Now that God has changed me from Miss Guided to becoming a Guide, I reflect on my process and I think I should develop some tools that document my process and share them with others.

Set Up For Service: An Acronym
Selected
Experiences
Transforming your

Understanding of your life's
Purpose

Faithful
Obedience bringing forth
Revelation

Sanctification
Elevation and
Restoration resulting in
Victorious
Inspired
Consecrated
Evangelism

God has been telling me that I have to stay focused. It is easy to get distracted when preparing for Ministry. He gave me what I call the 10 Tips To Staying Focused. In other words I had to learn how to mind my business. Too often when I have heard this statement I found it to be offensive. No matter whom the statement was directed to. Now that I am saved and trying to live right I see it as empowering.

10 Tips to Staying Focused: Mind Your Business

1. When you are minding your business you encounter fewer distractions.
2. When you mind your business you are able to focus on what God is doing to get you ready for what He has for you to do.
3. When you mind your business you are not holding on to bad feelings about other people that you told yourself you were over.

4. When you mind your business you are able to allow God to change things about you He doesn't like.
5. When you mind your business you don't sweat the big stuff and you know the small stuff is not worth it.
6. When you mind your business you are able to pay attention to what's happening around you. You are then able to see how these factors affect your walk.
7. When you mind your business you are able to hear God talking to you.
8. When you mind your business you will find that your assignment is your business and you should focus only on that.
9. When you mind your business your able to trust God.
10. When you mind your business you have plenty of time to develop, reflect on and present your testimony to those who need encouragement.

As I walk through restoration I start to understand that I'm still being guided through this process and I'm getting a lot of different things. I'm beginning to pull it all together. Before with each step I learned a new lesson, but the steps were like puzzle pieces and the pieces were being given to me at different points. Now that I am restored I am renewed.

Wow! I am now understanding why I went through the different things I went through. I am getting from God exactly what I'm supposed to do. I am truly hearing from God now daily. I think it's because I'm seeking Him daily. He took me through this Walk Through Model and as I walked and look back over my life I realized that it's all about personal relationship. I realize that it's no longer about religion. It's about developing a relationship with God and truly understanding. I had to truly take the time out to listen and understand what He was trying to tell me. Sometimes you have to shut everything down, friends, TV, children, work whatever is getting in the way of you hearing. I had to stop making my life about things I wanted to do and feel and in turn making them bigger than God. I had to make myself truly available to find out what it is I am supposed to be and what I'm supposed to be doing. Let's face it, I took six and a half years out of my life to go to college and graduate school to pursue a career that wasn't fulfilling.

Why didn't I pursue God like that? I don't know, but I am pursuing Him now and I am so happy and at peace.

I reflect back on the relationships I had with men in my life. I realize for so long I looked at what I lost, what I gave up and was left feeling defeated. Now I realize that I am victorious and gained so much from my experiences.

Mr. Contender taught me that I am a child of the King and I am royalty. My Father is a God of love. I now know who I am in relation to God and no one can take that from me. I will not allow any man to ever hit me or abuse me again because I know who I am, who I belong to and I am better than that.

Mr. Dis-ease taught me to seek God in all my decisions through prayer and wait for his direction, especially when you are contemplating marriage. I learned the importance of and the power of prayer. God has clearly defined choices and roles for husbands and wives. I know God is not going to select someone for you who is a mess. I am no longer going to create a mess and come back to God asking Him to bless my mess.

Mr. Man taught me that I have to read the Bible and know the Word for myself. He used what the Bible says about submission to control me. I was ignorant. When I read the Word for myself it says that wives are to submit to their husbands not girlfriends. I also know that the Word says that husbands are supposed to love their wives. It only makes sense to me if you are treating women with love, patience and kindness then she would want to submit. I'm just saying, why a man would need to use manipulation. If I am reading, studying and looking to the Lord for guidance no one can ever falsely use the Word against me to meet their needs.

Mr. Forbidden Fruit taught me how a sin filled life is a life of misery. Now I know how unfulfilling it is to pursue the works of the flesh. Although things may feel or seem good, that's temporary and lead to the absence of joy. This joy that I have now sin didn't give it to me but sin can take it away.

Mr. Manhattan Slick taught me that I have to put my faith in God and not in man. I learned all of my help comes from the Lord. I

This Walk Ain't Right! But, Help Is Along The Way

learned that I love hard and that's OK when that unconditional love is directed to God because He loves harder.

God has also allowed me to meet some awesome women who have inspired me. I have gotten guidance, advice and support from the Shepherd. Now I am starting to look at it as a whole and realize that it's a process and that it is a continuing process. I see things very clearly now.

When I approached the Mountain and even after I moved onto this Mountain I questioned why these situations kept happening to me. I saw them as isolated incidents. To me, it was a bunch of horrible things happening to me one thing after the next. Now that I am restored I see that everything has been a part of a process. I'm a guide now, but my process started off misguided because I had no relationship with God. Now that I am being guided I understand that there is a structure to this walk. There are footsteps to a destination called relationship. There is a road map with points of interest called virtues that must be obtained and that there is a courtship through the issues we face.

A person comes through this journey with clearly identified relaters that create pathways for the relationship development process. Throughout this whole process I have focused on the relaters. The footsteps are the things that happened to me that made me come to an understanding of what I gained.

This new knowledge awarded me the opportunity to develop skills and gain abilities that I will utilize in ministry. I get it now.

The Bible support in this model is the roadmap of references, insight and encouragement giving examples of people or situations that took this journey and successfully completed it. This roadmap inspires the person to complete his journey. As you walk through, you develop admirable qualities which are the virtues. You develop these virtues through a courtship with the relaters, which is to go through something. As a result of going through, you develop strength and you begin to recognize that you are being broken for glory. You are able to then look back at what's now left behind and not cringe but Praise! I think that's one of the keys to being restored, the ability to let go of the past and move forward leaving old issues, mistakes, situations and guilt, then recognizing that this process you went through was purposeful and part of a master plan designed by God. Now that you are restored God is given you your peace of mind. You are whole spiritually. You are renewed!

This goes back to being guided. Now that I am restored I am willing to allow God to guide me. God is blowing my mind because He is giving me so much insight, that I know I'm not coming up with. This stuff it's all Him. He is guiding me to do something and I may not have all the answers right now but I know I am being moved to a different place. I can feel it; it almost feels like I am being pushed in a specific direction. He is giving me a clear understanding that there is movement in this walk. I understand that it's going to take time though. I also understand that this does not mean I won't continue to be broken as He prepares me for higher dimensions in Him.

I was sitting under a tree enjoying the weather and putting some of my thoughts down on paper and the Shepherd appeared. We greeted each other and the Shepherd asked what I was up to. I explained that I was writing some things down so I will always remember this experience. He said this is good because you are going to need that when you face these trials in the future. I remember looking at him like he was crazy. I asked, "What do you mean isn't it over? Now that I know what I should be doing wont things go smoothly now?" He said, "No my dear this is just the beginning. You have been introduced to the steps but the Christian walk is a continual process. Just because you are almost at the top of the mountain does not mean that you are not going to continue to go through stuff, grow and develop. What it does mean is you will be able to handle things differently than you have in the past. There are multiple dimensions to this walk and there are different levels within each dimension. With the new levels there will be brokenness to get you ready. There will also be new devils trying to distract you every step of the way. What you just experienced you experienced for a reason, to get you exactly where you are now. Look at what you gained!"

The Shepherd Speaks on Restoration

Restored through God—Job 42:10-17: Double for your trouble. That's what we like to refer this story and specifically this text as. To go from top to bottom and from bottom back to top is the essence of the book of Job. We know that God once again was manifesting His wonder working power in the life of Job. As believers we must be mindful that at any given time, hell and high water can break out in our lives. The fabric of our faith in God will often come by way of us being tested by God. The testing is not meant to make us mean nor bitter, but rather to make us better.

God has a unique way of recommending us for trials, troubles and the snares of the Devil in order to show us just how strong we are. God being omniscient knows us better than we know ourselves. Whereas we might not think that we can handle the test, God has already given us the formula to pass the test. Job declared, "The Lord gave unto him, and has now taken away from him, blessed be the name of the Lord." (Job 1:21) Praise is what we ought to do whenever we are going through something, because God is truly in control. When God is in the midst of your situation, Isaiah stated weapons may be formed against you, but they shall not prosper (Isaiah 54:17).

On life's journey at some point or another, all of us are named Job. It is our task to prayerfully ride out the storm, knowing that Jesus is the Master of the raging sea. Even though your world may be turned upside down, in the end, if you remain faithful, God is able to give you back everything that was taken from you. He will give you double for your trouble!

Then the Shepherd told me he will be meeting me for the final step. He said you are now ready to go to the top of Mount Horeb; this is where you will meet God and go through a period of consecration before you begin your ministry. I said, "I don't have what I need to tell God what I should be doing. I haven't figured it out yet." He laughed and said, "You have everything you need." He said, "You do need to understand that you won't be telling God what you need. God is going to tell you what to do and he will supply you with everything you will need to make it happen." I said, "Oh yeah that's right. Sorry Shepherd some old habits are hard to break. You see how I just went there? It was like a reflex reaction." The Shepherd said, "We all do it from time to time. Just try to be conscious of what you think and say and don't be so hard on yourself. Remember it's a process." I thanked the Shepherd and pulled all my documents together and returned home. It was getting cold out and late. When I got in the house I settled down for the night.

My Prayer:
Dear God,
All I can say is I'm ready to give back. You have brought me through so much and I'm still standing. I know I am standing here for a reason. I want to be helpful to someone as they find their way, I want to give back. I want to effectively minister to people like me and the women who ministered to me. I want to use the skills you gave me during my set up to enhance your kingdom. Lord I am open for whatever it is You have for me to do. In Jesus name, Amen!

Ministry

The Eighth Set of Footprints:
Matthew 20:28

Lord, You Want Me . . . to Minister?
Lead Me, Guide Me!

I t's finally morning. I was so excited about today I could barely sleep last night. Today I begin my final step but more importantly I get to spend some alone time with God to get my assignment. It's funny, when you finally get it you realize that you have a partnership with God. You are working for Him; He is the CEO. In order to have a working relationship with God you have to be willing to be led and take steps in the right direction. You need to understand that it is a process and it is gradual. You have to allow yourself to be used by Him. In order for you to be used in the right way He has to prepare you, mold you so you represent Him accordingly. God is not going to let you represent Him tore up from the floor up. You got to be right!

MG's PRAYER
Good Morning God:
I can't wait to get to the top of the Mountain to see what You have in store for me. I can't believe how excited I am about going into Ministry. I now know what you were showing me at that Women's Conference years ago. You remember when I went into that trance like state and I came out of it saying me, Lord you want me to do that? What am I saying, of course, You remember you are God! I can be so slow sometimes God. But I guess You know that too. I remember feeling so humbled but I also remember feeling like I didn't know what "IT" was. I felt so unprepared and uninformed.

Ministry

NOT TODAY LORD! I'm ready! I'll meet You on the Mountain! In Jesus name I pray, Amen.

So I went outside and I started my final climb up to the top of Mount Horeb. When I reached the top of the mountain I was filled with so much emotion. You have to remember this walk got even more difficult for me when my back and legs went out while I was learning to trust. It took me longer than I originally anticipated because some days the pain held me back. It was rough climbing this mountain. There were times I wanted to give up and I thought I never would have made it. BUT GOD!!!! It's funny, but none of that negative stuff I experienced or the fact that it took longer than I expected really seem to matter now. All I know is I AM HERE!

Much to my surprise, I am not alone up here. I mean I knew I would not be alone because I came up here to be with God. But off in the distance I see my sister-friends who shared their testimonies with me during my process. The women were sitting together having a discussion. When they saw me they were thrilled. They greeted me with smiles and hugs. They said they were hoping I would make it through my journey. I asked why they were acting as if they were surprised that I made it up here. Taken Charge said, "In time you will see not everyone makes it through. Some people give up. She said that's why it's so important that we go back and help those who are struggling." The women talked about what had happened in their lives since I had last seen them. Each woman had undergone a change. They each have name changes just as God had revealed to me and are actively involved in ministry. Understanding said, "We understand you are now called Guide. You too have experienced great change." I was clearly puzzled by all of this. Understanding asked me what's wrong? She could tell something wasn't sitting right with me by the look of disappointment on my face. I said to the women you mean to tell me I came all the way up here to find out that you guys got name changes? God already told me that. All the women burst into laughter. Taking Charge said, "Oh Ye of little faith." She said, "No that's not it. You are here for consecration." Leader said, "Just like you we went through the journey and discovered our individual purposes and are currently on assignment. There is more to ministry than just wanting to do it. You have to be prepared. We are helping and encouraging others who are going through their process." Story said, "Each of us reviewed the lessons learned and developed a way to get the Word out using our spiritual gifts, and now we are walking in purpose." I was intrigued by all of this and asked if I could walk with them. Understanding told me that I could walk down with them but not quite yet. She told me that I had to spend some time on the top of Mount Horeb, alone talking to God, meditating and preparing to commit to ministry. Once I completed this final lesson I would be ready to formally minister and walk with them. Leader said, "Each of us is going to give you a test question. You must take these four test assignments and use them as a guide to completing this dimension you are in. You are about to enter into another dimension. But before you can do that you must spend time with God to get prepared for your assignment." Story said, "He will show you how to use the gifts and experiences you gained while traveling up the Mountain."

Each of my sisters gave me a test to complete and then went back down the Mountain to minister to others making the journey.

MY PRAYER:
Dear Lord, I come before You thanking you for what you have done in my life in spite of me. Lord I know now You have always been there for me and I thank You. I want to be used by You Lord in any way you see fit. If there is someone who needs help I will help them. Please show me how I can be used by You. In Jesus name I pray.

I sat there waiting, meditating. Then I got my answer.

GOD SAID
MY PEOPLE WILL NEVER TRULY UNDERSTAND HOW AND WHY I OPERATE THE WAY I DO BECAUSE MY THOUGHTS ARE NOT THEIR THOUGHTS AND MY WAYS ARE NOT THEIR WAYS. I NEED THEM TO UNDERSTAND THEIR TRANSFORMATION PROCESS AS MUCH AS THEY CAN AND I WANT YOU TO BE

Ministry

THEIR GUIDE, THEIR TEACHER. THIS IS WHY I CHANGED YOUR NAME. YOU ARE NO LONGER MISGUIDED BY THE HYPOCRITICAL RELIGIOUS BELIEFS AND PRACTICES. YOU ARE NO LONGER DRIVEN AND CONFORMING TO THE THINGS OF THE WORLD. I SEE HOW HARD YOU ARE TRYING MY DAUGHTER AND I WANT YOU TO CONTINUE TO DEVELOP WHILE SIMULTANEOUSLY HELPING OTHERS. I HAVE SENT YOU TO JOURNALISM SCHOOL WHERE YOU LEARNED TO WRITE, I HAVE SENT YOU TO SOCIAL WORK SCHOOL WHERE YOU LEARNED TO COUNSEL, I HAVE ALLOWED YOU TO BECOME SKILLED IN FACILITATING GROUPS WHERE YOU LEARNED TO MAKE A DIFFERENCE. I HAVE BROUGHT YOU THROUGH NUMEROUS ISSUES IN YOUR LIFE AND YOU NOW HAVE A TESTIMONY. I WANT YOU TO TAKE ALL I HAVE GIVEN TO YOU AND USE IT TO ASSIST IN THE DEVELOPMENT OF MY KINGDOM.

I then asked, "But how Lord? How am I this ordinary person, going to be able to do such an extraordinary task?" He then said

AS IT IS WRITTEN I HAVE ALWAYS USED ORDINARY PEOPLE, LOOK AT THE STORIES OF JOSEPH, MOSES, DAVID AND PAUL JUST TO NAME A FEW. GOD SAID ANSWER THE FOUR QUESTIONS MY DAUGHTERS HAVE GIVEN YOU. USE THE CREATIVITY I HAVE GIVEN YOU TO DEVELOP A PLAN FOR YOUR MINISTRY. AS LONG AS YOU COME TO ME FOR HELP YOU WILL NEVER GO WRONG. TAKE ALL YOUR ABILITIES AND EXPERIENCES AND USE THEM TO COMPLETE YOUR GOAL.

I took the test questions and started to meditate on each one. It was amazing because the answers were coming so fast I had a hard time writing them down.

Preparing for Ministry

Test One: What knowledge did you gain while on this journey that will assist you in Ministry?

1. Life is already set-up by God.
2. Everything that happens can be used for good.
3. Our time is different than God's time.
4. During your process you must surround yourself with people who are also trying to walk in purpose.
5. Even when you are going through you can be a light to someone else going through.
6. *The Walk Thru Model* can be used in any situation you are facing.

Test Two: What skills did you develop while on this journey that will assist you in Ministry?

1. I learned how to study the Bible
2. I learned how to pray
3. I learned how to fast
4. I learned how to praise
5. I learned how to worship
6. I learned how to forgive

Test Three: What abilities do you have that will assist you in Ministry?

1. I know how to love
2. I know how to be patient and kind
3. I am giving
4. I can write

5. I can counsel
6. I can facilitate groups
7. I know how to let go and let God use me

Test Four: What is your vision for your Ministry?

1. To write a book that clearly demonstrates and explains the process a person goes through when becoming what God wants them to be.
2. To develop and facilitate a series of experiential workgroups that give participants the opportunity to focus on their individual developmental process.
3. To exhort, encourage and support people as they go through their process.

At this point I sit on top of the mountain and meditate and pray that God gives me the ability to document my thoughts so I can share with others what I have learned. This is what God gave me:

The Components of Effective Ministry: Connection, Competence, Commitment

God prepared me for ministry. I had to get **connected** to Him through building a relationship. I had to become **competent** in my understanding of the Christian Development Process. I had to become **committed** to Kingdom building.

1. Development of Connectedness for Ministry
    - Relationship Building Process—by understanding the *Walk Thru Model*
    - Stay rooted in the Word—by reading the Bible daily
    - Pray without ceasing—by staying in constant communication with God
2. Development of Competence for Ministry

- Realization—by recognizing and answering the call on your life
- Discernment—by becoming a predictive visionary of God
- Capacity Building—by becoming informed and an obedient servant of God

3. Development of Commitment for Ministry
   - Falling in Love with God—by truly understanding who He is.
   - A sense of Gratitude—by understanding all He has done for me in spite of me.
   - Demonstrate a willingness to serve—by practicing obedience.

Where am I now? I know that it is vital that I honor God, worship God, and praise God. I know that I cannot put anyone else before God. I also know that the way of honoring God and my brothers and sisters is to fulfill my purpose. Now that I have gotten it all straightened out I developed an acronym with God's guidance, to define the "must haves" in developing a ministry.

Establishing Essential Connections in Ministry
Consider and Consult God first
Others come second
Need to know your Word
Need to know yourself
Excellence must always be the standard
Compassion is the practice
Testimony is crucial because it

1. Builds character
2. Draws people into the Kingdom
3. Inspires and encourages
4. Shows how God developed you for His use

God told me to describe the Three Dimensions of the Christian Development Process. This is what He gave me.

The Three Dimensions of the Christian Development Process

Dimension One: The Activated Christian: Becoming Mobilized by Embracing God the Father

Stage One—The Introduction *"Humble yourselves in the sight of the Lord, and he will lift you up."* **James 4:10** *NKJV*

During this stage the believer is in the beginning of his/her walk. The person knows that God exists and believes that God is the creator. His knowledge of God is very limited at this stage of the developmental process. The believer has no real relationship or connection with God. This belief is childlike in nature. The perception is that God is an external factor. God is sought in times of trouble as an escape or a "when all else fails I'll call on Him."

Stage Two—The Foundation . . . *"what must I do to be saved?"* **Acts 16:30** *NKJV*

During this stage the believer becomes engaged in the development process. This is where the ground work is laid. The person may have been "turned on" to God by watching Televangelists or visiting a church. This person is searching for a deeper understanding of who God is. The believer begins to connect with God through sermons he's heard or a passage of scripture he has read in the Bible or feeling encouraged while listening to gospel music. He may also have seen what God is doing in someone else's life or sees the joy that worshipers have and "wants some of that." This believer desires to change in his or her life and feels comforted when he prays or someone prays for him. The person begins to develop an understanding of what it means to become saved or "give your life" over to God.

Stage Three—The Launch *"He must increase, but I must decrease."* **John 3:30** *NKJV*

During this stage the believer moves from spectator to an active participant in the process. He gives his/her life over to God by accepting the Plan of Salvation. This stage is when the newly converted Christian sees God in a broader sense. They understand that God is not some distant stranger whom you go to only when you need something. The new convert becomes hungry, needs more than what they know. This new convert frequently attends Worship services and connects to the sermons and the Word on a deeper level. They feel as though a fire is lit inside of them. The new convert feels off balance when they miss a Sunday service. New converts also fall under attack by facing challenges and temptations Satan designed to lure them back to a life filled with sin. There is also a strong desire to gain a deeper understanding of God, learn more about Jesus, His time on earth and the second coming.

Dimension Two: The Focused Christian: Determined to Emulate God the Son

Stage One—The Motivation: "To live the Christian life is to allow Jesus to live his life in and through us." **Gal2:20** *NKJV*

During this stage the Christian develops a feeling of enthusiasm and shows interest or commitment to the process. There is a willingness and strong desire to know more or participate in more than just weekly Sunday services. The believer is connected to God and understands who Jesus is and why He gave His life. An emotional, cognitive force is activated and directs behavior. A deeper understanding of Jesus changes the Christian and effects their character and behavior. The Christian begins to understand that God must come first in their life. Around this time the Christian becomes interested and or involved in a Church ministry. This Christian begins to commit scriptures to memory, using them to support what he may be thinking, feeling or doing. The person becomes relationship focused and tries to understand the difference between Satan's attacks and God's trials.

Stage Two—The Preoccupation: "And do not be conformed to this world but be transformed by the renewing of your mind that you may prove what that is good and acceptable and perfect will of God." **Romans 12:2** *NKJV*

During this stage the Christian is constantly in thought about who Jesus is and how He relates to his/her life. There is a persistent interest in Jesus and His works. The Believer's attention is focused on learning more (bible study, workshops, conferences, and televangelism). There is a preoccupation with getting things right and questions everything (How do I know when God is speaking to me?). The Christian is fixated on what's in the bible and has a desire to read more and understand more. The Christian experiences ups and downs, high and low points in his life. He begins to understand grace, mercy and favor but he also experiences trials, temptations and at times tragedy. The person at times feels like he is on what feels like a rollercoaster doesn't always understand that this is a process and the Lord will see him through. At times the Christian gets weary and wants to give up, stop coming to church. This is usually connected to feelings of discouragement; they may become disillusioned and even depressed. They question why God allows bad things to happen "to good people." Even though he may want to give up there is a desire to hold on. He realizes that things may be tough right now but it's better than where he has been. The person begins to understand that there is a purpose for his life; He understands that he has a divine assignment. The Christian starts to feel an internal struggle with guilt from the past and even guilt related to current sins. He doesn't feel worthy of God's blessings. He begins to understand that guilt is a weapon used by Satan to distract you from your purpose. The Christian is determined to understand his purpose and walk in it. The Christian understands that he is supposed to help others. It's not just about what Jesus can do and has done for me, but what can I do for Jesus. The person understands Salvation. There is a desire that develops to help others who are hurting and lost. The person wants people they know to become saved. They understand that Jesus is love and to love Him is to be selfless and kind to others.

Stage Three-The Convergence: In my search for wisdom and in my observation of peoples burdens here on earth discovered that there is ceaseless activity day and night. I realized that no one can discover everything God is doing under the sun. "Not even the wisest people discover everything, no matter what they claim" ***Ecclesiastes 8:16-17 NLT***

During this stage there is a coming together from different directions. The Christian understands that there is a developmental process to their Christian walk. The person has moved from gaining knowledge to building faith to incorporating what has been learned into every day practice. They are able to reflect on their past, live in the present and believe that God will provide for them in the future with Jesus as the "go to" person. The Christian understands the difference between the Old Testament and the New Testament and draws knowledge from the stories. There is a transformation taking place. This is where the person truly understands who Jesus is, why He was sent, how He ministered and relates it to his own life. The person strives to be like Jesus. Hearing the Word and reading the Word are not enough for this person they are driven to incorporate the Word into their daily interactions. This is the stage when the "light bulb" truly goes on and they see that everything a person goes through is part of a process, a master plan designed by God as indicated in *Romans 8:28*. He begins to see trials as life lessons; he sees that he had to be broken in certain areas to walk in purpose. The person understands that he will go through some stuff but Jesus is there going through it with him. As he matures he becomes more patient during these times he is waiting on God to change things. A relationship is clearly developed at this stage. The person understands testimony and some of its uses. He understands that God must change a person, polish them up for His use. The person begins to understand the third part of the Trinity, the Holy Spirit. The person begins to develop a broader understanding of how the Holy Spirit works inside of him.

Dimension Three: The Integrated Christian: Spiritual Maturity and Driven by God the Holy Spirit

Stage One—The Absorption: "To walk in the Spirit is to obey the initial promptings of the spirit." ***Acts 10:19 NKJV***

Ministry

During this stage the mature Christian is actively engaged in and is a willing participant in the developmental process. This is a state in which the concentration of what's in your heart and what's in your mind are aligned and on a path of obedience to God. This is the time when the mature Christian makes a conscious, consistent effort to allow the Holy Spirit to guide his life. He, (the Holy Spirit) indwells, He sanctifies, He regenerates, He gives discernment, He bears fruit, He gives gifts and He comforts. The Holy Spirit also makes the mature Christian feel convicted when being disobedient.

Stage Two—The Assimilation: *"The steps of a good man are ordered by the LORD: and he delights in his way."* **Psalm 37:23** NKJV

This is the stage where a major transformation has taken place and the Christian is actively seeking The Holy Spirit for Guidance as they continue through the developmental process. There is a great deal of growth, adjustment and adaptation. This is a time of renewal, focusing on becoming more and more Like Jesus Christ. The Mature Christian wants to inherit the kingdom of God and avoids participating in the Works of the Flesh by Practicing the Fruit of the Spirit.

Stage Three—The Application: *"I therefore, the prisoner of the Lord, beseech you that ye walk worthy of the calling of which you were called, with all lowliness and gentleness, with longsuffering, bearing one another in love; endeavoring to keep the unity of the Spirit in the bond of peace."* **Ephesians 4:1-3** NKJV

During this stage the mature Christian is focused, understands his purpose and ready to walk in it. Unceasing prayer, bible study and meditation are a vital part of their daily lives. The mature Christian has a true relationship with God and strives to build on and maintain that relationship. These people are good stewards; they tithe, sow seeds and are committed to doing their part in Kingdom building. The mature Christian is upright in and outside of the church. He is committed to pleasing God, worshipping God, giving him all the glory and all the praise. This level of maturity understands that they will never be sinless but is committed to reducing the sin in their lives. They are humble people and walking in purpose. The mature Christian wants to get to heaven but also understands and recognizes that God expects us to live an obedient, fruitful and productive life prior to being called home.

God said state some of the barriers one may face.

What can impede the Christian Development Process? Tempted by Satan: What does this really mean? Why Me?

The devil's sole purpose is to stop the believer from believing. He knows that God has a purpose for every individual that He has created. He knows that our collective purpose is to build the Kingdom by serving God, encouraging non-believers to get saved and encouraging the believer not to give up and fulfill their individual purpose by accepting their assignment. The devil will use everything in his power to distract, discourage, dilute, dispute and disintegrate any hope, trust, belief and faith of an individual as they move towards their pre-destined purpose. Once the devil has knocked you off your mark, he:

Gets you to give up or quit saving souls.

Uses you to stop others from getting to the place they need to be.

Sometimes, actually most times, people don't even see him coming. If you have low self-esteem it is very easy for him to discourage you from fulfilling your purpose because he makes you think that God would never use you, to do great things. Too often the devil succeeds in making you believe this because you already believe that you are worthless so how could God want to use you. This is where the Bible stories come into play. The Bible is full of stories that show how God took ordinary people to do extraordinary things. It also shows how He took bad people and used them for good so anyone can be changed, used and broken for glory. Look at Paul who wrote most of the New Testament. Prior to becoming saved and used by God his job was to kill Christians. But God!!! Paul was broken for glory. God stripped him of all the characteristics he had that was not needed to fulfill his purpose and fixed him up with the characteristics and focus needed to build the Kingdom of God. Once God revealed the truth to Paul, he had to have moments where he felt unworthy especially knowing what he had done to Christians. The devil had to come after him, but he chose to turn away from a life of sin and follow God and fulfill his purpose.

Keep in mind that the devil is relentless in his attacks. He will try to wear you down. He will use the people, places and things closest to you. He tries to tire you out. He is a formidable opponent. You can't fight him alone. You must plead the blood of Jesus. Keep in mind when you are tired and ready to give up you are getting close to your breakthrough and he knows that so he comes at you even harder. Just know that you are moving to another dimension and you have to "Jesus up" and know this too shall pass. Remember this is a fight for your life, the life God has for you.

An Acronym highlighting Strategies, Techniques and Attitudes Satan Uses to Impede Your Process.

Interfere in the relationship between you and God
Mask reality
Prey on your weaknesses
Embarks on a mission to deceive you
Determines how to win his battle
Empowers guilt

Take what he knows about you and uses it to his advantage
Hinder your growth process
Encourages sin

Procrastination is used as a distraction
Relentless
On-going
Christians are targeted
Expert at his game
Successful
Sin focused

This Walk Ain't Right! But, Help Is Along The Way

How to Overcome the Guilt, the Shame, and Forgiving Yourself

Read and meditate on one, a couple or all of the following scriptures.
Acts 13:39;
1 John 1:9;
Colossians 1:22;
Isaiah 1:18;
Romans 8:39, Isaiah 43:25.

1. Determine/identify what you did and what you didn't do.
2. Confess your sins to God.
3. Forgive yourself and forgive others.
4. Ask for God's forgiveness and believe that He will forgive you.
5. Repent and try with all your will not to do it again.
6. Understand what you have been through is your testimony.
7. Believe that you are a Victor and not a Victim.
8. Use your Testimony to show others the truth about some of the challenges you faced while walking this walk.

Give God all the GLORY, all the PRAISE and all the CREDIT for your transformation, all the time.

When I was able to write down everything God had shown me I sat back in amazement. Once again, the Shepherd came out of nowhere.

The Shepherd Speaks On Ministry
Now you are ready to Minister for God—Matthew 28:18-20: Since God has done so many wonderful things for you, what have you done for God lately? Jesus Christ makes a clear mandate for us to preach, teach and reach each. Christ did not come down from Heaven to take a vacation, but "to do the will of God who sent him." (John 6:38) It is important for us to recognize that all who have been saved by God must work for God. To minister is more than just preaching, it's serving. It is the responsibility of every child of God to give back to God in a tangible way. The stewardship of our

time, talent and treasure is what God is standing in need of to do Kingdom building. Jesus gives us the Power—All authority comes from Him. The People—all nations, everywhere. The Purpose—make disciples out of them. The Principles—the teachings and commands of our Savior. The Promise—He is with us, always!

The Shepherd then said, "Guide, you have reflected on your journey and now realize how far you've come right?" I said yes, "it seemed like it was just yesterday I was driving my car in the rain and ended up so lost. BUT GOD!!! I feel as though my life is changed. I have an indescribable joy. I have purpose, a purpose for my life. I am on fire and can't wait to get started." So he said, "Well what are you waiting for? You have everything you need for now. But remember don't get so caught up in ministry that you forget who you are ministering for. Practice What You Teach!" I said, "OK Shepherd I will." I went to leave and then I stopped and turned around and said, "You still going to be stalking me right?" He laughed and said, "Yes you have been put under my care." I said, "Well that's good, because I got used to you being around." We both laughed and I ran down the mountain to begin working on my first formal Ministry assignment.

I was so excited. I could not get down the mountain fast enough. All I know is . . . I want to write. God has given me all the pieces to this puzzle called a "Set Up" and He has shown me the picture of what needs to be put together. Now I am ready to do what I have been placed here to do. No more distractions, no more mess I am going to get the job done. At that point I started running as fast as I could. My legs and my back weren't even hurting, I felt so free with the wind blowing through my hair. Then it happened, I was running so fast I wasn't paying attention. I stepped on something and I went sliding and knew I was about to fall. You know that feeling when you know you are about to go down and try to stop yourself but just keep on going down? If I didn't know better I would think someone or something put something there to slow me down. It's like someone who doesn't want me to achieve what God has for me to do. So here I am on the ground my leg is hurt and so is my back. I take my cell phone out to call someone for help but I have no bars left. It's getting dark and I can't get myself off the ground. I can't believe this is happening to me. I start to cry because I am in so much pain. I start to ask myself how and why is this happening. I know God did not bring me this far to leave me to die out here. It's getting darker and darker and colder and colder. I can hear wild animals in the distance. I start to get so scared wondering what's going to happen to me. As I sit there I start to have bad thoughts and the thoughts are coming to me as if someone is whispering in my ear. I'm hearing you are going to die here. You will never make it out of this situation. No one knows you are here. What made you think you could write a book anyway. Even if you write it no one is going to publish it. You misread everything. God never told you to write a book. Why would God talk to you, especially with what you have done in your past?

I really started to feel sorry for myself. At this point I felt something stirring up in me. I heard loud and clear NO! The Devil is a liar! You know what was told to you and you will do it! The only thing that can stop you is you! So pick yourself up and continue the journey! You are too close, you can do it! Don't give up!

At this point I started to recite whatever I could to encourage myself. NO WEAPON FORMED AGAINST ME SHALL PROSPER! GOD DIDN'T BRING ME THIS FAR TO LEAVE ME! BY HIS STRIPES I AM HEALED! I PLEAD THE BLOOD OF JESUS ON THIS SITUATION! I SHALL NOT BE MOVED! I BELIEVE! I BELIEVE! All of a sudden I felt strength that I didn't know I had. I slid down that mountain. No let me keep it real, I scooted down that mountain. You know what I mean. When you sit on your butt and you move slowly sliding on your butt using your feet to take you a small distance. I was in so much pain. I was crying but giving up was not an option. I just kept scooting and scooting. I just kept encouraging myself and encouraging myself. Then kept scooting and scooting and scooting and scooting.

I stopped to rest for a few minutes. I was sweating, crying and in so much pain. I started to think about all I had been through. I remembered that God had brought me through. I cried out "GOD PLEASE GIVE ME THE STRENGTH TO GET HOME!"

Ministry

    I started to think about how I finally developed a relationship with Him through the steps I took on my journey. I said, "I'm going to relate the steps to this struggle I'm going through right now." I am exposed to yet another crazy situation, challenge, issue. I have to accept that even when I think I have it all figured out and ready to complete my assignment distractions will still surface to try and stop me from completing my goal. The difference is now I know that I have to trust Him and He will see me through this. I also know that I have to wait because things happen in God's time. This is why it's OK for me to rest here for a little. I can rest but I can't give up because God will deliver me and give me the strength to continue, but we must do it together. So now I gain more strength and I continue to scoot and scoot and scoot and scoot my way down the mountain. I can see my house. I know I am close enough for someone to hear me. I call out to my daughter. Pooh comes out and helps me into the house. I get onto a chair and feel so good because I made it. I'm still hurting but I'm home. Pooh helps me clean myself up and I realize I have no broken bones just a little bruised. I put my leg up because I realize that I have to stay off the leg and allow it to heal. After a couple of hours, I realized the pain is not bad as long as I stay off the leg for a while. This works for me because I came home to write. As a matter of fact I feel so good being off this leg and out of the wilderness. I feel renewed. I feel restored. I am now truly ready to share what I have learned; I am ready to begin my ministry.

    I sat down at my computer and began writing my first book. The book is entitled *This Walk Ain't Easy: But Help is Along the Way!*

Survival Guide for Walkers

Anointed—God doing those things only He can do and doing them through a flesh-and-blood, earthly vessel. To be anointed by God is not only to be picked, but also to be empowered by Him for the task or position to which He has called you.

Baptism—The application of water to a person, as a sacrament or religious ceremony, by which he is initiated into the visible church of Christ. This is usually performed by sprinkling or immersion.

Blessing—God's help, approval, sanction, a miracle, a prayer of thanks before a meal.

Consecration—To make or declare to be sacred, by certain ceremonies or rites; to appropriate to sacred uses; to set apart, dedicate, or devote, to the service and worship of God.

Evangelist—One who proclaims Good News, either by preaching or writing. Without being fixed to any church, preaches wherever they were led by the Holy Spirit.

Fellowship—when a group of people come together who share common beliefs or activities; such as worship services, meals, etc.

Fruit of the Spirit—love, joy, peace, longsuffering, gentleness, goodness, faith, meekness and temperance.

Grace—the free and undeserved love and favor of God towards man as a sinner. It is only by the unmerited favor of God that we embrace the offer of mercy. Because He gave the life of His son, Jesus Christ, who died for our sins so that we may be redeemed. We are currently living under what is called the Dispensation of Grace.

Honor—To respect, show admiration, to revere, to hold high.

Mercy—It implies benevolence, tenderness, mildness, pity or compassion, and clemency given to us by God.

Obedience—To obey the Lord God; this has been and is the crucial question for every human being.

Omission—To show deliberate disobedience to the known will of God.

Omnipresent—God is everywhere; being present everywhere at once.

Omnipotent—God is all powerful; possessing unlimited power.

Omniscient—God is all knowing.

Pastor—A minister of the gospel who has the charge of a church and congregation, whose duty is to watch over the people of his charge, and instruct them in the sacred doctrines of the Christian religion.

Permissive will—allows things to happen.

Plan of Salvation—If you confess with your mouth, "Jesus is Lord," and believe in your heart that God raised Him from the dead, you will be saved. For it is with your heart that you believe and are justified, and it is with your mouth that you confess and are saved." *Romans 10:9-10.*

Praise—To extol in words or song; to magnify; to glorify on account of perfections or excellent works.

Purpose—God's plan for your life, the reason why you are here on earth

Reverence—the respect or devotion that people show somebody or something.

Righteous—virtuous, moral, good, just, upright, honorable, honest, respectable, decent.

Sanctification—Made holy; consecrated; set apart for sacred services.

Shepherd—A minister of the gospel who has the charge of a church and congregation, whose duty is to watch over the people of his charge, and instruct them in the sacred doctrines of the Christian religion.

Sin—an act, thought or way of behaving that goes against the teachings of Jesus Christ. Any thought, word, desire, action, or omission of action, contrary to the law of God, or defective when compared with it.

Spiritual Gifts—gifts bestowed on Christians on Christians by God the Holy Spirit. According to the Word, these gifts given for the strengthening of the Church. These spiritual gifts are not to be confused with talents or skills, but are considered supernatural—beyond human capabilities. These gifts are considered to be given, empowered, and led by the Holy Spirit, thus "spiritual" gifts.

Transformation—a complete change for the better and usefulness by God.

The Lord's Supper—another term for Holy Communion, the last meal Jesus shared with the Disciples before He was crucified.

Trinity—the unity of God as existing in three distinct entities. God the Father, God the Son and God the Holy Spirit.

Ultimate will—God's perfect will.

Works of the Flesh—adultery, fornication, uncleanness, lasciviousness, idolatry, witchcraft, hatred, variance, emulations, wrath, strife, seditions, heresies, envying, murders, drunkenness, reveling.

Worship—A title of honor, used in to adore; paying divine honor; reverencing with supreme respect.